Department of Economic
and Social Affairs
Statistics Division

World
Statistics
Pocketbook
2011

United Nations, New York, 2012

The **Department of Economic and Social Affairs** of the United Nations Secretariat is a vital interface between global policies in the economic, social and environmental spheres and national action. The Department works in three main interlinked areas: (i) it compiles, generates and analyses a wide range of economic, social and environmental data and information on which States Members of the United Nations draw to review common problems and to take stock of policy options; (ii) it facilitates the negotiations of Member States in many intergovernmental bodies on joint courses of action to address ongoing or emerging global challenges; and (iii) it advises interested Governments on the ways and means of translating policy frameworks developed in United Nations conferences and summits into programmes at the country level and, through technical assistance, helps build national capacities.

Note

The designations employed and the presentation of material in this publication do not imply the expression of any opinion whatsoever on the part of the Secretariat of the United Nations concerning the legal status of any country, territory, city or area or of its authorities, or concerning the delimitation of its frontiers or boundaries.

The term "country" as used in this publication also refers, as appropriate, to territories or areas.

Visit the United Nations World Wide Web site on the Internet:
For the Department of Economic and Social Affairs,
    http://www.un.org/esa/desa/
For statistics and statistical publications,
    http://unstats.un.org/unsd/
For UN publications, https://unp.un.org/

ST/ESA/STAT/SER.V/36
United Nations Publication
Sales No. E.12.XVII.4
ISBN-13: 978-92-1-161558-6

World Statistics Pocketbook 2011

Printed in the United States of America

Contents

Country profiles

Contents (*continued*)

Contents (*continued*)

Introduction

The *World Statistics Pocketbook* is the thirty-first in a series of annual compilations of key economic, social and environmental indicators, presented in one-page profiles for 216 countries or areas of the world. Prepared by the United Nations Statistics Division of the Department of Economic and Social Affairs, it responds to General Assembly resolution 2626 (XXV), in which the Secretary-General is requested to supply basic national data that will increase international public awareness of countries' development efforts.

The indicators shown are selected from the wealth of international statistical information compiled regularly by the Statistics Division and the Population Division of the United Nations, the statistical services of the United Nations specialized agencies and other international organizations and institutions. Special recognition is gratefully given for their assistance in continually providing data.

Time period

This issue of the *World Statistics Pocketbook* covers various years from 2000 to 2011. For the economic indicators, in general, three years - 2000, 2005 and 2010 - are shown, unless otherwise indicated. Due to space limitations, data for one year only are shown for the indicators in the social and environmental categories. For the six social indicators for which the range of years 2010-2015 is shown, the data refer to projections. When other ranges of years are shown, the data refer to the most recent year available within that range.

Organization of the Pocketbook

The country tables or profiles are presented alphabetically according to countries' names in English and contain the available data for the following broad categories:

- *General information:* includes each country's location by geographical region, currency, surface area, population and population density, capital city and United Nations membership date

- *Economic indicators:* includes national accounts (Gross domestic product (GDP), GDP growth rate, GDP per capita, gross national income per capita and gross fixed capital formation), exchange rates, balance of payments, consumer price index, production indices (industrial, agricultural and food), unemployment, employment, labour force participation, tourist arrivals, energy production, telephone subscribers and internet users

- *Trade:* contains the value of total exports, imports and the trade balance as well as the countries' main trading partners

- *Social indicators:* includes population (growth rates, urban percentage, age groups and sex ratios), life expectancy, infant mortality rate, total fertility

Introduction (*continued*)

rate, contraceptive prevalence, international migrant stock, refugees, education (expenditure and enrolment), deaths by assault and female participation in national parliaments

- *Environmental indicators:* includes threatened species, forested area, CO_2 emission estimates, energy consumption per capita and climatological information.

The complete set of indicators, listed by category and in the order in which they appear in the profiles, is shown at the beginning of the country profile section. Not all indicators are shown for each country or area due to different degrees of data availability.

The technical notes section, which follows the country profile pages, contains brief descriptions of the concepts and methodologies used in the compilation of the indicators as well as information on the statistical sources for the indicators. Readers interested in longer time-series data or more detailed descriptions of the concepts or methodologies should consult the primary sources of the data and the references listed in the section following the technical notes.

The index of indicators, at the back of this publication, lists the complete set of indicators in alphabetical order and shows the category in which each is presented in the country profiles along with the pages on which information on the concepts, definitions and the data sources are given. As noted above, the number of indicators actually shown for the countries varies according to data availability.

* * *

The *World Statistics Pocketbook* is prepared annually by the Statistical Services Branch of the Statistics Division, Department of Economic and Social Affairs of the United Nations Secretariat. The programme manager is Mary Jane Holupka, the editor is Iliana Vaca, and the software developer is Salomon Cameo. Comments on this publication are welcome and may be sent by e-mail to statistics@un.org.

Symbols, abbreviations and conversion factors

The following symbols and abbreviations have been used in the *World Statistics Pocketbook*:

...	Data not available
–	Magnitude zero
<	Magnitude not zero, but less than half of the unit employed
–<	Magnitude not zero, but negative and less than half of the unit employed
000	Thousands
°C	Degrees Celsius
°F	Degrees Fahrenheit
%	Percentage
60+	Aged sixty years and over
.	Decimal figures are always preceded by a period (.)
CFA	Coopération financière en Afrique centrale
CIF	Cost, Insurance and Freight
CO_2	Carbon dioxide
CPI	Consumer price index
f	Females
FOB	Free on board
GDP	Gross domestic product
GNI	Gross national income
ILO	International Labour Organization
ISIC	International Standard Industrial Classification
ISO	International Organization for Standardization
km	Kilometres
m	Males
mt	Metric tons
UN	United Nations
UNESCO	United Nations Educational, Scientific and Cultural Organization
UNHCR	Office of the United Nations High Commissioner for Refugees
UNSD	United Nations Statistics Division
US$	United States dollar

The metric system of weights and measures has been employed in the *World Statistics Pocketbook*. The equivalents of the basic British Imperial and United States weights and measures are as follows:

Area	1 square kilometre	= 0.386102 square mile
Weight or mass	1 ton	= 1.102311 short tons or
		= 0.987207 long ton
	1 kilogram	= 35.273962 avoirdupois ounces
		= 2.204623 avoirdupois pounds
Distance	1 kilometre	= 0.621371 mile
	1 millimetre	= 0.039 inch
Temperature	°C	= (°F - 32) × 5/9

Country profile information and indicator list*

General information
Region
Currency
Surface area (square kilometres)
Population in 2010 (estimated, 000)
Population density in 2010 (per square kilometre)
Capital city and population in 2011 (000)
United Nations membership date

Economic indicators
GDP: Gross domestic product (million current US$)
GDP: Growth rate at constant 2005 prices (annual %)
GDP per capita (current US$)
GNI: Gross national income per capita (current US$)
Gross fixed capital formation (% of GDP)
Exchange rates (national currency per US$)
Balance of payments, current account (million US$)
CPI: Consumer price index (2000=100)
Industrial production index (2005=100)
Agricultural production index (2004-2006=100)
Food production index (2004-2006=100)
Unemployment (% of labour force)
Employment in industrial sector (% of employed)
Employment in agricultural sector (% of employed)
Labour force participation, adult female population (%)
Labour force participation, adult male population (%)
Tourist arrivals at national borders (000)
Energy production, primary (000 mt oil equivalent)
Telephone subscribers, total (per 100 inhabitants)
Internet users (per 100 inhabitants)

Trade
Total trade (exports, imports and balance, million US$)
Major trading partners (exports and imports, %)

Social indicators
Population growth rate (average annual %)
Urban population growth rate (average annual %)
Rural population growth rate (average annual %)
Urban population (%)
Population aged 0-14 years (%)
Population aged 60+ years (females and males, % of total)
Sex ratio (males per 100 females)
Life expectancy at birth (females and males, years)
Infant mortality rate (per 1 000 live births)
Fertility rate, total (live births per woman)
Contraceptive prevalence (ages 15-49, %)
International migrant stock (000 and % of total population)
Refugees and others of concern to UNHCR
Education: Government expenditure (% of GDP)
Education: Primary and secondary gross enrolment ratio (females and males per 100)
Education: Female third-level students (% of total)
Deaths by assault (females and males, per 100 000)
Seats held by women in national parliaments (%)

Environmental indicators
Threatened species
Forested area (% of land area)
CO_2 emission estimates (000 metric tons and metric tons per capita)
Energy consumption per capita (kilograms oil equivalent)
Rainfall in the capital city, total mean (millimetres)
Temperature in the capital city, mean °C (minimum and maximum)

* The complete set of information and indicators listed here may not be shown for each
  country or area depending upon data availability.

Country profiles

Afghanistan

Region	South-central Asia
Currency	Afghani (AFN)[a]
Surface area (square kilometres)	652 864
Population in 2010 (estimated, 000)	31 412
Population density in 2010 (per square kilometre)	48.1
Capital city and population in 2011 (000)	Kabul (3 097)
United Nations membership date	19 November 1946

Economic indicators	2000	2005	2010
GDP: Gross domestic product (million current US$)	3 532	6 840	15 676
GDP: Growth rate at constant 2005 prices (annual %)	−5.5	14.5	8.2
GDP per capita (current US$)	154.5	247.7	499.0
GNI: Gross national income per capita (current US$)	154.5	247.7	499.0
Gross fixed capital formation (% of GDP)	14.3	31.3	26.5
Exchange rates (national currency per US$)[b]	...	50.41	45.27
Agricultural production index (2004-2006=100)	85	107	116
Food production index (2004-2006=100)	84	107	116
Labour force participation, adult female pop. (%)	13.4	13.9	15.5
Labour force participation, adult male pop. (%)	80.8	80.6	80.4
Energy production, primary (000 mt oil equivalent)	154[c]	85	420[d]
Telephone subscribers, total (per 100 inhabitants)	0.1[e]	4.7	41.8
Internet users (per 100 inhabitants)	0.1[f]	1.2	4.0

Total trade		Major trading partners			2010
	(million US$)	(% of exports)			(% of imports)
Exports	388.5	Pakistan	38.9	Uzbekistan	21.1
Imports	5 154.2	India	16.8	China	13.7
Balance	−4 765.7	Turkey	9.0	Pakistan	11.6

Social indicators		
Population growth rate (average annual %)	2010-2015	3.1
Urban population growth rate (average annual %)	2010-2015	4.4
Rural population growth rate (average annual %)	2010-2015	2.7
Urban population (%)	2011	23.5
Population aged 0-14 years (%)	2011	46.2
Population aged 60+ years (females and males, % of total)	2011	3.9/3.6
Sex ratio (males per 100 females)	2011	107.2
Life expectancy at birth (females and males, years)	2010-2015	49.5/49.2
Infant mortality rate (per 1 000 live births)	2010-2015	124.5
Fertility rate, total (live births per woman)	2010-2015	6.0
Contraceptive prevalence (ages 15-49, %)	2006-2010	22.8
International migrant stock (000 and % of total population)	mid-2010	90.9/0.3
Refugees and others of concern to UNHCR	end-2010	1 318 019
Education: Primary-secondary gross enrolment ratio (f/m per 100)	2005-2011	57.0/89.4
Education: Female third-level students (% of total)	2005-2011	18.0
Seats held by women in national parliaments (%)	2011	27.7

Environmental indicators		
Threatened species	2011	36
Forested area (% of land area)	2009	2.1
CO_2 emission estimates (000 metric tons and metric tons per capita)	2008	813/0.0
Energy consumption per capita (kilograms oil equivalent)	2009	71.0
Rainfall in the capital city, total mean (millimetres)		312
Temperature in the capital city, mean °C (minimum and maximum)		4.3/19.6

a Beginning October 2002, 1 new Afghani = 1000 old Afghanis. **b** Principal rate. **c** UNSD estimate. **d** 2009. **e** Main telephone lines only. **f** 2003.

Albania

Region	Southern Europe
Currency	Lek (ALL)
Surface area (square kilometres)	28 748
Population in 2010 (estimated, 000)	3 204
Population density in 2010 (per square kilometre)	111.5
Capital city and population in 2011 (000)	Tirana (419)
United Nations membership date	14 December 1955

Economic indicators	2000	2005	2010
GDP: Gross domestic product (million current US$)	3 640	8 159	11 783
GDP: Growth rate at constant 2005 prices (annual %)	6.6	5.8	3.5
GDP per capita (current US$)	1 184.8	2 596.8	3 677.2
GNI: Gross national income per capita (current US$)	1 218.2	2 647.7	3 729.0
Gross fixed capital formation (% of GDP)	31.7	37.0	25.1
Exchange rates (national currency per US$)[a]	142.64	103.58	104.00
Balance of payments, current account (million US$)	−156	−571	−1 403
CPI: Consumer price index (2000=100)	100	117	135
Industrial production index (2005=100)[b]	94[c]	100	194
Agricultural production index (2004-2006=100)	88	98	119
Food production index (2004-2006=100)	87	98	119
Employment in industrial sector (% of employed)	6.6[d]	13.5[d]	19.9[ef]
Employment in agricultural sector (% of employed)	71.8[d]	58.5[d]	44.1[ef]
Labour force participation, adult female pop. (%)	50.9	50.0	49.7
Labour force participation, adult male pop. (%)	73.0	71.7	71.3
Tourist arrivals at national borders (000)[gh]	317	748	2 417
Energy production, primary (000 mt oil equivalent)	732	945	1 050[f]
Telephone subscribers, total (per 100 inhabitants)	5.9	57.6	152.3
Internet users (per 100 inhabitants)	0.1	6.0	45.0

Total trade	Major trading partners				2010
(million US$)	(% of exports)				(% of imports)
Exports	1 550.0	Italy	50.8	Italy	28.2
Imports	4 602.8	Serbia	8.3	Greece	13.1
Balance	−3 052.8	Turkey	6.0	China	6.3

Social indicators		
Population growth rate (average annual %)	2010-2015	0.3
Urban population growth rate (average annual %)	2010-2015	2.3
Rural population growth rate (average annual %)	2010-2015	−2.0
Urban population (%)	2011	53.4
Population aged 0-14 years (%)	2011	22.1
Population aged 60+ years (females and males, % of total)	2011	14.1/12.9
Sex ratio (males per 100 females)	2011	100.2
Life expectancy at birth (females and males, years)	2010-2015	80.4/74.2
Infant mortality rate (per 1 000 live births)	2010-2015	16.6
Fertility rate, total (live births per woman)	2010-2015	1.5
Contraceptive prevalence (ages 15-49, %)	2006-2009	69.3
International migrant stock (000 and % of total population)[i]	mid-2010	89.1/2.8
Refugees and others of concern to UNHCR	end-2010	99
Education: Primary-secondary gross enrolment ratio (f/m per 100)	2005-2011	87.3/88.9
Education: Female third-level students (% of total)	2005-2011	62.1[j]
Seats held by women in national parliaments (%)	2011	16.4

Environmental indicators		
Threatened species	2011	107
Forested area (% of land area)	2009	28.4
CO_2 emission estimates (000 metric tons and metric tons per capita)	2008	4 173/1.3
Energy consumption per capita (kilograms oil equivalent)	2009	402.0

a Market rate. **b** The indices are shown in terms of ISIC Rev. 3. **c** 2003. **d** Official estimates. **e** Age group 15 to 64 years. **f** 2009. **g** Excludes nationals residing abroad. **h** Arrivals of non-resident visitors at national borders. **i** Data refer to foreign citizens. **j** 2004.

Algeria

Region	Northern Africa
Currency	Dinar (DZD)
Surface area (square kilometres)	2 381 741
Population in 2010 (estimated, 000)	35 468
Population density in 2010 (per square kilometre)	14.9
Capital city and population in 2011 (000)	Algiers (2 916)
United Nations membership date	8 October 1962

Economic indicators	2000	2005	2010
GDP: Gross domestic product (million current US$)	54 790	103 234	158 650
GDP: Growth rate at constant 2005 prices (annual %)	2.2	5.1	3.3
GDP per capita (current US$)	1 794.4	3 138.9	4 473.0
GNI: Gross national income per capita (current US$)	1 718.2	2 983.1	4 441.2
Gross fixed capital formation (% of GDP)	20.7	22.4	32.7
Exchange rates (national currency per US$) [a]	75.34	73.38	74.94
Balance of payments, current account (million US$)	...	21 084	160[b]
CPI: Consumer price index (2000=100)	100	117	146
Industrial production index (2005=100) [c]	94[d]	100	99
Agricultural production index (2004-2006=100)	69	99	124
Food production index (2004-2006=100)	69	99	124
Employment in industrial sector (% of employed) [e]	24.3[f]	26.0[g]	...
Employment in agricultural sector (% of employed) [e]	21.1[f]	20.7[g]	...
Labour force participation, adult female pop. (%)	12.0	13.0	14.7
Labour force participation, adult male pop. (%)	75.5	73.2	71.7
Tourist arrivals at national borders (000) [hi]	866	1 443	1 912[b]
Energy production, primary (000 mt oil equivalent)	165 360	189 329	173 267[b]
Telephone subscribers, total (per 100 inhabitants)	6.1	49.4	100.7
Internet users (per 100 inhabitants)	0.5	5.8	12.5

Total trade		Major trading partners			2010
	(million US$)	(% of exports)			(% of imports)
Exports	57 051.0	United States	24.2	France	14.9
Imports	40 999.9	Italy	15.4	China	11.2
Balance	16 051.1	Spain	10.4	Italy	10.0

Social indicators		
Population growth rate (average annual %)	2010-2015	1.4
Urban population growth rate (average annual %)	2010-2015	2.5
Rural population growth rate (average annual %)	2010-2015	−1.9
Urban population (%)	2011	73.0
Population aged 0-14 years (%)	2011	26.8
Population aged 60+ years (females and males, % of total)	2011	7.7/6.3
Sex ratio (males per 100 females)	2011	101.9
Life expectancy at birth (females and males, years)	2010-2015	75.0/71.9
Infant mortality rate (per 1 000 live births)	2010-2015	21.5
Fertility rate, total (live births per woman)	2010-2015	2.1
Contraceptive prevalence (ages 15-49, %)	2006-2010	61.4
International migrant stock (000 and % of total population) [jk]	mid-2010	242.3/0.7
Refugees and others of concern to UNHCR	end-2010	94 451[l]
Education: Government expenditure (% of GDP)	2005-2011	4.3
Education: Primary-secondary gross enrolment ratio (f/m per 100)	2005-2011	99.9/101.5
Education: Female third-level students (% of total)	2005-2011	58.3
Seats held by women in national parliaments (%)	2011	7.7

Environmental indicators		
Threatened species	2011	106
Forested area (% of land area)	2009	0.6
CO_2 emission estimates (000 metric tons and metric tons per capita)	2008	111 213/3.2
Energy consumption per capita (kilograms oil equivalent)	2009	1 117.0
Rainfall in the capital city, total mean (millimetres)		598
Temperature in the capital city, mean °C (minimum and maximum)		11.9/23.7

a Official rate. **b** 2009. **c** The indices are shown in terms of ISIC Rev. 3. **d** 2003. **e** September. **f** 2001. **g** 2004. **h** Includes nationals residing abroad. **i** Arrivals of non-resident visitors at national borders. **j** Data refer to foreign citizens. **k** Includes refugees. **l** According to the Government of Algeria, there are an estimated 165,000 Sahrawi refugees in the Tindouf camps.

American Samoa

Region	Oceania-Polynesia
Currency	U.S. Dollar (USD)
Surface area (square kilometres)	199
Population in 2010 (estimated, 000)	68
Population density in 2010 (per square kilometre)	343.8
Capital city and population in 2011 (000)	Pago Pago (65)

Economic indicators	2000	2005	2010
CPI: Consumer price index (2000=100) [a]	100	122	...
Agricultural production index (2004-2006=100)	73	107	108
Food production index (2004-2006=100)	73	107	108
Tourist arrivals at national borders (000)	44	24	25[b]
Telephone subscribers, total (per 100 inhabitants)	21.3	16.5[c]	15.2[c]

Social indicators		
Population growth rate (average annual %)	2010-2015	1.6
Urban population growth rate (average annual %)	2010-2015	1.9
Rural population growth rate (average annual %)	2010-2015	−1.9
Urban population (%)	2011	93.2
Population aged 0-14 years (%) [d]	2011	34.6
Population aged 60+ years (females and males, % of total) [d]	2011	7.9/6.9
Sex ratio (males per 100 females) [d]	2011	104.2
Life expectancy at birth (females and males, years) [e]	2010-2015	76.2/68.5[b]
Infant mortality rate (per 1 000 live births) [e]	2010-2015	11.3[f]
Fertility rate, total (live births per woman) [d]	2010-2015	4.0[g]
International migrant stock (000 and % of total population)	mid-2010	28.4/41.4

Environmental indicators		
Threatened species	2011	80
Forested area (% of land area)	2009	88.8

a Excludes rent. b 2006. c Main telephone lines only. d Data compiled by the Secretariat of the Pacific Community Demography Programme. e Data compiled by the United Nations Demographic Yearbook system. f 2006-2008. g 2000.

Andorra

Region	Southern Europe
Currency	Euro (EUR)
Surface area (square kilometres)	468
Population in 2010 (estimated, 000)	85
Population density in 2010 (per square kilometre)	181.3
Capital city and population in 2011 (000)	Andorra la Vella (24)
United Nations membership date	28 July 1993

Economic indicators	2000	2005	2010
GDP: Gross domestic product (million current US$)	1 387	3 179	3 491
GDP: Growth rate at constant 2005 prices (annual %)	1.2	6.6	-3.4
GDP per capita (current US$)	21 458.9	40 820.8	41 138.3
GNI: Gross national income per capita (current US$)	21 458.9	40 820.8	41 138.3
Gross fixed capital formation (% of GDP)	25.8	29.4	22.5
Exchange rates (national currency per US$) [a]	1.07	0.85	0.75
CPI: Consumer price index (2000=100) [bc]	100[d]	115	126
Tourist arrivals at national borders (000)	2 949	2 418	1 830[ef]
Energy production, primary (000 mt oil equivalent)	7[g]	7	5[eg]
Telephone subscribers, total (per 100 inhabitants)	89.4	128.4	122.2
Internet users (per 100 inhabitants)	10.5	37.6	81.0

Total trade		Major trading partners		2010
	(million US$)	(% of exports)[h]		(% of imports)
Exports	150.5[h]	Spain	69.6	
		France	15.1	
		Germany	6.2	

Social indicators		
Population growth rate (average annual %)	2010-2015	1.5
Urban population growth rate (average annual %)	2010-2015	0.9
Rural population growth rate (average annual %)	2010-2015	5.5
Urban population (%)	2011	87.3
Population aged 0-14 years (%) [ijk]	2011	14.0[l]
Population aged 60+ years (females and males, % of total) [ijk]	2011	18.8/18.4[l]
Sex ratio (males per 100 females) [ij]	2011	108.5[l]
Fertility rate, total (live births per woman) [j]	2010-2015	1.2[e]
International migrant stock (000 and % of total population) [m]	mid-2010	55.9/64.4
Education: Government expenditure (% of GDP)	2005-2011	3.1
Education: Primary-secondary gross enrolment ratio (f/m per 100)	2005-2011	86.8/84.4
Education: Female third-level students (% of total)	2005-2011	57.5
Seats held by women in national parliaments (%)	2011	50.0

Environmental indicators		
Threatened species	2011	11
Forested area (% of land area)	2009	34.0
CO_2 emission estimates (000 metric tons and metric tons per capita)	2008	539/6.4
Energy consumption per capita (kilograms oil equivalent)	2009	2 636.0

a Market rate. b December. c Index base 2001=100. d 2001. e 2009. f Change in methodology, therefore data are not strictly comparable with those of previous years. g UNSD estimate. h 2006. i De jure estimate. j Data compiled by the United Nations Demographic Yearbook system. k Data refer to the latest available census. l 2010. m Data refer to foreign citizens.

Angola

Region	Middle Africa
Currency	Kwanza (AOA)
Surface area (square kilometres)	1 246 700
Population in 2010 (estimated, 000)	19 082
Population density in 2010 (per square kilometre)	15.3
Capital city and population in 2011 (000)	Luanda (5 068)
United Nations membership date	1 December 1976

Economic indicators	2000	2005	2010
GDP: Gross domestic product (million current US$)	9 133	30 629	82 470
GDP: Growth rate at constant 2005 prices (annual %)	3.0	20.6	3.4
GDP per capita (current US$)	655.8	1 857.6	4 321.9
GNI: Gross national income per capita (current US$)	535.1	1 613.1	3 734.5
Gross fixed capital formation (% of GDP)	11.7	8.1	10.3
Exchange rates (national currency per US$) [a]	16.82	80.78	92.64
Balance of payments, current account (million US$)	796	5 138	7 421
CPI: Consumer price index (2000=100) [b]	100	1 846	3 003[c]
Agricultural production index (2004-2006=100)	71	106	151
Food production index (2004-2006=100)	71	106	152
Labour force participation, adult female pop. (%)	67.4	64.4	62.7
Labour force participation, adult male pop. (%)	75.4	76.3	77.0
Tourist arrivals at national borders (000)	51	210	425
Energy production, primary (000 mt oil equivalent)	37 689	63 896	92 954[c]
Telephone subscribers, total (per 100 inhabitants)	0.7	10.4	48.3
Internet users (per 100 inhabitants)	0.1	1.1	10.0

Social indicators		
Population growth rate (average annual %)	2010-2015	2.7
Urban population growth rate (average annual %)	2010-2015	4.0
Rural population growth rate (average annual %)	2010-2015	0.8
Urban population (%)	2011	59.2
Population aged 0-14 years (%)	2011	46.3
Population aged 60+ years (females and males, % of total)	2011	4.3/3.6
Sex ratio (males per 100 females)	2011	98.2
Life expectancy at birth (females and males, years)	2010-2015	53.2/50.2
Infant mortality rate (per 1 000 live births)	2010-2015	96.2
Fertility rate, total (live births per woman)	2010-2015	5.1
Contraceptive prevalence (ages 15-49, %)	2006-2010	6.2[d]
International migrant stock (000 and % of total population) [e]	mid-2010	65.4/0.3
Refugees and others of concern to UNHCR	end-2010	19 884
Education: Government expenditure (% of GDP)	2005-2011	2.7
Education: Primary-secondary gross enrolment ratio (f/m per 100)	2005-2011	73.5/93.2
Education: Female third-level students (% of total)	2005-2011	45.4
Seats held by women in national parliaments (%)	2011	38.6

Environmental indicators		
Threatened species	2011	122
Forested area (% of land area)	2009	47.0
CO$_2$ emission estimates (000 metric tons and metric tons per capita)	2008	24 351/1.4
Energy consumption per capita (kilograms oil equivalent)	2009	249.0
Temperature in the capital city, mean °C (minimum and maximum)		22.3/27.7

a Official rate. b Luanda. c 2009. d 2001. e Includes refugees.

Antigua and Barbuda

Region	Caribbean
Currency	E.C. Dollar (XCD)
Surface area (square kilometres)	442
Population in 2010 (estimated, 000)	89
Population density in 2010 (per square kilometre)	200.7
Capital city and population in 2011 (000)	St. John's (27)
United Nations membership date	11 November 1981

Economic indicators	2000	2005	2010
GDP: Gross domestic product (million current US$)	664	867	1 118
GDP: Growth rate at constant 2005 prices (annual %)	1.5	4.2	−4.1
GDP per capita (current US$)	8 552.9	10 329.6	12 602.4
GNI: Gross national income per capita (current US$)	7 979.6	9 628.7	11 855.7
Gross fixed capital formation (% of GDP)	48.1	59.2	72.0
Exchange rates (national currency per US$)[a]	2.70	2.70	2.70
Balance of payments, current account (million US$)	−42	−171	−113
Agricultural production index (2004-2006=100)	102	95	106
Food production index (2004-2006=100)	102	95	106
Employment in industrial sector (% of employed)	14.6[bcd]	15.6[e]	15.6[ef]
Employment in agricultural sector (% of employed)	2.6[bcd]	2.8[e]	2.8[ef]
Tourist arrivals at national borders (000)[g]	207	245[h]	230
Telephone subscribers, total (per 100 inhabitants)	77.7	146.0	230.3
Internet users (per 100 inhabitants)	6.5	34.7	80.0

Total trade		Major trading partners			2010
	(million US$)	(% of exports)			(% of imports)
Exports	34.8	United States	29.6	United States	45.7
Imports	361.3	United Kingdom	19.5	China	11.7
Balance	−326.5	Panama	12.6	United Kingdom	6.4

Social indicators		
Population growth rate (average annual %)	2010-2015	1.0
Urban population growth rate (average annual %)	2010-2015	1.0
Rural population growth rate (average annual %)	2010-2015	1.0
Urban population (%)	2011	29.8
Population aged 0-14 years (%)[ijk]	2011	28.3[l]
Population aged 60+ years (females and males, % of total)[ijk]	2011	9.8/8.8[l]
Sex ratio (males per 100 females)[jm]	2011	88.6[n]
Contraceptive prevalence (ages 15-49, %)[o]	2006-2010	52.6[p]
International migrant stock (000 and % of total population)	mid-2010	20.9/23.6
Refugees and others of concern to UNHCR	end-2010	0[q]
Education: Government expenditure (% of GDP)	2005-2011	2.5
Education: Primary-secondary gross enrolment ratio (f/m per 100)	2005-2011	100.9/105.5
Education: Female third-level students (% of total)	2005-2011	73.6
Seats held by women in national parliaments (%)	2011	10.5

Environmental indicators		
Threatened species	2011	41
Forested area (% of land area)	2009	22.3
CO_2 emission estimates (000 metric tons and metric tons per capita)	2008	447/5.2
Energy consumption per capita (kilograms oil equivalent)	2009	1 759.0[r]
Rainfall in the capital city, total mean (millimetres)		1 052
Temperature in the capital city, mean °C (minimum and maximum)		23.9/29.6

a Official rate. b 2001. c May. d Population census. e Official estimates. f 2008. g Excludes nationals residing abroad. h Air arrivals. i De facto estimate. j Data compiled by the United Nations Demographic Yearbook system. k Data refer to the latest available census. l 2005. m De facto national estimate. n 2007. o Age group 15 to 44 years. p 1988. q Value is zero, not available or not applicable. r UNSD estimate.

Argentina

Region	South America
Currency	Argentine Peso (ARS)
Surface area (square kilometres)	2 780 400
Population in 2010 (estimated, 000)	40 412
Population density in 2010 (per square kilometre)	14.5
Capital city and population in 2011 (000)	Buenos Aires (13 528)
United Nations membership date	24 October 1945

Economic indicators	2000	2005	2010
GDP: Gross domestic product (million current US$)	284 346	183 196	370 263
GDP: Growth rate at constant 2005 prices (annual %)	−0.8	9.2	9.2
GDP per capita (current US$)	7 699.4	4 736.1	9 162.1
GNI: Gross national income per capita (current US$)	7 495.0	4 575.5	8 922.2
Gross fixed capital formation (% of GDP)	16.2	21.5	22.0
Exchange rates (national currency per US$) [a]	1.00	3.01	3.96
Balance of payments, current account (million US$)	−8 981	5 275	3 082
CPI: Consumer price index (2000=100) [b]	100	162	249
Agricultural production index (2004-2006=100)	86	103	115
Food production index (2004-2006=100)	86	103	115
Unemployment (% of labour force) [cd]	13.6[e]	11.6	7.7
Employment in industrial sector (% of employed) [d]	22.7[fg]	23.5[fh]	23.1[cij]
Employment in agricultural sector (% of employed) [d]	0.7[fg]	1.1[fh]	1.2[cij]
Labour force participation, adult female pop. (%)	42.6	48.8	47.0
Labour force participation, adult male pop. (%)	74.3	76.6	74.9
Tourist arrivals at national borders (000)	2 909	3 823[k]	5 325
Energy production, primary (000 mt oil equivalent)	82 216	86 293	81 878[j]
Telephone subscribers, total (per 100 inhabitants)	39.0	81.7	166.5
Internet users (per 100 inhabitants)	7.0	17.7	36.0

Total trade		Major trading partners			2010
	(million US$)	(% of exports)			(% of imports)
Exports	68 134.1	Brazil	21.2	Brazil	31.3
Imports	56 501.3	China	8.5	China	13.5
Balance	11 632.8	Chile	6.6	United States	10.8

Social indicators		
Population growth rate (average annual %)	2010-2015	0.9
Urban population growth rate (average annual %)	2010-2015	1.0
Rural population growth rate (average annual %)	2010-2015	−1.2
Urban population (%)	2011	92.5
Population aged 0-14 years (%)	2011	24.7
Population aged 60+ years (females and males, % of total)	2011	16.8/12.7
Sex ratio (males per 100 females)	2011	95.8
Life expectancy at birth (females and males, years)	2010-2015	79.9/72.4
Infant mortality rate (per 1 000 live births)	2010-2015	12.3
Fertility rate, total (live births per woman)	2010-2015	2.2
Contraceptive prevalence (ages 15-49, %)	2006-2010	65.3[l]
International migrant stock (000 and % of total population)	mid-2010	1 449.3/3.6
Refugees and others of concern to UNHCR	end-2010	4 223
Education: Government expenditure (% of GDP)	2005-2011	6.0
Education: Primary-secondary gross enrolment ratio (f/m per 100)	2005-2011	105.1/100.7
Education: Female third-level students (% of total)	2005-2011	59.5
Deaths by assault (females and males, per 100 000)	2005-2008	1.3/7.6
Seats held by women in national parliaments (%)	2011	37.4

Environmental indicators		
Threatened species	2011	214
Forested area (% of land area)	2009	10.8
CO$_2$ emission estimates (000 metric tons and metric tons per capita)	2008	192 221/4.8
Energy consumption per capita (kilograms oil equivalent)	2009	1 774.0
Rainfall in the capital city, total mean (millimetres)		1 215
Temperature in the capital city, mean °C (minimum and maximum)		13.5/22.5

a Official rate. **b** Metropolitan areas. **c** 31 urban agglomerations. **d** Age group 10 years and over. **e** 2004. **f** 28 urban agglomerations. **g** Average of May and October. **h** Second semester. **i** Average of quarterly estimates. **j** 2009. **k** Change in methodology, therefore data are not strictly comparable with those of previous years. **l** 2001.

Armenia

Region	Western Asia
Currency	Dram (AMD)
Surface area (square kilometres)	29 743
Population in 2010 (estimated, 000)	3 092
Population density in 2010 (per square kilometre)	104.0
Capital city and population in 2011 (000)	Yerevan (1 116)
United Nations membership date	2 March 1992

Economic indicators	2000	2005	2010
GDP: Gross domestic product (million current US$)	1 912	4 900	9 371
GDP: Growth rate at constant 2005 prices (annual %)	5.9	13.9	2.1
GDP per capita (current US$)	621.4	1 598.4	3 030.7
GNI: Gross national income per capita (current US$)	613.8	1 641.6	3 122.0
Gross fixed capital formation (% of GDP)	18.4	29.8	33.1
Exchange rates (national currency per US$) [a]	552.18	450.19	363.44
Balance of payments, current account (million US$)	−278	−52	−1 373
CPI: Consumer price index (2000=100)	100	117[b]	142[c]
Agricultural production index (2004-2006=100)	67	103	101
Food production index (2004-2006=100)	67	103	101
Employment in industrial sector (% of employed) [d]	17.0[e]	15.9	16.8[f]
Employment in agricultural sector (% of employed) [d]	45.3[e]	46.2	44.2[f]
Labour force participation, adult female pop. (%)	57.7	52.1	49.0
Labour force participation, adult male pop. (%)	72.8	69.9	69.6
Tourist arrivals at national borders (000)	45	319	575[c]
Energy production, primary (000 mt oil equivalent)	281	386	388[c]
Telephone subscribers, total (per 100 inhabitants)	17.9	29.8	144.2
Internet users (per 100 inhabitants)	1.3	5.3	44.0

Total trade		Major trading partners			2010
	(million US$)	(% of exports)		(% of imports)	
Exports	1 011.4	Russian Federation	15.8	Russian Federation	21.9
Imports	3 781.8	Bulgaria	15.5	China	10.6
Balance	−2 770.4	Germany	13.1	Ukraine	6.1

Social indicators		
Population growth rate (average annual %)	2010-2015	0.3
Urban population growth rate (average annual %)	2010-2015	0.3
Rural population growth rate (average annual %)	2010-2015	0.1
Urban population (%)	2011	64.1
Population aged 0-14 years (%)	2011	20.1
Population aged 60+ years (females and males, % of total)	2011	16.9/12.4
Sex ratio (males per 100 females)	2011	87.1
Life expectancy at birth (females and males, years)	2010-2015	77.3/71.0
Infant mortality rate (per 1 000 live births)	2010-2015	24.3
Fertility rate, total (live births per woman)	2010-2015	1.7
Contraceptive prevalence (ages 15-49, %)	2006-2010	53.1[g]
International migrant stock (000 and % of total population) [h]	mid-2010	324.2/10.5
Refugees and others of concern to UNHCR	end-2010	85 844
Education: Government expenditure (% of GDP)	2005-2011	3.2
Education: Primary-secondary gross enrolment ratio (f/m per 100)	2005-2011	96.0/93.9
Education: Female third-level students (% of total)	2005-2011	55.9
Seats held by women in national parliaments (%)	2011	9.2

Environmental indicators		
Threatened species	2011	39
Forested area (% of land area)	2009	9.4
CO_2 emission estimates (000 metric tons and metric tons per capita)	2008	5 544/1.8
Energy consumption per capita (kilograms oil equivalent)	2009	728.0
Rainfall in the capital city, total mean (millimetres)		277
Temperature in the capital city, mean °C (minimum and maximum)		5.5/18.2

a Official rate. **b** Series linked to former series. **c** 2009. **d** Official estimates. **e** 2002. **f** 2008. **g** 2005. **h** Includes refugees.

Aruba

Region	Caribbean
Currency	Aruban Guilder (AWG)
Surface area (square kilometres)	180
Population in 2010 (estimated, 000)	107
Population density in 2010 (per square kilometre)	597.2
Capital city and population in 2011 (000)	Oranjestad (37)

Economic indicators	2000	2005	2010
GDP: Gross domestic product (million current US$)	1 873	2 331	2 456
GDP: Growth rate at constant 2005 prices (annual %)	4.5	1.0	−3.7
GDP per capita (current US$)	20 753.7	23 080.2	22 851.5
GNI: Gross national income per capita (current US$)	19 618.2	21 678.9	21 475.6
Gross fixed capital formation (% of GDP)	24.1	32.1	28.7
Exchange rates (national currency per US$) [a]	1.79	1.79	1.79
Balance of payments, current account (million US$)	204	−198	−410
CPI: Consumer price index (2000=100)	100	117	139
Employment in industrial sector (% of employed) [b]	16.4[c]	20.3[d]	...
Employment in agricultural sector (% of employed) [b]	0.5[c]	0.7[d]	...
Tourist arrivals at national borders (000)	721	733	813[e]
Energy production, primary (000 mt oil equivalent) [f]	121	121	124[e]
Telephone subscribers, total (per 100 inhabitants)	58.8	140.3	155.2
Internet users (per 100 inhabitants)	15.4	25.4	42.0

Total trade		Major trading partners			2010
	(million US$)	(% of exports)			(% of imports)
Exports	124.5	Colombia	27.1	United States	50.5
Imports	1 002.9	Panama	22.2	Netherlands	11.5
Balance	−878.4	Netherlands Antilles	15.2	United Kingdom	6.3

Social indicators		
Population growth rate (average annual %)	2010-2015	0.3
Urban population growth rate (average annual %)	2010-2015	0.5
Rural population growth rate (average annual %)	2010-2015	0.2
Urban population (%)	2011	46.9
Population aged 0-14 years (%)	2011	18.8
Population aged 60+ years (females and males, % of total)	2011	15.9/13.6
Sex ratio (males per 100 females)	2011	90.3
Life expectancy at birth (females and males, years)	2010-2015	77.8/73.0
Infant mortality rate (per 1 000 live births)	2010-2015	14.7
Fertility rate, total (live births per woman)	2010-2015	1.7
International migrant stock (000 and % of total population)	mid-2010	34.3/31.9
Refugees and others of concern to UNHCR	end-2010	1
Education: Government expenditure (% of GDP)	2005-2011	5.6
Education: Primary-secondary gross enrolment ratio (f/m per 100)	2005-2011	101.5/102.9
Education: Female third-level students (% of total)	2005-2011	57.2

Environmental indicators		
Threatened species	2011	22
Forested area (% of land area)	2009	2.2
CO$_2$ emission estimates (000 metric tons and metric tons per capita)	2008	2 286/21.7
Energy consumption per capita (kilograms oil equivalent)	2009	2 333.0[f]

a Official rate. b October. c Population census. d 2007. e 2009. f UNSD estimate.

Australia

Region	Oceania
Currency	Australian Dollar (AUD)
Surface area (square kilometres)	7 692 024
Population in 2010 (estimated, 000)	22 268 [a]
Population density in 2010 (per square kilometre)	2.9 [a]
Capital city and population in 2011 (000)	Canberra (399)
United Nations membership date	1 November 1945

Economic indicators	2000	2005	2010
GDP: Gross domestic product (million current US$)	411 009	764 765	1 271 950
GDP: Growth rate at constant 2005 prices (annual %)	2.1	3.1	2.5
GDP per capita (current US$)	21 446.5	37 482.0	57 118.9
GNI: Gross national income per capita (current US$)	20 863.4	36 064.1	54 863.5
Gross fixed capital formation (% of GDP)	23.0	27.9	27.4
Exchange rates (national currency per US$) [b]	1.81	1.36	0.98
Balance of payments, current account (million US$)	−14 763	−41 032	−31 991
CPI: Consumer price index (2000=100)	100	116	134
Industrial production index (2005=100) [c]	99 [d]	100	111
Agricultural production index (2004-2006=100)	106	108	99
Food production index (2004-2006=100)	103	108	101
Unemployment (% of labour force)	5.4 [e]	5.0	5.2
Employment in industrial sector (% of employed)	21.7 [f]	21.3 [f]	21.1 [gh]
Employment in agricultural sector (% of employed)	5.0 [f]	3.6 [f]	3.3 [gh]
Labour force participation, adult female pop. (%)	54.6	57.0	58.7
Labour force participation, adult male pop. (%)	72.4	72.2	72.5
Tourist arrivals at national borders (000) [ijk]	4 931	5 499	5 584 [h]
Energy production, primary (000 mt oil equivalent) [l]	230 742	278 077	308 655 [h]
Telephone subscribers, total (per 100 inhabitants)	97.1	139.9	139.9
Internet users (per 100 inhabitants)	46.8	63.0	76.0

Total trade		Major trading partners			2010
	(million US$)	(% of exports)			(% of imports)
Exports	206 705.1	China	25.3	China	18.7
Imports	188 740.7	Japan	18.9	United States	11.1
Balance	17 964.4	Republic of Korea	8.9	Japan	8.7

Social indicators		
Population growth rate (average annual %) [a]	2010-2015	1.3
Urban population growth rate (average annual %) [a]	2010-2015	1.5
Rural population growth rate (average annual %) [a]	2010-2015	−0.1
Urban population (%) [a]	2011	89.2
Population aged 0-14 years (%) [a]	2011	19.0
Population aged 60+ years (females and males, % of total) [a]	2011	20.3/18.2
Sex ratio (males per 100 females) [a]	2011	99.4
Life expectancy at birth (females and males, years) [a]	2010-2015	84.3/79.9
Infant mortality rate (per 1 000 live births) [a]	2010-2015	4.5
Fertility rate, total (live births per woman) [a]	2010-2015	2.0
Contraceptive prevalence (ages 15-49, %) [m]	2006-2010	70.8 [n]
International migrant stock (000 and % of total population) [a]	mid-2010	4 711.5/21.9
Refugees and others of concern to UNHCR	end-2010	25 565
Education: Government expenditure (% of GDP)	2005-2011	5.1
Education: Primary-secondary gross enrolment ratio (f/m per 100)	2005-2011	114.9/117.7
Education: Female third-level students (% of total)	2005-2011	55.8
Deaths by assault (females and males, per 100 000)	2005-2008	</0.8
Seats held by women in national parliaments (%)	2011	24.7

Environmental indicators		
Threatened species [o]	2011	849
Forested area (% of land area)	2009	19.6
CO_2 emission estimates (000 metric tons and metric tons per capita)	2008	398 892/18.9
Energy consumption per capita (kilograms oil equivalent) [l]	2009	5 929.0
Rainfall in the capital city, total mean (millimetres)		576
Temperature in the capital city, mean °C (minimum and maximum)		6.0/18.9

a Includes Christmas Island, Cocos (Keeling) Islands and Norfolk Island. **b** Market rate. **c** Average of 12 months ending 30 June of the year stated. **d** 2003. **e** 2004. **f** Average of February, May, August and November. **g** Average of quarterly estimates. **h** 2009. **i** Excludes nationals residing abroad. **j** Arrivals of non-resident visitors at national borders. **k** Excludes crew members. **l** Excludes the overseas territories. **m** Age group 16 to 59 years. **n** 2001-2002. **o** Excludes Christmas Island and Cocos (Keeling) Islands.

Austria

Region	Western Europe
Currency	Euro (EUR)
Surface area (square kilometres)	83 871
Population in 2010 (estimated, 000)	8 394
Population density in 2010 (per square kilometre)	100.1
Capital city and population in 2011 (000)	Vienna (1 720)
United Nations membership date	14 December 1955

Economic indicators	2000	2005	2010
GDP: Gross domestic product (million current US$)	192 071	304 984	379 047
GDP: Growth rate at constant 2005 prices (annual %)	3.7	2.4	2.3
GDP per capita (current US$)	23 994.7	37 047.7	45 158.8
GNI: Gross national income per capita (current US$)	23 589.6	36 688.1	44 919.7
Gross fixed capital formation (% of GDP)	24.3	22.0	21.1
Exchange rates (national currency per US$)[a]	1.07	0.85	0.75
Balance of payments, current account (million US$)	−1 339	6 245	11 461
CPI: Consumer price index (2000=100)	100	111	121
Industrial production index (2005=100)	90[b]	100	110
Agricultural production index (2004-2006=100)	97	101	97
Food production index (2004-2006=100)	97	101	98
Unemployment (% of labour force)	4.9[c]	5.2	4.4
Employment in industrial sector (% of employed)	30.3	27.5[d]	24.9[e]
Employment in agricultural sector (% of employed)	5.8	5.5[d]	5.2[e]
Labour force participation, adult female pop. (%)	48.4	51.2	53.9
Labour force participation, adult male pop. (%)	68.6	67.3	67.8
Tourist arrivals at national borders (000)[f]	17 982	19 952	22 004
Energy production, primary (000 mt oil equivalent)	6 854	6 066	6 878[g]
Telephone subscribers, total (per 100 inhabitants)	126.4	150.7	184.5
Internet users (per 100 inhabitants)	33.7	58.0	72.7

Total trade		Major trading partners			2010
	(million US$)	(% of exports)			(% of imports)
Exports	144 882.0	Germany	31.6	Germany	39.5
Imports	150 592.7	Italy	7.8	Italy	6.8
Balance	−5 710.7	Switzerland	5.1	Switzerland	5.4

Social indicators		
Population growth rate (average annual %)	2010-2015	0.2
Urban population growth rate (average annual %)	2010-2015	0.5
Rural population growth rate (average annual %)	2010-2015	−0.5
Urban population (%)	2011	67.7
Population aged 0-14 years (%)	2011	14.5
Population aged 60+ years (females and males, % of total)	2011	25.9/20.7
Sex ratio (males per 100 females)	2011	95.4
Life expectancy at birth (females and males, years)	2010-2015	83.6/78.4
Infant mortality rate (per 1 000 live births)	2010-2015	3.7
Fertility rate, total (live births per woman)	2010-2015	1.4
Contraceptive prevalence (ages 15-49, %)[h]	2006-2010	50.9[i]
International migrant stock (000 and % of total population)	mid-2010	1 310.2/15.6
Refugees and others of concern to UNHCR	end-2010	68 656
Education: Government expenditure (% of GDP)	2005-2011	5.5
Education: Primary-secondary gross enrolment ratio (f/m per 100)	2005-2011	98.1/101.4
Education: Female third-level students (% of total)	2005-2011	53.2
Deaths by assault (females and males, per 100 000)	2005-2008	0.6/0.6[j]
Seats held by women in national parliaments (%)	2011	27.9

Environmental indicators		
Threatened species	2011	99
Forested area (% of land area)	2009	47.1
CO_2 emission estimates (000 metric tons and metric tons per capita)	2008	67 670/8.1
Energy consumption per capita (kilograms oil equivalent)	2009	3 124.0
Rainfall in the capital city, total mean (millimetres)		620
Temperature in the capital city, mean °C (minimum and maximum)		6.7/14.5

a Market rate. **b** 2003. **c** 2004. **d** Excludes conscripts. **e** European Labour Force Survey (Eurostat). **f** Arrivals of non-resident tourists in all types of accommodation establishments. **g** 2009. **h** Age group 20 to 49 years. **i** 1995-1996. **j** Rate based on 30 or fewer events.

Azerbaijan

Region	Western Asia
Currency	Azerbaijan Manat (AZN)[a]
Surface area (square kilometres)	86 600
Population in 2010 (estimated, 000)	9 188[b]
Population density in 2010 (per square kilometre)	106.1
Capital city and population in 2011 (000)	Baku (2 123)
United Nations membership date	2 March 1992

Economic indicators	2000	2005	2010
GDP: Gross domestic product (million current US$)	5 273	13 246	51 797
GDP: Growth rate at constant 2005 prices (annual %)	11.1	26.5	5.0
GDP per capita (current US$)	650.1	1 542.4	5 637.6
GNI: Gross national income per capita (current US$)	638.4	1 366.4	6 348.1
Gross fixed capital formation (% of GDP)	23.1	41.3	16.9
Exchange rates (national currency per US$)[c]	0.91	0.92	0.80
Balance of payments, current account (million US$)	−168	167	15 040
CPI: Consumer price index (2000=100)	100	125	193[d]
Industrial production index (2005=100)	...	100	200
Agricultural production index (2004-2006=100)	73	104	118
Food production index (2004-2006=100)	73	103	123
Employment in industrial sector (% of employed)	10.9[e]	12.1[e]	12.9[d]
Employment in agricultural sector (% of employed)	41.0[e]	39.3[e]	38.6[d]
Labour force participation, adult female pop. (%)	57.3	59.3	61.1
Labour force participation, adult male pop. (%)	71.3	68.4	67.8
Tourist arrivals at national borders (000)[f]	681	1 177	1 963
Energy production, primary (000 mt oil equivalent)	19 711	28 101	68 543[d]
Telephone subscribers, total (per 100 inhabitants)	15.1	38.9	115.5
Internet users (per 100 inhabitants)	0.2	8.0	46.0

Total trade		Major trading partners			2010
	(million US$)		(% of exports)		(% of imports)
Exports	21 278.4	Italy	33.1	Russian Federation	17.4
Imports	6 596.8	France	8.7	Turkey	11.7
Balance	14 681.6	Israel	8.2	Germany	9.2

Social indicators		
Population growth rate (average annual %)[b]	2010-2015	1.2
Urban population growth rate (average annual %)	2010-2015	1.6
Rural population growth rate (average annual %)	2010-2015	0.7
Urban population (%)	2011	53.6
Population aged 0-14 years (%)[b]	2011	21.1
Population aged 60+ years (females and males, % of total)[b]	2011	10.1/7.7
Sex ratio (males per 100 females)[b]	2011	98.0
Life expectancy at birth (females and males, years)[b]	2010-2015	73.7/68.0
Infant mortality rate (per 1 000 live births)[b]	2010-2015	37.6
Fertility rate, total (live births per woman)[b]	2010-2015	2.2
Contraceptive prevalence (ages 15-49, %)	2006-2010	51.1
International migrant stock (000 and % of total population)[g]	mid-2010	263.9/3.0
Refugees and others of concern to UNHCR	end-2010	596 846
Education: Government expenditure (% of GDP)	2005-2011	3.2
Education: Primary-secondary gross enrolment ratio (f/m per 100)[h]	2005-2011	96.5/97.8
Education: Female third-level students (% of total)	2005-2011	49.4
Seats held by women in national parliaments (%)	2011	16.0

Environmental indicators		
Threatened species	2011	46
Forested area (% of land area)	2009	11.3
CO$_2$ emission estimates (000 metric tons and metric tons per capita)	2008	47 101/5.4
Energy consumption per capita (kilograms oil equivalent)	2009	1 309.0
Rainfall in the capital city, total mean (millimetres)		210
Temperature in the capital city, mean °C (minimum and maximum)		12.0/18.9

a Beginning January 2006, 1 new Manat = 5000 old Manats. b Includes Nagorno-Karabakh. c Official rate. d 2009. e Official estimates. f Arrivals of non-resident visitors at national borders. g Includes refugees. h National estimate.

Bahamas

Region	Caribbean
Currency	Bahamian Dollar (BSD)
Surface area (square kilometres)	13 943
Population in 2010 (estimated, 000)	343
Population density in 2010 (per square kilometre)	24.6
Capital city and population in 2011 (000)	Nassau (254)
United Nations membership date	18 September 1973

Economic indicators	2000	2005	2010
GDP: Gross domestic product (million current US$)	6 328	7 706	7 702
GDP: Growth rate at constant 2005 prices (annual %)	4.2	3.4	1.0
GDP per capita (current US$)	21 258.4	24 130.4	22 461.6
GNI: Gross national income per capita (current US$)	20 886.7	23 723.3	21 663.3
Gross fixed capital formation (% of GDP)	25.9	24.2	20.5
Exchange rates (national currency per US$)[a]	1.00	1.00	1.00
Balance of payments, current account (million US$)	−633	−701	−900
CPI: Consumer price index (2000=100)[b]	100	111	123[c]
Agricultural production index (2004-2006=100)	85	96	111
Food production index (2004-2006=100)	85	96	111
Employment in industrial sector (% of employed)[d]	17.0[e]	17.8	16.0[c]
Employment in agricultural sector (% of employed)[d]	4.2[e]	3.5	2.9[c]
Labour force participation, adult female pop. (%)	66.1	68.0	69.3
Labour force participation, adult male pop. (%)	75.2	78.0	79.4
Tourist arrivals at national borders (000)	1 544	1 608	1 370
Telephone subscribers, total (per 100 inhabitants)	49.0	* 113.0	162.7
Internet users (per 100 inhabitants)	8.0	25.0	43.0

Total trade		Major trading partners			2010
	(million US$)	(% of exports)		(% of imports)	
Exports	620.1	United States	76.0	United States	90.9
Imports	2 861.9	United Kingdom	5.0	Trinidad and Tobago	2.3
Balance	−2 241.8	Nigeria	3.7		

Social indicators		
Population growth rate (average annual %)	2010-2015	1.1
Urban population growth rate (average annual %)	2010-2015	1.4
Rural population growth rate (average annual %)	2010-2015	−0.1
Urban population (%)	2011	84.3
Population aged 0-14 years (%)	2011	22.2
Population aged 60+ years (females and males, % of total)	2011	12.0/9.4
Sex ratio (males per 100 females)	2011	95.7
Life expectancy at birth (females and males, years)	2010-2015	78.9/72.7
Infant mortality rate (per 1 000 live births)	2010-2015	14.1
Fertility rate, total (live births per woman)	2010-2015	1.9
Contraceptive prevalence (ages 15-49, %)[f]	2006-2010	61.7[g]
International migrant stock (000 and % of total population)	mid-2010	33.4/9.7
Refugees and others of concern to UNHCR	end-2010	37
Education: Government expenditure (% of GDP)[h]	2005-2011	3.3[i]
Education: Primary-secondary gross enrolment ratio (f/m per 100)	2005-2011	105.9/102.2
Deaths by assault (females and males, per 100 000)	2005-2008	5.4/29.1[j]
Seats held by women in national parliaments (%)	2011	12.2

Environmental indicators		
Threatened species	2011	67
Forested area (% of land area)	2009	51.5
CO_2 emission estimates (000 metric tons and metric tons per capita)	2008	2 154/6.4
Energy consumption per capita (kilograms oil equivalent)	2009	2 531.0[k]
Rainfall in the capital city, total mean (millimetres)		1 389
Temperature in the capital city, mean °C (minimum and maximum)		20.8/28.8

a Principal rate. **b** New Providence. **c** 2009. **d** April. **e** 2001. **f** Age group 15 to 44 years. **g** 1988. **h** UNESCO estimate. **i** 2000. **j** Rate based on 30 or fewer events. **k** UNSD estimate.

Bahrain

Region	Western Asia
Currency	Bahraini Dinar (BHD)
Surface area (square kilometres)	758
Population in 2010 (estimated, 000)	1 262
Population density in 2010 (per square kilometre)	1 665.8
Capital city and population in 2011 (000)	Manama (262)
United Nations membership date	21 September 1971

Economic indicators	2000	2005	2010
GDP: Gross domestic product (million current US$)	8 028	13 459	22 945
GDP: Growth rate at constant 2005 prices (annual %)	5.5	7.9	4.5
GDP per capita (current US$)	12 578.6	18 569.2	18 184.1
GNI: Gross national income per capita (current US$)	12 228.1	17 999.0	15 498.6
Gross fixed capital formation (% of GDP)	12.4	23.1	28.9
Exchange rates (national currency per US$) [a]	0.38	0.38	0.38
Balance of payments, current account (million US$)	830	1 474	770
CPI: Consumer price index (2000=100)	100	105	120
Agricultural production index (2004-2006=100)	123	92	117
Food production index (2004-2006=100)	123	92	117
Employment in industrial sector (% of employed) [b]	28.0[cd]	15.0[e]	...
Employment in agricultural sector (% of employed) [b]	1.5[cd]	0.8[e]	...
Labour force participation, adult female pop. (%)	35.0	36.1	39.2
Labour force participation, adult male pop. (%)	86.4	83.6	87.2
Tourist arrivals at national borders (000)	2 420	3 914	4 935[f]
Energy production, primary (000 mt oil equivalent)	17 658	16 759	18 345[g]
Telephone subscribers, total (per 100 inhabitants)	59.0	132.5	142.3
Internet users (per 100 inhabitants)	6.2	21.3	55.0

Total trade		Major trading partners	2010
	(million US$)	(% of exports)	(% of imports)
Exports	16 059.2		
Imports	16 001.6		
Balance	57.6		

Social indicators		
Population growth rate (average annual %)	2010-2015	2.1
Urban population growth rate (average annual %)	2010-2015	2.2
Rural population growth rate (average annual %)	2010-2015	1.5
Urban population (%)	2011	88.7
Population aged 0-14 years (%)	2011	20.3
Population aged 60+ years (females and males, % of total)	2011	4.3/3.1
Sex ratio (males per 100 females)	2011	167.3
Life expectancy at birth (females and males, years)	2010-2015	76.1/74.7
Infant mortality rate (per 1 000 live births)	2010-2015	6.7
Fertility rate, total (live births per woman)	2010-2015	2.4
Contraceptive prevalence (ages 15-49, %)	2006-2010	61.8[h]
International migrant stock (000 and % of total population) [i]	mid-2010	315.4/39.1
Refugees and others of concern to UNHCR	end-2010	234
Education: Government expenditure (% of GDP)	2005-2011	2.9
Education: Primary-secondary gross enrolment ratio (f/m per 100)	2005-2011	106.2/104.6
Education: Female third-level students (% of total)	2005-2011	45.9
Seats held by women in national parliaments (%)	2011	10.0

Environmental indicators		
Threatened species	2011	32
Forested area (% of land area)	2009	0.7
CO$_2$ emission estimates (000 metric tons and metric tons per capita)	2008	22 460/29.0
Energy consumption per capita (kilograms oil equivalent)	2009	8 656.0
Rainfall in the capital city, total mean (millimetres)		71
Temperature in the capital city, mean °C (minimum and maximum)		23.0/30.1

a Official rate. b November. c 2001. d Population census. e 2004. f 2007. g 2009. h 1995. i Data refer to foreign citizens.

Bangladesh

Region	South-central Asia
Currency	Taka (BDT)
Surface area (square kilometres)	143 998
Population in 2010 (estimated, 000)	148 692
Population density in 2010 (per square kilometre)	1 032.6
Capital city and population in 2011 (000)	Dhaka (15 391)
United Nations membership date	17 September 1974

Economic indicators	2000	2005	2010
GDP: Gross domestic product (million current US$)	45 470	57 628	99 689
GDP: Growth rate at constant 2005 prices (annual %)	5.9	6.0	6.1
GDP per capita (current US$)	350.9	409.9	670.4
GNI: Gross national income per capita (current US$)	363.8	430.8	720.2
Gross fixed capital formation (% of GDP)	23.0	24.5	24.9
Exchange rates (national currency per US$) [a]	54.00	66.21	70.75
Balance of payments, current account (million US$)	−306	−176	2 502
CPI: Consumer price index (2000=100) [b]	100	127	183
Industrial production index (2005=100) [c]	86[d]	100	148
Agricultural production index (2004-2006=100)	89	103	129
Food production index (2004-2006=100)	89	103	129
Employment in industrial sector (% of employed) [e]	10.3	14.5	...
Employment in agricultural sector (% of employed) [e]	62.1	48.1	...
Labour force participation, adult female pop. (%)	54.3	55.5	56.9
Labour force participation, adult male pop. (%)	85.8	85.0	84.4
Tourist arrivals at national borders (000)	199	208	267[f]
Energy production, primary (000 mt oil equivalent)	8 380	12 262	17 665[f]
Telephone subscribers, total (per 100 inhabitants)	0.6	7.2	46.8
Internet users (per 100 inhabitants)	0.1	0.2	3.7

Total trade		Major trading partners			2010
	(million US$)[g]	(% of exports)[g]			(% of imports)[g]
Exports	13 143.0	United States	25.7	China	15.6
Imports	17 622.9	Germany	15.2	India	13.2
Balance	−4 479.9	United Kingdom	9.5	Kuwait	7.2

Social indicators		
Population growth rate (average annual %)	2010-2015	1.3
Urban population growth rate (average annual %)	2010-2015	3.0
Rural population growth rate (average annual %)	2010-2015	0.6
Urban population (%)	2011	28.4
Population aged 0-14 years (%)	2011	30.6
Population aged 60+ years (females and males, % of total)	2011	6.9/6.5
Sex ratio (males per 100 females)	2011	102.4
Life expectancy at birth (females and males, years)	2010-2015	70.2/68.5
Infant mortality rate (per 1 000 live births)	2010-2015	41.8
Fertility rate, total (live births per woman)	2010-2015	2.2
Contraceptive prevalence (ages 15-49, %)	2006-2010	55.8
International migrant stock (000 and % of total population) [h]	mid-2010	1 085.3/0.7
Refugees and others of concern to UNHCR	end-2010	229 253
Education: Government expenditure (% of GDP)	2005-2011	2.2
Education: Female third-level students (% of total)	2005-2011	37.0
Seats held by women in national parliaments (%)	2011	18.6

Environmental indicators		
Threatened species	2011	122
Forested area (% of land area)	2009	11.1
CO_2 emission estimates (000 metric tons and metric tons per capita)	2008	46 489/0.3
Energy consumption per capita (kilograms oil equivalent)	2009	146.0
Rainfall in the capital city, total mean (millimetres)		2 154
Temperature in the capital city, mean °C (minimum and maximum)		21.5/30.6

a Principal rate. b Government officials. c The indices are shown in terms of ISIC Rev. 3. d 2003. e Year ending in June of the year indicated. f 2009. g 2007. h Includes refugees.

Barbados

Region	Caribbean
Currency	Barbados Dollar (BBD)
Surface area (square kilometres)	430
Population in 2010 (estimated, 000)	273
Population density in 2010 (per square kilometre)	635.7
Capital city and population in 2011 (000)	Bridgetown (122)
United Nations membership date	9 December 1966

Economic indicators	2000	2005	2010
GDP: Gross domestic product (million current US$)	2 913	3 685	3 963
GDP: Growth rate at constant 2005 prices (annual %)	2.3	3.9	−0.5
GDP per capita (current US$)	10 890.2	13 622.6	14 497.3
GNI: Gross national income per capita (current US$)	10 504.6	11 926.5	13 392.7
Gross fixed capital formation (% of GDP)	18.9	19.3	18.0
Exchange rates (national currency per US$) [a]	2.00	2.00	2.00
Balance of payments, current account (million US$)	−214	−510	−312[b]
CPI: Consumer price index (2000=100)	100	113	149
Industrial production index (2005=100) [c]	96[d]	100	88
Agricultural production index (2004-2006=100)	102	105	100
Food production index (2004-2006=100)	102	105	100
Unemployment (% of labour force)	9.6[e]	9.1	10.8
Employment in industrial sector (% of employed)	20.4	17.3[e]	...
Employment in agricultural sector (% of employed)	3.7	3.3[e]	...
Labour force participation, adult female pop. (%)	63.4	64.4	64.8
Labour force participation, adult male pop. (%)	76.1	76.1	76.3
Tourist arrivals at national borders (000)	545	548	532
Energy production, primary (000 mt oil equivalent)	115	90	56[b]
Telephone subscribers, total (per 100 inhabitants)	56.9	126.1	178.4
Internet users (per 100 inhabitants)	4.0	56.1	70.2

Total trade		Major trading partners			2010
	(million US$)	(% of exports)		(% of imports)	
Exports	313.7	United States	24.9	United States	43.9
Imports	1 196.2	United Kingdom	16.8	Trinidad and Tobago	7.2
Balance	−882.5	Trinidad and Tobago	8.4	United Kingdom	5.4

Social indicators		
Population growth rate (average annual %)	2010-2015	0.2
Urban population growth rate (average annual %)	2010-2015	1.4
Rural population growth rate (average annual %)	2010-2015	−0.7
Urban population (%)	2011	44.4
Population aged 0-14 years (%)	2011	17.1
Population aged 60+ years (females and males, % of total)	2011	19.0/14.4
Sex ratio (males per 100 females)	2011	98.5
Life expectancy at birth (females and males, years)	2010-2015	80.3/73.9
Infant mortality rate (per 1 000 live births)	2010-2015	12.3
Fertility rate, total (live births per woman)	2010-2015	1.6
Contraceptive prevalence (ages 15-49, %) [f]	2006-2010	55.0[g]
International migrant stock (000 and % of total population)	mid-2010	28.1/11.0
Education: Government expenditure (% of GDP)	2005-2011	6.7
Education: Primary-secondary gross enrolment ratio (f/m per 100) [h]	2005-2011	113.4/107.3
Education: Female third-level students (% of total)	2005-2011	68.5
Seats held by women in national parliaments (%)	2011	10.0

Environmental indicators		
Threatened species	2011	40
Forested area (% of land area)	2009	19.4
CO$_2$ emission estimates (000 metric tons and metric tons per capita)	2008	1 352/5.3
Energy consumption per capita (kilograms oil equivalent)	2009	1 742.0

a Official rate. b 2009. c The indices are shown in terms of ISIC Rev. 3. d 2003. e 2004. f Age group 15 to 44 years. g 1988. h National estimate.

Belarus

Region	Eastern Europe
Currency	Belarusian Ruble (BYR)
Surface area (square kilometres)	207 600
Population in 2010 (estimated, 000)	9 595
Population density in 2010 (per square kilometre)	46.2
Capital city and population in 2011 (000)	Minsk (1 861)
United Nations membership date	24 October 1945

Economic indicators	2000	2005	2010
GDP: Gross domestic product (million current US$)	10 418	30 210	54 713
GDP: Growth rate at constant 2005 prices (annual %)	5.8	9.4	7.6
GDP per capita (current US$)	1 035.8	3 074.8	5 702.0
GNI: Gross national income per capita (current US$)	1 031.5	3 080.4	5 562.9
Gross fixed capital formation (% of GDP)	25.2	26.5	38.7
Exchange rates (national currency per US$) [a]	1 180.00	2 152.00	3 000.00
Balance of payments, current account (million US$)	...	436	−8 317
CPI: Consumer price index (2000=100)	100	384	578[b]
Industrial production index (2005=100) [c]	...	100	146
Agricultural production index (2004-2006=100)	84	98	117
Food production index (2004-2006=100)	84	98	117
Labour force participation, adult female pop. (%)	52.6	51.0	50.0
Labour force participation, adult male pop. (%)	65.1	62.9	62.2
Tourist arrivals at national borders (000) [d]	60	91	119
Energy production, primary (000 mt oil equivalent)	2 570	2 542	2 454[b]
Telephone subscribers, total (per 100 inhabitants)	27.9	75.2	150.8
Internet users (per 100 inhabitants)	1.9	16.2[e]	31.7

Total trade		Major trading partners			2010
	(million US$)	(% of exports)		(% of imports)	
Exports	25 225.9	Russian Federation	38.5	Russian Federation	51.3
Imports	34 868.2	Netherlands	11.0	Germany	6.8
Balance	−9 642.3	Ukraine	10.1	Ukraine	5.4

Social indicators		
Population growth rate (average annual %)	2010-2015	−0.3
Urban population growth rate (average annual %)	2010-2015	0.2
Rural population growth rate (average annual %)	2010-2015	−2.0
Urban population (%)	2011	75.0
Population aged 0-14 years (%)	2011	15.1
Population aged 60+ years (females and males, % of total)	2011	22.8/13.9
Sex ratio (males per 100 females)	2011	86.9
Life expectancy at birth (females and males, years)	2010-2015	76.4/65.2
Infant mortality rate (per 1 000 live births)	2010-2015	6.5
Fertility rate, total (live births per woman)	2010-2015	1.5
Contraceptive prevalence (ages 15-49, %)	2006-2010	72.6[f]
International migrant stock (000 and % of total population)	mid-2010	1 090.4/11.4
Refugees and others of concern to UNHCR	end-2010	8 386
Education: Government expenditure (% of GDP)	2005-2011	4.5
Education: Primary-secondary gross enrolment ratio (f/m per 100)	2005-2011	97.0/95.9
Education: Female third-level students (% of total)	2005-2011	57.6
Deaths by assault (females and males, per 100 000)	2005-2008	3.9/10.0
Seats held by women in national parliaments (%)	2011	31.8

Environmental indicators		
Threatened species	2011	19
Forested area (% of land area)	2009	42.4
CO$_2$ emission estimates (000 metric tons and metric tons per capita)	2008	62 764/6.5
Energy consumption per capita (kilograms oil equivalent)	2009	2 529.0
Rainfall in the capital city, total mean (millimetres)		677
Temperature in the capital city, mean °C (minimum and maximum)		2.1/9.9

a Official rate. b 2009. c The indices are shown in terms of ISIC Rev. 3. d Organized tourism. e 2006. f 2005-2006.

Belgium

Region	Western Europe
Currency	Euro (EUR)
Surface area (square kilometres)	30 528
Population in 2010 (estimated, 000)	10 712
Population density in 2010 (per square kilometre)	350.9
Capital city and population in 2011 (000)	Brussels (1 892) [a]
United Nations membership date	27 December 1945

Economic indicators	2000	2005	2010
GDP: Gross domestic product (million current US$)	232 673	377 253	469 347
GDP: Growth rate at constant 2005 prices (annual %)	3.7	1.7	2.3
GDP per capita (current US$)	22 865.6	36 224.9	43 814.8
GNI: Gross national income per capita (current US$)	23 387.9	36 462.3	44 586.7
Gross fixed capital formation (% of GDP)	21.2	20.7	20.2
Exchange rates (national currency per US$) [b]	1.07	0.85	0.75
Balance of payments, current account (million US$)	11 611 [c]	7 703	6 349
CPI: Consumer price index (2000=100)	100	111	123
Industrial production index (2005=100)	91 [d]	100	116
Agricultural production index (2004-2006=100)	107	100	101
Food production index (2004-2006=100)	107	100	101
Unemployment (% of labour force)	8.4 [e]	8.4	8.3
Employment in industrial sector (% of employed) [f]	25.8	24.7	23.4
Employment in agricultural sector (% of employed) [f]	1.9	2.0	1.4
Labour force participation, adult female pop. (%)	43.5	45.8	47.6
Labour force participation, adult male pop. (%)	61.4	61.5	60.8
Tourist arrivals at national borders (000) [g]	6 457	6 747	7 186
Energy production, primary (000 mt oil equivalent)	4 496	4 321	4 638 [a]
Telephone subscribers, total (per 100 inhabitants)	104.8	138.3	156.8
Internet users (per 100 inhabitants)	29.4	59.8	75.0

Total trade		Major trading partners			2010
	(million US$)	(% of exports)			(% of imports)
Exports	411 084.8	Germany	18.6	Netherlands	18.9
Imports	390 091.1	France	16.6	Germany	16.3
Balance	20 993.7	Netherlands	11.9	France	11.3

Social indicators		
Population growth rate (average annual %)	2010-2015	0.3
Urban population growth rate (average annual %)	2010-2015	0.3
Rural population growth rate (average annual %)	2010-2015	−0.9
Urban population (%)	2011	97.5
Population aged 0-14 years (%)	2011	16.9
Population aged 60+ years (females and males, % of total)	2011	25.9/21.3
Sex ratio (males per 100 females)	2011	96.2
Life expectancy at birth (females and males, years)	2010-2015	82.8/77.2
Infant mortality rate (per 1 000 live births)	2010-2015	3.7
Fertility rate, total (live births per woman)	2010-2015	1.8
Contraceptive prevalence (ages 15-49, %)	2006-2010	74.6 [e]
International migrant stock (000 and % of total population) [h]	mid-2010	974.9/9.1
Refugees and others of concern to UNHCR	end-2010	36 871
Education: Government expenditure (% of GDP)	2005-2011	6.4
Education: Primary-secondary gross enrolment ratio (f/m per 100)	2005-2011	106.7/108.6
Education: Female third-level students (% of total)	2005-2011	54.8
Deaths by assault (females and males, per 100 000) [e]	2005-2008	1.6/1.9
Seats held by women in national parliaments (%)	2011	39.3

Environmental indicators		
Threatened species	2011	30
Forested area (% of land area)	2009	22.4
CO$_2$ emission estimates (000 metric tons and metric tons per capita)	2008	104 794/9.9
Energy consumption per capita (kilograms oil equivalent)	2009	3 611.0
Rainfall in the capital city, total mean (millimetres)		820
Temperature in the capital city, mean °C (minimum and maximum)		6.7/13.9

a 2009. **b** Market rate. **c** 2002. **d** 2003. **e** 2004. **f** European Labour Force Survey (Eurostat). **g** Arrivals of non-resident tourists in all types of accommodation establishments. **h** Data refer to foreign citizens.

Belize

Region	Central America
Currency	Belize Dollar (BZD)
Surface area (square kilometres)	22 966
Population in 2010 (estimated, 000)	312
Population density in 2010 (per square kilometre)	13.6
Capital city and population in 2011 (000)	Belmopan (14)
United Nations membership date	25 September 1981

Economic indicators	2000	2005	2010
GDP: Gross domestic product (million current US$)	832	1 115	1 401
GDP: Growth rate at constant 2005 prices (annual %)	12.9	3.1	2.7
GDP per capita (current US$)	3 320.2	3 968.0	4 495.8
GNI: Gross national income per capita (current US$)	3 065.6	3 531.2	3 938.7
Gross fixed capital formation (% of GDP)	28.7	18.5	17.8
Exchange rates (national currency per US$)[a]	2.00	2.00	2.00
Balance of payments, current account (million US$)	−162	−151	−46
CPI: Consumer price index (2000=100)	100	113	128
Agricultural production index (2004-2006=100)	86	96	91
Food production index (2004-2006=100)	86	96	91
Employment in industrial sector (% of employed)	...	17.9[bc]	...
Employment in agricultural sector (% of employed)	...	19.5[bc]	...
Labour force participation, adult female pop. (%)	40.2	44.8	48.0
Labour force participation, adult male pop. (%)	83.8	80.8	81.8
Tourist arrivals at national borders (000)	196	237	239
Energy production, primary (000 mt oil equivalent)	8	6	21[d]
Telephone subscribers, total (per 100 inhabitants)	21.0	46.2	72.0
Internet users (per 100 inhabitants)	6.0	9.2	14.0

Total trade		Major trading partners			2010
	(million US$)	(% of exports)		(% of imports)	
Exports	282.0	United States	49.1	United States	47.9
Imports	700.0	United Kingdom	26.1	Mexico	10.0
Balance	−418.0	Costa Rica	4.5	China	9.7

Social indicators		
Population growth rate (average annual %)	2010-2015	2.0
Urban population growth rate (average annual %)	2010-2015	1.5
Rural population growth rate (average annual %)	2010-2015	2.3
Urban population (%)	2011	44.7
Population aged 0-14 years (%)	2011	34.4
Population aged 60+ years (females and males, % of total)	2011	5.9/5.6
Sex ratio (males per 100 females)	2011	97.3
Life expectancy at birth (females and males, years)	2010-2015	77.8/74.9
Infant mortality rate (per 1 000 live births)	2010-2015	16.2
Fertility rate, total (live births per woman)	2010-2015	2.7
Contraceptive prevalence (ages 15-49, %)	2006-2010	34.3
International migrant stock (000 and % of total population)[e]	mid-2010	46.8/15.0
Refugees and others of concern to UNHCR	end-2010	164
Education: Government expenditure (% of GDP)	2005-2011	6.1
Education: Primary-secondary gross enrolment ratio (f/m per 100)	2005-2011	94.4/101.6
Education: Female third-level students (% of total)	2005-2011	61.8
Deaths by assault (females and males, per 100 000)	2005-2008	4.9/27.1[f]
Seats held by women in national parliaments (%)	2011	0.0

Environmental indicators		
Threatened species	2011	97
Forested area (% of land area)	2009	61.9
CO_2 emission estimates (000 metric tons and metric tons per capita)	2008	425/1.4
Energy consumption per capita (kilograms oil equivalent)	2009	587.0[g]
Rainfall in the capital city, total mean (millimetres)		1 842
Temperature in the capital city, mean °C (minimum and maximum)		20.5/31.2

a Official rate. **b** April. **c** Age group 14 years and over. **d** 2009. **e** Includes refugees. **f** Rate based on 30 or fewer events. **g** UNSD estimate.

Benin

Region	Western Africa
Currency	CFA Franc (XOF)
Surface area (square kilometres)	114 763
Population in 2010 (estimated, 000)	8 850
Population density in 2010 (per square kilometre)	77.1
Capital city and population in 2011 (000)	Porto-Novo (315)[a]
United Nations membership date	20 September 1960

Economic indicators	2000	2005	2010
GDP: Gross domestic product (million current US$)	2 359	4 358	6 558
GDP: Growth rate at constant 2005 prices (annual %)	4.9	2.9	2.6
GDP per capita (current US$)	362.0	570.9	741.1
GNI: Gross national income per capita (current US$)	344.1	557.9	735.1
Gross fixed capital formation (% of GDP)	18.0	19.4	20.5
Exchange rates (national currency per US$)[b]	704.95	556.04	490.91
Balance of payments, current account (million US$)	−111	−270	−756[c]
CPI: Consumer price index (2000=100)[d]	100	115	134[e]
Industrial production index (2005=100)[f]	101[g]	100	129
Agricultural production index (2004-2006=100)	88	101	116
Food production index (2004-2006=100)	85	102	122
Employment in industrial sector (% of employed)	9.5[g]	...	...
Employment in agricultural sector (% of employed)	42.7[g]	...	...
Labour force participation, adult female pop. (%)	64.0	66.1	67.1
Labour force participation, adult male pop. (%)	81.2	78.6	78.3
Tourist arrivals at national borders (000)	96	176[h]	199[h]
Telephone subscribers, total (per 100 inhabitants)	1.6	8.8	81.5
Internet users (per 100 inhabitants)	0.2	1.3	3.1

Total trade		Major trading partners			2010
	(million US$)	(% of exports)			(% of imports)
Exports	434.5	Nigeria	48.5	France	16.3
Imports	1 494.3	China	11.6	China	12.6
Balance	−1 059.8	India	5.2	Togo	10.9

Social indicators		
Population growth rate (average annual %)	2010-2015	2.7
Urban population growth rate (average annual %)	2010-2015	4.1
Rural population growth rate (average annual %)	2010-2015	1.5
Urban population (%)	2011	44.9
Population aged 0-14 years (%)	2011	43.6
Population aged 60+ years (females and males, % of total)	2011	5.4/3.9
Sex ratio (males per 100 females)	2011	97.4
Life expectancy at birth (females and males, years)	2010-2015	58.7/54.8
Infant mortality rate (per 1 000 live births)	2010-2015	76.7
Fertility rate, total (live births per woman)	2010-2015	5.1
Contraceptive prevalence (ages 15-49, %)	2006-2010	17.0
International migrant stock (000 and % of total population)[i] [j]	mid-2010	232.0/2.5
Refugees and others of concern to UNHCR	end-2010	7 240
Education: Government expenditure (% of GDP)	2005-2011	4.5
Education: Primary-secondary gross enrolment ratio (f/m per 100)[k]	2005-2011	59.6/85.2
Education: Female third-level students (% of total)[k]	2005-2011	19.8[l]
Seats held by women in national parliaments (%)	2011	8.4

Environmental indicators		
Threatened species	2011	63
Forested area (% of land area)	2009	41.7
CO$_2$ emission estimates (000 metric tons and metric tons per capita)	2008	4 063/0.5
Energy consumption per capita (kilograms oil equivalent)	2009	169.0
Rainfall in the capital city, total mean (millimetres)		1 308
Temperature in the capital city, mean °C (minimum and maximum)		24.3/30.1

a Porto-Novo is the constitutional capital, Cotonou is the seat of government. b Official rate. c 2009. d Cotonou. e Series linked to former series. f The indices are shown in terms of ISIC Rev. 3. g 2003. h Country estimates. i Data refer to foreign-born and foreign citizens. j Includes refugees. k UNESCO estimate. l 2001.

Bermuda

Region	Northern America
Currency	Bermudian Dollar (BMD)
Surface area (square kilometres)	53
Population in 2010 (estimated, 000)	65
Population density in 2010 (per square kilometre)	1 225.3
Capital city and population in 2011 (000)	Hamilton (11)

Economic indicators	2000	2005	2010
GDP: Gross domestic product (million current US$)	3 518	4 846	6 015
GDP: Growth rate at constant 2005 prices (annual %)	3.0	5.2	1.5
GDP per capita (current US$)	55 995.5	75 567.6	92 624.7
GNI: Gross national income per capita (current US$)	62 297.5	90 247.9	115 175.7
Gross fixed capital formation (% of GDP)	19.5	19.4	19.0
CPI: Consumer price index (2000=100)	100	116	136
Agricultural production index (2004-2006=100)	103	98	111
Food production index (2004-2006=100)	103	98	111
Employment in industrial sector (% of employed)	14.8[ab]	12.1[cd]	...
Employment in agricultural sector (% of employed)	1.4[ab]	1.7[c]	...
Tourist arrivals at national borders (000)[e]	332	270	232
Telephone subscribers, total (per 100 inhabitants)	109.9	164.0	224.8
Internet users (per 100 inhabitants)	43.0	65.5	84.2

Total trade	Major trading partners		2010
(million US$)	(% of exports)		(% of imports)
Imports 969.6		United States	71.7
		Canada	8.0
		Venezuela	7.1

Social indicators		
Population growth rate (average annual %)	2010-2015	0.2
Urban population growth rate (average annual %)	2010-2015	0.2
Rural population growth rate (average annual %)	2010-2015	0.0
Urban population (%)	2011	100.0
Population aged 0-14 years (%)[fgh]	2011	17.3[i]
Population aged 60+ years (females and males, % of total)[fgh]	2011	20.4/16.6[i]
Sex ratio (males per 100 females)[fg]	2011	90.8
Life expectancy at birth (females and males, years)[g]	2010-2015	82.3/76.9[i]
Fertility rate, total (live births per woman)[g]	2010-2015	1.8[i]
International migrant stock (000 and % of total population)	mid-2010	19.9/30.7
Education: Government expenditure (% of GDP)	2005-2011	2.7
Education: Primary-secondary gross enrolment ratio (f/m per 100)[k]	2005-2011	88.5/81.7
Education: Female third-level students (% of total)	2005-2011	67.4

Environmental indicators		
Threatened species	2011	54
Forested area (% of land area)	2009	20.0
CO_2 emission estimates (000 metric tons and metric tons per capita)	2008	388/6.0
Energy consumption per capita (kilograms oil equivalent)	2009	2 375.0[l]
Rainfall in the capital city, total mean (millimetres)		1 410
Temperature in the capital city, mean °C (minimum and maximum)		19.6/24.4

a May. b Population census. c 2004. d Excludes mining and quarrying. e Air arrivals. f De jure estimate.
g Data compiled by the United Nations Demographic Yearbook system. h Data refer to the latest available census. i 2010. j 2009. k UNESCO estimate. l UNSD estimate.

Bhutan

Region	South-central Asia
Currency	Ngultrum (BTN)
Surface area (square kilometres)	38 394
Population in 2010 (estimated, 000)	726
Population density in 2010 (per square kilometre)	18.9
Capital city and population in 2011 (000)	Thimphu (99)
United Nations membership date	21 September 1971

Economic indicators	2000	2005	2010
GDP: Gross domestic product (million current US$)	439	819	1 486
GDP: Growth rate at constant 2005 prices (annual %)	5.9	7.1	6.7
GDP per capita (current US$)	768.7	1 242.0	2 047.2
GNI: Gross national income per capita (current US$)	767.9	1 223.4	2 020.4
Gross fixed capital formation (% of GDP)	50.0	49.9	42.3
Exchange rates (national currency per US$) [a]	46.75	45.06	44.81
Balance of payments, current account (million US$)	...	−79[b]	−139
CPI: Consumer price index (2000=100)	100	117	156
Agricultural production index (2004-2006=100)	68	107	95
Food production index (2004-2006=100)	68	107	95
Employment in industrial sector (% of employed)	2.7[c]	17.2[de]	6.4[fg]
Employment in agricultural sector (% of employed)	79.8[c]	43.6[de]	65.4[fg]
Labour force participation, adult female pop. (%)	53.5	63.4	65.5
Labour force participation, adult male pop. (%)	79.1	77.6	76.0
Tourist arrivals at national borders (000)	8	14	27
Energy production, primary (000 mt oil equivalent)	191[h]	287	636[g]
Telephone subscribers, total (per 100 inhabitants)	2.5[i]	10.5	57.9
Internet users (per 100 inhabitants)	0.4	3.9	13.6

Total trade		Major trading partners			2010
	(million US$)	(% of exports)		(% of imports)	
Exports	413.5	India	82.4	India	75.1
Imports	853.8	China, Hong Kong SAR	11.6	Republic of Korea	5.1
Balance	−440.3	Bangladesh	4.8	Thailand	2.5

Social indicators		
Population growth rate (average annual %)	2010-2015	1.6
Urban population growth rate (average annual %)	2010-2015	3.7
Rural population growth rate (average annual %)	2010-2015	0.3
Urban population (%)	2011	35.6
Population aged 0-14 years (%)	2011	28.8
Population aged 60+ years (females and males, % of total)	2011	7.3/7.0
Sex ratio (males per 100 females)	2011	112.6
Life expectancy at birth (females and males, years)	2010-2015	69.8/65.9
Infant mortality rate (per 1 000 live births)	2010-2015	38.0
Fertility rate, total (live births per woman)	2010-2015	2.3
International migrant stock (000 and % of total population)	mid-2010	40.3/5.7
Education: Government expenditure (% of GDP)	2005-2011	4.0
Education: Primary-secondary gross enrolment ratio (f/m per 100)	2005-2011	92.8/90.9
Education: Female third-level students (% of total)	2005-2011	39.8
Seats held by women in national parliaments (%)	2011	8.5

Environmental indicators		
Threatened species	2011	61
Forested area (% of land area)	2009	84.3
CO_2 emission estimates (000 metric tons and metric tons per capita)	2008	733/1.1
Energy consumption per capita (kilograms oil equivalent)	2009	352.0
Rainfall in the capital city, total mean (millimetres)[j]		799
Temperature in the capital city, mean °C (minimum and maximum)[j]		14.0/24.3

a Official rate. **b** 2006. **c** 2003. **d** May. **e** Population census. **f** March to May. **g** 2009. **h** UNSD estimate. **i** Main telephone lines only. **j** Wangdi Phodrang.

Bolivia (Plurinational State of)

Region	South America
Currency	Boliviano (BOB)
Surface area (square kilometres)	1 098 581
Population in 2010 (estimated, 000)	9 930
Population density in 2010 (per square kilometre)	9.0
Capital city and population in 2011 (000)	Sucre (307)[a]
United Nations membership date	14 November 1945

Economic indicators	2000	2005	2010
GDP: Gross domestic product (million current US$)	8 398	9 549	19 640
GDP: Growth rate at constant 2005 prices (annual %)	2.5	4.4	4.1
GDP per capita (current US$)	1 010.9	1 044.0	1 977.9
GNI: Gross national income per capita (current US$)	983.8	1 011.5	1 890.7
Gross fixed capital formation (% of GDP)	17.9	13.0	16.6
Exchange rates (national currency per US$)[b]	6.39	8.04	6.99
Balance of payments, current account (million US$)	−446	622	874
CPI: Consumer price index (2000=100)[c]	100	117	156[d]
Agricultural production index (2004-2006=100)	85	101	115
Food production index (2004-2006=100)	85	101	116
Unemployment (% of labour force)[ef]	...	...	7.9[d]
Employment in industrial sector (% of employed)	19.5[gh]	19.4[e]	...
Employment in agricultural sector (% of employed)	36.8[gh]	38.6[e]	...
Labour force participation, adult female pop. (%)	59.6	61.1	63.8
Labour force participation, adult male pop. (%)	81.7	81.5	81.0
Tourist arrivals at national borders (000)	319	524	807
Energy production, primary (000 mt oil equivalent)	5.112	14 269	14 285[d]
Telephone subscribers, total (per 100 inhabitants)	13.2	33.5	80.8
Internet users (per 100 inhabitants)	1.4	5.2	20.0

Total trade		Major trading partners			2010
	(million US$)	(% of exports)			(% of imports)
Exports	6 965.4	Brazil	34.6	Brazil	18.0
Imports	5 603.9	United States	9.9	United States	13.1
Balance	1 361.5	Argentina	7.9	Argentina	12.7

Social indicators		
Population growth rate (average annual %)	2010-2015	1.6
Urban population growth rate (average annual %)	2010-2015	2.2
Rural population growth rate (average annual %)	2010-2015	0.3
Urban population (%)	2011	66.8
Population aged 0-14 years (%)	2011	35.6
Population aged 60+ years (females and males, % of total)	2011	7.8/6.5
Sex ratio (males per 100 females)	2011	99.6
Life expectancy at birth (females and males, years)	2010-2015	69.4/64.8
Infant mortality rate (per 1 000 live births)	2010-2015	40.7
Fertility rate, total (live births per woman)	2010-2015	3.2
Contraceptive prevalence (ages 15-49, %)	2006-2010	60.5
International migrant stock (000 and % of total population)	mid-2010	145.8/1.5
Refugees and others of concern to UNHCR	end-2010	736
Education: Government expenditure (% of GDP)	2005-2011	6.3
Education: Primary-secondary gross enrolment ratio (f/m per 100)	2005-2011	92.4/93.3
Education: Female third-level students (% of total)[i]	2005-2011	45.0
Seats held by women in national parliaments (%)	2011	25.4

Environmental indicators		
Threatened species	2011	166
Forested area (% of land area)	2009	53.1
CO_2 emission estimates (000 metric tons and metric tons per capita)	2008	12 824/1.3
Energy consumption per capita (kilograms oil equivalent)	2009	530.0

a La Paz is the capital and the seat of government; Sucre is the legal capital and the seat of the judiciary. **b** Market rate. **c** Urban areas. **d** 2009. **e** Age group 10 years and over. **f** 10 Urban agglomerations. **g** . November. **h** Data are derived from micro-sources. **i** National estimate.

Bosnia and Herzegovina

Region	Southern Europe
Currency	Convertible Marka (BAM)
Surface area (square kilometres)	51 209
Population in 2010 (estimated, 000)	3 760
Population density in 2010 (per square kilometre)	73.4
Capital city and population in 2011 (000)	Sarajevo (389)
United Nations membership date	22 May 1992

Economic indicators	2000	2005	2010
GDP: Gross domestic product (million current US$)	5 553	10 909	16 837
GDP: Growth rate at constant 2005 prices (annual %)	5.4	3.9	0.8
GDP per capita (current US$)	1 503.5	2 885.2	4 477.7
GNI: Gross national income per capita (current US$)	1 663.3	3 009.0	4 618.0
Gross fixed capital formation (% of GDP)	26.8	27.9	20.3
Exchange rates (national currency per US$)[a]	2.10	1.66	1.46
Balance of payments, current account (million US$)	–396	–1 844	–1 008
CPI: Consumer price index (2000=100)[b]	...	100	118
Agricultural production index (2004-2006=100)	62	96	102
Food production index (2004-2006=100)	62	96	102
Labour force participation, adult female pop. (%)	33.4	32.3	35.2
Labour force participation, adult male pop. (%)	57.7	56.7	58.5
Tourist arrivals at national borders (000)[c]	171	217	365
Energy production, primary (000 mt oil equivalent)	5 383	5 945	6 973[d]
Telephone subscribers, total (per 100 inhabitants)	23.7	67.8	109.3
Internet users (per 100 inhabitants)	1.1	21.3	52.0

Total trade		Major trading partners			2010
	(million US$)		(% of exports)		(% of imports)
Exports	4 803.1	Germany	15.3	Croatia	15.1
Imports	9 223.0	Croatia	15.1	Serbia	10.5
Balance	–4 419.9	Serbia	12.5	Germany	10.5

Social indicators		
Population growth rate (average annual %)	2010-2015	–0.2
Urban population growth rate (average annual %)	2010-2015	0.9
Rural population growth rate (average annual %)	2010-2015	–1.3
Urban population (%)	2011	48.3
Population aged 0-14 years (%)	2011	14.8
Population aged 60+ years (females and males, % of total)	2011	21.4/17.8
Sex ratio (males per 100 females)	2011	92.6
Life expectancy at birth (females and males, years)	2010-2015	78.4/73.3
Infant mortality rate (per 1 000 live births)	2010-2015	12.7
Fertility rate, total (live births per woman)	2010-2015	1.1
Contraceptive prevalence (ages 15-49, %)	2006-2010	35.7[e]
International migrant stock (000 and % of total population)[fg]	mid-2010	27.8/0.7
Refugees and others of concern to UNHCR	end-2010	179 433
Education: Primary-secondary gross enrolment ratio (f/m per 100)	2005-2011	89.9/87.9
Education: Female third-level students (% of total)	2005-2011	55.9
Seats held by women in national parliaments (%)	2011	16.7

Environmental indicators		
Threatened species	2011	75
Forested area (% of land area)	2009	42.8
CO$_2$ emission estimates (000 metric tons and metric tons per capita)	2008	31 250/8.3
Energy consumption per capita (kilograms oil equivalent)	2009	2 209.0
Rainfall in the capital city, total mean (millimetres)		931
Temperature in the capital city, mean °C (minimum and maximum)		4.8/15.0

a Market rate. **b** Index base 2005=100. **c** Arrivals of non-resident tourists in all types of accommodation establishments. **d** 2009. **e** 2005-2006. **f** Estimates. **g** Includes refugees.

Botswana

Region	Southern Africa
Currency	Pula (BWP)
Surface area (square kilometres)	582 000
Population in 2010 (estimated, 000)	2 007
Population density in 2010 (per square kilometre)	3.5
Capital city and population in 2011 (000)	Gaborone (202)
United Nations membership date	17 October 1966

Economic indicators	2000	2005	2010
GDP: Gross domestic product (million current US$)	5 633	10 256	14 857
GDP: Growth rate at constant 2005 prices (annual %)	5.9	1.7	7.2
GDP per capita (current US$)	3 204.2	5 467.7	7 402.9
GNI: Gross national income per capita (current US$)	2 574.7	5 022.2	7 101.1
Gross fixed capital formation (% of GDP)	25.8	24.5	25.8
Exchange rates (national currency per US$)[a]	5.36	5.51	6.44
Balance of payments, current account (million US$)	545	1 562	46
CPI: Consumer price index (2000=100)	100	146	227
Agricultural production index (2004-2006=100)	90	101	113
Food production index (2004-2006=100)	90	101	114
Employment in industrial sector (% of employed)[bc]	20.9	15.2[d]	...
Employment in agricultural sector (% of employed)[bc]	19.7	29.9[d]	...
Labour force participation, adult female pop. (%)	69.5	70.7	71.6
Labour force participation, adult male pop. (%)	80.4	80.8	81.5
Tourist arrivals at national borders (000)	1 104	1 474	2 145
Energy production, primary (000 mt oil equivalent)	658	689	517[e]
Telephone subscribers, total (per 100 inhabitants)	20.4	37.3	124.6
Internet users (per 100 inhabitants)	2.9	3.3	6.0

Total trade		Major trading partners			2010
	(million US$)	(% of exports)			(% of imports)
Exports	4 693.2	United Kingdom	55.5	South Africa	72.8
Imports	5 656.8	South Africa	12.9	United Kingdom	9.3
Balance	−963.6	Norway	9.3	China	4.9

Social indicators

Population growth rate (average annual %)	2010-2015	1.1
Urban population growth rate (average annual %)	2010-2015	2.1
Rural population growth rate (average annual %)	2010-2015	−0.7
Urban population (%)	2011	61.7
Population aged 0-14 years (%)	2011	32.3
Population aged 60+ years (females and males, % of total)	2011	7.2/5.5
Sex ratio (males per 100 females)	2011	101.9
Life expectancy at birth (females and males, years)	2010-2015	51.3/53.7
Infant mortality rate (per 1 000 live births)	2010-2015	35.1
Fertility rate, total (live births per woman)	2010-2015	2.6
Contraceptive prevalence (ages 15-49, %)	2006-2010	44.4[f]
International migrant stock (000 and % of total population)[g]	mid-2010	114.8/5.8
Refugees and others of concern to UNHCR	end-2010	3 235
Education: Government expenditure (% of GDP)	2005-2011	7.8
Education: Primary-secondary gross enrolment ratio (f/m per 100)	2005-2011	96.0/96.0
Education: Female third-level students (% of total)	2005-2011	53.2
Seats held by women in national parliaments (%)	2011	7.9

Environmental indicators

Threatened species	2011	19
Forested area (% of land area)	2009	20.5
CO_2 emission estimates (000 metric tons and metric tons per capita)	2008	4 836/2.5
Energy consumption per capita (kilograms oil equivalent)	2009	806.0

a Official rate. b Excludes conscripts. c Age group 12 years and over. d 2006. e 2009. f 2000. g Data refer to foreign citizens.

Brazil

Region	South America
Currency	Real (BRL)
Surface area (square kilometres)	8 514 877
Population in 2010 (estimated, 000)	194 947
Population density in 2010 (per square kilometre)	22.9
Capital city and population in 2011 (000)	Brasília (3 813)
United Nations membership date	24 October 1945

Economic indicators	2000	2005	2010
GDP: Gross domestic product (million current US$)	644 729	882 044	2 088 970
GDP: Growth rate at constant 2005 prices (annual %)	4.3	3.2	7.5
GDP per capita (current US$)	3 696.3	4 742.5	10 715.6
GNI: Gross national income per capita (current US$)	3 594.2	4 606.5	10 516.9
Gross fixed capital formation (% of GDP)	16.8	15.9	18.5
Exchange rates (national currency per US$)[a]	1.95	2.34	1.69
Balance of payments, current account (million US$)	−24 225	13 984	−47 365
CPI: Consumer price index (2000=100)	100	151	190
Industrial production index (2005=100)[b]	90[c]	100	115
Agricultural production index (2004-2006=100)	78	99	117
Food production index (2004-2006=100)	78	99	118
Unemployment (% of labour force)[de]	11.5[f]	9.9	6.7
Employment in industrial sector (% of employed)[d]	20.0[ghi]	21.4[h]	22.1[jk]
Employment in agricultural sector (% of employed)[d]	20.6[ghi]	20.5[h]	17.0[jk]
Labour force participation, adult female pop. (%)	54.8	58.9	59.4
Labour force participation, adult male pop. (%)	82.1	82.0	81.0
Tourist arrivals at national borders (000)	5 313	5 358	5 161
Energy production, primary (000 mt oil equivalent)	107 636	138 589	165 973[k]
Telephone subscribers, total (per 100 inhabitants)	31.0	67.8	125.7
Internet users (per 100 inhabitants)	2.9	21.0	40.7

Total trade		Major trading partners			2010
	(million US$)	(% of exports)			(% of imports)
Exports	197 356.4	China	15.6	United States	15.1
Imports	180 458.8	United States	9.7	China	14.2
Balance	16 897.6	Argentina	9.3	Argentina	8.0

Social indicators		
Population growth rate (average annual %)	2010-2015	0.8
Urban population growth rate (average annual %)	2010-2015	1.2
Rural population growth rate (average annual %)	2010-2015	−1.0
Urban population (%)	2011	84.6
Population aged 0-14 years (%)	2011	24.9
Population aged 60+ years (females and males, % of total)	2011	11.5/9.6
Sex ratio (males per 100 females)	2011	96.8
Life expectancy at birth (females and males, years)	2010-2015	77.4/70.7
Infant mortality rate (per 1 000 live births)	2010-2015	19.0
Fertility rate, total (live births per woman)	2010-2015	1.8
Contraceptive prevalence (ages 15-49, %)	2006-2010	80.3
International migrant stock (000 and % of total population)	mid-2010	688.0/0.4
Refugees and others of concern to UNHCR	end-2010	5 229
Education: Government expenditure (% of GDP)	2005-2011	5.4
Education: Primary-secondary gross enrolment ratio (f/m per 100)	2005-2011	112.5/109.8
Education: Female third-level students (% of total)	2005-2011	57.0
Seats held by women in national parliaments (%)	2011	8.6

Environmental indicators		
Threatened species	2011	784
Forested area (% of land area)	2009	61.7
CO_2 emission estimates (000 metric tons and metric tons per capita)	2008	392 898/2.1
Energy consumption per capita (kilograms oil equivalent)	2009	842.0
Rainfall in the capital city, total mean (millimetres)		1 304
Temperature in the capital city, mean °C (minimum and maximum)		16.0/26.6

a Market rate. **b** The indices are shown in terms of ISIC Rev. 3. **c** 2003. **d** Age group 10 years and over. **e** 6 metropolitan areas. **f** 2004. **g** 2001. **h** September. **i** Excludes rural population of Rondônia, Acre, Amazonas, Roraima, Pará and Amapá. **j** August. **k** 2009.

British Virgin Islands

Region	Caribbean		
Currency	U.S. Dollar (USD)		
Surface area (square kilometres)	151		
Population in 2010 (estimated, 000)	23		
Population density in 2010 (per square kilometre)	153.9		
Capital city and population in 2011 (000)	Road Town (10)		

Economic indicators	2000	2005	2010
GDP: Gross domestic product (million current US$)	751	870	909
GDP: Growth rate at constant 2005 prices (annual %)	8.5	14.3	4.5
GDP per capita (current US$)	36 617.3	39 564.9	39 113.3
GNI: Gross national income per capita (current US$)	34 343.1	39 336.1	40 120.7
Gross fixed capital formation (% of GDP)	24.1	24.1	24.0
CPI: Consumer price index (2000=100)	100	110	...
Agricultural production index (2004-2006=100)	98	100	101
Food production index (2004-2006=100)	98	100	101
Tourist arrivals at national borders (000)	272	337	330
Telephone subscribers, total (per 100 inhabitants)	50.7[a]	69.6[a]	191.9
Internet users (per 100 inhabitants)	18.9[b]	...	39.0

Social indicators		
Population growth rate (average annual %)	2010-2015	0.9
Urban population growth rate (average annual %)	2010-2015	1.5
Rural population growth rate (average annual %)	2010-2015	0.6
Urban population (%)	2011	40.6
Population aged 0-14 years (%) [cde]	2011	26.3[f]
Population aged 60+ years (females and males, % of total) [cde]	2011	7.3/7.5[f]
Sex ratio (males per 100 females) [cde]	2011	106.1[f]
International migrant stock (000 and % of total population)	mid-2010	8.5/36.6
Refugees and others of concern to UNHCR	end-2010	2
Education: Government expenditure (% of GDP)	2005-2011	2.6
Education: Primary-secondary gross enrolment ratio (f/m per 100) [g]	2005-2011	99.5/102.1
Education: Female third-level students (% of total)	2005-2011	64.7

Environmental indicators		
Threatened species	2011	47
Forested area (% of land area)	2009	24.3
CO$_2$ emission estimates (000 metric tons and metric tons per capita)	2008	103/4.6
Energy consumption per capita (kilograms oil equivalent)	2009	1 602.0[h]

a Main telephone lines only. **b** 2002. **c** De facto population count. **d** Data compiled by the United Nations Demographic Yearbook system. **e** Data refer to the latest available census. **f** 2001. **g** National estimate. **h** UNSD estimate.

Brunei Darussalam

Region	South-eastern Asia
Currency	Brunei Dollar (BND)
Surface area (square kilometres)	5 765
Population in 2010 (estimated, 000)	399
Population density in 2010 (per square kilometre)	69.2
Capital city and population in 2011 (000)	Bandar Seri Begawan (16)
United Nations membership date	21 September 1984

Economic indicators	2000	2005	2010
GDP: Gross domestic product (million current US$)	6 001	9 531	13 024
GDP: Growth rate at constant 2005 prices (annual %)	2.9	0.4	4.1
GDP per capita (current US$)	18 350.5	26 248.5	32 647.6
GNI: Gross national income per capita (current US$)	18 350.5	26 248.5	32 647.6
Gross fixed capital formation (% of GDP)	13.0	11.4	14.7
Exchange rates (national currency per US$) [a]	1.73	1.66	1.29
Balance of payments, current account (million US$)	1 951 [b]	4 033	3 977 [c]
CPI: Consumer price index (2000=100)	100	101	104 [d]
Agricultural production index (2004-2006=100)	86	87	134
Food production index (2004-2006=100)	86	87	134
Employment in industrial sector (% of employed)	21.4 [bef]	...	...
Employment in agricultural sector (% of employed)	1.4 [bef]	...	...
Labour force participation, adult female pop. (%)	55.4	56.1	55.7
Labour force participation, adult male pop. (%)	79.4	78.0	76.8
Tourist arrivals at national borders (000)	984 [g]	126 [h]	157 [ch]
Energy production, primary (000 mt oil equivalent)	20 496	21 407	20 126 [c]
Telephone subscribers, total (per 100 inhabitants)	53.7	87.2	129.1
Internet users (per 100 inhabitants)	9.0	36.5	50.0

Total trade		Major trading partners			2010
	(million US$) [i]	(% of exports) [i]			(% of imports) [i]
Exports	7 636.1	Japan	30.6	Malaysia	21.6
Imports	1 676.2	Indonesia	19.8	Singapore	17.4
Balance	5 959.9	Republic of Korea	15.1	Japan	12.8

Social indicators		
Population growth rate (average annual %)	2010-2015	1.7
Urban population growth rate (average annual %)	2010-2015	2.1
Rural population growth rate (average annual %)	2010-2015	0.1
Urban population (%)	2011	76.0
Population aged 0-14 years (%)	2011	25.9
Population aged 60+ years (females and males, % of total)	2011	5.8/6.3
Sex ratio (males per 100 females)	2011	102.0
Life expectancy at birth (females and males, years)	2010-2015	80.6/76.0
Infant mortality rate (per 1 000 live births)	2010-2015	4.5
Fertility rate, total (live births per woman)	2010-2015	2.0
International migrant stock (000 and % of total population)	mid-2010	148.1/36.4
Refugees and others of concern to UNHCR	end-2010	20 992
Education: Government expenditure (% of GDP)	2005-2011	2.1
Education: Primary-secondary gross enrolment ratio (f/m per 100)	2005-2011	110.2/107.7
Education: Female third-level students (% of total)	2005-2011	63.3

Environmental indicators		
Threatened species	2011	175
Forested area (% of land area)	2009	72.5
CO$_2$ emission estimates (000 metric tons and metric tons per capita)	2008	10 585/27.0
Energy consumption per capita (kilograms oil equivalent)	2009	8 776.0
Rainfall in the capital city, total mean (millimetres)		2 913
Temperature in the capital city, mean °C (minimum and maximum)		23.3/31.8

a Market rate. **b** 2001. **c** 2009. **d** 2008. **e** August. **f** Population census. **g** Arrivals of non-resident visitors at national borders. **h** Air arrivals. **i** 2006.

Bulgaria

Region	Eastern Europe
Currency	Lev (BGN)
Surface area (square kilometres)	110 879
Population in 2010 (estimated, 000)	7 494
Population density in 2010 (per square kilometre)	67.6
Capital city and population in 2011 (000)	Sofia (1 174)
United Nations membership date	14 December 1955

Economic indicators	2000	2005	2010
GDP: Gross domestic product (million current US$)	12 904	28 894	47 702
GDP: Growth rate at constant 2005 prices (annual %)	5.7	6.4	0.2
GDP per capita (current US$)	1 611.8	3 733.6	6 365.1
GNI: Gross national income per capita (current US$)	1 573.3	3 729.8	6 201.7
Gross fixed capital formation (% of GDP)	15.8	25.8	23.5
Exchange rates (national currency per US$) [a]	2.10	1.66	1.47
Balance of payments, current account (million US$)	−703	−3 347	−736
CPI: Consumer price index (2000=100)	100	130	178
Industrial production index (2005=100)	83[b]	100	98
Agricultural production index (2004-2006=100)	109	91	105
Food production index (2004-2006=100)	111	91	106
Unemployment (% of labour force)	12.0[c]	10.1	10.2
Employment in industrial sector (% of employed) [d]	32.7	34.2	33.3
Employment in agricultural sector (% of employed) [d]	13.1	8.9	6.8
Labour force participation, adult female pop. (%)	47.7	44.9	48.5
Labour force participation, adult male pop. (%)	57.4	56.5	60.0
Tourist arrivals at national borders (000)	2 785	4 837	6 047
Energy production, primary (000 mt oil equivalent)	6 208	6 661	6 359[e]
Telephone subscribers, total (per 100 inhabitants)	45.2	112.9	165.8
Internet users (per 100 inhabitants)	5.4	20.0	46.2

Total trade		Major trading partners			2010
	(million US$)	(% of exports)			(% of imports)
Exports	20 608.0	Germany	10.6	Russian Federation	16.1
Imports	25 359.9	Italy	9.7	Germany	11.7
Balance	−4 751.9	Romania	9.2	Italy	7.4

Social indicators		
Population growth rate (average annual %)	2010-2015	−0.7
Urban population growth rate (average annual %)	2010-2015	0.1
Rural population growth rate (average annual %)	2010-2015	−2.8
Urban population (%)	2011	73.1
Population aged 0-14 years (%)	2011	13.9
Population aged 60+ years (females and males, % of total)	2011	27.8/21.4
Sex ratio (males per 100 females)	2011	93.5
Life expectancy at birth (females and males, years)	2010-2015	77.1/70.3
Infant mortality rate (per 1 000 live births)	2010-2015	9.2
Fertility rate, total (live births per woman)	2010-2015	1.6
Contraceptive prevalence (ages 15-49, %) [f]	2006-2010	63.4[g]
International migrant stock (000 and % of total population)	mid-2010	107.2/1.4
Refugees and others of concern to UNHCR	end-2010	6 942
Education: Government expenditure (% of GDP)	2005-2011	4.4
Education: Primary-secondary gross enrolment ratio (f/m per 100)	2005-2011	91.1/93.5
Education: Female third-level students (% of total)	2005-2011	55.6
Deaths by assault (females and males, per 100 000)	2005-2008	1.1/2.3
Seats held by women in national parliaments (%)	2011	20.8

Environmental indicators		
Threatened species	2011	77
Forested area (% of land area)	2009	35.7
CO_2 emission estimates (000 metric tons and metric tons per capita)	2008	50 497/6.7
Energy consumption per capita (kilograms oil equivalent)	2009	1 843.0
Rainfall in the capital city, total mean (millimetres)		571
Temperature in the capital city, mean °C (minimum and maximum)		5.0/15.1

a Market rate. b 2003. c 2004. d European Labour Force Survey (Eurostat). e 2009. f Age group 20 to 44 years. g 1997-1998.

Burkina Faso

Region	Western Africa
Currency	CFA Franc (XOF)
Surface area (square kilometres)	272 967
Population in 2010 (estimated, 000)	16 469
Population density in 2010 (per square kilometre)	60.3
Capital city and population in 2011 (000)	Ouagadougou (2 053)
United Nations membership date	20 September 1960

Economic indicators	2000	2005	2010
GDP: Gross domestic product (million current US$)	2 633	5 463	8 559
GDP: Growth rate at constant 2005 prices (annual %)	1.9	8.7	5.8
GDP per capita (current US$)	214.1	384.7	519.7
GNI: Gross national income per capita (current US$)	212.5	381.7	518.5
Gross fixed capital formation (% of GDP)	21.2	19.7	27.1
Exchange rates (national currency per US$) [a]	704.95	556.04	490.91
Balance of payments, current account (million US$)	−392	−819	−766[b]
CPI: Consumer price index (2000=100) [c]	100	116	135[b]
Agricultural production index (2004-2006=100)	68	102	112
Food production index (2004-2006=100)	72	103	119
Employment in industrial sector (% of employed) [d]	3.4[e]	3.1	...
Employment in agricultural sector (% of employed) [d]	85.1[e]	84.8	...
Labour force participation, adult female pop. (%)	77.3	77.4	77.5
Labour force participation, adult male pop. (%)	90.6	90.6	90.5
Tourist arrivals at national borders (000) [f]	126	245	274
Energy production, primary (000 mt oil equivalent)	8	9	11[b]
Telephone subscribers, total (per 100 inhabitants)	0.6	5.1	35.5
Internet users (per 100 inhabitants)	0.1	0.5	1.4

Total trade		Major trading partners			2010
	(million US$)		(% of exports)		(% of imports)
Exports	1 288.1	Switzerland	63.5	Côte d'Ivoire	16.0
Imports	2 048.2	South Africa	11.2	France	10.3
Balance	−760.1	Singapore	4.9	China	9.7

Social indicators

Population growth rate (average annual %)	2010-2015	3.0
Urban population growth rate (average annual %)	2010-2015	6.0
Rural population growth rate (average annual %)	2010-2015	1.8
Urban population (%)	2011	26.5
Population aged 0-14 years (%)	2011	45.3
Population aged 60+ years (females and males, % of total)	2011	4.4/3.0
Sex ratio (males per 100 females)	2011	98.6
Life expectancy at birth (females and males, years)	2010-2015	57.0/55.0
Infant mortality rate (per 1 000 live births)	2010-2015	71.0
Fertility rate, total (live births per woman)	2010-2015	5.8
Contraceptive prevalence (ages 15-49, %)	2006-2010	17.4
International migrant stock (000 and % of total population) [g]	mid-2010	1 043.0/6.4
Refugees and others of concern to UNHCR	end-2010	1 065
Education: Government expenditure (% of GDP)	2005-2011	4.6
Education: Primary-secondary gross enrolment ratio (f/m per 100)	2005-2011	48.6/54.4
Education: Female third-level students (% of total)	2005-2011	31.9
Seats held by women in national parliaments (%)	2011	15.3

Environmental indicators

Threatened species	2011	25
Forested area (% of land area)	2009	20.9
CO_2 emission estimates (000 metric tons and metric tons per capita)	2008	1 854/0.1
Energy consumption per capita (kilograms oil equivalent)	2009	36.0

a Official rate. **b** 2009. **c** Ouagadougou. **d** Core Welfare Indicators Questionnaire (World Bank). **e** 2003. **f** Arrivals of non-resident tourists in hotels and similar establishments. **g** Includes refugees.

Burundi

Region	Eastern Africa
Currency	Burundi Franc (BIF)
Surface area (square kilometres)	27 834
Population in 2010 (estimated, 000)	8 383
Population density in 2010 (per square kilometre)	301.2
Capital city and population in 2011 (000)	Bujumbura (605)
United Nations membership date	18 September 1962

Economic indicators	2000	2005	2010
GDP: Gross domestic product (million current US$)	995	1 117	1 481
GDP: Growth rate at constant 2005 prices (annual %)	−0.9	0.9	3.9
GDP per capita (current US$)	156.1	154.0	176.6
GNI: Gross national income per capita (current US$)	155.8	151.6	175.3
Gross fixed capital formation (% of GDP)	13.2	18.4	13.4
Exchange rates (national currency per US$)[a]	778.20	997.78	1 232.50
Balance of payments, current account (million US$)	−103	−222	−323
CPI: Consumer price index (2000=100)[b]	100	145	161[c]
Agricultural production index (2004-2006=100)	86	100	50
Food production index (2004-2006=100)	87	101	50
Labour force participation, adult female pop. (%)	85.6	84.1	83.7
Labour force participation, adult male pop. (%)	84.3	82.3	81.9
Tourist arrivals at national borders (000)[d]	29	148	201[e]
Energy production, primary (000 mt oil equivalent)	10	10	14[f]
Telephone subscribers, total (per 100 inhabitants)	0.6	2.5	14.1
Internet users (per 100 inhabitants)	0.1	0.5	2.1

Total trade		Major trading partners			2010
	(million US$)	(% of exports)			(% of imports)
Exports	118.2	Switzerland	26.9	Belgium	12.0
Imports	404.1	United Kingdom	13.4	China	12.0
Balance	−285.9	Belgium	13.0	Japan	9.4

Social indicators		
Population growth rate (average annual %)	2010-2015	1.9
Urban population growth rate (average annual %)	2010-2015	4.5
Rural population growth rate (average annual %)	2010-2015	1.6
Urban population (%)	2011	10.9
Population aged 0-14 years (%)	2011	37.7
Population aged 60+ years (females and males, % of total)	2011	5.4/3.8
Sex ratio (males per 100 females)	2011	96.5
Life expectancy at birth (females and males, years)	2010-2015	52.6/49.6
Infant mortality rate (per 1 000 live births)	2010-2015	94.1
Fertility rate, total (live births per woman)	2010-2015	4.1
Contraceptive prevalence (ages 15-49, %)	2006-2010	9.1[g]
International migrant stock (000 and % of total population)[h]	mid-2010	60.8/0.7
Refugees and others of concern to UNHCR	end-2010	204 419
Education: Government expenditure (% of GDP)	2005-2011	9.2
Education: Primary-secondary gross enrolment ratio (f/m per 100)	2005-2011	83.2/88.7
Education: Female third-level students (% of total)	2005-2011	35.4
Seats held by women in national parliaments (%)	2011	32.1

Environmental indicators		
Threatened species	2011	54
Forested area (% of land area)	2009	6.8
CO$_2$ emission estimates (000 metric tons and metric tons per capita)	2008	180/0.0
Energy consumption per capita (kilograms oil equivalent)	2009	10.0

a Official rate. b Bujumbura. c 2007. d Includes nationals residing abroad. e 2006. f 2009. g 2005-2006. h Includes refugees.

Cambodia

Region	South-eastern Asia
Currency	Riel (KHR)
Surface area (square kilometres)	181 035
Population in 2010 (estimated, 000)	14 138
Population density in 2010 (per square kilometre)	78.1
Capital city and population in 2011 (000)	Phnom Penh (1 550)
United Nations membership date	14 December 1955

Economic indicators	2000	2005	2010
GDP: Gross domestic product (million current US$)	3 667	6 293	11 272
GDP: Growth rate at constant 2005 prices (annual %)	8.8	13.3	6.0
GDP per capita (current US$)	294.6	471.1	797.3
GNI: Gross national income per capita (current US$)	252.3	403.3	684.3
Gross fixed capital formation (% of GDP)	18.3	18.9	16.0
Exchange rates (national currency per US$) [a]	3 905.00	4 112.00	4 051.00
Balance of payments, current account (million US$)	−136	−307	−879
CPI: Consumer price index (2000=100) [b]	100	114	165
Agricultural production index (2004-2006=100)	75	104	150
Food production index (2004-2006=100)	74	104	150
Employment in industrial sector (% of employed)	8.4[cd]	...	8.6[efg]
Employment in agricultural sector (% of employed)	73.7[cd]	...	72.2[efg]
Labour force participation, adult female pop. (%)	76.5	76.4	79.3
Labour force participation, adult male pop. (%)	82.7	86.7	86.6
Tourist arrivals at national borders (000)	466[h]	1 333	2 399
Energy production, primary (000 mt oil equivalent)	4[i]	4	4[j]
Telephone subscribers, total (per 100 inhabitants)	1.3	8.2	60.2
Internet users (per 100 inhabitants)	0.1	0.3	1.3

Total trade		Major trading partners				2010
	(million US$)		(% of exports)			(% of imports)
Exports	5 590.1	United States	34.1	China		24.2
Imports	4 902.5	China, Hong Kong SAR	24.8	Thailand		14.1
Balance	687.6	Singapore	7.7	China, Hong Kong SAR		11.3

Social indicators		
Population growth rate (average annual %)	2010-2015	1.2
Urban population growth rate (average annual %)	2010-2015	2.1
Rural population growth rate (average annual %)	2010-2015	1.0
Urban population (%)	2011	20.0
Population aged 0-14 years (%)	2011	31.3
Population aged 60+ years (females and males, % of total)	2011	7.7/5.1
Sex ratio (males per 100 females)	2011	95.9
Life expectancy at birth (females and males, years)	2010-2015	65.1/62.2
Infant mortality rate (per 1 000 live births)	2010-2015	52.8
Fertility rate, total (live births per woman)	2010-2015	2.4
Contraceptive prevalence (ages 15-49, %)	2006-2010	40.0[k]
International migrant stock (000 and % of total population) [l]	mid-2010	335.8/2.2
Refugees and others of concern to UNHCR	end-2010	180
Education: Government expenditure (% of GDP)	2005-2011	2.6
Education: Primary-secondary gross enrolment ratio (f/m per 100) [m]	2005-2011	81.0/86.4
Education: Female third-level students (% of total)	2005-2011	34.4
Seats held by women in national parliaments (%)	2011	21.1

Environmental indicators		
Threatened species	2011	219
Forested area (% of land area)	2009	57.9
CO_2 emission estimates (000 metric tons and metric tons per capita)	2008	4 598/0.3
Energy consumption per capita (kilograms oil equivalent)	2009	107.0
Rainfall in the capital city, total mean (millimetres)		1 636
Temperature in the capital city, mean °C (minimum and maximum)		23.8/32.5

a Market rate. b Phnom Penh. c November. d Age group 10 years and over. e Population census. f 2008. g Age group 7 years and over. h Arrivals of non-resident visitors at national borders. i UNSD estimate. j 2009. k 2005. l Data refer to foreign citizens. m UNESCO estimate.

Cameroon

Region	Middle Africa
Currency	CFA Franc (XAF)
Surface area (square kilometres)	475 650
Population in 2010 (estimated, 000)	19 599
Population density in 2010 (per square kilometre)	41.2
Capital city and population in 2011 (000)	Yaoundé (2 432)
United Nations membership date	20 September 1960

Economic indicators	2000	2005	2010
GDP: Gross domestic product (million current US$)	9 287	16 588	23 649
GDP: Growth rate at constant 2005 prices (annual %)	4.2	2.3	3.0
GDP per capita (current US$)	592.4	945.0	1 206.6
GNI: Gross national income per capita (current US$)	566.5	909.6	1 196.2
Gross fixed capital formation (% of GDP)	16.0	17.7	17.6
Exchange rates (national currency per US$) [a]	704.95	556.04	490.91
Balance of payments, current account (million US$)	−218	−493	−856
CPI: Consumer price index (2000=100)	100[b]	111	123[c]
Industrial production index (2005=100) [d]	94[e]	100	102
Agricultural production index (2004-2006=100)	79	103	123
Food production index (2004-2006=100)	77	102	126
Employment in industrial sector (% of employed)	9.1[fg]	...	...
Employment in agricultural sector (% of employed)	61.3[fg]	...	...
Labour force participation, adult female pop. (%)	61.6	62.6	63.9
Labour force participation, adult male pop. (%)	76.9	76.9	77.3
Tourist arrivals at national borders (000)	277[h]	451[i]	573
Energy production, primary (000 mt oil equivalent)	7 718	4 902	4 427[j]
Telephone subscribers, total (per 100 inhabitants)	1.3	13.4	46.8
Internet users (per 100 inhabitants)	0.3	1.4	4.0

Total trade		Major trading partners			2010
	(million US$)	(% of exports)			(% of imports)
Exports	3 878.4	Spain	18.5	Nigeria	18.2
Imports	5 133.3	Netherlands	13.1	France	14.6
Balance	−1 254.9	Italy	9.7	China	10.6

Social indicators		
Population growth rate (average annual %)	2010-2015	2.1
Urban population growth rate (average annual %)	2010-2015	3.2
Rural population growth rate (average annual %)	2010-2015	0.9
Urban population (%)	2011	52.1
Population aged 0-14 years (%)	2011	40.5
Population aged 60+ years (females and males, % of total)	2011	5.8/5.0
Sex ratio (males per 100 females)	2011	99.7
Life expectancy at birth (females and males, years)	2010-2015	53.6/51.4
Infant mortality rate (per 1 000 live births)	2010-2015	84.9
Fertility rate, total (live births per woman)	2010-2015	4.3
Contraceptive prevalence (ages 15-49, %)	2006-2010	29.2
International migrant stock (000 and % of total population)	mid-2010	196.6/1.0
Refugees and others of concern to UNHCR	end-2010	106 658
Education: Government expenditure (% of GDP)	2005-2011	3.5
Education: Primary-secondary gross enrolment ratio (f/m per 100) [k]	2005-2011	73.9/86.5
Education: Female third-level students (% of total)	2005-2011	44.7
Seats held by women in national parliaments (%)	2011	13.9

Environmental indicators		
Threatened species	2011	630
Forested area (% of land area)	2009	42.6
CO$_2$ emission estimates (000 metric tons and metric tons per capita)	2008	5 298/0.3
Energy consumption per capita (kilograms oil equivalent)	2009	108.0
Rainfall in the capital city, total mean (millimetres)		1 628
Temperature in the capital city, mean °C (minimum and maximum)		18.6/28.4

a Official rate. b Douala and Yaoundé. c 2008. d The indices are shown in terms of ISIC Rev. 3. e 2003. f 2001. g October to November. h Arrivals of non-resident tourists in hotels and similar establishments. i 2006. j 2009. k UNESCO estimate.

Canada

Region	Northern America
Currency	Canadian Dollar (CAD)
Surface area (square kilometres)	9 984 670
Population in 2010 (estimated, 000)	34 017
Population density in 2010 (per square kilometre)	3.4
Capital city and population in 2011 (000)	Ottawa-Gatineau (1 208)[a]
United Nations membership date	9 November 1945

Economic indicators	2000	2005	2010
GDP: Gross domestic product (million current US$)	724 914	1 133 760	1 577 040
GDP: Growth rate at constant 2005 prices (annual %)	5.2	3.0	3.2
GDP per capita (current US$)	23 638.0	35 118.9	46 360.9
GNI: Gross national income per capita (current US$)	23 022.5	34 460.7	45 555.8
Gross fixed capital formation (% of GDP)	19.2	21.3	22.1
Exchange rates (national currency per US$)[b]	1.50	1.16	1.00
Balance of payments, current account (million US$)	19 622	21 714	−49 307
CPI: Consumer price index (2000=100)	100	112	122
Industrial production index (2005=100)[c]	96[d]	100	88
Agricultural production index (2004-2006=100)	93	102	102
Food production index (2004-2006=100)	93	102	102
Unemployment (% of labour force)	7.2[e]	6.8	8.0
Employment in industrial sector (% of employed)[f]	22.5	22.0	21.5[g]
Employment in agricultural sector (% of employed)[f]	3.3	2.7	2.4[g]
Labour force participation, adult female pop. (%)	58.7	60.9	61.8
Labour force participation, adult male pop. (%)	72.2	72.7	71.5
Tourist arrivals at national borders (000)	19 627	18 771	16 097
Energy production, primary (000 mt oil equivalent)	364 018	388 916	377 492[h]
Telephone subscribers, total (per 100 inhabitants)	96.4	108.9	120.7
Internet users (per 100 inhabitants)	51.3	71.7	81.6

Total trade		Major trading partners			2010
	(million US$)	(% of exports)		(% of imports)	
Exports	386 579.9	United States	74.9	United States	50.4
Imports	392 108.7	United Kingdom	4.1	China	11.0
Balance	−5 528.8	China	3.3	Mexico	5.5

Social indicators		
Population growth rate (average annual %)	2010-2015	0.9
Urban population growth rate (average annual %)	2010-2015	1.1
Rural population growth rate (average annual %)	2010-2015	0.4
Urban population (%)	2011	80.7
Population aged 0-14 years (%)	2011	16.4
Population aged 60+ years (females and males, % of total)	2011	21.9/18.8
Sex ratio (males per 100 females)	2011	98.5
Life expectancy at birth (females and males, years)	2010-2015	83.5/78.9
Infant mortality rate (per 1 000 live births)	2010-2015	4.9
Fertility rate, total (live births per woman)	2010-2015	1.7
Contraceptive prevalence (ages 15-49, %)[i]	2006-2010	74.0[j]
International migrant stock (000 and % of total population)	mid-2010	7 202.3/21.3
Refugees and others of concern to UNHCR	end-2010	216 574
Education: Government expenditure (% of GDP)	2005-2011	4.8
Education: Primary-secondary gross enrolment ratio (f/m per 100)	2005-2011	99.4/100.8
Education: Female third-level students (% of total)	2005-2011	56.4[j]
Deaths by assault (females and males, per 100 000)[e]	2005-2008	0.9/2.3
Seats held by women in national parliaments (%)	2011	24.7

Environmental indicators		
Threatened species	2011	83
Forested area (% of land area)	2009	34.1
CO₂ emission estimates (000 metric tons and metric tons per capita)	2008	543 646/16.3
Energy consumption per capita (kilograms oil equivalent)	2009	6 636.0
Rainfall in the capital city, total mean (millimetres)		862
Temperature in the capital city, mean °C (minimum and maximum)		2.2/12.2

a The capital is Ottawa. **b** Market rate. **c** The indices are shown in terms of ISIC Rev. 3. **d** 2003. **e** 2004. **f** Excludes residents of the Territories and indigenous persons living on reserves. **g** 2008. **h** 2009. **i** Age group 18 to 44 years. **j** 2002.

Cape Verde

Region	Western Africa
Currency	Cape Verde Escudo (CVE)
Surface area (square kilometres)	4 033
Population in 2010 (estimated, 000)	496
Population density in 2010 (per square kilometre)	123.0
Capital city and population in 2011 (000)	Praia (132)
United Nations membership date	16 September 1975

Economic indicators	2000	2005	2010
GDP: Gross domestic product (million current US$)	539	972	1 609
GDP: Growth rate at constant 2005 prices (annual %)	7.3	6.5	5.4
GDP per capita (current US$)	1 233.3	2 055.4	3 244.0
GNI: Gross national income per capita (current US$)	1 206.8	1 986.2	3 142.0
Gross fixed capital formation (% of GDP)	30.5	35.8	68.2
Exchange rates (national currency per US$) [a]	118.51	93.47	82.53
Balance of payments, current account (million US$)	−58	−41	−184
CPI: Consumer price index (2000=100)	100	105	127
Agricultural production index (2004-2006=100)	92	98	120
Food production index (2004-2006=100)	92	98	120
Labour force participation, adult female pop. (%)	46.0	48.0	50.2
Labour force participation, adult male pop. (%)	83.8	83.0	83.1
Tourist arrivals at national borders (000) [b]	115	198	382
Energy production, primary (000 mt oil equivalent)	1	1	0 [c]
Telephone subscribers, total (per 100 inhabitants)	17.0	32.4	89.5
Internet users (per 100 inhabitants)	1.8	6.1	30.0

Total trade		Major trading partners			2010
	(million US$)	(% of exports)			(% of imports)
Exports	46.6	Spain	68.2	Portugal	45.5
Imports	730.8	Portugal	24.9	Netherlands	13.5
Balance	−684.2			Spain	6.8

Social indicators		
Population growth rate (average annual %)	2010-2015	1.0
Urban population growth rate (average annual %)	2010-2015	2.1
Rural population growth rate (average annual %)	2010-2015	−1.1
Urban population (%)	2011	62.6
Population aged 0-14 years (%)	2011	31.0
Population aged 60+ years (females and males, % of total)	2011	8.5/5.7
Sex ratio (males per 100 females)	2011	98.3
Life expectancy at birth (females and males, years)	2010-2015	77.7/70.5
Infant mortality rate (per 1 000 live births)	2010-2015	18.5
Fertility rate, total (live births per woman)	2010-2015	2.3
Contraceptive prevalence (ages 15-49, %)	2006-2010	61.3 [d]
International migrant stock (000 and % of total population)	mid-2010	12.1/2.4
Education: Government expenditure (% of GDP)	2005-2011	5.6
Education: Primary-secondary gross enrolment ratio (f/m per 100)	2005-2011	100.2/96.1
Education: Female third-level students (% of total)	2005-2011	55.2
Seats held by women in national parliaments (%)	2011	20.8

Environmental indicators		
Threatened species	2011	35
Forested area (% of land area)	2009	21.0
CO_2 emission estimates (000 metric tons and metric tons per capita)	2008	308/0.6
Energy consumption per capita (kilograms oil equivalent)	2009	215.0
Rainfall in the capital city, total mean (millimetres) [e]		70
Temperature in the capital city, mean °C (minimum and maximum) [ef]		23.5/23.5

a Official rate. b Arrivals of non-resident tourists in hotels and similar establishments. c 2009. d 2005.
e Sal. f Refers to average temperature.

Cayman Islands

Region	Caribbean
Currency	Cayman Is. Dollar (KYD)
Surface area (square kilometres)	264
Population in 2010 (estimated, 000)	56
Population density in 2010 (per square kilometre)	213.0
Capital city and population in 2011 (000)	George Town (28)

Economic indicators	2000	2005	2010
GDP: Gross domestic product (million current US$)	2 277	3 042	3 208
GDP: Growth rate at constant 2005 prices (annual %)	1.0	6.5	−4.0
GDP per capita (current US$)	56 657.6	58 195.3	57 047.9
GNI: Gross national income per capita (current US$)	51 323.0	52 715.9	51 676.5
Gross fixed capital formation (% of GDP)	22.4	22.4	22.4
Exchange rates (national currency per US$) [a]	0.81	0.81	0.81
CPI: Consumer price index (2000=100)	100	117	124[b]
Agricultural production index (2004-2006=100)	153	94	103
Food production index (2004-2006=100)	153	94	103
Employment in industrial sector (% of employed) [c]	...	22.2	19.1[d]
Employment in agricultural sector (% of employed) [c]	...	1.7	1.9[d]
Tourist arrivals at national borders (000) [e]	354	168	288
Telephone subscribers, total (per 100 inhabitants)	113.7	227.6	244.1
Internet users (per 100 inhabitants)	...	38.0	66.0

Social indicators		
Population growth rate (average annual %)	2010-2015	0.9
Urban population growth rate (average annual %)	2010-2015	0.8
Rural population growth rate (average annual %)	2010-2015	0.0
Urban population (%)	2011	100.0
Population aged 0-14 years (%) [fgh]	2011	18.8[b]
Population aged 60+ years (females and males, % of total) [fgh]	2011	8.1/8.0[b]
Sex ratio (males per 100 females) [ghi]	2011	97.8[i]
Life expectancy at birth (females and males, years) [gk]	2010-2015	83.8/76.3[l]
Fertility rate, total (live births per woman) [g]	2010-2015	1.6[m]
International migrant stock (000 and % of total population)	mid-2010	35.7/63.0
Refugees and others of concern to UNHCR	end-2010	5
Education: Primary-secondary gross enrolment ratio (f/m per 100)	2005-2011	88.5/85.1
Education: Female third-level students (% of total)	2005-2011	68.9

Environmental indicators		
Threatened species	2011	37
Forested area (% of land area)	2009	52.9
CO$_2$ emission estimates (000 metric tons and metric tons per capita)	2008	557/10.0
Energy consumption per capita (kilograms oil equivalent)	2009	3 024.0
Rainfall in the capital city, total mean (millimetres)		1 435
Temperature in the capital city, mean °C (minimum and maximum)		21.2/32.0

a UN operational exchange rate. b 2009. c October. d 2008. e Air arrivals. f De jure estimate. g Data compiled by the United Nations Demographic Yearbook system. h Data refer to the latest available census. i De jure population count. j 2010. k The data are based on a small number of deaths. l 2006. m 2007.

Central African Republic

Region	Middle Africa
Currency	CFA Franc (XAF)
Surface area (square kilometres)	622 984
Population in 2010 (estimated, 000)	4 401
Population density in 2010 (per square kilometre)	7.1
Capital city and population in 2011 (000)	Bangui (740)
United Nations membership date	20 September 1960

Economic indicators	2000	2005	2010
GDP: Gross domestic product (million current US$)	914	1 350	1 984
GDP: Growth rate at constant 2005 prices (annual %)	1.9	2.4	3.3
GDP per capita (current US$)	247.0	336.0	450.8
GNI: Gross national income per capita (current US$)	243.8	333.8	425.3
Gross fixed capital formation (% of GDP)	11.1	9.8	11.4
Exchange rates (national currency per US$) [a]	704.95	556.04	490.91
CPI: Consumer price index (2000=100) [bc]	100	112	136[d]
Industrial production index (2005=100) [e]	...	100	143
Agricultural production index (2004-2006=100)	95	99	114
Food production index (2004-2006=100)	91	99	114
Labour force participation, adult female pop. (%)	70.7	71.7	72.5
Labour force participation, adult male pop. (%)	86.1	85.5	85.2
Tourist arrivals at national borders (000) [f]	11	12	52[d]
Energy production, primary (000 mt oil equivalent)	7[g]	12	12[d]
Telephone subscribers, total (per 100 inhabitants)	0.4	2.7	22.4
Internet users (per 100 inhabitants)	0.1	0.3	2.3

Total trade		Major trading partners			2010
	(million US$)[d]	(% of exports)[d]			(% of imports)[d]
Exports	80.5	Belgium	58.5	France	22.7
Imports	211.7	France	9.3	United States	15.6
Balance	−131.2	China	9.3	Cameroon	8.8

Social indicators		
Population growth rate (average annual %)	2010-2015	2.0
Urban population growth rate (average annual %)	2010-2015	2.6
Rural population growth rate (average annual %)	2010-2015	1.6
Urban population (%)	2011	39.1
Population aged 0-14 years (%)	2011	40.1
Population aged 60+ years (females and males, % of total)	2011	6.5/5.4
Sex ratio (males per 100 females)	2011	97.1
Life expectancy at birth (females and males, years)	2010-2015	51.3/47.7
Infant mortality rate (per 1 000 live births)	2010-2015	95.8
Fertility rate, total (live births per woman)	2010-2015	4.4
Contraceptive prevalence (ages 15-49, %)	2006-2010	19.0
International migrant stock (000 and % of total population) [h]	mid-2010	80.5/1.8
Refugees and others of concern to UNHCR	end-2010	215 371
Education: Government expenditure (% of GDP)	2005-2011	1.2
Education: Primary-secondary gross enrolment ratio (f/m per 100)	2005-2011	43.4/62.6
Education: Female third-level students (% of total)	2005-2011	24.5
Seats held by women in national parliaments (%)	2011	12.5

Environmental indicators		
Threatened species	2011	38
Forested area (% of land area)	2009	36.3
CO_2 emission estimates (000 metric tons and metric tons per capita)	2008	260/0.1
Energy consumption per capita (kilograms oil equivalent)	2009	21.0[g]

a Official rate. **b** Excludes rent. **c** Bangui. **d** 2009. **e** The indices are shown in terms of ISIC Rev. 3. **f** Air arrivals in Bangui only. **g** UNSD estimate. **h** Data refer to foreign citizens.

Chad

Region	Middle Africa
Currency	CFA Franc (XAF)
Surface area (square kilometres)	1 284 000
Population in 2010 (estimated, 000)	11 227
Population density in 2010 (per square kilometre)	8.7
Capital city and population in 2011 (000)	N'Djamena (1 079)
United Nations membership date	20 September 1960

Economic indicators	2000	2005	2010
GDP: Gross domestic product (million current US$)	1 385	5 873	8 166
GDP: Growth rate at constant 2005 prices (annual %)	−0.5	7.9	5.1
GDP per capita (current US$)	168.5	600.2	727.4
GNI: Gross national income per capita (current US$)	190.1	338.1	425.9
Gross fixed capital formation (% of GDP)	15.2	20.3	22.5
Exchange rates (national currency per US$) [a]	704.95	556.04	490.91
CPI: Consumer price index (2000=100) [b]	100	118	141[c]
Industrial production index (2005=100) [d]	93[e]	100	77
Agricultural production index (2004-2006=100)	78	104	102
Food production index (2004-2006=100)	78	104	106
Labour force participation, adult female pop. (%)	64.6	64.5	64.5
Labour force participation, adult male pop. (%)	80.2	80.1	80.2
Tourist arrivals at national borders (000) [f]	43	29	31[c]
Energy production, primary (000 mt oil equivalent)	...	8 899	5 793[c]
Telephone subscribers, total (per 100 inhabitants)	0.2	2.3	24.3
Internet users (per 100 inhabitants)	<	0.4	1.7

Social indicators		
Population growth rate (average annual %)	2010-2015	2.6
Urban population growth rate (average annual %)	2010-2015	3.0
Rural population growth rate (average annual %)	2010-2015	2.5
Urban population (%)	2011	21.8
Population aged 0-14 years (%)	2011	45.4
Population aged 60+ years (females and males, % of total)	2011	4.9/4.1
Sex ratio (males per 100 females)	2011	98.9
Life expectancy at birth (females and males, years)	2010-2015	51.6/48.6
Infant mortality rate (per 1 000 live births)	2010-2015	123.9
Fertility rate, total (live births per woman)	2010-2015	5.7
Contraceptive prevalence (ages 15-49, %)	2006-2010	2.8[g]
International migrant stock (000 and % of total population) [h]	mid-2010	388.3/3.4
Refugees and others of concern to UNHCR	end-2010	529 090
Education: Government expenditure (% of GDP)	2005-2011	2.8
Education: Primary-secondary gross enrolment ratio (f/m per 100)	2005-2011	46.5/71.2
Education: Female third-level students (% of total) [i]	2005-2011	14.8
Seats held by women in national parliaments (%)	2011	12.8

Environmental indicators		
Threatened species	2011	30
Forested area (% of land area)	2009	9.2
CO_2 emission estimates (000 metric tons and metric tons per capita)	2008	495/0.0
Energy consumption per capita (kilograms oil equivalent)	2009	6.0[j]
Rainfall in the capital city, total mean (millimetres)		510[k]
Temperature in the capital city, mean °C (minimum and maximum)		20.8/30.5

a Official rate. **b** N'Djamena. **c** 2009. **d** The indices are shown in terms of ISIC Rev. 3. **e** 2003. **f** Arrivals of non-resident tourists in hotels and similar establishments. **g** 2004. **h** Includes refugees. **i** UNESCO estimate. **j** UNSD estimate. **k** January to November only.

Chile

Region	South America
Currency	Chilean Peso (CLP)
Surface area (square kilometres)	756 102
Population in 2010 (estimated, 000)	17 114
Population density in 2010 (per square kilometre)	22.6
Capital city and population in 2011 (000)	Santiago (6 034)
United Nations membership date	24 October 1945

Economic indicators	2000	2005	2010
GDP: Gross domestic product (million current US$)	75 197	118 250	203 443
GDP: Growth rate at constant 2005 prices (annual %)	4.5	5.6	5.2
GDP per capita (current US$)	4 876.6	7 253.8	11 887.7
GNI: Gross national income per capita (current US$)	4 690.1	6 612.2	10 987.2
Gross fixed capital formation (% of GDP)	20.7	21.2	20.9
Exchange rates (national currency per US$) [a]	572.68	514.21	468.37
Balance of payments, current account (million US$)	−898	1 449	3 802
CPI: Consumer price index (2000=100) [b]	...	...	101
Agricultural production index (2004-2006=100)	83	100	107
Food production index (2004-2006=100)	82	100	107
Unemployment (% of labour force)	10.0[c]	9.2	8.1
Employment in industrial sector (% of employed)	23.4[d]	23.0[d]	23.2[ef]
Employment in agricultural sector (% of employed)	14.4[d]	13.2[d]	11.2[ef]
Labour force participation, adult female pop. (%)	35.4	38.2	46.8
Labour force participation, adult male pop. (%)	74.7	72.9	74.3
Tourist arrivals at national borders (000)	1 742	2 027	2 766
Energy production, primary (000 mt oil equivalent)	4 287	4 670	4 320[f]
Telephone subscribers, total (per 100 inhabitants)	43.5	85.9	136.2
Internet users (per 100 inhabitants)	16.6	31.2	45.0

Total trade	Major trading partners			2010
(million US$)	(% of exports)		(% of imports)	
Exports	70 631.5	China	24.6	China	17.6
Imports	56 220.8	Japan	10.8	United States	17.5
Balance	14 410.7	United States	10.0	Argentina	8.4

Social indicators

Population growth rate (average annual %)	2010-2015	0.9
Urban population growth rate (average annual %)	2010-2015	1.1
Rural population growth rate (average annual %)	2010-2015	−1.1
Urban population (%)	2011	89.2
Population aged 0-14 years (%)	2011	21.7
Population aged 60+ years (females and males, % of total)	2011	14.9/12.1
Sex ratio (males per 100 females)	2011	97.8
Life expectancy at birth (females and males, years)	2010-2015	82.4/76.2
Infant mortality rate (per 1 000 live births)	2010-2015	6.8
Fertility rate, total (live births per woman)	2010-2015	1.8
Contraceptive prevalence (ages 15-49, %) [g]	2006-2010	64.2
International migrant stock (000 and % of total population)	mid-2010	320.4/1.9
Refugees and others of concern to UNHCR	end-2010	1 895
Education: Government expenditure (% of GDP)	2005-2011	4.5
Education: Primary-secondary gross enrolment ratio (f/m per 100)	2005-2011	95.7/96.8
Education: Female third-level students (% of total)	2005-2011	50.7
Deaths by assault (females and males, per 100 000)	2005-2008	1.3/10.4
Seats held by women in national parliaments (%)	2011	14.2

Environmental indicators

Threatened species	2011	147
Forested area (% of land area)	2009	21.8
CO$_2$ emission estimates (000 metric tons and metric tons per capita)	2008	73 049/4.4
Energy consumption per capita (kilograms oil equivalent)	2009	1 359.0
Rainfall in the capital city, total mean (millimetres)		313
Temperature in the capital city, mean °C (minimum and maximum)		8.3/22.5

a Principal rate. b Index base 2009=100. c 2004. d Fourth quarter. e Average of quarterly estimates. f 2009. g Age group 15 to 44 years.

China[a]

Region	Eastern Asia
Currency	Renminbi (CNY)
Surface area (square kilometres)	9 596 961
Population in 2010 (estimated, 000)	1 341 335
Population density in 2010 (per square kilometre)	139.8
Capital city and population in 2011 (000)	Beijing (15 594)
United Nations membership date	24 October 1945

Economic indicators	2000	2005	2010
GDP: Gross domestic product (million current US$)	1 192 840	2 283 670	5 739 360
GDP: Growth rate at constant 2005 prices (annual %)	8.4	11.3	10.4
GDP per capita (current US$)	956.7	1 777.4	4 354.0
GNI: Gross national income per capita (current US$)	949.4	1 764.9	4 529.4
Gross fixed capital formation (% of GDP)	34.3	39.7	46.9
Exchange rates (national currency per US$)[b]	8.28	8.07	6.62
Balance of payments, current account (million US$)	20 518	134 082	305 374
CPI: Consumer price index (2000=100)	100	107	120[c]
Agricultural production index (2004-2006=100)	85	100	114
Food production index (2004-2006=100)	85	100	115
Employment in industrial sector (% of employed)[de]	22.5	23.8	27.2[c]
Employment in agricultural sector (% of employed)[de]	50.0	44.8	39.6[c]
Labour force participation, adult female pop. (%)	71.1	69.1	67.9
Labour force participation, adult male pop. (%)	82.6	81.2	80.2
Tourist arrivals at national borders (000)	31 229	46 809	55 664
Energy production, primary (000 mt oil equivalent)	920 520	1 439 360	1 814 966[f]
Telephone subscribers, total (per 100 inhabitants)	18.1	56.9	86.0
Internet users (per 100 inhabitants)	1.8	8.5	34.3

Total trade		Major trading partners			2010
	(million US$)	(% of exports)			(% of imports)
Exports	1 577 764.0	United States	18.0	Japan	12.7
Imports	1 396 002.0	China, Hong Kong SAR	13.8	Republic of Korea	9.9
Balance	181 762.1	Japan	7.7		

Social indicators		
Population growth rate (average annual %)	2010-2015	0.4
Urban population growth rate (average annual %)	2010-2015	2.9
Rural population growth rate (average annual %)	2010-2015	−2.3
Urban population (%)	2011	50.6
Population aged 0-14 years (%)	2011	19.1
Population aged 60+ years (females and males, % of total)	2011	13.7/12.0
Sex ratio (males per 100 females)	2011	108.0
Life expectancy at birth (females and males, years)	2010-2015	75.6/72.1
Infant mortality rate (per 1 000 live births)	2010-2015	19.6
Fertility rate, total (live births per woman)	2010-2015	1.6
Contraceptive prevalence (ages 15-49, %)	2006-2010	84.6
International migrant stock (000 and % of total population)[g]	mid-2010	685.8/0.1
Refugees and others of concern to UNHCR	end-2010	301 108[h]
Education: Government expenditure (% of GDP)	2005-2011	1.9[i]
Education: Primary-secondary gross enrolment ratio (f/m per 100)	2005-2011	95.7/92.5
Education: Female third-level students (% of total)	2005-2011	49.7
Seats held by women in national parliaments (%)	2011	21.3

Environmental indicators		
Threatened species	2011	888
Forested area (% of land area)	2009	21.9
CO_2 emission estimates (000 metric tons and metric tons per capita)	2008	7 026 164/5.2
Energy consumption per capita (kilograms oil equivalent)	2009	1 431.0
Rainfall in the capital city, total mean (millimetres)		576
Temperature in the capital city, mean °C (minimum and maximum)		7.7/19.0

a For statistical purposes the data for China do not include those for Hong Kong Special Administrative Region, Macao Special Administrative Region and Taiwan Province of China, except for statistics relating to population of Taiwan Province. **b** Principal rate. **c** 2008. **d** Official estimates. **e** Age group 16 years and over. **f** 2009. **g** Estimates. **h** The 300,000 Vietnamese refugees are well integrated and in practice receive protection from the Government of China. **i** 1999.

China, Hong Kong SAR

Region	Eastern Asia
Currency	Hong Kong Dollar (HKD)
Surface area (square kilometres)	1 104
Population in 2010 (estimated, 000)	7 053
Population density in 2010 (per square kilometre)	6 388.8
Capital city and population in 2011 (000)	Hong Kong (7 122)

Economic indicators	2000	2005	2010
GDP: Gross domestic product (million current US$)	169 121	177 772	224 459
GDP: Growth rate at constant 2005 prices (annual %)	8.0	7.1	7.0
GDP per capita (current US$)	24 931.9	26 105.1	31 823.7
GNI: Gross national income per capita (current US$)	25 097.5	26 136.2	32 491.1
Gross fixed capital formation (% of GDP)	26.4	20.9	21.5
Exchange rates (national currency per US$) [a]	7.80	7.75	7.77
Balance of payments, current account (million US$)	6 993	20 181	13 936
CPI: Consumer price index (2000=100)	100	94[b]	102[c]
Unemployment (% of labour force)	6.8[d]	5.6	4.3
Employment in industrial sector (% of employed) [e]	20.3	15.1	12.4[fg]
Employment in agricultural sector (% of employed) [e]	0.3	0.3	0.2[fg]
Labour force participation, adult female pop. (%)	49.0	51.8	51.0
Labour force participation, adult male pop. (%)	73.3	71.0	68.3
Tourist arrivals at national borders (000)	8 814	14 773	20 085
Telephone subscribers, total (per 100 inhabitants)	138.2	181.2	257.4
Internet users (per 100 inhabitants)	.27.8	56.9	72.0

Total trade		Major trading partners			2010
	(million US$)	(% of exports)			(% of imports)
Exports	400 692.0	China	52.5	China	44.7
Imports	441 369.2	United States	10.7	Japan	9.3
Balance	−40 677.2	Japan	4.1	Singapore	7.0

Social indicators		
Population growth rate (average annual %)	2010-2015	1.0
Urban population growth rate (average annual %)	2010-2015	1.0
Rural population growth rate (average annual %)	2010-2015	0.0
Urban population (%)	2011	100.0
Population aged 0-14 years (%)	2011	11.3
Population aged 60+ years (females and males, % of total)	2011	18.7/18.9
Sex ratio (males per 100 females)	2011	89.9
Life expectancy at birth (females and males, years)	2010-2015	86.4/80.2
Infant mortality rate (per 1 000 live births)	2010-2015	2.0
Fertility rate, total (live births per woman)	2010-2015	1.1
Contraceptive prevalence (ages 15-49, %)	2006-2010	79.5
International migrant stock (000 and % of total population)	mid-2010	2 741.8/38.8
Refugees and others of concern to UNHCR	end-2010	641
Education: Government expenditure (% of GDP)	2005-2011	3.6
Education: Primary-secondary gross enrolment ratio (f/m per 100)	2005-2011	90.6/89.1
Education: Female third-level students (% of total) [h]	2005-2011	50.5

Environmental indicators		
Threatened species	2011	54
CO_2 emission estimates (000 metric tons and metric tons per capita)	2008	38 542/5.5
Energy consumption per capita (kilograms oil equivalent)	2009	1 689.0
Rainfall in the capital city, total mean (millimetres)		2 383
Temperature in the capital city, mean °C (minimum and maximum)		21.1/25.6

a Market rate. b Series linked to former series. c 2008. d 2004. e Excludes marine and institutional populations. f Average of quarterly estimates. g 2009. h National estimate.

China, Macao SAR

Region	Eastern Asia		
Currency	Pataca (MOP)		
Surface area (square kilometres)	30		
Population in 2010 (estimated, 000)	544		
Population density in 2010 (per square kilometre)	18 121.9		
Capital city and population in 2011 (000)	Macao (556)		

Economic indicators	2000	2005	2010
GDP: Gross domestic product (million current US$)	6 302	11 502	27 177
GDP: Growth rate at constant 2005 prices (annual %)	5.8	8.3	26.2
GDP per capita (current US$)	14 592.4	23 893.0	49 990.2
GNI: Gross national income per capita (current US$)	14 821.7	22 281.8	47 022.5
Gross fixed capital formation (% of GDP)	11.0	26.4	12.6
Exchange rates (national currency per US$) [a]	8.03	7.99	8.02
Balance of payments, current account (million US$)	2 324[b]	2 942	12 233
CPI: Consumer price index (2000=100)	100	99[c]	124
Industrial production index (2005=100) [d]	114[e]	100	45
Unemployment (% of labour force) [f]	4.8[g]	4.1	2.8
Employment in industrial sector (% of employed)	28.2[h]	25.0[h]	16.0[fij]
Employment in agricultural sector (% of employed)	0.2[h]	0.1[h]	0.2[fj]
Labour force participation, adult female pop. (%)	55.7	59.1	66.3
Labour force participation, adult male pop. (%)	75.5	73.3	76.9
Tourist arrivals at national borders (000) [k]	5 197	9 014	11 926[l]
Telephone subscribers, total (per 100 inhabitants)	73.6	146.9	237.3
Internet users (per 100 inhabitants)	13.6	34.9	56.8

Total trade		Major trading partners		2010
	(million US$)	(% of exports)		(% of imports)
Exports	869.8	China	30.5
Imports	5 629.5	China, Hong Kong SAR	10.3
Balance	−4 759.7	France	9.0

Social indicators		
Population growth rate (average annual %)	2010-2015	2.0
Urban population growth rate (average annual %)	2010-2015	2.0
Rural population growth rate (average annual %)	2010-2015	0.0
Urban population (%)	2011	100.0
Population aged 0-14 years (%)	2011	12.9
Population aged 60+ years (females and males, % of total)	2011	11.1/13.0
Sex ratio (males per 100 females)	2011	92.4
Life expectancy at birth (females and males, years)	2010-2015	83.8/79.1
Infant mortality rate (per 1 000 live births)	2010-2015	4.1
Fertility rate, total (live births per woman)	2010-2015	1.2
International migrant stock (000 and % of total population)	mid-2010	299.7/54.7
Refugees and others of concern to UNHCR	end-2010	10
Education: Government expenditure (% of GDP)	2005-2011	2.6
Education: Primary-secondary gross enrolment ratio (f/m per 100)	2005-2011	90.6/95.0
Education: Female third-level students (% of total)	2005-2011	51.1

Environmental indicators		
Threatened species	2011	9
CO$_2$ emission estimates (000 metric tons and metric tons per capita)	2008	1 334/2.5
Energy consumption per capita (kilograms oil equivalent)	2009	1 320.0
Rainfall in the capital city, total mean (millimetres)		2 123
Temperature in the capital city, mean °C (minimum and maximum)		20.2/25.2

a Market rate. b 2002. c Series linked to former series. d The indices are shown in terms of ISIC Rev. 3.
e 2003. f Age group 16 years and over. g 2004. h Age group 14 years and over. i Excludes mining and
quarrying. j 2009. k Country estimates. l Excludes other non-residents namely workers, students, etc.

Colombia

Region	South America
Currency	Colombian Peso (COP)
Surface area (square kilometres)	1 141 748
Population in 2010 (estimated, 000)	46 295
Population density in 2010 (per square kilometre)	40.6
Capital city and population in 2011 (000)	Bogotá (8 744)
United Nations membership date	5 November 1945

Economic indicators	2000	2005	2010
GDP: Gross domestic product (million current US$)	99 876	146 566	288 086
GDP: Growth rate at constant 2005 prices (annual %)	2.9	4.7	4.3
GDP per capita (current US$)	2 511.7	3 405.3	6 222.9
GNI: Gross national income per capita (current US$)	2 472.4	3 320.1	6 041.2
Gross fixed capital formation (% of GDP)	14.1	19.7	22.4
Exchange rates (national currency per US$) [a]	2 187.02	2 284.22	1 989.88
Balance of payments, current account (million US$)	795	−1 886	−8 855
CPI: Consumer price index (2000=100) [b]	100	140	177
Agricultural production index (2004-2006=100)	87	99	103
Food production index (2004-2006=100)	87	99	106
Unemployment (% of labour force) [c]	13.6[d]	11.8	11.8
Employment in industrial sector (% of employed) [e]	25.5[fgh]	20.3	20.0
Employment in agricultural sector (% of employed) [e]	1.1[fgh]	21.4	17.9
Labour force participation, adult female pop. (%)	48.5	52.9	55.3
Labour force participation, adult male pop. (%)	81.8	81.0	79.7
Tourist arrivals at national borders (000) [ij]	707	981	2 494[kl]
Energy production, primary (000 mt oil equivalent)	69 548	76 092	95 843[k]
Telephone subscribers, total (per 100 inhabitants)	23.8	68.6	111.6
Internet users (per 100 inhabitants)	2.2	11.0	36.5

Total trade		Major trading partners			2010
	(million US$)	(% of exports)			(% of imports)
Exports	39 819.5	United States	43.1	United States	25.9
Imports	40 682.5	China	4.9	China	13.5
Balance	−863.0	Ecuador	4.6	Mexico	9.5

Social indicators		
Population growth rate (average annual %)	2010-2015	1.3
Urban population growth rate (average annual %)	2010-2015	1.7
Rural population growth rate (average annual %)	2010-2015	0.2
Urban population (%)	2011	75.3
Population aged 0-14 years (%)	2011	28.4
Population aged 60+ years (females and males, % of total)	2011	9.7/8.0
Sex ratio (males per 100 females)	2011	96.8
Life expectancy at birth (females and males, years)	2010-2015	77.7/70.4
Infant mortality rate (per 1 000 live births)	2010-2015	16.7
Fertility rate, total (live births per woman)	2010-2015	2.3
Contraceptive prevalence (ages 15-49, %)	2006-2010	78.2[m]
International migrant stock (000 and % of total population)	mid-2010	110.3/0.2
Refugees and others of concern to UNHCR	end-2010	3 672 478
Education: Government expenditure (% of GDP)	2005-2011	4.8
Education: Primary-secondary gross enrolment ratio (f/m per 100)	2005-2011	107.0/103.1
Education: Female third-level students (% of total)	2005-2011	51.6
Seats held by women in national parliaments (%)	2011	12.7

Environmental indicators		
Threatened species	2011	692
Forested area (% of land area)	2009	54.6
CO_2 emission estimates (000 metric tons and metric tons per capita)	2008	67 645/1.5
Energy consumption per capita (kilograms oil equivalent)	2009	520.0
Rainfall in the capital city, total mean (millimetres)		799
Temperature in the capital city, mean °C (minimum and maximum)		7.4/16.0

a Official rate. **b** Low income group. **c** Age group 12 years and over in urban areas and 10 years and over in rural areas. **d** 2004. **e** Age group 12 years and over. **f** September. **g** Seven main cities. **h** Estimates based on 1993 population census results. **i** Includes cruise passengers. **j** Arrivals of non-resident visitors at national borders. **k** 2009. **l** Includes arrivals of the foreign travellers at terrestrial frontier points. **m** 2004-2005.

Comoros

Region	Eastern Africa
Currency	Comorian Franc (KMF)
Surface area (square kilometres)	2 235
Population in 2010 (estimated, 000)	735
Population density in 2010 (per square kilometre)	328.8
Capital city and population in 2011 (000)	Moroni (54)
United Nations membership date	12 November 1975

Economic indicators	2000	2005	2010
GDP: Gross domestic product (million current US$)	202	387	541
GDP: Growth rate at constant 2005 prices (annual %)	1.4	4.2	2.1
GDP per capita (current US$)	359.0	602.0	736.6
GNI: Gross national income per capita (current US$)	359.6	600.3	736.4
Gross fixed capital formation (% of GDP)	10.1	9.3	16.5
Exchange rates (national currency per US$)[a]	528.71	417.03	368.18
Agricultural production index (2004-2006=100)	91	95	93
Food production index (2004-2006=100)	91	95	93
Labour force participation, adult female pop. (%)	30.3	32.5	34.7
Labour force participation, adult male pop. (%)	78.6	79.7	80.4
Tourist arrivals at national borders (000)	24	26	15[b]
Telephone subscribers, total (per 100 inhabitants)	1.2[c]	5.0	25.4
Internet users (per 100 inhabitants)	0.3	3.2	5.1

Total trade		Major trading partners			2010
	(million US$)[d]	(% of exports)[d]		(% of imports)[d]	
Exports	12.6	France	43.7	United Arab Emirates	29.4
Imports	181.5	Singapore	23.8	France	21.4
Balance	−168.9	Netherlands	6.3	Pakistan	14.7

Social indicators

Population growth rate (average annual %)	2010-2015	2.5
Urban population growth rate (average annual %)	2010-2015	2.8
Rural population growth rate (average annual %)	2010-2015	2.4
Urban population (%)	2011	28.0
Population aged 0-14 years (%)	2011	42.7
Population aged 60+ years (females and males, % of total)	2011	4.6/3.8
Sex ratio (males per 100 females)	2011	101.5
Life expectancy at birth (females and males, years)	2010-2015	63.2/60.3
Infant mortality rate (per 1 000 live births)	2010-2015	62.8
Fertility rate, total (live births per woman)	2010-2015	4.7
Contraceptive prevalence (ages 15-49, %)	2006-2010	25.7[e]
International migrant stock (000 and % of total population)	mid-2010	13.5/2.0
Refugees and others of concern to UNHCR	end-2010	0[f]
Education: Government expenditure (% of GDP)	2005-2011	7.6
Education: Primary-secondary gross enrolment ratio (f/m per 100)[g]	2005-2011	72.9/86.4
Education: Female third-level students (% of total)	2005-2011	42.0
Seats held by women in national parliaments (%)	2011	3.0

Environmental indicators

Threatened species	2011	91
Forested area (% of land area)	2009	1.8
CO_2 emission estimates (000 metric tons and metric tons per capita)	2008	125/0.2
Energy consumption per capita (kilograms oil equivalent)	2009	59.0[h]
Rainfall in the capital city, total mean (millimetres)		2 700
Temperature in the capital city, mean °C (minimum and maximum)		21.2/29.5

a Official rate. **b** 2007. **c** Main telephone lines only. **d** 2009. **e** 2000. **f** Value is zero, not available or not applicable. **g** UNESCO estimate. **h** UNSD estimate.

Congo

Region	Middle Africa
Currency	CFA Franc (XAF)
Surface area (square kilometres)	342 000
Population in 2010 (estimated, 000)	4 043
Population density in 2010 (per square kilometre)	11.8
Capital city and population in 2011 (000)	Brazzaville (1 611)
United Nations membership date	20 September 1960

Economic indicators	2000	2005	2010
GDP: Gross domestic product (million current US$)	3 220	6 087	10 775
GDP: Growth rate at constant 2005 prices (annual %)	7.6	7.7	8.7
GDP per capita (current US$)	1 026.8	1 722.8	2 665.1
GNI: Gross national income per capita (current US$)	769.8	1 249.6	2 180.9
Gross fixed capital formation (% of GDP)	18.0	24.2	44.9
Exchange rates (national currency per US$) [a]	704.95	556.04	490.91
Balance of payments, current account (million US$)	648	696	−2 181[b]
CPI: Consumer price index (2000=100) [c]	100	110	135[d]
Agricultural production index (2004-2006=100)	83	99	125
Food production index (2004-2006=100)	83	99	125
Employment in industrial sector (% of employed)	...	20.6[ef]	...
Employment in agricultural sector (% of employed)	...	35.4[ef]	...
Labour force participation, adult female pop. (%)	65.1	67.5	68.2
Labour force participation, adult male pop. (%)	71.4	71.6	72.7
Tourist arrivals at national borders (000) [g]	19	35	85[d]
Energy production, primary (000 mt oil equivalent)	13 975	12 798	14 361[d]
Telephone subscribers, total (per 100 inhabitants)	2.9	16.3	94.2
Internet users (per 100 inhabitants)	<	1.5	5.0

Total trade		Major trading partners			2010
	(million US$)	(% of exports)			(% of imports)
Exports	6 917.6	China	20.9	Angola	15.0
Imports	4 369.4	Angola	13.1	France	12.2
Balance	2 548.2	France	12.5	Singapore	10.1

Social indicators		
Population growth rate (average annual %)	2010-2015	2.2
Urban population growth rate (average annual %)	2010-2015	2.8
Rural population growth rate (average annual %)	2010-2015	1.0
Urban population (%)	2011	63.7
Population aged 0-14 years (%)	2011	40.6
Population aged 60+ years (females and males, % of total)	2011	6.0/5.1
Sex ratio (males per 100 females)	2011	100.2
Life expectancy at birth (females and males, years)	2010-2015	59.3/56.6
Infant mortality rate (per 1 000 live births)	2010-2015	66.7
Fertility rate, total (live births per woman)	2010-2015	4.4
Contraceptive prevalence (ages 15-49, %)	2006-2010	44.3[h]
International migrant stock (000 and % of total population)	mid-2010	143.2/3.8
Refugees and others of concern to UNHCR	end-2010	138 737
Education: Government expenditure (% of GDP)	2005-2011	6.2
Education: Primary-secondary gross enrolment ratio (f/m per 100) [i]	2005-2011	74.9/81.9[j]
Education: Female third-level students (% of total)	2005-2011	17.3
Seats held by women in national parliaments (%)	2011	7.3

Environmental indicators		
Threatened species	2011	103
Forested area (% of land area)	2009	65.7
CO$_2$ emission estimates (000 metric tons and metric tons per capita)	2008	1 935/0.6
Energy consumption per capita (kilograms oil equivalent)	2009	158.0

a Official rate. **b** 2007. **c** Brazzaville. **d** 2009. **e** Core Welfare Indicators Questionnaire (World Bank). **f** June to August. **g** Arrivals of non-resident tourists in hotels and similar establishments. **h** 2005. **i** UNESCO estimate. **j** 2004.

Cook Islands

Region	Oceania-Polynesia
Currency	New Zealand Dollar (NZD)
Surface area (square kilometres)	236[a]
Population in 2010 (estimated, 000)	20
Population density in 2010 (per square kilometre)	86.0
Capital city and population in 2011 (000)	Avarua (...)[b]

Economic indicators	2000	2005	2010
GDP: Gross domestic product (million current US$)	92	183	248
GDP: Growth rate at constant 2005 prices (annual %)	13.9	-1.1	-2.4
GDP per capita (current US$)	5 139.2	9 409.2	12 212.1
GNI: Gross national income per capita (current US$)	5 139.2	9 409.2	12 212.1
Gross fixed capital formation (% of GDP)	13.8	13.1	15.4
Exchange rates (national currency per US$)[c]	2.26	1.46	1.31
CPI: Consumer price index (2000=100)[d]	100	118	144
Agricultural production index (2004-2006=100)	190	100	106
Food production index (2004-2006=100)	190	100	106
Tourist arrivals at national borders (000)	73	88	104
Telephone subscribers, total (per 100 inhabitants)	35.0	54.9	74.1
Internet users (per 100 inhabitants)	15.7	26.2	35.7

Total trade		Major trading partners		2010
	(million US$)	(% of exports)[e]		(% of imports)
Exports	4.1[e]	Japan	48.8	
		China	26.8	
		New Zealand	12.2	

Social indicators		
Population growth rate (average annual %)	2010-2015	0.5
Urban population growth rate (average annual %)	2010-2015	0.9
Rural population growth rate (average annual %)	2010-2015	-0.4
Urban population (%)	2011	73.5
Population aged 0-14 years (%)[f]	2011	27.3
Population aged 60+ years (females and males, % of total)[f]	2011	12.5/11.9
Sex ratio (males per 100 females)[f]	2011	103.2
Life expectancy at birth (females and males, years)[f]	2010-2015	76.3/69.6[g]
Infant mortality rate (per 1 000 live births)[f]	2010-2015	11.6[h]
Fertility rate, total (live births per woman)[f]	2010-2015	2.5[i]
Contraceptive prevalence (ages 15-49, %)	2006-2010	43.2[i]
International migrant stock (000 and % of total population)	mid-2010	2.8/14.1
Education: Primary-secondary gross enrolment ratio (f/m per 100)[k]	2005-2011	99.6/89.8

Environmental indicators		
Threatened species	2011	55
Forested area (% of land area)	2009	64.6
CO_2 emission estimates (000 metric tons and metric tons per capita)	2008	70/3.6
Energy consumption per capita (kilograms oil equivalent)	2009	1 167.0[l]

a Excludes Niue. **b** Population estimates for Avarua are not available. Avarua is located on the island of Rarotonga, the population of which is 15.007. **c** UN operational exchange rate. **d** Rarotonga. **e** 2008. **f** Data compiled by the Secretariat of the Pacific Community Demography Programme. **g** 2001-2006. **h** 2005-2009. **i** 2005-2006. **j** 1999. **k** National estimate. **l** UNSD estimate.

Costa Rica

Region	Central America
Currency	Costa Rican Colon (CRC)
Surface area (square kilometres)	51 100
Population in 2010 (estimated, 000)	4 659
Population density in 2010 (per square kilometre)	91.2
Capital city and population in 2011 (000)	San José (1 515)
United Nations membership date	2 November 1945

Economic indicators	2000	2005	2010
GDP: Gross domestic product (million current US$)	15 947	19 965	35 891
GDP: Growth rate at constant 2005 prices (annual %)	1.8	5.9	4.2
GDP per capita (current US$)	4 068.9	4 632.9	7 703.8
GNI: Gross national income per capita (current US$)	3 750.0	4 451.6	7 502.8
Gross fixed capital formation (% of GDP)	17.8	18.7	19.7
Exchange rates (national currency per US$)[a]	318.02	496.68	512.97
Balance of payments, current account (million US$)	−707	−981	−1 439
CPI: Consumer price index (2000=100)[b]	100	170	268
Agricultural production index (2004-2006=100)	90	99	107
Food production index (2004-2006=100)	88	98	108
Employment in industrial sector (% of employed)[c]	22.3[d]	21.6[d]	21.6[e]
Employment in agricultural sector (% of employed)[c]	20.4[d]	15.2[d]	12.3[e]
Labour force participation, adult female pop. (%)	37.1	44.0	46.0
Labour force participation, adult male pop. (%)	81.4	80.4	78.9
Tourist arrivals at national borders (000)	1 088	1 679	2 100
Energy production, primary (000 mt oil equivalent)	588	681	751[e]
Telephone subscribers, total (per 100 inhabitants)	28.3	57.8	96.9
Internet users (per 100 inhabitants)	5.8	22.1	36.5

Total trade		Major trading partners			2010
	(million US$)	(% of exports)		(% of imports)	
Exports	9 044.8	United States	37.4	United States	46.8
Imports	13 920.2	Netherlands	7.0	China	7.1
Balance	−4 875.4	China, Hong Kong SAR	4.8	Mexico	6.4

Social indicators		
Population growth rate (average annual %)	2010-2015	1.4
Urban population growth rate (average annual %)	2010-2015	2.1
Rural population growth rate (average annual %)	2010-2015	<
Urban population (%)	2011	64.7
Population aged 0-14 years (%)	2011	24.4
Population aged 60+ years (females and males, % of total)	2011	10.5/9.2
Sex ratio (males per 100 females)	2011	103.1
Life expectancy at birth (females and males, years)	2010-2015	82.0/77.1
Infant mortality rate (per 1 000 live births)	2010-2015	9.2
Fertility rate, total (live births per woman)	2010-2015	1.8
Contraceptive prevalence (ages 15-49, %)[f]	2006-2010	80.0[g]
International migrant stock (000 and % of total population)[h]	mid-2010	489.2/10.5
Refugees and others of concern to UNHCR	end-2010	19 880
Education: Government expenditure (% of GDP)	2005-2011	6.3
Education: Primary-secondary gross enrolment ratio (f/m per 100)	2005-2011	106.1/104.2
Education: Female third-level students (% of total)[i]	2005-2011	54.3
Deaths by assault (females and males, per 100 000)	2005-2008	1.7/13.5
Seats held by women in national parliaments (%)	2011	38.6

Environmental indicators		
Threatened species	2011	291
Forested area (% of land area)	2009	50.6
CO_2 emission estimates (000 metric tons and metric tons per capita)	2008	8 010/1.8
Energy consumption per capita (kilograms oil equivalent)	2009	666.0
Rainfall in the capital city, total mean (millimetres)		1 866
Temperature in the capital city, mean °C (minimum and maximum)		16.2/24.9

a Market rate. **b** Central area. **c** Age group 12 years and over. **d** July. **e** 2009. **f** Age group 18 to 44 years. **g** 1999. **h** Includes refugees. **i** UNESCO estimate.

Côte d'Ivoire

Region	Western Africa
Currency	CFA Franc (XOF)
Surface area (square kilometres)	322 463
Population in 2010 (estimated, 000)	19 738
Population density in 2010 (per square kilometre)	61.2
Capital city and population in 2011 (000)	Yamoussoukro (966)[a]
United Nations membership date	20 September 1960

Economic indicators	2000	2005	2010
GDP: Gross domestic product (million current US$)	10 682	16 354	22 780
GDP: Growth rate at constant 2005 prices (annual %)	−2.7	1.8	2.6
GDP per capita (current US$)	644.2	907.5	1 154.1
GNI: Gross national income per capita (current US$)	607.6	920.6	1 170.8
Gross fixed capital formation (% of GDP)	12.3	9.3	7.8
Exchange rates (national currency per US$)[b]	704.95	556.04	490.91
Balance of payments, current account (million US$)	−241	40	1 670[c]
CPI: Consumer price index (2000=100)[d]	100	117	131[c]
Industrial production index (2005=100)[e]	85[f]	100	103
Agricultural production index (2004-2006=100)	102	99	106
Food production index (2004-2006=100)	95	98	106
Labour force participation, adult female pop. (%)	48.8	50.2	51.5
Labour force participation, adult male pop. (%)	81.9	81.7	81.3
Energy production, primary (000 mt oil equivalent)	1 684	3 757	4 238[c]
Telephone subscribers, total (per 100 inhabitants)	4.4	14.5	77.6
Internet users (per 100 inhabitants)	0.2	1.0	2.6

Total trade		Major trading partners			2010
	(million US$)	(% of exports)			(% of imports)
Exports	10 283.5	Netherlands	14.2	Nigeria	26.3
Imports	7 849.3	United States	10.3	France	11.9
Balance	2 434.2	Ghana	7.6		

Social indicators		
Population growth rate (average annual %)	2010-2015	2.2
Urban population growth rate (average annual %)	2010-2015	3.6
Rural population growth rate (average annual %)	2010-2015	0.7
Urban population (%)	2011	51.3
Population aged 0-14 years (%)	2011	40.6
Population aged 60+ years (females and males, % of total)	2011	5.6/6.3
Sex ratio (males per 100 females)	2011	103.7
Life expectancy at birth (females and males, years)	2010-2015	57.7/55.3
Infant mortality rate (per 1 000 live births)	2010-2015	68.8
Fertility rate, total (live births per woman)	2010-2015	4.2
Contraceptive prevalence (ages 15-49, %)	2006-2010	12.9
International migrant stock (000 and % of total population)[g]	mid-2010	2 406.7/11.2
Refugees and others of concern to UNHCR	end-2010	563 660
Education: Government expenditure (% of GDP)	2005-2011	4.6
Education: Primary-secondary gross enrolment ratio (f/m per 100)[h]	2005-2011	42.8/62.5[i]
Education: Female third-level students (% of total)	2005-2011	33.3
Seats held by women in national parliaments (%)	2011	8.9

Environmental indicators		
Threatened species	2011	213
Forested area (% of land area)	2009	32.7
CO_2 emission estimates (000 metric tons and metric tons per capita)	2008	7 009/0.3
Energy consumption per capita (kilograms oil equivalent)	2009	138.0

a Yamoussoukro is the capital, Abidjan is the seat of government. **b** Official rate. **c** 2009. **d** Abidjan. **e** The indices are shown in terms of ISIC Rev. 3. **f** 2003. **g** Data refer to foreign-born and foreign citizens. **h** UNESCO estimate. **i** 2002.

Croatia

Region	Southern Europe
Currency	Kuna (HRK)
Surface area (square kilometres)	56 594
Population in 2010 (estimated, 000)	4 403
Population density in 2010 (per square kilometre)	77.8
Capital city and population in 2011 (000)	Zagreb (686)
United Nations membership date	22 May 1992

Economic indicators	2000	2005	2010
GDP: Gross domestic product (million current US$)	21 518	44 821	60 852
GDP: Growth rate at constant 2005 prices (annual %)	3.8	4.3	−1.2
GDP per capita (current US$)	4 775.9	10 090.4	13 819.5
GNI: Gross national income per capita (current US$)	4 881.7	10 370.2	14 388.0
Gross fixed capital formation (% of GDP)	19.0	24.7	21.6
Exchange rates (national currency per US$) [a]	8.16	6.23	5.57
Balance of payments, current account (million US$)	−533	−2 455	−918
CPI: Consumer price index (2000=100)	100	114[b]	133
Industrial production index (2005=100)	93[c]	100	99
Agricultural production index (2004-2006=100)	96	98	100
Food production index (2004-2006=100)	96	98	100
Unemployment (% of labour force)	13.6[d]	12.6	11.8
Employment in industrial sector (% of employed)	28.8[e]	28.6[e]	27.3[f]
Employment in agricultural sector (% of employed)	14.5[e]	17.3[e]	14.9[f]
Labour force participation, adult female pop. (%)	45.1	46.4	46.0
Labour force participation, adult male pop. (%)	63.0	61.4	59.6
Tourist arrivals at national borders (000) [g]	5 831	7 743	9 111
Energy production, primary (000 mt oil equivalent)	3 352	3 653	3 860[h]
Telephone subscribers, total (per 100 inhabitants)	61.1	124.5	186.9
Internet users (per 100 inhabitants)	6.6	33.1	60.3

Total trade		Major trading partners			2010
	(million US$)	(% of exports)		(% of imports)	
Exports	11 810.7	Italy	18.7	Italy	15.2
Imports	20 067.0	Bosnia-Herzegovina	11.6	Germany	12.5
Balance	−8 256.3	Germany	10.3	Russian Federation	9.1

Social indicators		
Population growth rate (average annual %)	2010-2015	−0.2
Urban population growth rate (average annual %)	2010-2015	0.3
Rural population growth rate (average annual %)	2010-2015	−0.9
Urban population (%)	2011	57.8
Population aged 0-14 years (%)	2011	14.9
Population aged 60+ years (females and males, % of total)	2011	27.0/20.2
Sex ratio (males per 100 females)	2011	92.8
Life expectancy at birth (females and males, years)	2010-2015	80.4/73.3
Infant mortality rate (per 1 000 live births)	2010-2015	5.6
Fertility rate, total (live births per woman)	2010-2015	1.5
Contraceptive prevalence (ages 15-49, %) [i]	2006-2010	58.0[j]
International migrant stock (000 and % of total population) [k]	mid-2010	700.0/15.9
Refugees and others of concern to UNHCR	end-2010	25 903
Education: Government expenditure (% of GDP)	2005-2011	4.3
Education: Primary-secondary gross enrolment ratio (f/m per 100)	2005-2011	95.9/93.6
Education: Female third-level students (% of total)	2005-2011	55.0
Deaths by assault (females and males, per 100 000)	2005-2008	1.0/2.6[l]
Seats held by women in national parliaments (%)	2011	23.5

Environmental indicators		
Threatened species	2011	145
Forested area (% of land area)	2009	34.3
CO$_2$ emission estimates (000 metric tons and metric tons per capita)	2008	23 285/5.3
Energy consumption per capita (kilograms oil equivalent)	2009	1 936.0
Rainfall in the capital city, total mean (millimetres)		856
Temperature in the capital city, mean °C (minimum and maximum)		5.4/15.7

a Market rate. **b** Series linked to former series. **c** 2003. **d** 2004. **e** Excludes conscripts. **f** European Labour Force Survey (Eurostat). **g** Arrivals of non-resident tourists in all types of accommodation establishments. **h** 2009. **i** Age group 15 to 44 years. **j** 1970. **k** Includes refugees. **l** Rate based on 30 or fewer events.

Cuba

Region	Caribbean
Currency	Cuban Peso (CUP) [a]
Surface area (square kilometres)	109 886
Population in 2010 (estimated, 000)	11 258
Population density in 2010 (per square kilometre)	102.5
Capital city and population in 2011 (000)	Havana (2 116)
United Nations membership date	24 October 1945

Economic indicators	2000	2005	2010
GDP: Gross domestic product (million current US$)	30 565	42 644	64 220
GDP: Growth rate at constant 2005 prices (annual %)	5.9	11.2	2.1
GDP per capita (current US$)	2 752.6	3 789.2	5 704.4
GNI: Gross national income per capita (current US$)	2 696.6	3 732.9	5 621.1
Gross fixed capital formation (% of GDP)	11.9	9.0	9.9
CPI: Consumer price index (2000=100)	100	109	125 [b]
Agricultural production index (2004-2006=100)	115	97	88
Food production index (2004-2006=100)	115	97	88
Employment in industrial sector (% of employed) [c]	19.1 [d]	19.1 [d]	18.1 [be]
Employment in agricultural sector (% of employed) [c]	27.1 [d]	20.2 [d]	18.6 [be]
Labour force participation, adult female pop. (%)	37.8	38.8	43.1
Labour force participation, adult male pop. (%)	70.2	67.3	70.1
Tourist arrivals at national borders (000) [f]	1 741	2 261	2 507
Energy production, primary (000 mt oil equivalent)	3 298	3 953	3 982 [g]
Telephone subscribers, total (per 100 inhabitants)	4.5	8.8	19.3
Internet users (per 100 inhabitants)	0.5	9.7	15.9

Total trade	Major trading partners		2010
(million US$) [h]	(% of exports) [h]		(% of imports) [h]
Exports	2 980.2		
Imports	10 173.6		
Balance	−7 193.4		

Social indicators		
Population growth rate (average annual %)	2010-2015	−0.1
Urban population growth rate (average annual %)	2010-2015	−0.1
Rural population growth rate (average annual %)	2010-2015	<
Urban population (%)	2011	75.2
Population aged 0-14 years (%)	2011	16.9
Population aged 60+ years (females and males, % of total)	2011	18.4/16.4
Sex ratio (males per 100 females)	2011	101.2
Life expectancy at birth (females and males, years)	2010-2015	81.3/77.4
Infant mortality rate (per 1 000 live births)	2010-2015	5.0
Fertility rate, total (live births per woman)	2010-2015	1.5
Contraceptive prevalence (ages 15-49, %)	2006-2010	72.6
International migrant stock (000 and % of total population)	mid-2010	15.3/0.1
Refugees and others of concern to UNHCR	end-2010	422
Education: Government expenditure (% of GDP)	2005-2011	13.4
Education: Primary-secondary gross enrolment ratio (f/m per 100)	2005-2011	94.9/96.5
Education: Female third-level students (% of total)	2005-2011	61.0
Deaths by assault (females and males, per 100 000)	2005-2008	2.5/7.6
Seats held by women in national parliaments (%)	2011	43.2

Environmental indicators		
Threatened species	2011	311
Forested area (% of land area)	2009	26.6
CO_2 emission estimates (000 metric tons and metric tons per capita)	2008	31 393/2.8
Energy consumption per capita (kilograms oil equivalent)	2009	788.0
Rainfall in the capital city, total mean (millimetres)		1 189
Temperature in the capital city, mean °C (minimum and maximum)		21.6/28.8

a The Cuban Convertible Peso is only exchangeable within the country. **b** 2008. **c** Age group for males 17 to 60 years and for females 17 to 55 years. **d** December. **e** February to April. **f** Air arrivals. **g** 2009. **h** 2006.

Cyprus[a]

Region	Western Asia
Currency	Euro (EUR)[b]
Surface area (square kilometres)	9 251
Population in 2010 (estimated, 000)	1 104[c]
Population density in 2010 (per square kilometre)	119.3
Capital city and population in 2011 (000)	Nicosia (253)
United Nations membership date	20 September 1960

Economic indicators	2000	2005	2010
GDP: Gross domestic product (million current US$)	9 174	16 902	22 957
GDP: Growth rate at constant 2005 prices (annual %)	5.0	3.9	1.1
GDP per capita (current US$)	13 226.5	22 298.4	28 364.3
GNI: Gross national income per capita (current US$)	12 352.5	21 372.2	27 585.7
Gross fixed capital formation (% of GDP)	17.2	19.4	18.6
Exchange rates (national currency per US$)	0.62[de]	0.48[de]	0.75[f]
Balance of payments, current account (million US$)	−488	−971	−2 803
CPI: Consumer price index (2000=100)	100	115	129
Industrial production index (2005=100)	...	100	100
Agricultural production index (2004-2006=100)	107	98	86
Food production index (2004-2006=100)	107	98	86
Unemployment (% of labour force)	...	5.3	6.2
Employment in industrial sector (% of employed)[g]	23.8	24.1	20.8
Employment in agricultural sector (% of employed)[g]	5.2	4.6	3.8
Labour force participation, adult female pop. (%)	49.7	53.6	57.1
Labour force participation, adult male pop. (%)	71.9	73.1	71.3
Tourist arrivals at national borders (000)	2 686	2 470	2 173
Telephone subscribers, total (per 100 inhabitants)	69.8	116.5	131.1
Internet users (per 100 inhabitants)	15.3	32.8	53.0

Total trade		Major trading partners			2010
	(million US$)	(% of exports)			(% of imports)
Exports	1 506.5	Greece	21.3	Greece	18.7
Imports	8 644.7			Italy	9.3
Balance	−7 138.2			Germany	9.0

Social indicators

Population growth rate (average annual %)[c]	2010-2015	1.1
Urban population growth rate (average annual %)[c]	2010-2015	1.4
Rural population growth rate (average annual %)[c]	2010-2015	0.4
Urban population (%)[c]	2011	70.5
Population aged 0-14 years (%)[c]	2011	17.5
Population aged 60+ years (females and males, % of total)[c]	2011	18.2/15.0
Sex ratio (males per 100 females)[c]	2011	104.4
Life expectancy at birth (females and males, years)[c]	2010-2015	82.1/77.7
Infant mortality rate (per 1 000 live births)[c]	2010-2015	4.4
Fertility rate, total (live births per woman)[c]	2010-2015	1.5
International migrant stock (000 and % of total population)	mid-2010	154.3/17.5
Refugees and others of concern to UNHCR	end-2010	8 790
Education: Government expenditure (% of GDP)	2005-2011	7.4
Education: Primary-secondary gross enrolment ratio (f/m per 100)[h]	2005-2011	101.6/101.4
Education: Female third-level students (% of total)	2005-2011	46.8
Deaths by assault (females and males, per 100 000)	2005-2008	0.5/2.3[i]
Seats held by women in national parliaments (%)	2011	10.7

Environmental indicators

Threatened species	2011	55
Forested area (% of land area)	2009	18.7
CO_2 emission estimates (000 metric tons and metric tons per capita)	2008	8 548/9.9
Energy consumption per capita (kilograms oil equivalent)	2009	2 207.0
Rainfall in the capital city, total mean (millimetres)		308
Temperature in the capital city, mean °C (minimum and maximum)		12.8/26.0

a Data generally refer to the government-controlled area unless otherwise indicated. **b** Beginning 1 January 2008, the Cyprus Pound (CYP) was replaced by the euro (1 EUR=0.585274 CYP). **c** Includes Northern-Cyprus. **d** Official rate. **e** Currency = Cyprus Pound. **f** Market rate. **g** European Labour Force Survey (Eurostat). **h** National estimate. **i** Rate based on 30 or fewer events.

Czech Republic

Region	Eastern Europe
Currency	Czech Koruna (CZK)
Surface area (square kilometres)	78 865
Population in 2010 (estimated, 000)	10 493
Population density in 2010 (per square kilometre)	133.1
Capital city and population in 2011 (000)	Prague (1 276)
United Nations membership date	19 January 1993

Economic indicators	2000	2005	2010
GDP: Gross domestic product (million current US$)	58 803	130 066	197 674
GDP: Growth rate at constant 2005 prices (annual %)	4.2	6.8	2.7
GDP per capita (current US$)	5 740.8	12 725.9	18 838.8
GNI: Gross national income per capita (current US$)	5 642.1	12 189.5	17 570.3
Gross fixed capital formation (% of GDP)	28.9	25.9	24.6
Exchange rates (national currency per US$) [a]	37.81	24.59	18.75
Balance of payments, current account (million US$)	−2 690	−1 210	−5 992
CPI: Consumer price index (2000=100)	100	112	125 [b]
Industrial production index (2005=100)	87 [c]	100	112
Agricultural production index (2004-2006=100)	102	100	90
Food production index (2004-2006=100)	102	100	90
Unemployment (% of labour force)	8.3 [d]	7.9	7.3
Employment in industrial sector (% of employed)	39.5	39.5	38.0 [e]
Employment in agricultural sector (% of employed)	5.1	4.0	3.1 [e]
Labour force participation, adult female pop. (%)	51.7	50.7	49.3
Labour force participation, adult male pop. (%)	69.8	68.8	68.2
Tourist arrivals at national borders (000)	4 773 [f]	8 767 [g]	8 185
Energy production, primary (000 mt oil equivalent)	27 034	26 843	24 088 [h]
Telephone subscribers, total (per 100 inhabitants)	80.2	146.7	160.1
Internet users (per 100 inhabitants)	9.8	35.3	68.8

Total trade		Major trading partners			2010
	(million US$)	(% of exports)			(% of imports)
Exports	132 140.9	Germany	31.9	Germany	25.5
Imports	125 690.7	Slovakia	8.8	China	12.2
Balance	6 450.2	Poland	6.2	Poland	6.4

Social indicators		
Population growth rate (average annual %)	2010-2015	0.3
Urban population growth rate (average annual %)	2010-2015	0.2
Rural population growth rate (average annual %)	2010-2015	0.4
Urban population (%)	2011	73.4
Population aged 0-14 years (%)	2011	14.1
Population aged 60+ years (females and males, % of total)	2011	25.3/19.3
Sex ratio (males per 100 females)	2011	96.4
Life expectancy at birth (females and males, years)	2010-2015	81.0/74.7
Infant mortality rate (per 1 000 live births)	2010-2015	3.0
Fertility rate, total (live births per woman)	2010-2015	1.5
Contraceptive prevalence (ages 15-49, %) [i]	2006-2010	72.0 [j]
International migrant stock (000 and % of total population)	mid-2010	453.0/4.4
Refugees and others of concern to UNHCR	end-2010	3 514
Education: Government expenditure (% of GDP)	2005-2011	4.1
Education: Primary-secondary gross enrolment ratio (f/m per 100)	2005-2011	95.5/95.0
Education: Female third-level students (% of total)	2005-2011	56.5
Deaths by assault (females and males, per 100 000)	2005-2008	0.5/1.0 [k]
Seats held by women in national parliaments (%)	2011	22.0

Environmental indicators		
Threatened species	2011	42
Forested area (% of land area)	2009	34.4
CO_2 emission estimates (000 metric tons and metric tons per capita)	2008	116 900/11.3
Energy consumption per capita (kilograms oil equivalent)	2009	3 239.0
Rainfall in the capital city, total mean (millimetres)		526
Temperature in the capital city, mean °C (minimum and maximum)		3.6/12.5

a Official rate. **b** 2008. **c** 2003. **d** 2004. **e** European Labour Force Survey (Eurostat). **f** Arrivals of non-resident tourists in all types of accommodation establishments. **g** 2006. **h** 2009. **i** Age group 15 to 44 years. **j** 1997. **k** Rate based on 30 or fewer events.

Democratic People's Republic of Korea

Region	Eastern Asia
Currency	North Korean Won (KPW)
Surface area (square kilometres)	120 538
Population in 2010 (estimated, 000)	24 346
Population density in 2010 (per square kilometre)	202.0
Capital city and population in 2011 (000)	P'yongyang (2 843)
United Nations membership date	17 September 1991

Economic indicators	2000	2005	2010
GDP: Gross domestic product (million current US$)	10 608	13 031	12 278
GDP: Growth rate at constant 2005 prices (annual %)	0.4	3.8	0.8
GDP per capita (current US$)	462.0	548.4	504.0
GNI: Gross national income per capita (current US$)	461.3	547.2	503.4
Exchange rates (national currency per US$)[a]	2.14	141.00	139.00
Agricultural production index (2004-2006=100)	84	101	97
Food production index (2004-2006=100)	84	101	96
Labour force participation, adult female pop. (%)	73.7	72.6	71.8
Labour force participation, adult male pop. (%)	87.7	85.8	83.9
Energy production, primary (000 mt oil equivalent)	19 669	23 187	21 214[b]
Telephone subscribers, total (per 100 inhabitants)	2.2[c]	4.2[c]	6.6

Social indicators		
Population growth rate (average annual %)	2010-2015	0.4
Urban population growth rate (average annual %)	2010-2015	0.6
Rural population growth rate (average annual %)	2010-2015	0.1
Urban population (%)	2011	60.3
Population aged 0-14 years (%)	2011	22.5
Population aged 60+ years (females and males, % of total)	2011	16.6/10.8
Sex ratio (males per 100 females)	2011	96.4
Life expectancy at birth (females and males, years)	2010-2015	72.1/65.9
Infant mortality rate (per 1 000 live births)	2010-2015	25.1
Fertility rate, total (live births per woman)	2010-2015	2.0
Contraceptive prevalence (ages 15-49, %)	2006-2010	68.6[d]
International migrant stock (000 and % of total population)[e]	mid-2010	37.1/0.2
Seats held by women in national parliaments (%)	2011	15.6

Environmental indicators		
Threatened species	2011	57
Forested area (% of land area)	2009	48.1
CO_2 emission estimates (000 metric tons and metric tons per capita)	2008	78 307/3.3
Energy consumption per capita (kilograms oil equivalent)	2009	826.0
Rainfall in the capital city, total mean (millimetres)		940
Temperature in the capital city, mean °C (minimum and maximum)		5.6/15.7

a UN operational exchange rate. b 2009. c Main telephone lines only. d 2002. e Estimates.

Democratic Republic of the Congo

Region	Middle Africa
Currency	Franc Congolais (CDF)
Surface area (square kilometres)	2 344 858
Population in 2010 (estimated, 000)	65 966
Population density in 2010 (per square kilometre)	28.1
Capital city and population in 2011 (000)	Kinshasa (8 798)
United Nations membership date	20 September 1960

Economic indicators	2000	2005	2010
GDP: Gross domestic product (million current US$)	5 268	7 166	13 230
GDP: Growth rate at constant 2005 prices (annual %)	−6.9	7.8	7.2
GDP per capita (current US$)	106.1	124.8	200.6
GNI: Gross national income per capita (current US$)	96.6	118.8	186.4
Gross fixed capital formation (% of GDP)	3.5	14.0	26.4
Exchange rates (national currency per US$) [a]	50.00	431.28	915.13
Agricultural production index (2004-2006=100)	103	100	104
Food production index (2004-2006=100)	103	100	104
Labour force participation, adult female pop. (%)	70.6	70.5	70.2
Labour force participation, adult male pop. (%)	72.9	72.3	72.4
Tourist arrivals at national borders (000)	103	61	53[bc]
Energy production, primary (000 mt oil equivalent)	1 764	2 002	1 891[c]
Telephone subscribers, total (per 100 inhabitants)	0.1	4.8	18.0
Internet users (per 100 inhabitants)	<	0.2	0.7

Social indicators		
Population growth rate (average annual %)	2010-2015	2.6
Urban population growth rate (average annual %)	2010-2015	4.2
Rural population growth rate (average annual %)	2010-2015	1.8
Urban population (%)	2011	34.3
Population aged 0-14 years (%)	2011	46.1
Population aged 60+ years (females and males, % of total)	2011	4.7/3.8
Sex ratio (males per 100 females)	2011	99.0
Life expectancy at birth (females and males, years)	2010-2015	50.6/47.3
Infant mortality rate (per 1 000 live births)	2010-2015	109.5
Fertility rate, total (live births per woman)	2010-2015	5.5
Contraceptive prevalence (ages 15-49, %)	2006-2010	20.6
International migrant stock (000 and % of total population) [d]	mid-2010	444.7/0.7
Refugees and others of concern to UNHCR	end-2010	2 366 035
Education: Primary-secondary gross enrolment ratio (f/m per 100)	2005-2011	60.2/76.7
Education: Female third-level students (% of total)	2005-2011	23.6
Seats held by women in national parliaments (%) [e]	2011	10.4

Environmental indicators		
Threatened species	2011	300
Forested area (% of land area)	2009	68.1
CO$_2$ emission estimates (000 metric tons and metric tons per capita)	2008	2 814/0.0
Energy consumption per capita (kilograms oil equivalent)	2009	22.0

a Market rate. **b** Air arrivals. **c** 2009. **d** Includes refugees. **e** As of 31 October 2011.

Denmark

Region	Northern Europe
Currency	Danish Krone (DKK)
Surface area (square kilometres)	43 094
Population in 2010 (estimated, 000)	5 550
Population density in 2010 (per square kilometre)	128.8
Capital city and population in 2011 (000)	Copenhagen (1 206)
United Nations membership date	24 October 1945

Economic indicators	2000	2005	2010
GDP: Gross domestic product (million current US$)	160 082	257 676	309 866
GDP: Growth rate at constant 2005 prices (annual %)	3.5	2.5	1.8
GDP per capita (current US$)	29 980.7	47 546.5	55 830.2
GNI: Gross national income per capita (current US$)	29 346.8	48 209.5	56 875.0
Gross fixed capital formation (% of GDP)	20.3	19.7	16.8
Exchange rates (national currency per US$) [a]	8.02	6.32	5.61
Balance of payments, current account (million US$)	2 262	11 104	17 134
CPI: Consumer price index (2000=100)	100	110	122
Industrial production index (2005=100)	99[b]	100	87
Agricultural production index (2004-2006=100)	97	101	99
Food production index (2004-2006=100)	97	101	99
Unemployment (% of labour force)	5.5[c]	4.8	7.5
Employment in industrial sector (% of employed)	25.2[d]	23.4[e]	19.6[f]
Employment in agricultural sector (% of employed)	3.3[d]	2.8[e]	2.4[f]
Labour force participation, adult female pop. (%)	60.1	60.6	60.0
Labour force participation, adult male pop. (%)	71.7	71.5	69.4
Tourist arrivals at national borders (000) [g]	3 535	9 178	8 744
Energy production, primary (000 mt oil equivalent) [h]	26 566	29 772	22 067[i]
Telephone subscribers, total (per 100 inhabitants)	134.8	162.3	172.1
Internet users (per 100 inhabitants)	39.2	82.7	88.7

Total trade		Major trading partners			2010
	(million US$)[h]	(% of exports)[h]			(% of imports)[h]
Exports	96 811.6	Germany	15.0	Germany	20.6
Imports	84 468.3	Sweden	12.8	Sweden	13.4
Balance	12 343.3			China	7.5

Social indicators		
Population growth rate (average annual %)	2010-2015	0.3
Urban population growth rate (average annual %)	2010-2015	0.5
Rural population growth rate (average annual %)	2010-2015	−0.7
Urban population (%)	2011	86.9
Population aged 0-14 years (%)	2011	17.9
Population aged 60+ years (females and males, % of total)	2011	25.2/21.9
Sex ratio (males per 100 females)	2011	98.4
Life expectancy at birth (females and males, years)	2010-2015	81.4/76.7
Infant mortality rate (per 1 000 live births)	2010-2015	3.9
Fertility rate, total (live births per woman)	2010-2015	1.9
Contraceptive prevalence (ages 15-49, %) [j]	2006-2010	78.0[k]
International migrant stock (000 and % of total population)	mid-2010	483.7/8.8
Refugees and others of concern to UNHCR	end-2010	24 501
Education: Government expenditure (% of GDP)	2005-2011	7.7
Education: Primary-secondary gross enrolment ratio (f/m per 100)	2005-2011	109.0/107.7
Education: Female third-level students (% of total)	2005-2011	58.2
Deaths by assault (females and males, per 100 000)	2005-2008	</0.9[l]
Seats held by women in national parliaments (%)	2011	39.1

Environmental indicators		
Threatened species	2011	36
Forested area (% of land area)	2009	12.8
CO_2 emission estimates (000 metric tons and metric tons per capita)	2008	45 987/8.4
Energy consumption per capita (kilograms oil equivalent)	2009	2 799.0
Rainfall in the capital city, total mean (millimetres)		525
Temperature in the capital city, mean °C (minimum and maximum)		5.0/11.1

a Market rate. **b** 2003. **c** 2004. **d** Age group 15 to 66 years. **e** Age group 15 to 74 years. **f** European Labour Force Survey (Eurostat). **g** Arrivals of non-resident tourists in all types of accommodation establishments. **h** Excludes Faeroe Islands and Greenland. **i** 2009. **j** Age group 15 to 44 years. **k** 1988. **l** Rate based on 30 or fewer events.

Djibouti

Region	Eastern Africa
Currency	Djibouti Franc (DJF)
Surface area (square kilometres)	23 200
Population in 2010 (estimated, 000)	889
Population density in 2010 (per square kilometre)	38.3
Capital city and population in 2011 (000)	Djibouti (496)
United Nations membership date	20 September 1977

Economic indicators	2000	2005	2010
GDP: Gross domestic product (million current US$)	557	709	1 140
GDP: Growth rate at constant 2005 prices (annual %)	1.3	3.2	4.5
GDP per capita (current US$)	761.1	876.6	1 282.7
GNI: Gross national income per capita (current US$)	782.9	959.5	1 369.5
Gross fixed capital formation (% of GDP)	12.2	16.6	17.3
Exchange rates (national currency per US$) [a]	177.72	177.72	177.72
Balance of payments, current account (million US$)	−19	20	50
Agricultural production index (2004-2006=100)	85	95	208
Food production index (2004-2006=100)	85	95	208
Labour force participation, adult female pop. (%)	31.4	33.4	35.5
Labour force participation, adult male pop. (%)	66.5	66.5	67.0
Tourist arrivals at national borders (000) [b]	20	30	53[c]
Telephone subscribers, total (per 100 inhabitants)	1.4	6.8	20.7
Internet users (per 100 inhabitants)	0.2	1.0	6.5

Total trade		Major trading partners			2010
	(million US$)[d]	(% of exports)[d]		(% of imports)[d]	
Exports	363.7	Ethiopia	35.4	France	30.5
Imports	647.6	France	20.1	United Arab Emirates	18.5
Balance	−283.9	Somalia	11.9	Saudi Arabia	6.0

Social indicators		
Population growth rate (average annual %)	2010-2015	1.9
Urban population growth rate (average annual %)	2010-2015	2.0
Rural population growth rate (average annual %)	2010-2015	1.5
Urban population (%)	2011	77.1
Population aged 0-14 years (%)	2011	35.4
Population aged 60+ years (females and males, % of total)	2011	6.0/5.0
Sex ratio (males per 100 females)	2011	100.1
Life expectancy at birth (females and males, years)	2010-2015	60.0/57.0
Infant mortality rate (per 1 000 live births)	2010-2015	75.0
Fertility rate, total (live births per woman)	2010-2015	3.6
Contraceptive prevalence (ages 15-49, %)	2006-2010	17.8
International migrant stock (000 and % of total population) [e]	mid-2010	114.2/13.0
Refugees and others of concern to UNHCR	end-2010	15 843
Education: Government expenditure (% of GDP)	2005-2011	8.4
Education: Primary-secondary gross enrolment ratio (f/m per 100)	2005-2011	42.1/49.4
Education: Female third-level students (% of total)	2005-2011	39.9
Seats held by women in national parliaments (%)	2011	13.8

Environmental indicators		
Threatened species	2011	84
Forested area (% of land area)	2009	<
CO$_2$ emission estimates (000 metric tons and metric tons per capita)	2008	524/0.6
Energy consumption per capita (kilograms oil equivalent)	2009	180.0
Rainfall in the capital city, total mean (millimetres)		164
Temperature in the capital city, mean °C (minimum and maximum)		25.9/33.9

a Official rate. b Arrivals of non-resident tourists in hotels and similar establishments. c 2008. d 2009.
e Includes refugees.

Dominica

Region	Caribbean
Currency	E.C. Dollar (XCD)
Surface area (square kilometres)	751
Population in 2010 (estimated, 000)	68
Population density in 2010 (per square kilometre)	90.2
Capital city and population in 2011 (000)	Roseau (14)
United Nations membership date	18 December 1978

Economic indicators	2000	2005	2010
GDP: Gross domestic product (million current US$)	324	362	476
GDP: Growth rate at constant 2005 prices (annual %)	0.6	−0.5	2.1
GDP per capita (current US$)	4 656.5	5 246.0	7 020.8
GNI: Gross national income per capita (current US$)	4 092.2	4 825.6	6 672.8
Gross fixed capital formation (% of GDP)	20.5	20.2	24.7
Exchange rates (national currency per US$)[a]	2.70	2.70	2.70
Balance of payments, current account (million US$)	−60	−76	−97
CPI: Consumer price index (2000=100)[b]	100	106	120[c]
Agricultural production index (2004-2006=100)	120	95	113
Food production index (2004-2006=100)	120	95	114
Employment in industrial sector (% of employed)	19.8[def]	...	...
Employment in agricultural sector (% of employed)	21.0[def]	...	...
Tourist arrivals at national borders (000)	70	79	77
Energy production, primary (000 mt oil equivalent)	3	2	2[c]
Telephone subscribers, total (per 100 inhabitants)	34.3	103.0	178.7
Internet users (per 100 inhabitants)	8.8	38.5	47.5

Total trade		Major trading partners			2010
	(million US$)	(% of exports)		(% of imports)	
Exports	34.1	Saint Kitts and Nevis	17.6	United States	41.8
Imports	224.6	Jamaica	17.3	Trinidad and Tobago	15.3
Balance	−190.5	Trinidad and Tobago	13.8	Venezuela	7.3

Social indicators		
Population growth rate (average annual %)	2010-2015	<
Urban population growth rate (average annual %)	2010-2015	0.2
Rural population growth rate (average annual %)	2010-2015	−0.4
Urban population (%)	2011	67.1
Population aged 0-14 years (%)[ghi]	2011	29.5[j]
Population aged 60+ years (females and males, % of total)[ghi]	2011	15.1/11.7[j]
Sex ratio (males per 100 females)[hk]	2011	103.8[j]
Life expectancy at birth (females and males, years)[h]	2010-2015	78.2/73.8[l]
Fertility rate, total (live births per woman)[h]	2010-2015	3.0[d]
Contraceptive prevalence (ages 15-49, %)[m]	2006-2010	49.8[n]
International migrant stock (000 and % of total population)	mid-2010	5.5/8.3
Refugees and others of concern to UNHCR	end-2010	0[o]
Education: Government expenditure (% of GDP)	2005-2011	3.6
Education: Primary-secondary gross enrolment ratio (f/m per 100)	2005-2011	107.1/103.9
Education: Female third-level students (% of total)	2005-2011	76.0
Seats held by women in national parliaments (%)	2011	12.5

Environmental indicators		
Threatened species	2011	51
Forested area (% of land area)	2009	59.9
CO_2 emission estimates (000 metric tons and metric tons per capita)	2008	128/1.9
Energy consumption per capita (kilograms oil equivalent)	2009	663.0
Rainfall in the capital city, total mean (millimetres)[p]		2 575
Temperature in the capital city, mean °C (minimum and maximum)[p]		23.1/29.3

a Official rate. **b** Index base 2001=100. **c** 2009. **d** 2001. **e** May. **f** Population census. **g** De facto estimate. **h** Data compiled by the United Nations Demographic Yearbook system. **i** Data refer to the latest available census. **j** 2006. **k** De facto national estimate. **l** 2008. **m** Age group 15 to 44 years. **n** 1987. **o** Value is zero, not available or not applicable. **p** Melville Hall airport.

Dominican Republic

Region	Caribbean
Currency	Dominican Peso (DOP)
Surface area (square kilometres)	48 671
Population in 2010 (estimated, 000)	9 927
Population density in 2010 (per square kilometre)	204.0
Capital city and population in 2011 (000)	Santo Domingo (2 191)
United Nations membership date	24 October 1945

Economic indicators	2000	2005	2010
GDP: Gross domestic product (million current US$)	23 655	33 542	51 576
GDP: Growth rate at constant 2005 prices (annual %)	5.7	9.3	7.8
GDP per capita (current US$)	2 753.2	3 620.6	5 195.4
GNI: Gross national income per capita (current US$)	2 632.1	3 416.9	4 952.5
Gross fixed capital formation (% of GDP)	20.5	16.4	16.3
Exchange rates (national currency per US$)[a]	16.67	34.88	37.54
Balance of payments, current account (million US$)	-1 027	-473	-4 435
CPI: Consumer price index (2000=100)	100	230	314
Industrial production index (2005=100)[b]	94[c]	100	114
Agricultural production index (2004-2006=100)	82	98	125
Food production index (2004-2006=100)	81	98	127
Employment in industrial sector (% of employed)[d]	24.3	22.3	21.9[e]
Employment in agricultural sector (% of employed)[d]	15.9	14.6	14.5[e]
Labour force participation, adult female pop. (%)	46.3	48.9	50.8
Labour force participation, adult male pop. (%)	80.0	80.3	78.7
Tourist arrivals at national borders (000)[fg]	2 978	3 691	4 125
Energy production, primary (000 mt oil equivalent)	66	164	126[e]
Telephone subscribers, total (per 100 inhabitants)	18.6	48.8	99.8
Internet users (per 100 inhabitants)	3.7	11.5	39.5

Total trade		Major trading partners			2010
	(million US$)	(% of exports)		(% of imports)	
Exports	4 766.7	United States	57.7	United States	39.0
Imports	15 138.2	Haiti	16.8	China	10.7
Balance	-10 371.5	China	2.6	Venezuela	7.2

Social indicators		
Population growth rate (average annual %)	2010-2015	1.2
Urban population growth rate (average annual %)	2010-2015	2.0
Rural population growth rate (average annual %)	2010-2015	-0.7
Urban population (%)	2011	69.7
Population aged 0-14 years (%)	2011	30.7
Population aged 60+ years (females and males, % of total)	2011	9.3/8.8
Sex ratio (males per 100 females)	2011	100.6
Life expectancy at birth (females and males, years)	2010-2015	76.6/71.2
Infant mortality rate (per 1 000 live births)	2010-2015	21.6
Fertility rate, total (live births per woman)	2010-2015	2.5
Contraceptive prevalence (ages 15-49, %)	2006-2010	72.9
International migrant stock (000 and % of total population)	mid-2010	434.3/4.3
Refugees and others of concern to UNHCR	end-2010	2 358
Education: Government expenditure (% of GDP)	2005-2011	2.2
Education: Primary-secondary gross enrolment ratio (f/m per 100)	2005-2011	91.4/93.9
Education: Female third-level students (% of total)[h]	2005-2011	61.3[i]
Seats held by women in national parliaments (%)	2011	20.8

Environmental indicators		
Threatened species	2011	131
Forested area (% of land area)	2009	40.8
CO_2 emission estimates (000 metric tons and metric tons per capita)	2008	21 599/2.2
Energy consumption per capita (kilograms oil equivalent)	2009	641.0
Rainfall in the capital city, total mean (millimetres)		1 447
Temperature in the capital city, mean °C (minimum and maximum)		21.5/30.4

a Principal rate. **b** The indices are shown in terms of ISIC Rev. 3. **c** 2003. **d** Age group 10 years and over.
e 2009. **f** Air arrivals. **g** Includes nationals residing abroad. **h** UNESCO estimate. **i** 2004.

Ecuador

Region	South America
Currency	U.S. Dollar (USD)[a]
Surface area (square kilometres)	256 369
Population in 2010 (estimated, 000)	14 465
Population density in 2010 (per square kilometre)	56.4
Capital city and population in 2011 (000)	Quito (1 622)
United Nations membership date	21 December 1945

Economic indicators	2000	2005	2010
GDP: Gross domestic product (million current US$)	16 283	36 942	58 910
GDP: Growth rate at constant 2005 prices (annual %)	4.2	5.7	3.2
GDP per capita (current US$)	1 319.0	2 751.5	4 072.7
GNI: Gross national income per capita (current US$)	1 204.7	2 606.9	3 908.7
Gross fixed capital formation (% of GDP)	20.1	22.1	25.8
Balance of payments, current account (million US$)	926	347	−1 785
CPI: Consumer price index (2000=100)	100	175[b]	219
Agricultural production index (2004-2006=100)	80	98	119
Food production index (2004-2006=100)	79	98	120
Unemployment (% of labour force)[c]	...	7.4[d]	7.6
Employment in industrial sector (% of employed)[e]	19.9[f]	17.2[g]	18.8[h]
Employment in agricultural sector (% of employed)[e]	29.3[f]	31.5[g]	28.7[h]
Labour force participation, adult female pop. (%)	49.6	55.2	53.7
Labour force participation, adult male pop. (%)	83.5	84.6	82.6
Tourist arrivals at national borders (000)[ij]	627	860	1 047
Energy production, primary (000 mt oil equivalent)	22 160	29 184	27 025[h]
Telephone subscribers, total (per 100 inhabitants)	13.8	59.0	116.6
Internet users (per 100 inhabitants)	1.5	6.0	29.0

Total trade		Major trading partners			2010
	(million US$)	(% of exports)		(% of imports)	
Exports	17 489.9	United States	34.7	United States	27.9
Imports	20 590.8	Panama	12.2	Colombia	9.8
Balance	−3 100.9	Peru	7.6	China	7.8

Social indicators		
Population growth rate (average annual %)	2010-2015	1.3
Urban population growth rate (average annual %)	2010-2015	2.1
Rural population growth rate (average annual %)	2010-2015	−0.5
Urban population (%)	2011	67.5
Population aged 0-14 years (%)	2011	30.0
Population aged 60+ years (females and males, % of total)	2011	9.7/8.6
Sex ratio (males per 100 females)	2011	100.3
Life expectancy at birth (females and males, years)	2010-2015	78.9/73.0
Infant mortality rate (per 1 000 live births)	2010-2015	19.1
Fertility rate, total (live births per woman)	2010-2015	2.4
Contraceptive prevalence (ages 15-49, %)	2006-2010	72.7[k]
International migrant stock (000 and % of total population)[l]	mid-2010	393.6/2.9
Refugees and others of concern to UNHCR	end-2010	171 136
Education: Government expenditure (% of GDP)[m]	2005-2011	1.0[n]
Education: Primary-secondary gross enrolment ratio (f/m per 100)	2005-2011	99.2/96.5
Education: Female third-level students (% of total)	2005-2011	52.9
Seats held by women in national parliaments (%)	2011	32.3

Environmental indicators		
Threatened species	2011	2 260
Forested area (% of land area)	2009	40.5
CO_2 emission estimates (000 metric tons and metric tons per capita)	2008	26 802/2.0
Energy consumption per capita (kilograms oil equivalent)	2009	751.0
Rainfall in the capital city, total mean (millimetres)		1 014

a Beginning 15 September 2000 the Ecuadorian sucre (ECS) was replaced by the US Dollar (1 USD=25000 ECS). **b** Series linked to former series. **c** Urban areas. **d** 2007. **e** Age group 10 years and over. **f** November. **g** Fourth quarter. **h** 2009. **i** Excludes nationals residing abroad. **j** Arrivals of non-resident visitors at national borders. **k** 2004. **l** Includes refugees. **m** UNESCO estimate. **n** 2001.

Egypt

Region	Northern Africa
Currency	Egyptian Pound (EGP)
Surface area (square kilometres)	1 002 000
Population in 2010 (estimated, 000)	81 121
Population density in 2010 (per square kilometre)	81.0
Capital city and population in 2011 (000)	Cairo (11 169)
United Nations membership date	24 October 1945

Economic indicators	2000	2005	2010
GDP: Gross domestic product (million current US$)	95 688	94 461	215 272
GDP: Growth rate at constant 2005 prices (annual %)	5.4	4.5	5.2
GDP per capita (current US$)	1 414.5	1 273.0	2 653.7
GNI: Gross national income per capita (current US$)	1 412.7	1 259.4	2 684.6
Gross fixed capital formation (% of GDP)	17.1	16.9	18.6
Exchange rates (national currency per US$) [a]	3.69	5.73	5.79
Balance of payments, current account (million US$)	−971	2 103	−4 504
CPI: Consumer price index (2000=100)	100	134	232
Agricultural production index (2004-2006=100)	87	99	110
Food production index (2004-2006=100)	87	99	111
Unemployment (% of labour force)	10.7[b]	11.0	9.0
Employment in industrial sector (% of employed) [cd]	21.3	21.5	23.0[e]
Employment in agricultural sector (% of employed) [cd]	29.6	30.9	31.6[e]
Labour force participation, adult female pop. (%)	19.9	20.6	23.5
Labour force participation, adult male pop. (%)	73.1	75.8	74.2
Tourist arrivals at national borders (000)	5 116	8 244	14 051
Energy production, primary (000 mt oil equivalent)	63 427	83 649	98 163[f]
Telephone subscribers, total (per 100 inhabitants)	10.1	32.5	99.0
Internet users (per 100 inhabitants)	0.6	11.7	26.7

Total trade		Major trading partners			2010
	(million US$)	(% of exports)			(% of imports)
Exports	26 331.8	Italy	8.4	United States	9.4
Imports	53 003.4	Spain	6.2	China	9.2
Balance	−26 671.6	Saudi Arabia	5.9	Germany	7.6

Social indicators

Population growth rate (average annual %)	2010-2015	1.7
Urban population growth rate (average annual %)	2010-2015	2.0
Rural population growth rate (average annual %)	2010-2015	1.4
Urban population (%)	2011	43.5
Population aged 0-14 years (%)	2011	31.3
Population aged 60+ years (females and males, % of total)	2011	8.9/7.5
Sex ratio (males per 100 females)	2011	100.8
Life expectancy at birth (females and males, years)	2010-2015	75.5/71.6
Infant mortality rate (per 1 000 live births)	2010-2015	22.0
Fertility rate, total (live births per woman)	2010-2015	2.6
Contraceptive prevalence (ages 15-49, %)	2006-2010	60.3
International migrant stock (000 and % of total population) [g]	mid-2010	244.7/0.3
Refugees and others of concern to UNHCR	end-2010	109 419
Education: Government expenditure (% of GDP)	2005-2011	3.8
Education: Primary-secondary gross enrolment ratio (f/m per 100) [h]	2005-2011	89.3/94.4[b]
Education: Female third-level students (% of total) [h]	2005-2011	42.7[b]

Environmental indicators

Threatened species	2011	123
Forested area (% of land area)	2009	<
CO_2 emission estimates (000 metric tons and metric tons per capita)	2008	210 149/2.6
Energy consumption per capita (kilograms oil equivalent)	2009	894.0
Rainfall in the capital city, total mean (millimetres)		25
Temperature in the capital city, mean °C (minimum and maximum)		15.8/27.7

a Principal rate. **b** 2004. **c** Average of May and November. **d** Age group 15 to 64 years. **e** 2008. **f** 2009. **g** Includes refugees. **h** UNESCO estimate.

El Salvador

Region	Central America
Currency	U.S. Dollar (USD)[a]
Surface area (square kilometres)	21 041[b]
Population in 2010 (estimated, 000)	6 193
Population density in 2010 (per square kilometre)	294.3
Capital city and population in 2011 (000)	San Salvador (1 605)
United Nations membership date	24 October 1945

Economic indicators	2000	2005	2010
GDP: Gross domestic product (million current US$)	13 134	17 094	21 215
GDP: Growth rate at constant 2005 prices (annual %)	2.2	3.6	1.4
GDP per capita (current US$)	2 211.0	2 825.2	3 425.6
GNI: Gross national income per capita (current US$)	2 168.4	2 744.1	3 364.1
Gross fixed capital formation (% of GDP)	16.9	15.3	13.3
Exchange rates (national currency per US$)[c]	8.76	8.75	8.75
Balance of payments, current account (million US$)	−431	−622	−488
CPI: Consumer price index (2000=100)[d]	100	118[e]	140
Industrial production index (2005=100)[f]	98[g]	100	106
Agricultural production index (2004-2006=100)	96	99	112
Food production index (2004-2006=100)	93	98	112
Employment in industrial sector (% of employed)	24.2[hi]	22.2[hi]	20.7[jk]
Employment in agricultural sector (% of employed)	21.6[hi]	20.0[hi]	20.9[jk]
Labour force participation, adult female pop. (%)	44.7	44.6	47.1
Labour force participation, adult male pop. (%)	78.6	77.6	78.7
Tourist arrivals at national borders (000)	795	1 127	1 150
Energy production, primary (000 mt oil equivalent)	169	234	260[k]
Telephone subscribers, total (per 100 inhabitants)	23.1	55.9	140.5
Internet users (per 100 inhabitants)	1.2	4.2	15.9

Total trade		Major trading partners			2010
	(million US$)	(% of exports)		(% of imports)	
Exports	4 499.2	United States	48.4	United States	36.9
Imports	8 484.6	Guatemala	14.0	Guatemala	9.5
Balance	−3 985.4	Honduras	12.9	Mexico	8.9

Social indicators		
Population growth rate (average annual %)	2010-2015	0.6
Urban population growth rate (average annual %)	2010-2015	1.4
Rural population growth rate (average annual %)	2010-2015	−0.8
Urban population (%)	2011	64.8
Population aged 0-14 years (%)	2011	31.3
Population aged 60+ years (females and males, % of total)	2011	10.4/8.7
Sex ratio (males per 100 females)	2011	90.3
Life expectancy at birth (females and males, years)	2010-2015	77.1/67.7
Infant mortality rate (per 1 000 live births)	2010-2015	19.0
Fertility rate, total (live births per woman)	2010-2015	2.2
Contraceptive prevalence (ages 15-49, %)[l]	2006-2010	72.5
International migrant stock (000 and % of total population)[m]	mid-2010	40.3/0.7
Refugees and others of concern to UNHCR	end-2010	58
Education: Government expenditure (% of GDP)	2005-2011	3.2
Education: Primary-secondary gross enrolment ratio (f/m per 100)	2005-2011	87.5/89.7
Education: Female third-level students (% of total)	2005-2011	54.2
Seats held by women in national parliaments (%)	2011	19.0

Environmental indicators		
Threatened species	2011	74
Forested area (% of land area)	2009	14.1
CO_2 emission estimates (000 metric tons and metric tons per capita)	2008	6 108/1.0
Energy consumption per capita (kilograms oil equivalent)	2009	345.0
Rainfall in the capital city, total mean (millimetres)		1 734
Temperature in the capital city, mean °C (minimum and maximum)		18.4/30.1

a Beginning 1 January 2001 the Salvadoran colón (SVC) was replaced by the US Dollar (1 USD=8.75 SVC). **b** The total surface is 21040.79 square kilometres, without taking into account the last ruling of The Hague. **c** Principal rate. **d** Urban areas. **e** Series linked to former series. **f** The indices are shown in terms of ISIC Rev. 3. **g** 2003. **h** December. **i** Age group 10 years and over. **j** Age group 16 years and over. **k** 2009. **l** Age group 15 to 44 years. **m** Includes refugees.

Equatorial Guinea

Region	Middle Africa
Currency	CFA Franc (XAF)
Surface area (square kilometres)	28 051
Population in 2010 (estimated, 000)	700
Population density in 2010 (per square kilometre)	25.0
Capital city and population in 2011 (000)	Malabo (137)
United Nations membership date	12 November 1968

Economic indicators	2000	2005	2010
GDP: Gross domestic product (million current US$)	1 177	7 206	11 803
GDP: Growth rate at constant 2005 prices (annual %)	13.1	8.9	-0.8
GDP per capita (current US$)	2 262.6	11 856.3	16 852.4
GNI: Gross national income per capita (current US$)	1 551.1	6 020.9	11 523.7
Gross fixed capital formation (% of GDP)	61.9	21.7	61.1
Exchange rates (national currency per US$)[a]	704.95	556.04	490.91
CPI: Consumer price index (2000=100)[b]	100	145[c]	...
Agricultural production index (2004-2006=100)	93	100	108
Food production index (2004-2006=100)	90	101	112
Labour force participation, adult female pop. (%)	80.4	80.4	80.6
Labour force participation, adult male pop. (%)	93.3	92.5	92.3
Energy production, primary (000 mt oil equivalent)	6 732	24 609	23 206[d]
Telephone subscribers, total (per 100 inhabitants)	2.1	17.6	58.9
Internet users (per 100 inhabitants)	0.1	1.2	6.0

Social indicators		
Population growth rate (average annual %)	2010-2015	2.7
Urban population growth rate (average annual %)	2010-2015	3.2
Rural population growth rate (average annual %)	2010-2015	2.4
Urban population (%)	2011	39.5
Population aged 0-14 years (%)	2011	39.2
Population aged 60+ years (females and males, % of total)	2011	4.4/4.5
Sex ratio (males per 100 females)	2011	105.1
Life expectancy at birth (females and males, years)	2010-2015	52.9/50.3
Infant mortality rate (per 1 000 live births)	2010-2015	93.3
Fertility rate, total (live births per woman)	2010-2015	5.0
Contraceptive prevalence (ages 15-49, %)	2006-2010	10.1[e]
International migrant stock (000 and % of total population)[f]	mid-2010	7.5/1.1
Refugees and others of concern to UNHCR	end-2010	0[g]
Education: Government expenditure (% of GDP)[h]	2005-2011	0.6[i]
Education: Primary-secondary gross enrolment ratio (f/m per 100)[h]	2005-2011	60.9/73.5[j]
Education: Female third-level students (% of total)	2005-2011	30.3[e]
Seats held by women in national parliaments (%)	2011	10.0

Environmental indicators		
Threatened species	2011	132
Forested area (% of land area)	2009	58.4
CO$_2$ emission estimates (000 metric tons and metric tons per capita)	2008	4 811/7.3
Energy consumption per capita (kilograms oil equivalent)	2009	2 559.0[k]

a Official rate. **b** Malabo. **c** 2006. **d** 2009. **e** 2000. **f** Data refer to foreign citizens. **g** Value is zero, not available or not applicable. **h** UNESCO estimate. **i** 2003. **j** 2002. **k** UNSD estimate.

Eritrea

Region	Eastern Africa		
Currency	Nakfa (ERN)		
Surface area (square kilometres)	117 600		
Population in 2010 (estimated, 000)	5 254		
Population density in 2010 (per square kilometre)	44.7		
Capital city and population in 2011 (000)	Asmara (712)		
United Nations membership date	28 May 1993		

Economic indicators	2000	2005	2010
GDP: Gross domestic product (million current US$)	706	1 098	2 254
GDP: Growth rate at constant 2005 prices (annual %)	−12.4	2.6	1.8
GDP per capita (current US$)	192.6	244.9	429.1
GNI: Gross national income per capita (current US$)	192.5	246.8	433.1
Gross fixed capital formation (% of GDP)	22.0	20.3	12.3
Exchange rates (national currency per US$)[a]	10.20	15.38	15.38
Balance of payments, current account (million US$)	−105	...	...
Agricultural production index (2004-2006=100)	79	107	101
Food production index (2004-2006=100)	79	107	101
Labour force participation, adult female pop. (%)	74.6	78.0	79.6
Labour force participation, adult male pop. (%)	90.3	89.8	90.0
Tourist arrivals at national borders (000)[bc]	70	83	84
Telephone subscribers, total (per 100 inhabitants)	0.8[d]	1.7	4.6
Internet users (per 100 inhabitants)	0.1	1.8	5.4

Social indicators		
Population growth rate (average annual %)	2010-2015	2.9
Urban population growth rate (average annual %)	2010-2015	5.0
Rural population growth rate (average annual %)	2010-2015	2.3
Urban population (%)	2011	21.3
Population aged 0-14 years (%)	2011	41.6
Population aged 60+ years (females and males, % of total)	2011	4.9/3.3
Sex ratio (males per 100 females)	2011	97.2
Life expectancy at birth (females and males, years)	2010-2015	64.4/59.7
Infant mortality rate (per 1 000 live births)	2010-2015	47.5
Fertility rate, total (live births per woman)	2010-2015	4.2
Contraceptive prevalence (ages 15-49, %)	2006-2010	8.0[e]
International migrant stock (000 and % of total population)[f]	mid-2010	16.5/0.3
Refugees and others of concern to UNHCR	end-2010	4 946
Education: Government expenditure (% of GDP)	2005-2011	2.1
Education: Primary-secondary gross enrolment ratio (f/m per 100)	2005-2011	33.5/41.8
Education: Female third-level students (% of total)	2005-2011	25.0
Seats held by women in national parliaments (%)	2011	22.0

Environmental indicators		
Threatened species	2011	100
Forested area (% of land area)	2009	15.2
CO_2 emission estimates (000 metric tons and metric tons per capita)	2008	414/0.1
Energy consumption per capita (kilograms oil equivalent)	2009	32.0
Rainfall in the capital city, total mean (millimetres)		533
Temperature in the capital city, mean °C (minimum and maximum)		8.9/23.2

a Official rate. b Includes nationals residing abroad. c Arrivals of non-resident visitors at national borders. d Main telephone lines only. e 2002. f Estimates.

Estonia

Region	Northern Europe
Currency	Kroon (EEK)
Surface area (square kilometres)	45 227
Population in 2010 (estimated, 000)	1 341
Population density in 2010 (per square kilometre)	29.7
Capital city and population in 2011 (000)	Tallinn (400)
United Nations membership date	17 September 1991

Economic indicators	2000	2005	2010
GDP: Gross domestic product (million current US$)	5 680	13 903	18 958
GDP: Growth rate at constant 2005 prices (annual %)	10.0	8.9	2.3
GDP per capita (current US$)	4 143.7	10 330.5	14 135.4
GNI: Gross national income per capita (current US$)	4 008.2	9 937.4	13 430.6
Gross fixed capital formation (% of GDP)	25.8	32.1	18.8
Exchange rates (national currency per US$) [a]	16.82	13.22	11.71
Balance of payments, current account (million US$)	−299	−1 386	673
CPI: Consumer price index (2000=100)	100	119	146[b]
Industrial production index (2005=100)	82[c]	100	102
Agricultural production index (2004-2006=100)	101	103	106
Food production index (2004-2006=100)	101	103	106
Unemployment (% of labour force)	9.7[d]	7.9	16.9
Employment in industrial sector (% of employed) [e]	33.3[f]	33.8[f]	30.1[g]
Employment in agricultural sector (% of employed) [e]	7.1[f]	5.2[f]	4.2[g]
Labour force participation, adult female pop. (%)	51.7	53.4	56.5
Labour force participation, adult male pop. (%)	66.8	65.4	67.7
Tourist arrivals at national borders (000)	1 220	1 917	2 120
Energy production, primary (000 mt oil equivalent)	2 668	3 184	3 305[h]
Telephone subscribers, total (per 100 inhabitants)	78.8	140.2	159.2
Internet users (per 100 inhabitants)	28.6	61.5	74.1

Total trade		Major trading partners			2010
	(million US$)		(% of exports)		(% of imports)
Exports	12 823.0	Finland	15.3	Finland	11.6
Imports	13 182.5	Russian Federation	14.8	Germany	10.6
Balance	−359.5	Sweden	14.1	Russian Federation	10.5

Social indicators		
Population growth rate (average annual %)	2010-2015	−0.1
Urban population growth rate (average annual %)	2010-2015	<
Rural population growth rate (average annual %)	2010-2015	−0.3
Urban population (%)	2011	69.5
Population aged 0-14 years (%)	2011	15.6
Population aged 60+ years (females and males, % of total)	2011	27.6/17.6
Sex ratio (males per 100 females)	2011	85.6
Life expectancy at birth (females and males, years)	2010-2015	80.0/69.8
Infant mortality rate (per 1 000 live births)	2010-2015	4.4
Fertility rate, total (live births per woman)	2010-2015	1.7
Contraceptive prevalence (ages 15-49, %) [i]	2006-2010	70.3[j]
International migrant stock (000 and % of total population)	mid-2010	182.5/13.6
Refugees and others of concern to UNHCR	end-2010	101 032
Education: Government expenditure (% of GDP)	2005-2011	5.7
Education: Primary-secondary gross enrolment ratio (f/m per 100)	2005-2011	101.9/101.3
Education: Female third-level students (% of total)	2005-2011	61.9
Deaths by assault (females and males, per 100 000)	2005-2008	2.8/11.5[k]
Seats held by women in national parliaments (%)	2011	19.8

Environmental indicators		
Threatened species	2011	15
Forested area (% of land area)	2009	52.5
CO$_2$ emission estimates (000 metric tons and metric tons per capita)	2008	18 276/13.6
Energy consumption per capita (kilograms oil equivalent)	2009	3 361.0
Rainfall in the capital city, total mean (millimetres)		675
Temperature in the capital city, mean °C (minimum and maximum)		1.8/8.9

a Official rate. **b** 2008. **c** 2003. **d** 2004. **e** Age group 15 to 74 years. **f** Excludes conscripts. **g** European Labour Force Survey (Eurostat). **h** 2009. **i** Age group 20 to 49 years. **j** 1994. **k** Rate based on 30 or fewer events.

Ethiopia

Region	Eastern Africa		
Currency	Birr (ETB)		
Surface area (square kilometres)	1 104 300		
Population in 2010 (estimated, 000)	82 950		
Population density in 2010 (per square kilometre)	75.1		
Capital city and population in 2011 (000)	Addis Ababa (2 979)		
United Nations membership date	13 November 1945		

Economic indicators	2000	2005	2010
GDP: Gross domestic product (million current US$)	8 111	12 286	26 928
GDP: Growth rate at constant 2005 prices (annual %)	6.1	11.8	12.4
GDP per capita (current US$)	123.7	165.4	324.6
GNI: Gross national income per capita (current US$)	123.3	165.6	324.2
Gross fixed capital formation (% of GDP)	20.3	23.8	22.4
Exchange rates (national currency per US$) [a]	8.31	8.68	16.55
Balance of payments, current account (million US$)	13	−1 568	−425
CPI: Consumer price index (2000=100) [b]	100 [c]	138	313
Agricultural production index (2004-2006=100)	75	102	125
Food production index (2004-2006=100)	74	103	125
Employment in industrial sector (% of employed)	...	6.6 [de]	...
Employment in agricultural sector (% of employed)	...	79.3 [de]	...
Labour force participation, adult female pop. (%)	72.8	78.4	78.3
Labour force participation, adult male pop. (%)	90.9	91.1	89.9
Tourist arrivals at national borders (000) [f]	136	227	330 [g]
Energy production, primary (000 mt oil equivalent)	143	244	309 [h]
Telephone subscribers, total (per 100 inhabitants)	0.4	1.4	9.4
Internet users (per 100 inhabitants)	<	0.2	0.8

Total trade		Major trading partners			2010
	(million US$)	(% of exports)			(% of imports)
Exports	2 329.8	Germany	11.4	China	24.0
Imports	8 601.8	China	10.4	Saudi Arabia	11.9
Balance	−6 272.0	Somalia	9.6	India	7.2

Social indicators		
Population growth rate (average annual %)	2010-2015	2.1
Urban population growth rate (average annual %)	2010-2015	3.6
Rural population growth rate (average annual %)	2010-2015	1.8
Urban population (%)	2011	17.0
Population aged 0-14 years (%)	2011	40.8
Population aged 60+ years (females and males, % of total)	2011	5.6/5.0
Sex ratio (males per 100 females)	2011	99.1
Life expectancy at birth (females and males, years)	2010-2015	61.6/58.3
Infant mortality rate (per 1 000 live births)	2010-2015	62.9
Fertility rate, total (live births per woman)	2010-2015	3.9
Contraceptive prevalence (ages 15-49, %)	2006-2010	14.7 [i]
International migrant stock (000 and % of total population) [j]	mid-2010	548.0/0.6
Refugees and others of concern to UNHCR	end-2010	155 329
Education: Government expenditure (% of GDP)	2005-2011	4.7
Education: Primary-secondary gross enrolment ratio (f/m per 100)	2005-2011	66.6/75.0
Education: Female third-level students (% of total)	2005-2011	26.5
Seats held by women in national parliaments (%)	2011	27.8

Environmental indicators		
Threatened species	2011	120
Forested area (% of land area)	2009	12.4
CO$_2$ emission estimates (000 metric tons and metric tons per capita)	2008	7 101/0.1
Energy consumption per capita (kilograms oil equivalent)	2009	31.0
Rainfall in the capital city, total mean (millimetres)		1 055
Temperature in the capital city, mean °C (minimum and maximum)		15.9/23.2

a Official rate. **b** Index base 2001=100. **c** 2001. **d** March. **e** Age group 10 years and over. **f** Includes nationals residing abroad. **g** 2008. **h** 2009. **i** 2005. **j** Includes refugees.

Faeroe Islands

Region	Northern Europe
Currency	Danish Krone (DKK)
Surface area (square kilometres)	1 393
Population in 2010 (estimated, 000)	49
Population density in 2010 (per square kilometre)	35.0
Capital city and population in 2011 (000)	Tórshavn (20)

Economic indicators	2000	2005	2010
Exchange rates (national currency per US$) [a]	8.02	6.32	5.61
Balance of payments, current account (million US$)	99	...	...
CPI: Consumer price index (2000=100)	100	109	121[b]
Agricultural production index (2004-2006=100)	102	100	102
Food production index (2004-2006=100)	102	100	102
Employment in industrial sector (% of employed)	...	22.2[cd]	...
Employment in agricultural sector (% of employed)	...	11.1[cd]	...
Energy production, primary (000 mt oil equivalent)	7	9	9[b]
Telephone subscribers, total (per 100 inhabitants)	91.7	136.5	163.5
Internet users (per 100 inhabitants)	32.9	67.9	75.2

Total trade	(million US$)[b]	Major trading partners (% of exports)[b]			2010 (% of imports)[b]
Exports	761.7	United Kingdom	17.3	Denmark	30.4
Imports	783.4	Denmark	11.0	Norway	18.1
Balance	-21.7	France	10.8	Chile	6.6

Social indicators		
Population growth rate (average annual %)	2010-2015	0.5
Urban population growth rate (average annual %)	2010-2015	1.0
Rural population growth rate (average annual %)	2010-2015	0.1
Urban population (%)	2011	41.1
Population aged 0-14 years (%) [efg]	2011	22.0[h]
Population aged 60+ years (females and males, % of total) [efg]	2011	20.5/18.1[h]
Sex ratio (males per 100 females) [fgi]	2011	108.2[h]
Life expectancy at birth (females and males, years) [f]	2010-2015	82.3/76.8[h]
Fertility rate, total (live births per woman) [f]	2010-2015	2.5[j]
International migrant stock (000 and % of total population)	mid-2010	3.3/6.5

Environmental indicators		
Threatened species	2011	13
Forested area (% of land area)	2009	<
CO2 emission estimates (000 metric tons and metric tons per capita)	2008	707/14.2
Energy consumption per capita (kilograms oil equivalent)	2009	4 857.0[k]
Rainfall in the capital city, total mean (millimetres)		1 284
Temperature in the capital city, mean °C (minimum and maximum)		4.5/8.6

a Market rate. b 2009. c September. d Age group 16 years and over. e De jure estimate. f Data compiled by the United Nations Demographic Yearbook system. g Data refer to the latest available census. h 2008. i De jure population count. j 2007. k UNSD estimate.

Fiji

Region	Oceania-Melanesia
Currency	Fiji Dollar (FJD)
Surface area (square kilometres)	18 272
Population in 2010 (estimated, 000)	861
Population density in 2010 (per square kilometre)	47.1
Capital city and population in 2011 (000)	Suva (177)
United Nations membership date	13 October 1970

Economic indicators	2000	2005	2010
GDP: Gross domestic product (million current US$)	1 723	3 006	3 052
GDP: Growth rate at constant 2005 prices (annual %)	8.7	5.4	0.1
GDP per capita (current US$)	2 122.4	3 655.0	3 545.7
GNI: Gross national income per capita (current US$)	2 277.7	3 821.0	3 551.1
Gross fixed capital formation (% of GDP)	15.7	15.7	15.5
Exchange rates (national currency per US$) [a]	2.19	1.74	1.82
Balance of payments, current account (million US$)	−26	−302	−416
CPI: Consumer price index (2000=100)	100	115	146
Industrial production index (2005=100) [b]	103[c]	100	101
Agricultural production index (2004-2006=100)	102	99	82
Food production index (2004-2006=100)	102	99	82
Labour force participation, adult female pop. (%)	39.1	39.6	39.3
Labour force participation, adult male pop. (%)	78.5	79.6	79.6
Tourist arrivals at national borders (000) [d]	294	545	632
Energy production, primary (000 mt oil equivalent)	36	29	40[e]
Telephone subscribers, total (per 100 inhabitants)	17.4	38.6	96.2
Internet users (per 100 inhabitants)	1.5	8.5	14.8

Total trade		Major trading partners			2010
	(million US$)	(% of exports)			(% of imports)
Exports	846.6	Australia	20.7	Singapore	33.0
Imports	1 820.7			Australia	20.4
Balance	−974.1			New Zealand	16.0

Social indicators

Population growth rate (average annual %)	2010-2015	0.8
Urban population growth rate (average annual %)	2010-2015	1.6
Rural population growth rate (average annual %)	2010-2015	−<
Urban population (%)	2011	52.2
Population aged 0-14 years (%)	2011	28.9
Population aged 60+ years (females and males, % of total)	2011	8.7/7.6
Sex ratio (males per 100 females)	2011	104.2
Life expectancy at birth (females and males, years)	2010-2015	72.3/66.9
Infant mortality rate (per 1 000 live births)	2010-2015	17.2
Fertility rate, total (live births per woman)	2010-2015	2.6
Contraceptive prevalence (ages 15-49, %)	2006-2010	40.9[f]
International migrant stock (000 and % of total population)	mid-2010	18.5/2.2
Refugees and others of concern to UNHCR	end-2010	7
Education: Government expenditure (% of GDP)	2005-2011	4.5
Education: Primary-secondary gross enrolment ratio (f/m per 100)	2005-2011	96.7/93.2
Education: Female third-level students (% of total) [g]	2005-2011	53.1

Environmental indicators

Threatened species	2011	195
Forested area (% of land area)	2009	55.3
CO_2 emission estimates (000 metric tons and metric tons per capita)	2008	1 253/1.5
Energy consumption per capita (kilograms oil equivalent)	2009	358.0
Rainfall in the capital city, total mean (millimetres)		3 040
Temperature in the capital city, mean °C (minimum and maximum)		22.2/28.7

a Official rate. **b** The indices are shown in terms of ISIC Rev. 3. **c** 2003. **d** Excludes nationals residing abroad. **e** 2009. **f** 1974. **g** UNESCO estimate.

Finland

Region	Northern Europe
Currency	Euro (EUR)
Surface area (square kilometres)	336 861 [a]
Population in 2010 (estimated, 000)	5 365 [a]
Population density in 2010 (per square kilometre)	15.9 [a]
Capital city and population in 2011 (000)	Helsinki (1 134)
United Nations membership date	14 December 1955

Economic indicators	2000	2005	2010
GDP: Gross domestic product (million current US$)	121 715	195 626	238 731
GDP: Growth rate at constant 2005 prices (annual %)	5.3	2.9	3.6
GDP per capita (current US$)	23 527.3	37 302.4	44 501.7
GNI: Gross national income per capita (current US$)	23 347.4	37 474.3	45 275.9
Gross fixed capital formation (% of GDP)	20.1	20.1	18.8
Exchange rates (national currency per US$) [b]	1.07	0.85	0.75
Balance of payments, current account (million US$)	10 526	6 993	4 459
CPI: Consumer price index (2000=100)	100	106	116
Industrial production index (2005=100)	95 [c]	100	100
Agricultural production index (2004-2006=100)	99	102	94
Food production index (2004-2006=100)	99	102	94
Unemployment (% of labour force) [d]	8.8 [e]	8.4	8.4
Employment in industrial sector (% of employed) [d]	27.2	25.6	23.2 [f]
Employment in agricultural sector (% of employed) [d]	6.0 [g]	4.8	4.4 [f]
Labour force participation, adult female pop. (%)	56.7	56.8	56.1
Labour force participation, adult male pop. (%)	67.1	65.3	64.5
Tourist arrivals at national borders (000)	2 714	3 140	3 670
Energy production, primary (000 mt oil equivalent)	4 407	5 376	5 516 [h]
Telephone subscribers, total (per 100 inhabitants)	127.1	140.9	179.7
Internet users (per 100 inhabitants)	37.3	74.5	86.9

Total trade		Major trading partners			2010
	(million US$)	(% of exports)			(% of imports)
Exports	70 116.5	Sweden	11.3	Russian Federation	17.7
Imports	68 767.1	Germany	9.4	Germany	13.1
Balance	1 349.4	Russian Federation	8.8	Sweden	10.0

Social indicators

Population growth rate (average annual %) [a]	2010-2015	0.3
Urban population growth rate (average annual %) [a]	2010-2015	0.5
Rural population growth rate (average annual %) [a]	2010-2015	−0.5
Urban population (%) [a]	2011	83.7
Population aged 0-14 years (%) [a]	2011	16.5
Population aged 60+ years (females and males, % of total) [a]	2011	27.9/22.7
Sex ratio (males per 100 females) [a]	2011	96.4
Life expectancy at birth (females and males, years) [a]	2010-2015	83.3/77.2
Infant mortality rate (per 1 000 live births) [a]	2010-2015	2.8
Fertility rate, total (live births per woman) [a]	2010-2015	1.9
Contraceptive prevalence (ages 15-49, %) [i]	2006-2010	77.4 [j]
International migrant stock (000 and % of total population) [a]	mid-2010	225.7/4.2
Refugees and others of concern to UNHCR	end-2010	13 946
Education: Government expenditure (% of GDP)	2005-2011	6.1
Education: Primary-secondary gross enrolment ratio (f/m per 100)	2005-2011	104.7/102.2
Education: Female third-level students (% of total)	2005-2011	54.0
Deaths by assault (females and males, per 100 000)	2005-2008	1.5/3.0
Seats held by women in national parliaments (%)	2011	42.5

Environmental indicators

Threatened species	2011	22
Forested area (% of land area)	2009	72.9
CO_2 emission estimates (000 metric tons and metric tons per capita)	2008	56 466/10.7
Energy consumption per capita (kilograms oil equivalent)	2009	4 555.0
Rainfall in the capital city, total mean (millimetres)		650
Temperature in the capital city, mean °C (minimum and maximum)		1.0/8.7

a Includes Åland Islands. b Market rate. c 2003. d Age group 15 to 74 years. e 2004. f European Labour Force Survey (Eurostat). g Excludes conscripts. h 2009. i Age group 25 to 49 years. j 1989.

France

Region	Western Europe
Currency	Euro (EUR)
Surface area (square kilometres)	551 500
Population in 2010 (estimated, 000)	62 787
Population density in 2010 (per square kilometre)	113.9
Capital city and population in 2011 (000)	Paris (10 620)
United Nations membership date	24 October 1945

Economic indicators	2000	2005	2010
GDP: Gross domestic product (million current US$)	1 326 330	2 136 560	2 559 850
GDP: Growth rate at constant 2005 prices (annual %)	3.7	1.8	1.5
GDP per capita (current US$)	21 827.5	34 001.9	39 545.9
GNI: Gross national income per capita (current US$)	22 194.0	34 477.7	40 268.5
Gross fixed capital formation (% of GDP)	19.0	19.4	19.3
Exchange rates (national currency per US$) [a]	1.07	0.85	0.75
Balance of payments, current account (million US$)	19 670	−10 260	−44 500
CPI: Consumer price index (2000=100)	100	110	119
Industrial production index (2005=100)	98[b]	100	92
Agricultural production index (2004-2006=100)	104	100	96
Food production index (2004-2006=100)	104	100	95
Unemployment (% of labour force)	8.9[c]	8.9	9.4
Employment in industrial sector (% of employed) [d]	26.3	23.7	22.2
Employment in agricultural sector (% of employed) [d]	4.1	3.6	2.9
Labour force participation, adult female pop. (%)	48.3	50.2	51.2
Labour force participation, adult male pop. (%)	62.7	62.5	62.1
Tourist arrivals at national borders (000)	77 190[e]	74 988[f]	77 148[f]
Energy production, primary (000 mt oil equivalent) [g]	48 111	46 788	45 299[h]
Telephone subscribers, total (per 100 inhabitants)	106.8	134.1	156.9
Internet users (per 100 inhabitants)	14.3	42.9	80.1

Total trade		Major trading partners			2010
	(million US$)[g]	(% of exports)[g]			(% of imports)[g]
Exports	511 651.0	Germany	16.2	Germany	17.3
Imports	599 171.5	Italy	8.1	China	8.2
Balance	−87 520.5	Belgium	7.5	Belgium	7.8

Social indicators		
Population growth rate (average annual %)	2010-2015	0.5
Urban population growth rate (average annual %)	2010-2015	1.1
Rural population growth rate (average annual %)	2010-2015	−3.3
Urban population (%)	2011	85.8
Population aged 0-14 years (%)	2011	18.4
Population aged 60+ years (females and males, % of total)	2011	25.6/21.0
Sex ratio (males per 100 females)	2011	94.8
Life expectancy at birth (females and males, years)	2010-2015	84.9/78.5
Infant mortality rate (per 1 000 live births)	2010-2015	3.3
Fertility rate, total (live births per woman)	2010-2015	2.0
Contraceptive prevalence (ages 15-49, %) [i]	2006-2010	76.6[i]
International migrant stock (000 and % of total population)	mid-2010	6 684.8/10.7
Refugees and others of concern to UNHCR	end-2010	250 394
Education: Government expenditure (% of GDP)	2005-2011	5.6
Education: Primary-secondary gross enrolment ratio (f/m per 100)	2005-2011	111.6/112.0
Education: Female third-level students (% of total)	2005-2011	55.2
Deaths by assault (females and males, per 100 000)	2005-2008	</0.7
Seats held by women in national parliaments (%)	2011	18.9

Environmental indicators		
Threatened species	2011	216
Forested area (% of land area)	2009	29.0
CO_2 emission estimates (000 metric tons and metric tons per capita) [g]	2008	376 678/6.1
Energy consumption per capita (kilograms oil equivalent) [g]	2009	2 778.0
Rainfall in the capital city, total mean (millimetres)		650
Temperature in the capital city, mean °C (minimum and maximum)		8.5/15.5

a Market rate. **b** 2003. **c** 2004. **d** European Labour Force Survey (Eurostat). **e** Estimates based on surveys at national borders. **f** Non-resident visitor survey (EVE). **g** Includes Monaco. **h** 2009. **i** Metropolitan France only. **j** 2004-2005.

French Guiana

Region	South America
Currency	Euro (EUR)
Surface area (square kilometres)	83 534
Population in 2010 (estimated, 000)	231
Population density in 2010 (per square kilometre)	2.8
Capital city and population in 2011 (000)	Cayenne (67)

Economic indicators	2000	2005	2010
Exchange rates (national currency per US$) [a]	1.07	0.85	0.75
CPI: Consumer price index (2000=100)	100	108	119
Agricultural production index (2004-2006=100)	106	96	88
Food production index (2004-2006=100)	106	96	88
Labour force participation, adult female pop. (%)	53.4	53.5	53.8
Labour force participation, adult male pop. (%)	68.3	67.1	64.9
Tourist arrivals at national borders (000)	65[b]	95	109[c]
Energy production, primary (000 mt oil equivalent) [d]	...	53	61[e]
Telephone subscribers, total (per 100 inhabitants)	54.5	25.3[f]	19.7[f]
Internet users (per 100 inhabitants)	9.7	20.8	25.7[e]

Social indicators		
Population growth rate (average annual %)	2010-2015	2.5
Urban population growth rate (average annual %)	2010-2015	2.8
Rural population growth rate (average annual %)	2010-2015	1.8
Urban population (%)	2011	76.4
Population aged 0-14 years (%)	2011	33.0
Population aged 60+ years (females and males, % of total)	2011	7.2/7.3
Sex ratio (males per 100 females)	2011	100.2
Life expectancy at birth (females and males, years)	2010-2015	80.5/73.4
Infant mortality rate (per 1 000 live births)	2010-2015	12.7
Fertility rate, total (live births per woman)	2010-2015	3.1
International migrant stock (000 and % of total population)	mid-2010	107.5/46.5

Environmental indicators		
Threatened species	2011	59
Forested area (% of land area)	2009	98.4
CO$_2$ emission estimates (000 metric tons and metric tons per capita)	2008	912/4.1
Energy consumption per capita (kilograms oil equivalent)	2009	1 260.0[d]
Rainfall in the capital city, total mean (millimetres) [g]		3 674
Temperature in the capital city, mean °C (minimum and maximum) [g]		22.5/30.1

a Market rate. b 2001. c 2007. d UNSD estimate. e 2009. f Main telephone lines only. g Rochambeau.

French Polynesia

Region	Oceania-Polynesia
Currency	CFP Franc (XPF)
Surface area (square kilometres)	4 000
Population in 2010 (estimated, 000)	271
Population density in 2010 (per square kilometre)	67.7
Capital city and population in 2011 (000)	Papeete (137)

Economic indicators	2000	2005	2010
GDP: Gross domestic product (million current US$)	3 444	5 463	6 679
GDP: Growth rate at constant 2005 prices (annual %)	5.1	1.3	1.6
GDP per capita (current US$)	14 491.7	21 434.2	24 669.0
GNI: Gross national income per capita (current US$)	14 491.7	21 434.2	24 669.0
Gross fixed capital formation (% of GDP)	15.4	17.0	17.1
Exchange rates (national currency per US$) [a]	128.17	100.84	90.81
CPI: Consumer price index (2000=100)	100	106	116
Agricultural production index (2004-2006=100)	91	106	130
Food production index (2004-2006=100)	91	106	130
Employment in industrial sector (% of employed)	17.9[bcd]	...	...
Employment in agricultural sector (% of employed)	9.4[bcd]	...	...
Labour force participation, adult female pop. (%)	48.1	47.4	47.9
Labour force participation, adult male pop. (%)	69.5	66.9	66.7
Tourist arrivals at national borders (000) [e]	252	208	154
Energy production, primary (000 mt oil equivalent)	12	15	18[f]
Telephone subscribers, total (per 100 inhabitants)	39.4	68.0	100.0
Internet users (per 100 inhabitants)	6.4	21.5	49.0

Total trade		Major trading partners			2010
	(million US$)	(% of exports)			(% of imports)
Exports	153.2	China, Hong Kong SAR	30.0	France	28.1
Imports	1 725.8	Japan	20.2	Singapore	12.7
Balance	−1 572.6	France	13.2	United States	10.1

Social indicators		
Population growth rate (average annual %)	2010-2015	1.0
Urban population growth rate (average annual %)	2010-2015	1.1
Rural population growth rate (average annual %)	2010-2015	1.0
Urban population (%)	2011	51.4
Population aged 0-14 years (%)	2011	24.8
Population aged 60+ years (females and males, % of total)	2011	10.0/9.3
Sex ratio (males per 100 females)	2011	104.9
Life expectancy at birth (females and males, years)	2010-2015	78.1/73.1
Infant mortality rate (per 1 000 live births)	2010-2015	7.2
Fertility rate, total (live births per woman)	2010-2015	2.0
International migrant stock (000 and % of total population)	mid-2010	34.8/12.8

Environmental indicators		
Threatened species	2011	162
Forested area (% of land area)	2009	41.0
CO_2 emission estimates (000 metric tons and metric tons per capita)	2008	890/3.3
Energy consumption per capita (kilograms oil equivalent)	2009	1 141.0
Rainfall in the capital city, total mean (millimetres) [g]		1 761
Temperature in the capital city, mean °C (minimum and maximum) [g]		22.3/29.5

a UN operational exchange rate. b 2002. c Population census. d November. e Excludes nationals residing abroad. f 2009. g Tahiti.

Gabon

Region	Middle Africa
Currency	CFA Franc (XAF)
Surface area (square kilometres)	267 668
Population in 2010 (estimated, 000)	1 505
Population density in 2010 (per square kilometre)	5.6
Capital city and population in 2011 (000)	Libreville (686)
United Nations membership date	20 September 1960

Economic indicators	2000	2005	2010
GDP: Gross domestic product (million current US$)	5 487	9 459	18 771
GDP: Growth rate at constant 2005 prices (annual %)	−1.3	5.6	5.6
GDP per capita (current US$)	4 442.3	6 900.7	12 468.8
GNI: Gross national income per capita (current US$)	3 716.3	6 187.0	10 294.1
Gross fixed capital formation (% of GDP)	16.8	19.8	24.0
Exchange rates (national currency per US$) [a]	704.95	556.04	490.91
Balance of payments, current account (million US$)	1 001	1 983	...
CPI: Consumer price index (2000=100) [b]	100	105	123
Industrial production index (2005=100) [c]	92[d]	100	114
Agricultural production index (2004-2006=100)	100	100	111
Food production index (2004-2006=100)	100	100	110
Employment in industrial sector (% of employed)	...	11.8[e]	...
Employment in agricultural sector (% of employed)	...	24.2[e]	...
Labour force participation, adult female pop. (%)	54.6	55.1	56.0
Labour force participation, adult male pop. (%)	67.2	65.0	64.9
Tourist arrivals at national borders (000) [f]	155	269	358[g]
Energy production, primary (000 mt oil equivalent)	14 122	13 822	12 402[h]
Telephone subscribers, total (per 100 inhabitants)	12.9	56.6	109.0
Internet users (per 100 inhabitants)	1.2	4.9	7.2

Total trade		Major trading partners			2010
	(million US$) [h]	(% of exports) [h]		(% of imports) [h]	
Exports	5 356.0	United States	59.0	France	32.9
Imports	2 500.9	China	8.0	Belgium	15.7
Balance	2 855.1	Spain	5.3	United States	7.1

Social indicators		
Population growth rate (average annual %)	2010-2015	1.9
Urban population growth rate (average annual %)	2010-2015	2.3
Rural population growth rate (average annual %)	2010-2015	−0.4
Urban population (%)	2011	86.2
Population aged 0-14 years (%)	2011	35.0
Population aged 60+ years (females and males, % of total)	2011	6.9/6.2
Sex ratio (males per 100 females)	2011	100.7
Life expectancy at birth (females and males, years)	2010-2015	64.3/62.3
Infant mortality rate (per 1 000 live births)	2010-2015	43.8
Fertility rate, total (live births per woman)	2010-2015	3.2
Contraceptive prevalence (ages 15-49, %)	2006-2011	32.7[i]
International migrant stock (000 and % of total population) [j]	mid-2010	284.1/18.9
Refugees and others of concern to UNHCR	end-2010	13 147
Education: Government expenditure (% of GDP) [k]	2005-2011	3.8[i]
Education: Primary-secondary gross enrolment ratio (f/m per 100) [k]	2005-2011	90.9/94.8[i]
Education: Female third-level students (% of total)	2005-2011	35.7[l]
Seats held by women in national parliaments (%)	2011	14.7

Environmental indicators		
Threatened species	2011	205
Forested area (% of land area)	2009	85.4
CO_2 emission estimates (000 metric tons and metric tons per capita)	2008	2 470/1.7
Energy consumption per capita (kilograms oil equivalent)	2009	456.0
Rainfall in the capital city, total mean (millimetres)		2 842
Temperature in the capital city, mean °C (minimum and maximum)		23.3/28.6

a Official rate. **b** Libreville. **c** The indices are shown in terms of ISIC Rev. 3. **d** 2003. **e** Core Welfare Indicators Questionnaire (World Bank). **f** Arrivals of non-resident tourists at Libreville airport. **g** 2008. **h** 2009. **i** 2000. **j** Data refer to foreign citizens. **k** UNESCO estimate. **l** 1999.

Gambia

Region	Western Africa
Currency	Dalasi (GMD)
Surface area (square kilometres)	11 295
Population in 2010 (estimated, 000)	1 728
Population density in 2010 (per square kilometre)	153.0
Capital city and population in 2011 (000)	Banjul (506)
United Nations membership date	21 September 1965

Economic indicators	2000	2005	2010
GDP: Gross domestic product (million current US$)	783	630	1 001
GDP: Growth rate at constant 2005 prices (annual %)	6.1	−0.9	6.1
GDP per capita (current US$)	603.6	418.7	579.1
GNI: Gross national income per capita (current US$)	574.1	380.8	545.8
Gross fixed capital formation (% of GDP)	4.6	29.2	27.5
Exchange rates (national currency per US$) [a]	14.89	28.13	28.39
Balance of payments, current account (million US$)	...	−51	17
CPI: Consumer price index (2000=100) [c]	100	157	193
Agricultural production index (2004-2006=100)	98	94	133
Food production index (2004-2006=100)	98	94	133
Labour force participation, adult female pop. (%)	71.1	71.8	72.4
Labour force participation, adult male pop. (%)	83.4	83.4	83.2
Tourist arrivals at national borders (000) [d]	79	108	91
Telephone subscribers, total (per 100 inhabitants)	3.0	19.4	88.4
Internet users (per 100 inhabitants)	0.9	3.8	9.2

Total trade		Major trading partners			2010
	(million US$)		(% of exports)		(% of imports)
Exports	35.0	United Kingdom	25.4	Côte d'Ivoire	19.7
Imports	285.0	France	16.0	Brazil	13.0
Balance	−250.0	Senegal	16.0	China	7.5

Social indicators

Population growth rate (average annual %)	2010-2015	2.7
Urban population growth rate (average annual %)	2010-2015	3.6
Rural population growth rate (average annual %)	2010-2015	1.4
Urban population (%)	2011	57.3
Population aged 0-14 years (%)	2011	43.7
Population aged 60+ years (females and males, % of total)	2011	3.3/3.7
Sex ratio (males per 100 females)	2011	97.5
Life expectancy at birth (females and males, years)	2010-2015	60.3/57.7
Infant mortality rate (per 1 000 live births)	2010-2015	66.4
Fertility rate, total (live births per woman)	2010-2015	4.7
Contraceptive prevalence (ages 15-49, %)	2006-2010	17.5[e]
International migrant stock (000 and % of total population)	mid-2010	290.1/16.6
Refugees and others of concern to UNHCR	end-2010	8 452
Education: Government expenditure (% of GDP)	2005-2011	5.0
Education: Primary-secondary gross enrolment ratio (f/m per 100) [f]	2005-2011	69.4/69.9
Education: Female third-level students (% of total)	2005-2011	19.2[g]
Seats held by women in national parliaments (%)	2011	7.5

Environmental indicators

Threatened species	2011	47
Forested area (% of land area)	2009	47.8
CO_2 emission estimates (000 metric tons and metric tons per capita)	2008	410/0.3
Energy consumption per capita (kilograms oil equivalent)	2009	88.0
Rainfall in the capital city, total mean (millimetres)		977
Temperature in the capital city, mean °C (minimum and maximum)		19.9/32.0

a Market rate. **b** 2003. **c** Banjul and Kombo St. Mary only. **d** Charter tourists only. **e** 2001. **f** UNESCO estimate. **g** 2004.

Georgia

Region	Western Asia
Currency	Lari (GEL)
Surface area (square kilometres)	69 700
Population in 2010 (estimated, 000)	4 352 [a]
Population density in 2010 (per square kilometre)	62.4
Capital city and population in 2011 (000)	Tbilisi (1 121)
United Nations membership date	31 July 1992

Economic indicators	2000	2005	2010
GDP: Gross domestic product (million current US$)	3 058	6 411	11 665
GDP: Growth rate at constant 2005 prices (annual %)	1.8	9.6	6.4
GDP per capita (current US$)	644.4	1 432.0	2 680.3
GNI: Gross national income per capita (current US$)	669.1	1 453.0	2 637.3
Gross fixed capital formation (% of GDP)	25.5	28.1	17.3
Exchange rates (national currency per US$) [b]	1.98	1.79	1.77
Balance of payments, current account (million US$)	−249	−772	−1 465
CPI: Consumer price index (2000=100) [c]	100	132	174 [d]
Industrial production index (2005=100) [e]	71 [f]	100	140
Agricultural production index (2004-2006=100)	98	121	65
Food production index (2004-2006=100)	97	121	65
Employment in industrial sector (% of employed)	9.8	9.3	...
Employment in agricultural sector (% of employed)	52.1	54.3	...
Labour force participation, adult female pop. (%)	54.7	55.4	55.6
Labour force participation, adult male pop. (%)	74.0	73.3	73.8
Tourist arrivals at national borders (000) [g]	387	560	2 033
Energy production, primary (000 mt oil equivalent)	681	619	778 [h]
Telephone subscribers, total (per 100 inhabitants)	14.8	39.0	116.9
Internet users (per 100 inhabitants)	0.5	6.1	26.9

Total trade		Major trading partners			2010
	(million US$)	(% of exports)			(% of imports)
Exports	1 583.3	Azerbaijan	15.4	Turkey	17.3
Imports	5 095.2	Turkey	13.6	Ukraine	10.9
Balance	−3 511.9	United States	11.4	Azerbaijan	9.1

Social indicators		
Population growth rate (average annual %) [a]	2010-2015	−0.6
Urban population growth rate (average annual %)	2010-2015	−0.4
Rural population growth rate (average annual %)	2010-2015	−0.9
Urban population (%)	2011	52.8
Population aged 0-14 years (%) [a]	2011	16.5
Population aged 60+ years (females and males, % of total) [a]	2011	22.0/16.4
Sex ratio (males per 100 females) [a]	2011	89.0
Life expectancy at birth (females and males, years) [a]	2010-2015	77.3/70.5
Infant mortality rate (per 1 000 live births) [a]	2010-2015	25.6
Fertility rate, total (live births per woman) [a]	2010-2015	1.5
Contraceptive prevalence (ages 15-49, %) [i]	2006-2010	47.3 [j]
International migrant stock (000 and % of total population)	mid-2010	167.3/4.0
Refugees and others of concern to UNHCR	end-2010	362 228
Education: Government expenditure (% of GDP) [k]	2005-2011	3.2
Education: Primary-secondary gross enrolment ratio (f/m per 100)	2005-2011	97.2/100.6
Education: Female third-level students (% of total)	2005-2011	55.3
Seats held by women in national parliaments (%)	2011	6.5

Environmental indicators		
Threatened species	2011	49
Forested area (% of land area)	2009	39.5
CO_2 emission estimates (000 metric tons and metric tons per capita)	2008	5 199/1.2
Energy consumption per capita (kilograms oil equivalent)	2009	634.0
Rainfall in the capital city, total mean (millimetres)		496
Temperature in the capital city, mean °C (minimum and maximum) [l]		13.0/13.0

a Includes Abkhazia and South Ossetia. **b** Official rate. **c** 5 cities. **d** 2008. **e** The indices are shown in terms of ISIC Rev. 3. **f** 2003. **g** Arrivals of non-resident visitors at national borders. **h** 2009. **i** Age group 15 to 44 years. **j** 2005. **k** National estimate. **l** Refers to average temperature.

Germany

Region	Western Europe
Currency	Euro (EUR)
Surface area (square kilometres)	357 114
Population in 2010 (estimated, 000)	82 302
Population density in 2010 (per square kilometre)	230.5
Capital city and population in 2011 (000)	Berlin (3 462)
United Nations membership date	18 September 1973

Economic indicators	2000	2005	2010
GDP: Gross domestic product (million current US$)	1 886 400	2 766 250	3 280 330
GDP: Growth rate at constant 2005 prices (annual %)	3.1	0.7	3.7
GDP per capita (current US$)	22 907.4	33 513.8	39 857.1
GNI: Gross national income per capita (current US$)	22 665.4	33 893.3	40 596.5
Gross fixed capital formation (% of GDP)	21.5	17.3	17.6
Exchange rates (national currency per US$) [a]	1.07	0.85	0.75
Balance of payments, current account (million US$)	−32 280	140 620	187 940
CPI: Consumer price index (2000=100)	100	108	117
Industrial production index (2005=100)	93[b]	100	104
Agricultural production index (2004-2006=100)	102	100	102
Food production index (2004-2006=100)	102	100	102
Unemployment (% of labour force)	...	11.2	7.1
Employment in industrial sector (% of employed) [c]	33.5	29.7	28.4
Employment in agricultural sector (% of employed) [c]	2.6	2.3	1.6
Labour force participation, adult female pop. (%)	49.2	50.6	52.9
Labour force participation, adult male pop. (%)	67.9	66.8	66.7
Tourist arrivals at national borders (000) [d]	18 983	21 500	26 875
Energy production, primary (000 mt oil equivalent)	99 173	96 432	82 591[e]
Telephone subscribers, total (per 100 inhabitants)	119.5	162.4	182.5
Internet users (per 100 inhabitants)	30.2	68.7	82.0

Total trade		Major trading partners			2010
	(million US$)	(% of exports)			(% of imports)
Exports	1 271 096.0	France	9.5	China	9.5
Imports	1 066 817.0	United States	6.8	Netherlands	8.5
Balance	204 279.5	Netherlands	6.6	France	7.7

Social indicators		
Population growth rate (average annual %)	2010-2015	−0.2
Urban population growth rate (average annual %)	2010-2015	─<
Rural population growth rate (average annual %)	2010-2015	−0.7
Urban population (%)	2011	73.9
Population aged 0-14 years (%)	2011	13.4
Population aged 60+ years (females and males, % of total)	2011	28.8/23.8
Sex ratio (males per 100 females)	2011	96.2
Life expectancy at birth (females and males, years)	2010-2015	83.0/78.2
Infant mortality rate (per 1 000 live births)	2010-2015	3.5
Fertility rate, total (live births per woman)	2010-2015	1.5
Contraceptive prevalence (ages 15-49, %) [f]	2006-2010	70.1[g]
International migrant stock (000 and % of total population)	mid-2010	10 758.1/13.1
Refugees and others of concern to UNHCR	end-2010	670 462
Education: Government expenditure (% of GDP)	2005-2011	4.6
Education: Primary-secondary gross enrolment ratio (f/m per 100)	2005-2011	100.3/104.4
Deaths by assault (females and males, per 100 000)	2005-2008	0.5/0.6
Seats held by women in national parliaments (%)	2011	32.8

Environmental indicators		
Threatened species	2011	79
Forested area (% of land area)	2009	31.8
CO_2 emission estimates (000 metric tons and metric tons per capita)	2008	786 016/9.6
Energy consumption per capita (kilograms oil equivalent)	2009	3 241.0
Rainfall in the capital city, total mean (millimetres)		571
Temperature in the capital city, mean °C (minimum and maximum)		5.9/13.4

a Market rate. **b** 2003. **c** European Labour Force Survey (Eurostat). **d** Arrivals of non-resident tourists in all types of accommodation establishments. **e** 2009. **f** Age group 20 to 39 years. **g** 1992.

Ghana

Region	Western Africa	
Currency	(new) Cedi (GHS) [a]	
Surface area (square kilometres)	238 533	
Population in 2010 (estimated, 000)	24 392	
Population density in 2010 (per square kilometre)	102.3	
Capital city and population in 2011 (000)	Accra (2 573)	
United Nations membership date	8 March 1957	

Economic indicators	2000	2005	2010
GDP: Gross domestic product (million current US$)	7 985	17 198	32 520
GDP: Growth rate at constant 2005 prices (annual %)	4.2	6.2	7.7
GDP per capita (current US$)	416.7	794.8	1 333.2
GNI: Gross national income per capita (current US$)	404.4	785.1	1 318.0
Gross fixed capital formation (% of GDP)	17.3	20.6	19.0
Exchange rates (national currency per US$) [b]	0.70	0.91	1.47
Balance of payments, current account (million US$)	−387	−1 105	−2 700
CPI: Consumer price index (2000=100)	100	251	511
Agricultural production index (2004-2006=100)	79	100	125
Food production index (2004-2006=100)	79	100	125
Employment in industrial sector (% of employed)	...	13.6[cdef]	...
Employment in agricultural sector (% of employed)	...	57.2[cdef]	...
Labour force participation, adult female pop. (%)	72.6	67.7	66.8
Labour force participation, adult male pop. (%)	76.6	72.0	71.6
Tourist arrivals at national borders (000) [g]	399	429	698[h]
Energy production, primary (000 mt oil equivalent)	568	484	591[i]
Telephone subscribers, total (per 100 inhabitants)	1.8	14.8	72.6
Internet users (per 100 inhabitants)	0.2	1.8	9.6

Total trade		Major trading partners			2010
	(million US$)	(% of exports)			(% of imports)
Exports	5 233.4	South Africa	53.5	United States	13.7
Imports	8 057.1	United Arab Emirates	6.8	China	13.2
Balance	−2 823.7	Netherlands	5.6	France	6.2

Social indicators		
Population growth rate (average annual %)	2010-2015	2.3
Urban population growth rate (average annual %)	2010-2015	3.5
Rural population growth rate (average annual %)	2010-2015	0.9
Urban population (%)	2011	51.9
Population aged 0-14 years (%)	2011	38.4
Population aged 60+ years (females and males, % of total)	2011	6.2/5.7
Sex ratio (males per 100 females)	2011	103.6
Life expectancy at birth (females and males, years)	2010-2015	65.8/63.7
Infant mortality rate (per 1 000 live births)	2010-2015	43.9
Fertility rate, total (live births per woman)	2010-2015	4.0
Contraceptive prevalence (ages 15-49, %)	2006-2010	23.5
International migrant stock (000 and % of total population)	mid-2010	1 851.8/7.6
Refugees and others of concern to UNHCR	end-2010	14 578
Education: Government expenditure (% of GDP)	2005-2011	5.5
Education: Primary-secondary gross enrolment ratio (f/m per 100)	2005-2011	80.8/83.9
Education: Female third-level students (% of total)	2005-2011	37.3
Seats held by women in national parliaments (%)	2011	8.3

Environmental indicators		
Threatened species	2011	210
Forested area (% of land area)	2009	22.2
CO_2 emission estimates (000 metric tons and metric tons per capita)	2008	8 585/0.4
Energy consumption per capita (kilograms oil equivalent)	2009	111.0
Rainfall in the capital city, total mean (millimetres)		807
Temperature in the capital city, mean °C (minimum and maximum)		23.4/30.8

a Beginning 1 July 2007, 1 new Cedi = 10000 old Cedis. **b** Principal rate. **c** 2006. **d** Age group 15 to 64 years. **e** Living standards survey. **f** September of the preceding year to September of the current year. **g** Includes nationals residing abroad. **h** 2008. **i** 2009.

Greece

Region	Southern Europe
Currency	Euro (EUR)
Surface area (square kilometres)	131 957
Population in 2010 (estimated, 000)	11 359
Population density in 2010 (per square kilometre)	86.1
Capital city and population in 2011 (000)	Athens (3 414)
United Nations membership date	25 October 1945

Economic indicators	2000	2005	2010
GDP: Gross domestic product (million current US$)	127 088	240 076	301 065
GDP: Growth rate at constant 2005 prices (annual %)	4.5	2.3	-3.5
GDP per capita (current US$)	11 567.2	21 467.7	26 503.8
GNI: Gross national income per capita (current US$)	11 598.4	21 155.3	25 781.1
Gross fixed capital formation (% of GDP)	21.6	20.7	16.6
Exchange rates (national currency per US$)[a]	365.62[b]	0.85	0.75
Balance of payments, current account (million US$)	-9 820	-18 233	-30 897
CPI: Consumer price index (2000=100)	100	118[c]	139
Industrial production index (2005=100)	101[d]	100	85
Agricultural production index (2004-2006=100)	106	103	82
Food production index (2004-2006=100)	105	103	85
Unemployment (% of labour force)	10.5[e]	9.8	12.5
Employment in industrial sector (% of employed)[f]	22.6	22.4	19.7
Employment in agricultural sector (% of employed)[f]	17.4	12.4	12.5
Labour force participation, adult female pop. (%)	40.3	42.3	44.5
Labour force participation, adult male pop. (%)	65.3	65.0	64.9
Tourist arrivals at national borders (000)[g]	13 096	14 765	15 007
Energy production, primary (000 mt oil equivalent)	8 944	9 251	9 047[h]
Telephone subscribers, total (per 100 inhabitants)	105.5	148.2	154.0
Internet users (per 100 inhabitants)	9.1	24.0	44.4

Total trade		Major trading partners			2010
	(million US$)	(% of exports)			(% of imports)
Exports	21 559.7	Germany	10.9	Germany	10.5
Imports	63 320.7	Italy	10.8	Italy	9.9
Balance	-41 761.0	Cyprus	7.1	Russian Federation	9.8

Social indicators		
Population growth rate (average annual %)	2010-2015	0.2
Urban population growth rate (average annual %)	2010-2015	0.6
Rural population growth rate (average annual %)	2010-2015	-0.4
Urban population (%)	2011	61.4
Population aged 0-14 years (%)	2011	14.7
Population aged 60+ years (females and males, % of total)	2011	26.8/22.2
Sex ratio (males per 100 females)	2011	98.0
Life expectancy at birth (females and males, years)	2010-2015	82.6/77.6
Infant mortality rate (per 1 000 live births)	2010-2015	4.5
Fertility rate, total (live births per woman)	2010-2015	1.5
Contraceptive prevalence (ages 15-49, %)[i]	2006-2010	76.2[j]
International migrant stock (000 and % of total population)[k]	mid-2010	1 132.8/10.1
Refugees and others of concern to UNHCR	end-2010	57 428
Education: Government expenditure (% of GDP)	2005-2011	4.1
Education: Primary-secondary gross enrolment ratio (f/m per 100)	2005-2011	99.0/101.7
Education: Female third-level students (% of total)	2005-2011	50.4
Deaths by assault (females and males, per 100 000)	2005-2008	0.7/2.0
Seats held by women in national parliaments (%)	2011	17.3

Environmental indicators		
Threatened species	2011	156
Forested area (% of land area)	2009	30.0
CO$_2$ emission estimates (000 metric tons and metric tons per capita)	2008	97 734/8.8
Energy consumption per capita (kilograms oil equivalent)	2009	2 852.0
Rainfall in the capital city, total mean (millimetres)		414
Temperature in the capital city, mean °C (minimum and maximum)		12.3/22.5

a Market rate. b Currency = Drachma. c Series linked to former series. d 2003. e 2004. f European Labour Force Survey (Eurostat). g Information based on administrative data. h 2009. i Age group 16 to 45 years. j 2001. k Data refer to foreign citizens.

Greenland

Region	Northern America
Currency	Danish Krone (DKK)
Surface area (square kilometres)	2 166 086
Population in 2010 (estimated, 000)	57
Population density in 2010 (per square kilometre)	0.0
Capital city and population in 2011 (000)	Nuuk (16)

Economic indicators	2000	2005	2010
GDP: Gross domestic product (million current US$)	1 068	1 703	2 022
GDP: Growth rate at constant 2005 prices (annual %)	7.1	2.0	1.8
GDP per capita (current US$)	19 005.4	29 770.0	35 292.7
GNI: Gross national income per capita (current US$)	18 565.1	29 064.3	34 792.3
Gross fixed capital formation (% of GDP)	23.2	28.3	30.5
Exchange rates (national currency per US$) [a]	8.02	6.32	5.61
CPI: Consumer price index (2000=100)	100	113	132
Agricultural production index (2004-2006=100)	91	100	98
Food production index (2004-2006=100)	91	99	99
Telephone subscribers, total (per 100 inhabitants)	73.5	137.5	138.2
Internet users (per 100 inhabitants)	31.8	57.7	63.0

Total trade		Major trading partners			2010
	(million US$) [b]		(% of exports) [b]		(% of imports) [b]
Exports	319.8	Denmark	84.4	Denmark	66.6
Imports	432.3	Canada	10.0	Sweden	15.7
Balance	−112.5	Iceland	1.7	Germany	3.8

Social indicators

Population growth rate (average annual %)	2010-2015	−<
Urban population growth rate (average annual %)	2010-2015	0.3
Rural population growth rate (average annual %)	2010-2015	−1.9
Urban population (%)	2011	84.7
Population aged 0-14 years (%) [cde]	2011	22.6 [f]
Population aged 60+ years (females and males, % of total) [cde]	2011	10.7/11.0 [f]
Sex ratio (males per 100 females) [cd]	2011	112.6 [f]
Life expectancy at birth (females and males, years) [d]	2010-2015	71.6/66.6 [g]
Fertility rate, total (live births per woman) [d]	2010-2015	2.2 [h]
International migrant stock (000 and % of total population)	mid-2010	5.8/10.2

Environmental indicators

Threatened species	2011	14
Forested area (% of land area)	2009	0.0
CO_2 emission estimates (000 metric tons and metric tons per capita)	2008	575/10.0
Energy consumption per capita (kilograms oil equivalent)	2009	3 333.0
Rainfall in the capital city, total mean (millimetres)		754
Temperature in the capital city, mean °C (minimum and maximum)		−4.0/1.3

a Market rate. b 2007. c De jure estimate. d Data compiled by the United Nations Demographic Yearbook system. e Data refer to the latest available census. f 2010. g 2004-2008. h 2008.

Grenada

Region	Caribbean
Currency	E.C. Dollar (XCD)
Surface area (square kilometres)	344
Population in 2010 (estimated, 000)	104
Population density in 2010 (per square kilometre)	303.7
Capital city and population in 2011 (000)	St.George's (41)
United Nations membership date	17 September 1974

Economic indicators	2000	2005	2010
GDP: Gross domestic product (million current US$)	520	697	776
GDP: Growth rate at constant 2005 prices (annual %)	12.0	12.0	0.4
GDP per capita (current US$)	5 119.6	6 788.4	7 429.0
GNI: Gross national income per capita (current US$)	4 770.3	6 441.8	6 882.9
Gross fixed capital formation (% of GDP)	34.5	40.0	16.7
Exchange rates (national currency per US$)[a]	2.70	2.70	2.70
Balance of payments, current account (million US$)	−88	−193	−218
CPI: Consumer price index (2000=100)	100	113	133[b]
Agricultural production index (2004-2006=100)	107	80	93
Food production index (2004-2006=100)	107	80	94
Tourist arrivals at national borders (000)	129	99	114[b]
Telephone subscribers, total (per 100 inhabitants)	35.1	72.3	143.9
Internet users (per 100 inhabitants)	4.1	20.5	33.5

Total trade	Major trading partners		2010
(million US$)	(% of exports)		(% of imports)[b]
Imports 281.8[b]		United States	31.9
		Trinidad and Tobago	25.2
		United Kingdom	4.2

Social indicators		
Population growth rate (average annual %)	2010-2015	0.4
Urban population growth rate (average annual %)	2010-2015	1.2
Rural population growth rate (average annual %)	2010-2015	−0.2
Urban population (%)	2011	39.1
Population aged 0-14 years (%)	2011	27.3
Population aged 60+ years (females and males, % of total)	2011	11.1/8.1
Sex ratio (males per 100 females)	2011	100.1
Life expectancy at birth (females and males, years)	2010-2015	77.7/74.5
Infant mortality rate (per 1 000 live births)	2010-2015	13.0
Fertility rate, total (live births per woman)	2010-2015	2.2
Contraceptive prevalence (ages 15-49, %)[c]	2006-2010	54.3[d]
International migrant stock (000 and % of total population)	mid-2010	12.6/12.1
Refugees and others of concern to UNHCR	end-2010	3
Education: Government expenditure (% of GDP)	2005-2011	3.9[e]
Education: Primary-secondary gross enrolment ratio (f/m per 100)	2005-2011	105.1/105.7
Education: Female third-level students (% of total)	2005-2011	57.1
Seats held by women in national parliaments (%)	2011	13.3

Environmental indicators		
Threatened species	2011	42
Forested area (% of land area)	2009	50.0
CO_2 emission estimates (000 metric tons and metric tons per capita)	2008	245/2.4
Energy consumption per capita (kilograms oil equivalent)	2009	795.0

a Official rate. b 2009. c Age group 15 to 44 years. d 1990. e 2003.

Guadeloupe

Region	Caribbean
Currency	Euro (EUR)
Surface area (square kilometres)	1 705
Population in 2010 (estimated, 000)	461 [a]
Population density in 2010 (per square kilometre)	270.2
Capital city and population in 2011 (000)	Basse-Terre (13)

Economic indicators	2000	2005	2010
Exchange rates (national currency per US$) [b]	1.07	0.85	0.75
CPI: Consumer price index (2000=100)	100	112	122
Agricultural production index (2004-2006=100)	118	103	103
Food production index (2004-2006=100)	118	103	103
Labour force participation, adult female pop. (%)	55.1	54.5	54.3
Labour force participation, adult male pop. (%)	70.0	67.5	65.3
Tourist arrivals at national borders (000) [c d]	603 [e]	372 [f]	347 [g]
Energy production, primary (000 mt oil equivalent) [h]	...	22	47 [g]
Telephone subscribers, total (per 100 inhabitants)	87.7	51.6 [i]	55.5 [i]
Internet users (per 100 inhabitants)	5.8	18.7	23.4 [g]

Social indicators		
Population growth rate (average annual %) [a]	2010-2015	0.5
Urban population growth rate (average annual %)	2010-2015	0.5
Rural population growth rate (average annual %)	2010-2015	0.1
Urban population (%) [a]	2011	98.4
Population aged 0-14 years (%) [a]	2011	22.2
Population aged 60+ years (females and males, % of total) [a]	2011	18.8/16.2
Sex ratio (males per 100 females) [a]	2011	89.2
Life expectancy at birth (females and males, years) [a]	2010-2015	83.6/76.1
Infant mortality rate (per 1 000 live births) [a]	2010-2015	6.7
Fertility rate, total (live births per woman) [a]	2010-2015	2.1
Contraceptive prevalence (ages 15-49, %)	2006-2010	29.4 [i]
International migrant stock (000 and % of total population)	mid-2010	104.9/22.5

Environmental indicators		
Threatened species	2011	57
Forested area (% of land area)	2009	38.3
CO$_2$ emission estimates (000 metric tons and metric tons per capita)	2008	2 198/4.7
Energy consumption per capita (kilograms oil equivalent)	2009	1 282.0 [h]
Rainfall in the capital city, total mean (millimetres) [k]		1 779
Temperature in the capital city, mean °C (minimum and maximum) [k]		22.1/30.5

a Includes Saint-Barthélemy and Saint-Martin (French part). **b** Market rate. **c** Air arrivals. **d** Excludes Saint-Barthélemy and Saint-Martin (French part). **e** Non-resident tourists staying in all types of accommodation establishments. **f** Data based on a survey conducted at Guadeloupe airport. **g** 2009. **h** UNSD estimate. **i** Main telephone lines only. **j** 1975-1976. **k** Le Raizet.

Guam

	Region	Oceania-Micronesia
	Currency	U.S. Dollar (USD)
Surface area (square kilometres)		549
Population in 2010 (estimated, 000)		180
Population density in 2010 (per square kilometre)		327.7
Capital city and population in 2011 (000)		Hagåtña (169)

Economic indicators	2000	2005	2010
CPI: Consumer price index (2000=100)	100	116	154
Agricultural production index (2004-2006=100)	98	100	138
Food production index (2004-2006=100)	98	100	138
Labour force participation, adult female pop. (%)	49.8	48.6	47.5
Labour force participation, adult male pop. (%)	76.7	75.4	73.8
Tourist arrivals at national borders (000)	1 287	1 228	1 196
Telephone subscribers, total (per 100 inhabitants)	65.5	38.9[a]	36.4[a]
Internet users (per 100 inhabitants)	16.1	38.6	50.6[b]

Social indicators		
Population growth rate (average annual %)	2010-2015	1.2
Urban population growth rate (average annual %)	2010-2015	1.2
Rural population growth rate (average annual %)	2010-2015	0.7
Urban population (%)	2011	93.2
Population aged 0-14 years (%)	2011	27.0
Population aged 60+ years (females and males, % of total)	2011	12.0/10.5
Sex ratio (males per 100 females)	2011	103.4
Life expectancy at birth (females and males, years)	2010-2015	78.8/74.1
Infant mortality rate (per 1 000 live births)	2010-2015	8.1
Fertility rate, total (live births per woman)	2010-2015	2.4
Contraceptive prevalence (ages 15-49, %)[c]	2006-2010	66.6[d]
International migrant stock (000 and % of total population)	mid-2010	78.9/43.9

Environmental indicators		
Threatened species	2011	36
Forested area (% of land area)	2009	47.9

a Main telephone lines only. b 2009. c Age group 18 to 44 years. d 2002.

Guatemala

Region	Central America
Currency	Quetzal (GTQ)
Surface area (square kilometres)	108 889
Population in 2010 (estimated, 000)	14 389
Population density in 2010 (per square kilometre)	132.1
Capital city and population in 2011 (000)	Guatemala City (1 168)
United Nations membership date	21 November 1945

Economic indicators	2000	2005	2010
GDP: Gross domestic product (million current US$)	17 196	27 211	41 473
GDP: Growth rate at constant 2005 prices (annual %)	3.6	3.3	2.6
GDP per capita (current US$)	1 530.3	2 139.7	2 882.3
GNI: Gross national income per capita (current US$)	1 511.1	2 113.3	2 823.9
Gross fixed capital formation (% of GDP)	19.1	18.3	15.8
Exchange rates (national currency per US$) [a]	7.73	7.61	8.02
Balance of payments, current account (million US$)	−1 050	−1 301	−878
CPI: Consumer price index (2000=100) [b]	100	144	193
Agricultural production index (2004-2006=100)	85	101	124
Food production index (2004-2006=100)	82	101	126
Employment in industrial sector (% of employed) [c]	22.5	22.8[d]	...
Employment in agricultural sector (% of employed) [c]	39.8	33.2[d]	...
Labour force participation, adult female pop. (%)	41.9	44.9	48.8
Labour force participation, adult male pop. (%)	86.1	87.5	88.3
Tourist arrivals at national borders (000) [e]	826	1 316	1 876
Energy production, primary (000 mt oil equivalent)	1 231	1 378	925[f]
Telephone subscribers, total (per 100 inhabitants)	13.7	45.3	136.0
Internet users (per 100 inhabitants)	0.7	5.7	10.5

Total trade		Major trading partners			2010
	(million US$)	(% of exports)			(% of imports)
Exports	8 460.2	United States	38.8	United States	37.1
Imports	13 830.3	El Salvador	11.7	Mexico	11.2
Balance	−5 370.1	Honduras	8.3	China	7.1

Social indicators		
Population growth rate (average annual %)	2010-2015	2.5
Urban population growth rate (average annual %)	2010-2015	3.4
Rural population growth rate (average annual %)	2010-2015	1.6
Urban population (%)	2011	49.8
Population aged 0-14 years (%)	2011	41.1
Population aged 60+ years (females and males, % of total)	2011	6.7/6.2
Sex ratio (males per 100 females)	2011	95.1
Life expectancy at birth (females and males, years)	2010-2015	75.1/68.0
Infant mortality rate (per 1 000 live births)	2010-2015	26.3
Fertility rate, total (live births per woman)	2010-2015	3.8
Contraceptive prevalence (ages 15-49, %)	2006-2010	43.3[g]
International migrant stock (000 and % of total population) [h]	mid-2010	59.5/0.4
Refugees and others of concern to UNHCR	end-2010	140
Education: Government expenditure (% of GDP)	2005-2011	3.2
Education: Primary-secondary gross enrolment ratio (f/m per 100)	2005-2011	89.4/94.4
Education: Female third-level students (% of total)	2005-2011	50.8
Seats held by women in national parliaments (%) [i]	2011	12.0

Environmental indicators		
Threatened species	2011	237
Forested area (% of land area)	2009	34.7
CO₂ emission estimates (000 metric tons and metric tons per capita)	2008	11 904/0.9
Energy consumption per capita (kilograms oil equivalent)	2009	335.0
Rainfall in the capital city, total mean (millimetres)		1 186
Temperature in the capital city, mean °C (minimum and maximum)		14.7/25.0

a Market rate. **b** Guatemala City. **c** Age group 10 years and over. **d** 2006. **e** Arrivals of non-resident visitors at national borders. **f** 2009. **g** 2002. **h** Includes refugees. **i** As of 31 August 2011.

Guinea

Region	Western Africa
Currency	Guinean Franc (GNF)
Surface area (square kilometres)	245 857
Population in 2010 (estimated, 000)	9 982
Population density in 2010 (per square kilometre)	40.6
Capital city and population in 2011 (000)	Conakry (1 786)
United Nations membership date	12 December 1958

Economic indicators	2000	2005	2010
GDP: Gross domestic product (million current US$)	3 192	2 937	4 267
GDP: Growth rate at constant 2005 prices (annual %)	2.9	3.0	1.9
GDP per capita (current US$)	382.5	324.9	427.5
GNI: Gross national income per capita (current US$)	373.0	294.0	382.7
Gross fixed capital formation (% of GDP)	35.4	27.6	18.0
Exchange rates (national currency per US$)[a]	1 882.27	4 500.00	5 160.96[b]
Balance of payments, current account (million US$)	−155	−160	−329
CPI: Consumer price index (2000=100)[c]	100	185	439
Agricultural production index (2004-2006=100)	84	101	113
Food production index (2004-2006=100)	82	101	113
Labour force participation, adult female pop. (%)	63.3	63.7	65.2
Labour force participation, adult male pop. (%)	78.3	78.3	78.3
Tourist arrivals at national borders (000)[d]	33	45	30[e]
Energy production, primary (000 mt oil equivalent)	44	43	45[f]
Telephone subscribers, total (per 100 inhabitants)	0.8	2.4	40.3
Internet users (per 100 inhabitants)	0.1	0.5	1.0

Total trade		Major trading partners			2010
	(million US$)[b]	(% of exports)[b]			(% of imports)[b]
Exports	1 430.5	France	24.5	Netherlands	20.6
Imports	1 835.5	Switzerland	19.5	France	10.1
Balance	−405.0	Russian Federation	10.6	United Kingdom	7.9

Social indicators		
Population growth rate (average annual %)	2010-2015	2.5
Urban population growth rate (average annual %)	2010-2015	3.9
Rural population growth rate (average annual %)	2010-2015	1.8
Urban population (%)	2011	35.4
Population aged 0-14 years (%)	2011	42.8
Population aged 60+ years (females and males, % of total)	2011	5.5/4.6
Sex ratio (males per 100 females)	2011	102.2
Life expectancy at birth (females and males, years)	2010-2015	56.4/53.2
Infant mortality rate (per 1 000 live births)	2010-2015	84.2
Fertility rate, total (live births per woman)	2010-2015	5.0
Contraceptive prevalence (ages 15-49, %)	2006-2010	9.1[g]
International migrant stock (000 and % of total population)[hi]	mid-2010	394.6/3.8
Refugees and others of concern to UNHCR	end-2010	14 878
Education: Government expenditure (% of GDP)	2005-2011	2.4
Education: Primary-secondary gross enrolment ratio (f/m per 100)[j]	2005-2011	56.7/73.7
Education: Female third-level students (% of total)	2005-2011	24.4

Environmental indicators		
Threatened species	2011	136
Forested area (% of land area)	2009	26.8
CO$_2$ emission estimates (000 metric tons and metric tons per capita)	2008	1 392/0.2
Energy consumption per capita (kilograms oil equivalent)	2009	46.0[k]
Rainfall in the capital city, total mean (millimetres)		3 776
Temperature in the capital city, mean °C (minimum and maximum)		22.9/29.9

a Market rate. **b** 2008. **c** Conakry. **d** Air arrivals at Conakry airport. **e** 2007. **f** 2009. **g** 2005. **h** Data refer to foreign citizens. **i** Includes refugees. **j** UNESCO estimate. **k** UNSD estimate.

Guinea-Bissau

Region	Western Africa
Currency	CFA Franc (XOF)
Surface area (square kilometres)	36 125
Population in 2010 (estimated, 000)	1 515
Population density in 2010 (per square kilometre)	41.9
Capital city and population in 2011 (000)	Bissau (423)
United Nations membership date	17 September 1974

Economic indicators	2000	2005	2010
GDP: Gross domestic product (million current US$)	371	573	817
GDP: Growth rate at constant 2005 prices (annual %)	7.5	4.0	1.6
GDP per capita (current US$)	299.2	419.1	539.4
GNI: Gross national income per capita (current US$)	282.0	410.6	532.7
Gross fixed capital formation (% of GDP)	11.3	6.2	7.2
Exchange rates (national currency per US$)[a]	704.95	556.04	490.91
Balance of payments, current account (million US$)	−27[b]	−46	−114[c]
CPI: Consumer price index (2000=100)[de]	100[f]	104	123[g]
Agricultural production index (2004-2006=100)	87	99	120
Food production index (2004-2006=100)	87	99	120
Labour force participation, adult female pop. (%)	63.1	66.1	67.8
Labour force participation, adult male pop. (%)	78.5	78.3	78.2
Tourist arrivals at national borders (000)[h]	8[b]	5	30[i]
Telephone subscribers, total (per 100 inhabitants)	0.9[j]	7.9	39.5
Internet users (per 100 inhabitants)	0.2	1.9	2.5

Social indicators		
Population growth rate (average annual %)	2010-2015	2.1
Urban population growth rate (average annual %)	2010-2015	3.6
Rural population growth rate (average annual %)	2010-2015	0.9
Urban population (%)	2011	43.9
Population aged 0-14 years (%)	2011	41.2
Population aged 60+ years (females and males, % of total)	2011	5.7/5.0
Sex ratio (males per 100 females)	2011	98.3
Life expectancy at birth (females and males, years)	2010-2015	50.4/47.3
Infant mortality rate (per 1 000 live births)	2010-2015	109.8
Fertility rate, total (live births per woman)	2010-2015	4.9
Contraceptive prevalence (ages 15-49, %)	2006-2010	10.3
International migrant stock (000 and % of total population)[k]	mid-2010	19.2/1.2
Refugees and others of concern to UNHCR	end-2010	8 009
Education: Government expenditure (% of GDP)	2005-2011	5.3[l]
Education: Primary-secondary gross enrolment ratio (f/m per 100)	2005-2011	42.2/64.5[m]
Education: Female third-level students (% of total)[n]	2005-2011	15.6[b]
Seats held by women in national parliaments (%)	2011	10.0

Environmental indicators		
Threatened species	2011	56
Forested area (% of land area)	2009	72.3
CO_2 emission estimates (000 metric tons and metric tons per capita)	2008	282/0.2
Energy consumption per capita (kilograms oil equivalent)	2009	65.0[o]
Rainfall in the capital city, total mean (millimetres)		1 756[p]
Temperature in the capital city, mean °C (minimum and maximum)		19.7/32.1[p]

a Official rate. **b** 2001. **c** 2009. **d** Bissau. **e** Index base 2003=100. **f** 2003. **g** 2008. **h** Air arrivals. **i** 2007. **j** Main telephone lines only. **k** Includes refugees. **l** 1999. **m** 2000. **n** UNESCO estimate. **o** UNSD estimate. **p** January to November only.

Guyana

Region	South America
Currency	Guyana Dollar (GYD)
Surface area (square kilometres)	214 969
Population in 2010 (estimated, 000)	754
Population density in 2010 (per square kilometre)	3.5
Capital city and population in 2011 (000)	Georgetown (127)
United Nations membership date	20 September 1966

Economic indicators	2000	2005	2010
GDP: Gross domestic product (million current US$)	1 137	1 315	2 260
GDP: Growth rate at constant 2005 prices (annual %)	−1.4	−2.0	3.6
GDP per capita (current US$)	1 550.3	1 762.8	2 996.0
GNI: Gross national income per capita (current US$)	1 482.0	1 751.4	2 952.2
Gross fixed capital formation (% of GDP)	24.2	20.3	25.8
Exchange rates (national currency per US$)[a]	184.75	200.25	203.50
Balance of payments, current account (million US$)	−82	−96	−160
CPI: Consumer price index (2000=100)[b]	100	128	177
Agricultural production index (2004-2006=100)	96	94	98
Food production index (2004-2006=100)	97	94	98
Employment in industrial sector (% of employed)	22.6[c]	...	...
Employment in agricultural sector (% of employed)	27.8[c]	...	...
Labour force participation, adult female pop. (%)	39.2	39.2	41.3
Labour force participation, adult male pop. (%)	81.3	81.7	79.6
Tourist arrivals at national borders (000)	105	117[d]	150[d]
Telephone subscribers, total (per 100 inhabitants)	14.8	52.5	93.5
Internet users (per 100 inhabitants)	6.6	18.2[e]	29.9

Total trade		Major trading partners			2010
	(million US$)		(% of exports)		(% of imports)
Exports	936.7	United States	21.8	United States	28.1
Imports	1 448.3	Canada	18.5	Trinidad and Tobago	17.1
Balance	−511.6	United Kingdom	9.5	Netherlands Antilles	8.9

Social indicators		
Population growth rate (average annual %)	2010-2015	0.2
Urban population growth rate (average annual %)	2010-2015	0.5
Rural population growth rate (average annual %)	2010-2015	0.1
Urban population (%)	2011	28.4
Population aged 0-14 years (%)	2011	32.4
Population aged 60+ years (females and males, % of total)	2011	7.7/5.7
Sex ratio (males per 100 females)	2011	100.9
Life expectancy at birth (females and males, years)	2010-2015	73.5/67.2
Infant mortality rate (per 1 000 live births)	2010-2015	36.8
Fertility rate, total (live births per woman)	2010-2015	2.2
Contraceptive prevalence (ages 15-49, %)	2006-2010	42.5
International migrant stock (000 and % of total population)	mid-2010	11.6/1.5
Refugees and others of concern to UNHCR	end-2010	7
Education: Government expenditure (% of GDP)	2005-2011	3.7
Education: Primary-secondary gross enrolment ratio (f/m per 100)	2005-2011	90.5/84.7
Education: Female third-level students (% of total)	2005-2011	70.8
Seats held by women in national parliaments (%)[f]	2011	30.0

Environmental indicators		
Threatened species	2011	73
Forested area (% of land area)	2009	77.2
CO_2 emission estimates (000 metric tons and metric tons per capita)	2008	1 524/2.0
Energy consumption per capita (kilograms oil equivalent)	2009	686.0
Rainfall in the capital city, total mean (millimetres)		2 260
Temperature in the capital city, mean °C (minimum and maximum)		24.0/29.6

a Principal rate. b Georgetown. c 2001. d Arrivals at Timehri airport only. e 2008. f As of 31 October 2011.

Haiti

Region	Caribbean
Currency	Gourde (HTG)
Surface area (square kilometres)	27 750
Population in 2010 (estimated, 000)	9 993
Population density in 2010 (per square kilometre)	360.1
Capital city and population in 2011 (000)	Port-au-Prince (2 207)
United Nations membership date	24 October 1945

Economic indicators	2000	2005	2010
GDP: Gross domestic product (million current US$)	3 358	3 807	6 123
GDP: Growth rate at constant 2005 prices (annual %)	0.9	1.8	−5.1
GDP per capita (current US$)	388.4	407.3	612.7
GNI: Gross national income per capita (current US$)	387.0	400.4	611.7
Gross fixed capital formation (% of GDP)	14.3	14.3	13.1
Exchange rates (national currency per US$)[a]	22.52	43.00	39.88
Balance of payments, current account (million US$)	−114	−361	−1 956
CPI: Consumer price index (2000=100)[b]	100	255	380
Agricultural production index (2004-2006=100)	99	102	107
Food production index (2004-2006=100)	99	102	108
Labour force participation, adult female pop. (%)	56.9	58.2	59.8
Labour force participation, adult male pop. (%)	69.0	69.5	70.5
Tourist arrivals at national borders (000)[c]	140	112	423[de]
Energy production, primary (000 mt oil equivalent)	24	23	18[e]
Telephone subscribers, total (per 100 inhabitants)	1.5	6.9	40.5
Internet users (per 100 inhabitants)	0.2	6.4	8.4

Social indicators		
Population growth rate (average annual %)	2010-2015	1.3
Urban population growth rate (average annual %)	2010-2015	3.7
Rural population growth rate (average annual %)	2010-2015	−1.7
Urban population (%)	2011	53.4
Population aged 0-14 years (%)	2011	35.6
Population aged 60+ years (females and males, % of total)	2011	7.1/6.1
Sex ratio (males per 100 females)	2011	98.4
Life expectancy at birth (females and males, years)	2010-2015	63.9/61.1
Infant mortality rate (per 1 000 live births)	2010-2015	58.3
Fertility rate, total (live births per woman)	2010-2015	3.2
Contraceptive prevalence (ages 15-49, %)	2006-2010	32.0[f]
International migrant stock (000 and % of total population)	mid-2010	35.0/0.3
Refugees and others of concern to UNHCR	end-2010	5
Seats held by women in national parliaments (%)	2011	4.2

Environmental indicators		
Threatened species	2011	142
Forested area (% of land area)	2009	3.7
CO_2 emission estimates (000 metric tons and metric tons per capita)	2008	2 433/0.3
Energy consumption per capita (kilograms oil equivalent)	2009	74.0

a Principal rate. b Metropolitan areas. c Air arrivals. d Includes nationals residing abroad. e 2009. f 2005-2006.

Honduras

Region	Central America
Currency	Lempira (HNL)
Surface area (square kilometres)	112 492
Population in 2010 (estimated, 000)	7 601
Population density in 2010 (per square kilometre)	67.6
Capital city and population in 2011 (000)	Tegucigalpa (1 088)
United Nations membership date	17 December 1945

Economic indicators	2000	2005	2010
GDP: Gross domestic product (million current US$)	7 187	9 757	15 400
GDP: Growth rate at constant 2005 prices (annual %)	5.8	6.1	2.8
GDP per capita (current US$)	1 155.9	1 418.3	2 026.2
GNI: Gross national income per capita (current US$)	1 120.0	1 351.9	1 946.9
Gross fixed capital formation (% of GDP)	25.8	24.9	23.4
Exchange rates (national currency per US$) [a]	15.14	18.90	18.90
Balance of payments, current account (million US$)	−508	−304	−955
CPI: Consumer price index (2000=100)	100	150	208
Industrial production index (2005=100) [b]	99[c]	100	101
Agricultural production index (2004-2006=100)	71	101	109
Food production index (2004-2006=100)	68	102	108
Employment in industrial sector (% of employed) [d]	22.2[ef]	20.9[g]	...
Employment in agricultural sector (% of employed) [d]	36.9[ef]	39.2[g]	...
Labour force participation, adult female pop. (%)	44.4	39.6	41.9
Labour force participation, adult male pop. (%)	88.0	83.7	82.9
Tourist arrivals at national borders (000)	471	673	896
Energy production, primary (000 mt oil equivalent)	194	148	240[h]
Telephone subscribers, total (per 100 inhabitants)	7.3	25.8	133.9
Internet users (per 100 inhabitants)	1.2	6.5	11.1

Total trade		Major trading partners			2010
	(million US$)[h]	(% of exports)[h]			(% of imports)[h]
Exports	2 628.3	United States	47.7	United States	36.0
Imports	5 953.5	El Salvador	7.0	Guatemala	10.6
Balance	−3 325.2	Germany	6.5	Mexico	6.6

Social indicators		
Population growth rate (average annual %)	2010-2015	2.0
Urban population growth rate (average annual %)	2010-2015	3.1
Rural population growth rate (average annual %)	2010-2015	0.8
Urban population (%)	2011	52.2
Population aged 0-14 years (%)	2011	36.2
Population aged 60+ years (females and males, % of total)	2011	6.6/6.0
Sex ratio (males per 100 females)	2011	100.0
Life expectancy at birth (females and males, years)	2010-2015	75.9/71.3
Infant mortality rate (per 1 000 live births)	2010-2015	23.5
Fertility rate, total (live births per woman)	2010-2015	3.0
Contraceptive prevalence (ages 15-49, %)	2006-2010	65.2[i]
International migrant stock (000 and % of total population)[i]	mid-2010	24.3/0.3
Refugees and others of concern to UNHCR	end-2010	14
Education: Primary-secondary gross enrolment ratio (f/m per 100)	2005-2011	100.2/93.5
Education: Female third-level students (% of total) [k]	2005-2011	60.0
Seats held by women in national parliaments (%)	2011	18.0

Environmental indicators		
Threatened species	2011	249
Forested area (% of land area)	2009	47.5
CO$_2$ emission estimates (000 metric tons and metric tons per capita)	2008	8 665/1.2
Energy consumption per capita (kilograms oil equivalent)	2009	331.0
Rainfall in the capital city, total mean (millimetres)		872
Temperature in the capital city, mean °C (minimum and maximum)		16.7/27.9

a Principal rate. b The indices are shown in terms of ISIC Rev. 3. c 2003. d Age group 10 years and over.
e 2001. f Excludes the provinces of Gracias a Dios and Islas de la Bahía. g September. h 2009. i 2005-2006.
j Includes refugees. k National estimate.

Hungary

Region	Eastern Europe
Currency	Forint (HUF)
Surface area (square kilometres)	93 027
Population in 2010 (estimated, 000)	9 984
Population density in 2010 (per square kilometre)	107.3
Capital city and population in 2011 (000)	Budapest (1 737)
United Nations membership date	14 December 1955

Economic indicators	2000	2005	2010
GDP: Gross domestic product (million current US$)	46 386	110 322	128 629
GDP: Growth rate at constant 2005 prices (annual %)	4.2	4.0	1.3
GDP per capita (current US$)	4 542.9	10 937.1	12 884.0
GNI: Gross national income per capita (current US$)	4 317.6	10 346.8	12 257.1
Gross fixed capital formation (% of GDP)	24.4	22.8	18.0
Exchange rates (national currency per US$) [a]	284.73	213.58	208.65
Balance of payments, current account (million US$)	...	−8 238	1 417
CPI: Consumer price index (2000=100)	100	133	165[b]
Industrial production index (2005=100)	87[c]	100	108
Agricultural production index (2004-2006=100)	91	96	81
Food production index (2004-2006=100)	91	96	81
Unemployment (% of labour force)	6.1[d]	7.2	11.2
Employment in industrial sector (% of employed) [e]	33.7[f]	32.4[f]	30.7[g]
Employment in agricultural sector (% of employed) [e]	6.5[f]	5.0[f]	4.5[g]
Labour force participation, adult female pop. (%)	41.4	42.9	43.8
Labour force participation, adult male pop. (%)	58.0	58.3	58.4
Tourist arrivals at national borders (000)	2 992[h]	9 979	9 510
Energy production, primary (000 mt oil equivalent)	8 601	7 028	6 879[b]
Telephone subscribers, total (per 100 inhabitants)	67.3	126.3	150.1
Internet users (per 100 inhabitants)	7.0	39.0	65.3

Total trade		Major trading partners			2010
	(million US$)	(% of exports)		(% of imports)	
Exports	94 748.7	Germany	25.1	Germany	24.0
Imports	87 432.1	Italy	5.5	Russian Federation	7.8
Balance	7 316.6	United Kingdom	5.4	China	7.1

Social indicators		
Population growth rate (average annual %)	2010-2015	−0.2
Urban population growth rate (average annual %)	2010-2015	0.5
Rural population growth rate (average annual %)	2010-2015	−1.7
Urban population (%)	2011	69.5
Population aged 0-14 years (%)	2011	14.7
Population aged 60+ years (females and males, % of total)	2011	26.7/18.7
Sex ratio (males per 100 females)	2011	90.4
Life expectancy at birth (females and males, years)	2010-2015	78.5/70.8
Infant mortality rate (per 1 000 live births)	2010-2015	5.3
Fertility rate, total (live births per woman)	2010-2015	1.4
Contraceptive prevalence (ages 15-49, %) [i]	2006-2010	80.6[j]
International migrant stock (000 and % of total population) [k]	mid-2010	368.1/3.7
Refugees and others of concern to UNHCR	end-2010	5 843
Education: Government expenditure (% of GDP)	2005-2011	5.1
Education: Primary-secondary gross enrolment ratio (f/m per 100)	2005-2011	98.6/99.9
Education: Female third-level students (% of total)	2005-2011	56.8
Deaths by assault (females and males, per 100 000)	2005-2008	1.6/2.5
Seats held by women in national parliaments (%)	2011	9.1

Environmental indicators		
Threatened species	2011	47
Forested area (% of land area)	2009	22.3
CO₂ emission estimates (000 metric tons and metric tons per capita)	2008	54 594/5.5
Energy consumption per capita (kilograms oil equivalent)	2009	2 103.0
Rainfall in the capital city, total mean (millimetres)		516
Temperature in the capital city, mean °C (minimum and maximum)		6.3/15.0

a Official rate. b 2009. c 2003. d 2004. e Age group 15 to 74 years. f Excludes conscripts. g European Labour Force Survey (Eurostat). h Arrivals of non-resident tourists in all types of accommodation establishments. i Age group 18 to 41 years. j 1992-1993. k Includes refugees.

Iceland

Region	Northern Europe
Currency	Icelandic Krona (ISK)
Surface area (square kilometres)	103 000
Population in 2010 (estimated, 000)	320
Population density in 2010 (per square kilometre)	3.1
Capital city and population in 2011 (000)	Reykjavík (206)
United Nations membership date	19 November 1946

Economic indicators	2000	2005	2010
GDP: Gross domestic product (million current US$)	8 697	16 286	12 574
GDP: Growth rate at constant 2005 prices (annual %)	4.3	7.2	−4.0
GDP per capita (current US$)	30 928.2	54 883.6	39 278.0
GNI: Gross national income per capita (current US$)	30 072.8	52 906.3	31 158.6
Gross fixed capital formation (% of GDP)	22.9	28.3	13.0
Exchange rates (national currency per US$) [a]	84.70	62.98	115.05
Balance of payments, current account (million US$)	−847	−2 648	−1 417
CPI: Consumer price index (2000=100) [b]	100	123	155[c]
Agricultural production index (2004-2006=100)	96	99	109
Food production index (2004-2006=100)	95	99	109
Unemployment (% of labour force) [d]	3.0[e]	2.5	7.6
Employment in industrial sector (% of employed) [f]	23.0[g]	21.7	17.9[h]
Employment in agricultural sector (% of employed) [f]	8.3[g]	6.5	5.5[h]
Labour force participation, adult female pop. (%)	71.5	70.8	70.8
Labour force participation, adult male pop. (%)	82.2	80.2	78.2
Tourist arrivals at national borders (000) [i]	634	871	1 213
Energy production, primary (000 mt oil equivalent)	836	953	1 691[j]
Telephone subscribers, total (per 100 inhabitants)	146.2	160.7	167.0
Internet users (per 100 inhabitants)	44.5	87.0	95.0

Total trade	Major trading partners				2010
(million US$)	(% of exports)			(% of imports)	
Exports	4 603.1	Netherlands	34.0	Norway	9.1
Imports	3 914.3	Germany	14.0	Brazil	8.7
Balance	688.8	United Kingdom	10.1	Netherlands	8.5

Social indicators

Population growth rate (average annual %)	2010-2015	1.2
Urban population growth rate (average annual %)	2010-2015	1.3
Rural population growth rate (average annual %)	2010-2015	−0.6
Urban population (%)	2011	93.7
Population aged 0-14 years (%)	2011	20.8
Population aged 60+ years (females and males, % of total)	2011	18.1/16.2
Sex ratio (males per 100 females)	2011	101.5
Life expectancy at birth (females and males, years)	2010-2015	83.8/80.3
Infant mortality rate (per 1 000 live births)	2010-2015	2.1
Fertility rate, total (live births per woman)	2010-2015	2.1
International migrant stock (000 and % of total population)	mid-2010	37.2/11.3
Refugees and others of concern to UNHCR	end-2010	235
Education: Government expenditure (% of GDP)	2005-2011	7.6
Education: Primary-secondary gross enrolment ratio (f/m per 100)	2005-2011	104.3/102.7
Education: Female third-level students (% of total)	2005-2011	64.3
Deaths by assault (females and males, per 100 000)	2005-2008	0.6/...[k]
Seats held by women in national parliaments (%)	2011	42.9

Environmental indicators

Threatened species	2011	17
Forested area (% of land area)	2009	<
CO$_2$ emission estimates (000 metric tons and metric tons per capita)	2008	2 228/7.1
Energy consumption per capita (kilograms oil equivalent)	2009	7 377.0
Rainfall in the capital city, total mean (millimetres)		798
Temperature in the capital city, mean °C (minimum and maximum)		1.9/7.0

a Official rate. b Annual averages are based on the months February-December and January of the following year. c 2008. d Age group 16 years and over. e 2004. f Age group 16 to 74 years. g Average of April and November. h European Labour Force Survey (Eurostat). i Arrivals of non-resident tourists in all types of accommodation establishments. j 2009. k Rate based on 30 or fewer events.

India

Region	South-central Asia
Currency	Indian Rupee (INR)
Surface area (square kilometres)	3 287 263
Population in 2010 (estimated, 000)	1 224 614
Population density in 2010 (per square kilometre)	372.5
Capital city and population in 2011 (000)	New Delhi (...)[a]
United Nations membership date	30 October 1945

Economic indicators	2000	2005	2010
GDP: Gross domestic product (million current US$)	467 788	837 299	1 722 330
GDP: Growth rate at constant 2005 prices (annual %)	4.0	9.3	8.8
GDP per capita (current US$)	443.9	734.4	1 406.4
GNI: Gross national income per capita (current US$)	439.1	729.3	1 394.7
Gross fixed capital formation (% of GDP)	23.4	31.5	31.5
Exchange rates (national currency per US$)[b]	46.75	45.06	44.81
Balance of payments, current account (million US$)	−4 601	−10 284	−51 781
CPI: Consumer price index (2000=100)	100	122	183
Industrial production index (2005=100)[c]	83[d]	100	152
Agricultural production index (2004-2006=100)	90	100	119
Food production index (2004-2006=100)	91	100	118
Employment in industrial sector (% of employed)[efg]	16.1	19.0	22.4
Employment in agricultural sector (% of employed)[efg]	59.8	55.8	51.1
Labour force participation, adult female pop. (%)	34.3	37.0	29.0
Labour force participation, adult male pop. (%)	83.0	83.3	80.7
Tourist arrivals at national borders (000)[h]	2 649	3 919	5 776
Energy production, primary (000 mt oil equivalent)	253 768	314 739	403 962[i]
Telephone subscribers, total (per 100 inhabitants)	3.4	12.3	64.3
Internet users (per 100 inhabitants)	0.5	2.4	7.5

Total trade		Major trading partners			2010
	(million US$)	(% of exports)		(% of imports)	
Exports	220 408.5	United Arab Emirates	12.4	China	11.8
Imports	350 029.4	United States	10.7	United Arab Emirates	8.8
Balance	−129 620.9	China	7.9	Switzerland	6.3

Social indicators		
Population growth rate (average annual %)	2010-2015	1.3
Urban population growth rate (average annual %)	2010-2015	2.5
Rural population growth rate (average annual %)	2010-2015	0.8
Urban population (%)	2011	31.3
Population aged 0-14 years (%)	2011	30.2
Population aged 60+ years (females and males, % of total)	2011	8.4/7.2
Sex ratio (males per 100 females)	2011	106.8
Life expectancy at birth (females and males, years)	2010-2015	67.6/64.4
Infant mortality rate (per 1 000 live births)	2010-2015	47.9
Fertility rate, total (live births per woman)	2010-2015	2.5
Contraceptive prevalence (ages 15-49, %)	2006-2010	56.3[j]
International migrant stock (000 and % of total population)[k]	mid-2010	5 436.0/0.5
Refugees and others of concern to UNHCR	end-2010	188 567
Education: Government expenditure (% of GDP)	2005-2011	3.1
Education: Primary-secondary gross enrolment ratio (f/m per 100)	2005-2011	77.6/84.2
Education: Female third-level students (% of total)	2005-2011	38.6
Seats held by women in national parliaments (%)	2011	10.8

Environmental indicators		
Threatened species	2011	919
Forested area (% of land area)	2009	23.0
CO$_2$ emission estimates (000 metric tons and metric tons per capita)	2008	1 741 272/1.5
Energy consumption per capita (kilograms oil equivalent)	2009	439.0
Rainfall in the capital city, total mean (millimetres)		790
Temperature in the capital city, mean °C (minimum and maximum)		19.8/32.2

a The population of New Delhi was estimated at 249,998 in the year 2011. New Delhi is included in the urban agglomeration of Delhi, the population of which is 22,653,600. **b** Market rate. **c** The indices are shown in terms of ISIC Rev. 3. **d** 2003. **e** Data are based on the national sample survey conducted every five years. **f** Excludes Leh and Kargil of Jammu and Kashmi districts, some villages in Nagaland, Andaman and Nicobar Islands. **g** July of the preceding year to June of the current year. **h** Excludes nationals residing abroad. **i** 2009. **j** 2005-2006. **k** Includes refugees.

Indonesia

Region	South-eastern Asia
Currency	Rupiah (IDR)
Surface area (square kilometres)	1 910 931
Population in 2010 (estimated, 000)	239 871
Population density in 2010 (per square kilometre)	125.5
Capital city and population in 2011 (000)	Jakarta (9 769)
United Nations membership date	28 September 1950

Economic indicators	2000	2005	2010
GDP: Gross domestic product (million current US$)	165 021	285 869	707 448
GDP: Growth rate at constant 2005 prices (annual %)	4.9	5.7	6.1
GDP per capita (current US$)	773.3	1 257.7	2 949.3
GNI: Gross national income per capita (current US$)	717.0	1 109.2	2 611.5
Gross fixed capital formation (% of GDP)	19.9	23.6	32.2
Exchange rates (national currency per US$)[a]	9 595.00	9 830.00	8 991.00
Balance of payments, current account (million US$)	7 992	278	5 643
CPI: Consumer price index (2000=100)	100	156	227
Agricultural production index (2004-2006=100)	78	99	122
Food production index (2004-2006=100)	78	100	122
Unemployment (% of labour force)	...	10.8	7.3
Employment in industrial sector (% of employed)[b]	17.4	18.7	19.3
Employment in agricultural sector (% of employed)[b]	45.3	44.0	38.3
Labour force participation, adult female pop. (%)	50.4	50.0	51.0
Labour force participation, adult male pop. (%)	84.8	85.3	84.2
Tourist arrivals at national borders (000)	5 064	5 002	7 003
Energy production, primary (000 mt oil equivalent)	167 454[c]	219 724	293 181[d]
Telephone subscribers, total (per 100 inhabitants)	4.8	26.6	107.6
Internet users (per 100 inhabitants)	0.9	3.6	9.9

Total trade	Major trading partners				2010
(million US$)		(% of exports)			(% of imports)
Exports	157 779.1	Japan	16.3	China	15.1
Imports	135 663.3	China	9.9	Singapore	14.9
Balance	22 115.8	United States	9.1	Japan	12.5

Social indicators		
Population growth rate (average annual %)	2010-2015	1.0
Urban population growth rate (average annual %)	2010-2015	2.5
Rural population growth rate (average annual %)	2010-2015	−0.6
Urban population (%)	2011	50.7
Population aged 0-14 years (%)	2011	26.7
Population aged 60+ years (females and males, % of total)	2011	9.1/7.6
Sex ratio (males per 100 females)	2011	99.4
Life expectancy at birth (females and males, years)	2010-2015	71.8/68.3
Infant mortality rate (per 1 000 live births)	2010-2015	24.9
Fertility rate, total (live births per woman)	2010-2015	2.1
Contraceptive prevalence (ages 15-49, %)	2006-2010	61.4
International migrant stock (000 and % of total population)[ef]	mid-2010	122.9/0.1
Refugees and others of concern to UNHCR	end-2010	2 882
Education: Government expenditure (% of GDP)	2005-2011	4.6
Education: Primary-secondary gross enrolment ratio (f/m per 100)	2005-2011	98.1/97.0
Education: Female third-level students (% of total)	2005-2011	46.7
Seats held by women in national parliaments (%)	2011	18.0

Environmental indicators		
Threatened species	2011	1 149
Forested area (% of land area)	2009	52.5
CO$_2$ emission estimates (000 metric tons and metric tons per capita)	2008	405 696/1.8
Energy consumption per capita (kilograms oil equivalent)	2009	549.0
Rainfall in the capital city, total mean (millimetres)		1 655
Temperature in the capital city, mean °C (minimum and maximum)		25.0/31.8

a Market rate. **b** August. **c** Includes Timor-Leste. **d** 2009. **e** Data refer to foreign citizens. **f** Includes refugees.

Ireland

Region	Northern Europe	
Currency	Euro (EUR)	
Surface area (square kilometres)	70 273	
Population in 2010 (estimated, 000)	4 470	
Population density in 2010 (per square kilometre)	63.6	
Capital city and population in 2011 (000)	Dublin (1 121)	
United Nations membership date	14 December 1955	

Economic indicators	2000	2005	2010
GDP: Gross domestic product (million current US$)	97 525	203 280	206 600
GDP: Growth rate at constant 2005 prices (annual %)	9.3	5.3	−0.4
GDP per capita (current US$)	25 639.0	48 888.4	46 220.3
GNI: Gross national income per capita (current US$)	22 130.2	42 172.7	38 311.7
Gross fixed capital formation (% of GDP)	23.1	26.6	11.6
Exchange rates (national currency per US$) [a]	1.07	0.85	0.75
Balance of payments, current account (million US$)	−516	−7 150	954
CPI: Consumer price index (2000=100)	100	119	128
Industrial production index (2005=100)	95[b]	100	109
Agricultural production index (2004-2006=100)	103	99	100
Food production index (2004-2006=100)	103	99	100
Unemployment (% of labour force)	4.5[c]	4.3	13.6
Employment in industrial sector (% of employed)	27.7[d]	27.9[d]	19.5[e]
Employment in agricultural sector (% of employed)	6.5[d]	5.9[d]	4.6[e]
Labour force participation, adult female pop. (%)	47.2	51.9	52.4
Labour force participation, adult male pop. (%)	71.2	72.5	68.3
Tourist arrivals at national borders (000) [f]	6 646	7 333	7 189[g]
Energy production, primary (000 mt oil equivalent)	2 180	1 502	1 356[g]
Telephone subscribers, total (per 100 inhabitants)	112.9	152.0	151.7
Internet users (per 100 inhabitants)	17.9	41.6	69.9

Total trade		Major trading partners			2010
	(million US$)	(% of exports)		(% of imports)	
Exports	118 337.5	United States	23.3	United Kingdom	32.2
Imports	60 549.6	United Kingdom	15.5	United States	14.1
Balance	57 787.9	Belgium	15.1	Germany	7.6

Social indicators		
Population growth rate (average annual %)	2010-2015	1.1
Urban population growth rate (average annual %)	2010-2015	1.6
Rural population growth rate (average annual %)	2010-2015	0.3
Urban population (%)	2011	62.2
Population aged 0-14 years (%)	2011	21.4
Population aged 60+ years (females and males, % of total)	2011	17.9/15.7
Sex ratio (males per 100 females)	2011	100.2
Life expectancy at birth (females and males, years)	2010-2015	83.2/78.4
Infant mortality rate (per 1 000 live births)	2010-2015	3.9
Fertility rate, total (live births per woman)	2010-2015	2.1
Contraceptive prevalence (ages 15-49, %) [h]	2006-2010	64.8[i]
International migrant stock (000 and % of total population)	mid-2010	898.6/19.6
Refugees and others of concern to UNHCR	end-2010	14 236
Education: Government expenditure (% of GDP)	2005-2011	5.7
Education: Primary-secondary gross enrolment ratio (f/m per 100)	2005-2011	112.8/109.8
Education: Female third-level students (% of total)	2005-2011	53.9
Deaths by assault (females and males, per 100 000)	2005-2008	</1.6[j]
Seats held by women in national parliaments (%)	2011	15.1

Environmental indicators		
Threatened species	2011	27
Forested area (% of land area)	2009	10.6
CO$_2$ emission estimates (000 metric tons and metric tons per capita)	2008	43 569/9.8
Energy consumption per capita (kilograms oil equivalent)	2009	3 253.0
Rainfall in the capital city, total mean (millimetres)		733
Temperature in the capital city, mean °C (minimum and maximum)		6.3/12.8

a Market rate. **b** 2003. **c** 2004. **d** Second quarter. **e** European Labour Force Survey (Eurostat). **f** Includes tourists from Northern Ireland. **g** 2009. **h** Age group 18 to 49 years. **i** 2004-2005. **j** Rate based on 30 or fewer events.

Israel

Region	Western Asia
Currency	Shekel (ILS)
Surface area (square kilometres)	22 072
Population in 2010 (estimated, 000)	7 418
Population density in 2010 (per square kilometre)	336.1
Capital city and population in 2011 (000)	Jerusalem (791)
United Nations membership date	11 May 1949

Economic indicators	2000	2005	2010
GDP: Gross domestic product (million current US$)	124 894	133 968	217 445
GDP: Growth rate at constant 2005 prices (annual %)	9.3	4.9	4.9
GDP per capita (current US$)	20 764.0	20 284.1	29 311.6
GNI: Gross national income per capita (current US$)	19 381.1	20 071.5	28 464.3
Gross fixed capital formation (% of GDP)	18.8	16.6	17.8
Exchange rates (national currency per US$) [a]	4.04	4.60	3.55
Balance of payments, current account (million US$)	−2 056	4 101	6 342
CPI: Consumer price index (2000=100)	100	109	124
Industrial production index (2005=100) [b]	90[c]	100	125
Agricultural production index (2004-2006=100)	87	100	106
Food production index (2004-2006=100)	87	100	107
Unemployment (% of labour force)	10.4[d]	9.0	6.6
Employment in industrial sector (% of employed)	23.7	21.4	20.4[ef]
Employment in agricultural sector (% of employed)	2.2	2.0	1.7[f]
Labour force participation, adult female pop. (%)	48.1	50.0	52.5
Labour force participation, adult male pop. (%)	60.6	60.8	62.4
Tourist arrivals at national borders (000) [g]	2 417	1 903	2 803
Energy production, primary (000 mt oil equivalent)	101	1 529	2 511[f]
Telephone subscribers, total (per 100 inhabitants)	122.6	161.9	177.3
Internet users (per 100 inhabitants)	20.9	25.2	67.2

Total trade		Major trading partners		2010
	(million US$)		(% of exports)	(% of imports)
Exports	58 413.0	United States	31.7	
Imports	59 193.9	China, Hong Kong SAR	6.7	
Balance	−780.9	Belgium	5.3	

Social indicators		
Population growth rate (average annual %)	2010-2015	1.7
Urban population growth rate (average annual %)	2010-2015	1.7
Rural population growth rate (average annual %)	2010-2015	0.9
Urban population (%)	2011	91.9
Population aged 0-14 years (%)	2011	27.3
Population aged 60+ years (females and males, % of total)	2011	16.7/13.6
Sex ratio (males per 100 females)	2011	97.5
Life expectancy at birth (females and males, years)	2010-2015	84.2/79.6
Infant mortality rate (per 1 000 live births)	2010-2015	3.4
Fertility rate, total (live births per woman)	2010-2015	2.9
Contraceptive prevalence (ages 15-49, %) [h]	2006-2010	68.0[i]
International migrant stock (000 and % of total population) [j]	mid-2010	2 940.5/40.4
Refugees and others of concern to UNHCR	end-2010	31 055
Education: Government expenditure (% of GDP)	2005-2011	5.9
Education: Primary-secondary gross enrolment ratio (f/m per 100)	2005-2011	103.2/101.9
Education: Female third-level students (% of total)	2005-2011	55.7
Deaths by assault (females and males, per 100 000)	2005-2008	1.4/4.1
Seats held by women in national parliaments (%)	2011	19.2

Environmental indicators		
Threatened species	2011	134
Forested area (% of land area)	2009	7.1
CO$_2$ emission estimates (000 metric tons and metric tons per capita)	2008	67 535/9.6
Energy consumption per capita (kilograms oil equivalent)	2009	2 918.0
Rainfall in the capital city, total mean (millimetres)		448
Temperature in the capital city, mean °C (minimum and maximum)		14.0/22.2

a Market rate. **b** The indices are shown in terms of ISIC Rev. 3. **c** 2003. **d** 2004. **e** Excludes mining and quarrying. **f** 2009. **g** Excludes nationals residing abroad. **h** Age group 18 to 39 years. **i** 1987-1988. **j** Includes refugees.

Italy

Region	Southern Europe
Currency	Euro (EUR)
Surface area (square kilometres)	301 336
Population in 2010 (estimated, 000)	60 551
Population density in 2010 (per square kilometre)	200.9
Capital city and population in 2011 (000)	Rome (3 298)
United Nations membership date	14 December 1955

Economic indicators	2000	2005	2010
GDP: Gross domestic product (million current US$)	1 097 340	1 777 690	2 051 290
GDP: Growth rate at constant 2005 prices (annual %)	3.7	0.7	1.3
GDP per capita (current US$)	19 256.3	30 299.3	33 877.2
GNI: Gross national income per capita (current US$)	19 112.0	30 204.1	33 423.1
Gross fixed capital formation (% of GDP)	20.6	20.9	19.6
Exchange rates (national currency per US$) [a]	1.07	0.85	0.75
Balance of payments, current account (million US$)	−5 781	−29 744	−72 015
CPI: Consumer price index (2000=100) [b]	100	112	123
Industrial production index (2005=100)	101[c]	100	89
Agricultural production index (2004-2006=100)	100	101	93
Food production index (2004-2006=100)	100	100	93
Unemployment (% of labour force)	8.0[d]	7.7	8.4
Employment in industrial sector (% of employed) [e]	31.8	30.8	28.8
Employment in agricultural sector (% of employed) [e]	5.2	4.2	3.8
Labour force participation, adult female pop. (%)	35.4	37.7	37.7
Labour force participation, adult male pop. (%)	61.2	61.1	59.6
Tourist arrivals at national borders (000) [f]	41 181	36 513	43 626
Energy production, primary (000 mt oil equivalent) [g]	24 605	21 749	18 655[h]
Telephone subscribers, total (per 100 inhabitants)	121.8	164.6	185.1
Internet users (per 100 inhabitants)	23.1	35.0	53.7

Total trade		Major trading partners			2010
	(million US$)[g]	(% of exports)[g]			(% of imports)[g]
Exports	446 839.8	Germany	12.9	Germany	16.0
Imports	486 984.4	France	11.6	France	8.7
Balance	−40 144.6	United States	6.0	China	7.8

Social indicators		
Population growth rate (average annual %)	2010-2015	0.2
Urban population growth rate (average annual %)	2010-2015	0.5
Rural population growth rate (average annual %)	2010-2015	−0.4
Urban population (%)	2011	68.4
Population aged 0-14 years (%)	2011	14.1
Population aged 60+ years (females and males, % of total)	2011	29.6/23.9
Sex ratio (males per 100 females)	2011	95.9
Life expectancy at birth (females and males, years)	2010-2015	84.6/79.2
Infant mortality rate (per 1 000 live births)	2010-2015	3.4
Fertility rate, total (live births per woman)	2010-2015	1.5
Contraceptive prevalence (ages 15-49, %) [i]	2006-2010	62.7[j]
International migrant stock (000 and % of total population)	mid-2010	4 463.4/7.4
Refugees and others of concern to UNHCR	end-2010	61 327
Education: Government expenditure (% of GDP)	2005-2011	4.6
Education: Primary-secondary gross enrolment ratio (f/m per 100)	2005-2011	99.9/101.1
Education: Female third-level students (% of total)	2005-2011	57.7
Deaths by assault (females and males, per 100 000)	2005-2008	</1.5
Seats held by women in national parliaments (%)	2011	21.3

Environmental indicators		
Threatened species	2011	174
Forested area (% of land area)	2009	30.8
CO_2 emission estimates (000 metric tons and metric tons per capita) [g]	2008	444 755/7.5
Energy consumption per capita (kilograms oil equivalent) [g]	2009	2 637.0
Rainfall in the capital city, total mean (millimetres)		733
Temperature in the capital city, mean °C (minimum and maximum)		10.6/20.3

a Market rate. **b** Excludes tobacco. **c** 2003. **d** 2004. **e** European Labour Force Survey (Eurostat). **f** Excludes seasonal and border workers. **g** Includes San Marino. **h** 2009. **i** Age group 20 to 49 years. **j** 1995-1996.

Jamaica

Region	Caribbean
Currency	Jamaican Dollar (JMD)
Surface area (square kilometres)	10 991
Population in 2010 (estimated, 000)	2 741
Population density in 2010 (per square kilometre)	249.4
Capital city and population in 2011 (000)	Kingston (571)
United Nations membership date	18 September 1962

Economic indicators	2000	2005	2010
GDP: Gross domestic product (million current US$)	8 958	11 163	13 428
GDP: Growth rate at constant 2005 prices (annual %)	0.7	1.4	−1.1
GDP per capita (current US$)	3 470.0	4 162.6	4 899.0
GNI: Gross national income per capita (current US$)	3 336.7	3 910.5	4 652.5
Gross fixed capital formation (% of GDP)	23.3	26.8	17.9
Exchange rates (national currency per US$) [a]	45.41	64.38	85.60
Balance of payments, current account (million US$)	−367	−1 071	−934
CPI: Consumer price index (2000=100)	100	166	296
Agricultural production index (2004-2006=100)	98	95	101
Food production index (2004-2006=100)	98	95	99
Unemployment (% of labour force) [b]	12.2[c]	11.3	12.4
Employment in industrial sector (% of employed) [b]	16.9	17.7	16.6[de]
Employment in agricultural sector (% of employed) [b]	20.8	18.1	20.2[de]
Labour force participation, adult female pop. (%)	59.2	57.5	56.0
Labour force participation, adult male pop. (%)	77.7	76.2	72.0
Tourist arrivals at national borders (000) [fg]	1 323	1 479	1 922
Energy production, primary (000 mt oil equivalent)	10	17	14[e]
Telephone subscribers, total (per 100 inhabitants)	33.3	85.8	125.7
Internet users (per 100 inhabitants)	3.1	12.8	26.1

Total trade		Major trading partners			2010
	(million US$)	(% of exports)		(% of imports)	
Exports	1 327.6	United States	49.6	United States	35.9
Imports	5 225.2	Canada	12.3	Venezuela	14.0
Balance	−3 897.6	United Kingdom	6.3	Trinidad and Tobago	13.8

Social indicators		
Population growth rate (average annual %)	2010-2015	0.4
Urban population growth rate (average annual %)	2010-2015	0.5
Rural population growth rate (average annual %)	2010-2015	0.2
Urban population (%)	2011	52.0
Population aged 0-14 years (%)	2011	28.6
Population aged 60+ years (females and males, % of total)	2011	11.3/10.2
Sex ratio (males per 100 females)	2011	96.9
Life expectancy at birth (females and males, years)	2010-2015	76.0/70.9
Infant mortality rate (per 1 000 live births)	2010-2015	22.0
Fertility rate, total (live births per woman)	2010-2015	2.3
Contraceptive prevalence (ages 15-49, %)	2006-2010	69.0[h]
International migrant stock (000 and % of total population)	mid-2010	30.0/1.1
Refugees and others of concern to UNHCR	end-2010	21
Education: Government expenditure (% of GDP) [i]	2005-2011	6.1
Education: Primary-secondary gross enrolment ratio (f/m per 100)	2005-2011	90.1/91.1
Education: Female third-level students (% of total)	2005-2011	68.7
Seats held by women in national parliaments (%)	2011	13.3

Environmental indicators		
Threatened species	2011	286
Forested area (% of land area)	2009	31.2
CO_2 emission estimates (000 metric tons and metric tons per capita)	2008	12 194/4.5
Energy consumption per capita (kilograms oil equivalent)	2009	984.0
Rainfall in the capital city, total mean (millimetres)		813
Temperature in the capital city, mean °C (minimum and maximum)		22.9/31.4

a Market rate. **b** Age group 14 years and over. **c** 2004. **d** Average of quarterly estimates. **e** 2009. **f** Includes nationals residing abroad. **g** Air arrivals of non-resident tourists. **h** 2002-2003. **i** UNESCO estimate.

Japan

Region	Eastern Asia
Currency	Yen (JPY)
Surface area (square kilometres)	377 930
Population in 2010 (estimated, 000)	126 536
Population density in 2010 (per square kilometre)	334.8
Capital city and population in 2011 (000)	Tokyo (37 217)
United Nations membership date	18 December 1956

Economic indicators	2000	2005	2010
GDP: Gross domestic product (million current US$)	4 667 450	4 552 190	5 458 870
GDP: Growth rate at constant 2005 prices (annual %)	2.8	1.9	4.0
GDP per capita (current US$)	37 125.7	36 016.2	43 140.9
GNI: Gross national income per capita (current US$)	37 599.6	36 866.7	44 268.5
Gross fixed capital formation (% of GDP)	25.2	23.3	20.5
Exchange rates (national currency per US$) [a]	114.90	117.97	81.45
Balance of payments, current account (million US$)	119 660	165 780	195 760
CPI: Consumer price index (2000=100)	100	98	97
Industrial production index (2005=100)	94 [b]	100	95
Agricultural production index (2004-2006=100)	104	101	96
Food production index (2004-2006=100)	104	101	97
Unemployment (% of labour force)	4.7 [c]	4.4	5.1
Employment in industrial sector (% of employed)	31.2	27.9 [d]	25.3 [d]
Employment in agricultural sector (% of employed)	5.1	4.4 [d]	3.7 [d]
Labour force participation, adult female pop. (%)	49.3	48.4	49.5
Labour force participation, adult male pop. (%)	76.4	73.4	72.0
Tourist arrivals at national borders (000) [ef]	4 757	6 728	8 611
Energy production, primary (000 mt oil equivalent)	41 043	38 138	36 399 [g]
Telephone subscribers, total (per 100 inhabitants)	102.4	122.3	127.3
Internet users (per 100 inhabitants)	30.0	66.9	78.2

Total trade		Major trading partners			2010
	(million US$)	(% of exports)			(% of imports)
Exports	769 773.8	China	19.4	China	22.1
Imports	694 059.2	United States	15.6	United States	10.0
Balance	75 714.6	Republic of Korea	8.1	Australia	6.5

Social indicators		
Population growth rate (average annual %)	2010-2015	−0.1
Urban population growth rate (average annual %)	2010-2015	0.6
Rural population growth rate (average annual %)	2010-2015	−7.6
Urban population (%)	2011	91.3
Population aged 0-14 years (%)	2011	13.3
Population aged 60+ years (females and males, % of total)	2011	33.8/28.2
Sex ratio (males per 100 females)	2011	95.0
Life expectancy at birth (females and males, years)	2010-2015	87.1/80.1
Infant mortality rate (per 1 000 live births)	2010-2015	2.6
Fertility rate, total (live births per woman)	2010-2015	1.4
Contraceptive prevalence (ages 15-49, %) [h]	2006-2010	54.3 [i]
International migrant stock (000 and % of total population) [j]	mid-2010	2 176.2/1.7
Refugees and others of concern to UNHCR	end-2010	7 061
Education: Government expenditure (% of GDP)	2005-2011	3.8
Education: Primary-secondary gross enrolment ratio (f/m per 100)	2005-2011	102.2/102.1
Education: Female third-level students (% of total)	2005-2011	45.8
Deaths by assault (females and males, per 100 000)	2005-2008	</<
Seats held by women in national parliaments (%)	2011	11.3

Environmental indicators		
Threatened species	2011	340
Forested area (% of land area)	2009	68.5
CO$_2$ emission estimates (000 metric tons and metric tons per capita)	2008	1 207 174/9.5
Energy consumption per capita (kilograms oil equivalent)	2009	3 003.0
Rainfall in the capital city, total mean (millimetres)		1 467
Temperature in the capital city, mean °C (minimum and maximum)		12.6/19.7

a Market rate. **b** 2003. **c** 2004. **d** Average of monthly estimates. **e** Excludes nationals residing abroad. **f** Arrivals of non-resident visitors at national borders. **g** 2009. **h** Age group 20 to 49 years. **i** 2005. **j** Data refer to foreign citizens.

Jordan

Region	Western Asia
Currency	Jordanian Dinar (JOD)
Surface area (square kilometres)	89 342
Population in 2010 (estimated, 000)	6 187
Population density in 2010 (per square kilometre)	69.3
Capital city and population in 2011 (000)	Amman (1 179)
United Nations membership date	14 December 1955

Economic indicators	2000	2005	2010
GDP: Gross domestic product (million current US$)	8 461	12 589	27 504
GDP: Growth rate at constant 2005 prices (annual %)	4.3	8.2	3.1
GDP per capita (current US$)	1 752.8	2 356.5	4 445.3
GNI: Gross national income per capita (current US$)	1 773.5	2 419.5	4 553.5
Gross fixed capital formation (% of GDP)	21.1	30.6	24.8
Exchange rates (national currency per US$) [a]	0.71	0.71	0.71
Balance of payments, current account (million US$)	27	−2 272	−1 312
CPI: Consumer price index (2000=100)	100	113	149
Industrial production index (2005=100) [b]	81[c]	100	105
Agricultural production index (2004-2006=100)	81	98	122
Food production index (2004-2006=100)	81	97	122
Employment in industrial sector (% of employed)	21.8	20.7	18.7
Employment in agricultural sector (% of employed)	4.9	3.4	2.0
Labour force participation, adult female pop. (%)	12.5	12.1	15.3
Labour force participation, adult male pop. (%)	68.2	66.9	65.4
Tourist arrivals at national borders (000) [d]	1 580	2 987	4 557
Energy production, primary (000 mt oil equivalent)	221	205	186[e]
Telephone subscribers, total (per 100 inhabitants)	20.9	70.5	114.8
Internet users (per 100 inhabitants)	2.6	12.9	38.0

Total trade		Major trading partners			2010
	(million US$)	(% of exports)			(% of imports)
Exports	7 023.1	Iraq	16.0	Saudi Arabia	19.8
Imports	15 262.0	United States	13.2	China	10.8
Balance	−8 238.9	India	11.1	Germany	6.1

Social indicators		
Population growth rate (average annual %)	2010-2015	1.9
Urban population growth rate (average annual %)	2010-2015	2.2
Rural population growth rate (average annual %)	2010-2015	0.5
Urban population (%)	2011	82.7
Population aged 0-14 years (%)	2011	36.9
Population aged 60+ years (females and males, % of total)	2011	5.9/5.8
Sex ratio (males per 100 females)	2011	105.8
Life expectancy at birth (females and males, years)	2010-2015	75.2/72.2
Infant mortality rate (per 1 000 live births)	2010-2015	19.1
Fertility rate, total (live births per woman)	2010-2015	2.9
Contraceptive prevalence (ages 15-49, %)	2006-2010	59.3
International migrant stock (000 and % of total population) [fg]	mid-2010	2 973.0/45.9
Refugees and others of concern to UNHCR	end-2010	453 074[h]
Education: Government expenditure (% of GDP)	2005-2011	4.9[i]
Education: Primary-secondary gross enrolment ratio (f/m per 100)	2005-2011	95.4/93.1
Education: Female third-level students (% of total)	2005-2011	51.3
Seats held by women in national parliaments (%)	2011	10.8

Environmental indicators		
Threatened species	2011	91
Forested area (% of land area)	2009	1.1
CO$_2$ emission estimates (000 metric tons and metric tons per capita)	2008	21 365/3.5
Energy consumption per capita (kilograms oil equivalent)	2009	1 280.0
Rainfall in the capital city, total mean (millimetres)		269
Temperature in the capital city, mean °C (minimum and maximum)		11.3/23.5

a Official rate. **b** The indices are shown in terms of ISIC Rev. 3. **c** 2003. **d** Includes nationals residing abroad. **e** 2009. **f** Data refer to foreign citizens. **g** Includes refugees. **h** Refugee figures for Iraqis in Jordan are Government estimates. **i** 1999.

Kazakhstan

Region	South-central Asia
Currency	Tenge (KZT)
Surface area (square kilometres)	2 724 900
Population in 2010 (estimated, 000)	16 026
Population density in 2010 (per square kilometre)	5.9
Capital city and population in 2011 (000)	Astana (664)
United Nations membership date	2 March 1992

Economic indicators	2000	2005	2010
GDP: Gross domestic product (million current US$)	18 292	57 124	146 908
GDP: Growth rate at constant 2005 prices (annual %)	9.9	9.7	7.0
GDP per capita (current US$)	1 223.0	3 765.1	9 166.7
GNI: Gross national income per capita (current US$)	1 146.6	3 411.4	8 084.5
Gross fixed capital formation (% of GDP)	17.3	28.0	24.3
Exchange rates (national currency per US$) [a]	144.50	133.98	147.50
Balance of payments, current account (million US$)	366	−1 056	3 013
CPI: Consumer price index (2000=100)	100	140	198[b]
Agricultural production index (2004-2006=100)	78	100	107
Food production index (2004-2006=100)	79	100	108
Unemployment (% of labour force)	8.4[c]	8.1	5.8
Employment in industrial sector (% of employed)	16.3[d]	18.0	18.9[e]
Employment in agricultural sector (% of employed)	35.5[d]	32.4	29.4[e]
Labour force participation, adult female pop. (%)	64.7	64.4	66.4
Labour force participation, adult male pop. (%)	76.3	75.0	76.8
Tourist arrivals at national borders (000)	1 471	3 143	3 393
Energy production, primary (000 mt oil equivalent)	80 002	124 792	157 318[e]
Telephone subscribers, total (per 100 inhabitants)	13.6	53.4	146.4
Internet users (per 100 inhabitants)	0.7	3.0	34.0

Total trade		Major trading partners			2010
	(million US$)		(% of exports)		(% of imports)
Exports	57 244.1	China	17.7	Russian Federation	22.8
Imports	24 023.6	Italy	16.7	China	16.5
Balance	33 220.5	France	7.7	Germany	7.6

Social indicators

Population growth rate (average annual %)	2010-2015	1.0
Urban population growth rate (average annual %)	2010-2015	0.9
Rural population growth rate (average annual %)	2010-2015	1.3
Urban population (%)	2011	53.6
Population aged 0-14 years (%)	2011	25.0
Population aged 60+ years (females and males, % of total)	2011	12.5/7.4
Sex ratio (males per 100 females)	2011	92.4
Life expectancy at birth (females and males, years)	2010-2015	72.8/62.3
Infant mortality rate (per 1 000 live births)	2010-2015	23.7
Fertility rate, total (live births per woman)	2010-2015	2.5
Contraceptive prevalence (ages 15-49, %)	2006-2010	50.7
International migrant stock (000 and % of total population)	mid-2010	3 079.5/19.6
Refugees and others of concern to UNHCR	end-2010	12 686
Education: Government expenditure (% of GDP)	2005-2011	3.1
Education: Primary-secondary gross enrolment ratio (f/m per 100)	2005-2011	102.6/104.4
Education: Female third-level students (% of total)	2005-2011	58.4
Seats held by women in national parliaments (%)	2011	17.8

Environmental indicators

Threatened species	2011	74
Forested area (% of land area)	2009	1.2
CO_2 emission estimates (000 metric tons and metric tons per capita)	2008	236 760/15.2
Energy consumption per capita (kilograms oil equivalent)	2009	4 398.0
Rainfall in the capital city, total mean (millimetres)		298
Temperature in the capital city, mean °C (minimum and maximum)		−2.6/9.2

a Official rate. **b** 2008. **c** 2004. **d** 2001. **e** 2009.

Kenya

Region	Eastern Africa
Currency	Kenyan Shilling (KES)
Surface area (square kilometres)	581 313
Population in 2010 (estimated, 000)	40 513
Population density in 2010 (per square kilometre)	69.7
Capital city and population in 2011 (000)	Nairobi (3 363)
United Nations membership date	16 December 1963

Economic indicators	2000	2005	2010
GDP: Gross domestic product (million current US$)	12 604	18 739	32 483
GDP: Growth rate at constant 2005 prices (annual %)	0.5	5.9	5.6
GDP per capita (current US$)	403.3	526.2	801.8
GNI: Gross national income per capita (current US$)	399.0	523.1	797.9
Gross fixed capital formation (% of GDP)	16.8	18.7	19.9
Exchange rates (national currency per US$) [a]	78.04	72.37	80.75
Balance of payments, current account (million US$)	−199	−252	−2 512
CPI: Consumer price index (2000=100) [b]	...	...	127 [c]
Agricultural production index (2004-2006=100)	78	97	124
Food production index (2004-2006=100)	77	97	125
Employment in industrial sector (% of employed)	...	6.7 [d]	...
Employment in agricultural sector (% of employed)	...	61.1 [d]	...
Labour force participation, adult female pop. (%)	63.1	60.0	61.2
Labour force participation, adult male pop. (%)	73.2	69.9	71.5
Tourist arrivals at national borders (000)	899	1 399	1 469
Energy production, primary (000 mt oil equivalent)	151	347	297 [c]
Telephone subscribers, total (per 100 inhabitants)	1.3	13.8	62.6
Internet users (per 100 inhabitants)	0.3	3.1	25.9

Total trade		Major trading partners			2010
	(million US$)	(% of exports)			(% of imports)
Exports	5 169.1	Uganda	12.7	China	12.6
Imports	12 092.9	United Kingdom	9.8	United Arab Emirates	12.1
Balance	−6 923.8	United Rep. Tanzania	8.1	India	10.8

Social indicators		
Population growth rate (average annual %)	2010-2015	2.7
Urban population growth rate (average annual %)	2010-2015	4.4
Rural population growth rate (average annual %)	2010-2015	2.1
Urban population (%)	2011	24.0
Population aged 0-14 years (%)	2011	42.4
Population aged 60+ years (females and males, % of total)	2011	4.6/3.9
Sex ratio (males per 100 females)	2011	99.8
Life expectancy at birth (females and males, years)	2010-2015	59.2/56.7
Infant mortality rate (per 1 000 live births)	2010-2015	58.1
Fertility rate, total (live births per woman)	2010-2015	4.6
Contraceptive prevalence (ages 15-49, %)	2006-2010	45.5
International migrant stock (000 and % of total population) [e]	mid-2010	817.8/2.0
Refugees and others of concern to UNHCR	end-2010	751 196
Education: Government expenditure (% of GDP)	2005-2011	6.7
Education: Primary-secondary gross enrolment ratio (f/m per 100)	2005-2011	86.9/91.1
Education: Female third-level students (% of total)	2005-2011	41.2
Seats held by women in national parliaments (%)	2011	9.8

Environmental indicators		
Threatened species	2011	341
Forested area (% of land area)	2009	6.1
CO$_2$ emission estimates (000 metric tons and metric tons per capita)	2008	10 384/0.3
Energy consumption per capita (kilograms oil equivalent)	2009	90.0
Rainfall in the capital city, total mean (millimetres)		1 024
Temperature in the capital city, mean °C (minimum and maximum)		12.0/23.4

a Official rate. **b** Index base 2007=100. **c** 2009. **d** Household income and expenditure survey. **e** Includes refugees.

Kiribati

Region	Oceania-Micronesia
Currency	Australian Dollar (AUD)
Surface area (square kilometres)	726 [a]
Population in 2010 (estimated, 000)	100
Population density in 2010 (per square kilometre)	137.1
Capital city and population in 2011 (000)	Bairiki (...) [b]
United Nations membership date	14 September 1999

Economic indicators	2000	2005	2010
GDP: Gross domestic product (million current US$)	67	106	146
GDP: Growth rate at constant 2005 prices (annual %)	5.7	0.0	−0.4
GDP per capita (current US$)	794.8	1 147.8	1 468.2
GNI: Gross national income per capita (current US$)	1 054.7	1 383.4	1 738.9
Gross fixed capital formation (% of GDP)	33.2	60.6	58.6
Exchange rates (national currency per US$) [c]	1.81	1.36	0.98
CPI: Consumer price index (2000=100) [d]	100	110	125 [e]
Agricultural production index (2004-2006=100)	78	99	131
Food production index (2004-2006=100)	78	99	131
Employment in industrial sector (% of employed)	7.4 [f]	...	...
Employment in agricultural sector (% of employed)	2.8 [f]	...	...
Tourist arrivals at national borders (000) [g][h]	5	4	5
Telephone subscribers, total (per 100 inhabitants)	4.4	5.3	14.2
Internet users (per 100 inhabitants)	1.8	4.0	9.0

Total trade		Major trading partners		2010
	(million US$)	(% of exports)		(% of imports) [i]
Imports	68.1 [i]	Australia		29.4
		Fiji		25.8
		France		6.9

Social indicators

Population growth rate (average annual %)	2010-2015	1.5
Urban population growth rate (average annual %)	2010-2015	1.8
Rural population growth rate (average annual %)	2010-2015	1.3
Urban population (%)	2011	43.9
Population aged 0-14 years (%) [j]	2011	34.9
Population aged 60+ years (females and males, % of total) [j]	2011	6.5/4.8
Sex ratio (males per 100 females) [j]	2011	98.6
Life expectancy at birth (females and males, years) [k]	2010-2015	63.1/58.9 [l]
Infant mortality rate (per 1 000 live births) [k]	2010-2015	52.0 [m]
Fertility rate, total (live births per woman) [j]	2010-2015	3.5 [n]
International migrant stock (000 and % of total population)	mid-2010	2.0/2.0
Education: Government expenditure (% of GDP) [o]	2005-2011	11.6 [p]
Education: Primary-secondary gross enrolment ratio (f/m per 100)	2005-2011	104.0/97.3
Seats held by women in national parliaments (%)	2011	8.7

Environmental indicators

Threatened species	2011	91
Forested area (% of land area)	2009	15.0
CO_2 emission estimates (000 metric tons and metric tons per capita)	2008	29/0.3
Energy consumption per capita (kilograms oil equivalent)	2009	185.0 [q]

a Land area only. Excludes 84 square km of uninhabited islands. **b** Population estimates for Bairiki are not available. Bairiki is located on the island of Tarawa; the estimated population of South Tarawa is 44,385. **c** Official rate. **d** Tarawa. **e** 2008. **f** Population census. **g** Air arrivals. **h** Tarawa and Christmas Island. **i** 2009. **j** Data compiled by the Secretariat of the Pacific Community Demography Programme. **k** Data compiled by the United Nations Demographic Yearbook system. **l** 2005. **m** 2003. **n** 2004-2005. **o** UNESCO estimate. **p** 2002. **q** UNSD estimate.

Kuwait

Region	Western Asia
Currency	Kuwaiti Dinar (KWD)
Surface area (square kilometres)	17 818
Population in 2010 (estimated, 000)	2 737
Population density in 2010 (per square kilometre)	153.6
Capital city and population in 2011 (000)	Kuwait City (2 406)
United Nations membership date	14 May 1963

Economic indicators	2000	2005	2010
GDP: Gross domestic product (million current US$)	37 718	80 798	124 331
GDP: Growth rate at constant 2005 prices (annual %)	4.7	10.6	2.0
GDP per capita (current US$)	19 434.3	35 687.9	45 430.4
GNI: Gross national income per capita (current US$)	22 886.1	39 599.6	48 290.0
Gross fixed capital formation (% of GDP)	10.5	14.6	19.0
Exchange rates (national currency per US$)[a]	0.31	0.29	0.28
Balance of payments, current account (million US$)	14 672	30 071	36 822
CPI: Consumer price index (2000=100)	100	109	136
Agricultural production index (2004-2006=100)	80	96	114
Food production index (2004-2006=100)	80	96	114
Employment in industrial sector (% of employed)	18.3[b]	20.6[c]	...
Employment in agricultural sector (% of employed)	0.0[b]	2.7[c]	...
Labour force participation, adult female pop. (%)	44.3	44.7	43.3
Labour force participation, adult male pop. (%)	81.9	81.7	82.2
Tourist arrivals at national borders (000)[d]	1 944	3 474	5 208
Energy production, primary (000 mt oil equivalent)	114 508	146 560	129 448[e]
Telephone subscribers, total (per 100 inhabitants)	48.6	122.9	181.5
Internet users (per 100 inhabitants)	6.7	25.9	38.3

Total trade	Major trading partners		2010
(million US$)	(% of exports)[e]		(% of imports)
Exports	51 936.6[e]		

Social indicators		
Population growth rate (average annual %)	2010-2015	2.4
Urban population growth rate (average annual %)	2010-2015	2.4
Rural population growth rate (average annual %)	2010-2015	1.7
Urban population (%)	2011	98.3
Population aged 0-14 years (%)	2011	26.7
Population aged 60+ years (females and males, % of total)	2011	3.8/4.3
Sex ratio (males per 100 females)	2011	147.7
Life expectancy at birth (females and males, years)	2010-2015	75.9/74.0
Infant mortality rate (per 1 000 live births)	2010-2015	7.6
Fertility rate, total (live births per woman)	2010-2015	2.3
Contraceptive prevalence (ages 15-49, %)	2006-2010	52.0[f]
International migrant stock (000 and % of total population)[gh]	mid-2010	2 097.5/68.8
Refugees and others of concern to UNHCR	end-2010	96 459
Education: Government expenditure (% of GDP)[i]	2005-2011	3.8
Education: Primary-secondary gross enrolment ratio (f/m per 100)	2005-2011	105.7/100.5
Education: Female third-level students (% of total)[i]	2005-2011	64.3[j]
Seats held by women in national parliaments (%)	2011	7.7

Environmental indicators		
Threatened species	2011	41
Forested area (% of land area)	2009	<
CO_2 emission estimates (000 metric tons and metric tons per capita)	2008	76 680/26.3
Energy consumption per capita (kilograms oil equivalent)	2009	12 169.0
Rainfall in the capital city, total mean (millimetres)		107
Temperature in the capital city, mean °C (minimum and maximum)		18.7/32.5

a Official rate. b 2003. c Population census. d Arrivals of non-resident visitors at national borders. e 2009. f 1999. g Data refer to foreign citizens. h Includes refugees. i UNESCO estimate. j 2004.

Kyrgyzstan

Region	South-central Asia
Currency	Som (KGS)
Surface area (square kilometres)	199 951
Population in 2010 (estimated, 000)	5 334
Population density in 2010 (per square kilometre)	26.7
Capital city and population in 2011 (000)	Bishkek (839)
United Nations membership date	2 March 1992

Economic indicators	2000	2005	2010
GDP: Gross domestic product (million current US$)	1 370	2 460	4 616
GDP: Growth rate at constant 2005 prices (annual %)	5.4	−0.2	−1.4
GDP per capita (current US$)	276.5	487.9	865.4
GNI: Gross national income per capita (current US$)	260.2	471.9	844.7
Gross fixed capital formation (% of GDP)	18.3	16.2	28.1
Exchange rates (national currency per US$)[a]	48.30	41.30	47.10
Balance of payments, current account (million US$)	−123	−62	−467
CPI: Consumer price index (2000=100)	100	122	...
Agricultural production index (2004-2006=100)	96	98	104
Food production index (2004-2006=100)	95	98	106
Employment in industrial sector (% of employed)	10.5[b]	17.6[c]	20.6[cd]
Employment in agricultural sector (% of employed)	53.1[b]	38.5[c]	34.0[cd]
Labour force participation, adult female pop. (%)	56.2	54.1	55.2
Labour force participation, adult male pop. (%)	74.1	75.9	78.2
Tourist arrivals at national borders (000)	59	319	1 316
Energy production, primary (000 mt oil equivalent)	1 417	1 423	1 116[e]
Telephone subscribers, total (per 100 inhabitants)	7.8	19.5	108.1
Internet users (per 100 inhabitants)	1.0	10.5	20.0

Total trade		Major trading partners			2010
	(million US$)	(% of exports)		(% of imports)	
Exports	1 488.4	Switzerland	26.1	Russian Federation	33.6
Imports	3 222.6	United Arab Emirates	20.3	China	20.7
Balance	−1 734.2	Russian Federation	17.3	Kazakhstan	12.0

Social indicators		
Population growth rate (average annual %)	2010-2015	1.1
Urban population growth rate (average annual %)	2010-2015	1.3
Rural population growth rate (average annual %)	2010-2015	0.9
Urban population (%)	2011	35.4
Population aged 0-14 years (%)	2011	30.0
Population aged 60+ years (females and males, % of total)	2011	7.4/5.3
Sex ratio (males per 100 females)	2011	97.3
Life expectancy at birth (females and males, years)	2010-2015	72.4/64.3
Infant mortality rate (per 1 000 live births)	2010-2015	32.8
Fertility rate, total (live births per woman)	2010-2015	2.6
Contraceptive prevalence (ages 15-49, %)	2006-2010	47.8[f]
International migrant stock (000 and % of total population)	mid-2010	222.7/4.0
Refugees and others of concern to UNHCR	end-2010	304 169
Education: Government expenditure (% of GDP)	2005-2011	6.2
Education: Primary-secondary gross enrolment ratio (f/m per 100)[g]	2005-2011	88.7/89.7
Education: Female third-level students (% of total)	2005-2011	56.4
Seats held by women in national parliaments (%)	2011	23.3

Environmental indicators		
Threatened species	2011	40
Forested area (% of land area)	2009	4.9
CO_2 emission estimates (000 metric tons and metric tons per capita)	2008	6 203/1.1
Energy consumption per capita (kilograms oil equivalent)	2009	552.0
Rainfall in the capital city, total mean (millimetres)		442
Temperature in the capital city, mean °C (minimum and maximum)		4.8/17.0

a Official rate. **b** Official estimates. **c** November. **d** 2008. **e** 2009. **f** 2005-2006. **g** National estimate.

Lao People's Democratic Republic

Region	South-eastern Asia
Currency	Kip (LAK)
Surface area (square kilometres)	236 800
Population in 2010 (estimated, 000)	6 201
Population density in 2010 (per square kilometre)	26.2
Capital city and population in 2011 (000)	Vientiane (810)
United Nations membership date	14 December 1955

Economic indicators	2000	2005	2010
GDP: Gross domestic product (million current US$)	1 653	2 740	6 496
GDP: Growth rate at constant 2005 prices (annual %)	5.8	7.3	7.8
GDP per capita (current US$)	311.0	476.2	1 047.6
GNI: Gross national income per capita (current US$)	298.3	451.8	1 005.4
Gross fixed capital formation (% of GDP)	28.3	34.5	37.1
Exchange rates (national currency per US$)[a]	8 218.00	10 743.00	8 058.78
Balance of payments, current account (million US$)	−8	−174	29
CPI: Consumer price index (2000=100)	100	163	208
Agricultural production index (2004-2006=100)	86	100	125
Food production index (2004-2006=100)	83	100	125
Labour force participation, adult female pop. (%)	78.9	77.8	76.6
Labour force participation, adult male pop. (%)	81.4	80.2	79.4
Tourist arrivals at national borders (000)	191	672	1 670
Energy production, primary (000 mt oil equivalent)	527	615	721[bc]
Telephone subscribers, total (per 100 inhabitants)	1.0	13.0	66.2
Internet users (per 100 inhabitants)	0.1	0.9	7.0

Social indicators		
Population growth rate (average annual %)	2010-2015	1.3
Urban population growth rate (average annual %)	2010-2015	4.4
Rural population growth rate (average annual %)	2010-2015	−0.4
Urban population (%)	2011	34.3
Population aged 0-14 years (%)	2011	33.7
Population aged 60+ years (females and males, % of total)	2011	6.6/5.4
Sex ratio (males per 100 females)	2011	99.7
Life expectancy at birth (females and males, years)	2010-2015	69.4/66.4
Infant mortality rate (per 1 000 live births)	2010-2015	36.8
Fertility rate, total (live births per woman)	2010-2015	2.5
Contraceptive prevalence (ages 15-49, %)	2006-2010	38.0[d]
International migrant stock (000 and % of total population)[ef]	mid-2010	18.9/0.3
Refugees and others of concern to UNHCR	end-2010	0[g]
Education: Government expenditure (% of GDP)	2005-2011	3.3
Education: Primary-secondary gross enrolment ratio (f/m per 100)	2005-2011	73.2/84.0
Education: Female third-level students (% of total)	2005-2011	43.2
Seats held by women in national parliaments (%)	2011	25.0

Environmental indicators		
Threatened species	2011	167
Forested area (% of land area)	2009	68.6
CO_2 emission estimates (000 metric tons and metric tons per capita)	2008	1 532/0.3
Energy consumption per capita (kilograms oil equivalent)	2009	109.0[c]
Rainfall in the capital city, total mean (millimetres)		1 661
Temperature in the capital city, mean °C (minimum and maximum)		21.8/31.1

a Market rate. b 2009. c UNSD estimate. d 2005. e Data refer to foreign citizens. f Includes refugees.
g Value is zero, not available or not applicable.

Latvia

Region	Northern Europe
Currency	Lats (LVL)
Surface area (square kilometres)	64 559
Population in 2010 (estimated, 000)	2 252
Population density in 2010 (per square kilometre)	34.9
Capital city and population in 2011 (000)	Riga (701)
United Nations membership date	17 September 1991

Economic indicators	2000	2005	2010
GDP: Gross domestic product (million current US$)	7 776	15 938	24 014
GDP: Growth rate at constant 2005 prices (annual %)	6.1	10.1	−0.3
GDP per capita (current US$)	3 260.4	6 912.9	10 663.1
GNI: Gross national income per capita (current US$)	3 252.4	6 824.9	10 885.8
Gross fixed capital formation (% of GDP)	24.6	31.0	19.5
Exchange rates (national currency per US$) [a]	0.61	0.59	0.54
Balance of payments, current account (million US$)	−371	−1 992	731
CPI: Consumer price index (2000=100)	100	122	169
Industrial production index (2005=100)	87[b]	100	98
Agricultural production index (2004-2006=100)	89	105	108
Food production index (2004-2006=100)	89	105	108
Unemployment (% of labour force)	10.4[c]	8.9	18.7
Employment in industrial sector (% of employed)	26.3[d]	25.8[de]	24.0[ef]
Employment in agricultural sector (% of employed)	14.5[d]	12.1[de]	8.8[ef]
Labour force participation, adult female pop. (%)	48.6	50.8	54.7
Labour force participation, adult male pop. (%)	64.7	66.1	66.3
Tourist arrivals at national borders (000) [g]	509	1 116	1 373
Energy production, primary (000 mt oil equivalent)	258	294	356[h]
Telephone subscribers, total (per 100 inhabitants)	47.6	112.9	126.0
Internet users (per 100 inhabitants)	6.3	46.0	71.1

Total trade		Major trading partners			2010
	(million US$)	(% of exports)			(% of imports)
Exports	8 850.8	Lithuania	16.2	Lithuania	17.1
Imports	11 143.3	Estonia	13.5	Germany	11.5
Balance	−2 292.5	Russian Federation	10.6	Russian Federation	10.0

Social indicators		
Population growth rate (average annual %)	2010-2015	−0.4
Urban population growth rate (average annual %)	2010-2015	−0.4
Rural population growth rate (average annual %)	2010-2015	−0.4
Urban population (%)	2011	67.7
Population aged 0-14 years (%)	2011	14.0
Population aged 60+ years (females and males, % of total)	2011	27.8/17.4
Sex ratio (males per 100 females)	2011	85.2
Life expectancy at birth (females and males, years)	2010-2015	78.5/68.8
Infant mortality rate (per 1 000 live births)	2010-2015	6.7
Fertility rate, total (live births per woman)	2010-2015	1.5
Contraceptive prevalence (ages 15-49, %) [i]	2006-2010	67.8[j]
International migrant stock (000 and % of total population)	mid-2010	335.0/15.0
Refugees and others of concern to UNHCR	end-2010	327 027
Education: Government expenditure (% of GDP)	2005-2011	5.6
Education: Primary-secondary gross enrolment ratio (f/m per 100)	2005-2011	96.7/98.3
Education: Female third-level students (% of total)	2005-2011	62.8
Deaths by assault (females and males, per 100 000)	2005-2008	4.5/11.2
Seats held by women in national parliaments (%)	2011	21.0

Environmental indicators		
Threatened species	2011	23
Forested area (% of land area)	2009	53.8
CO$_2$ emission estimates (000 metric tons and metric tons per capita)	2008	7 584/3.4
Energy consumption per capita (kilograms oil equivalent)	2009	1 327.0
Rainfall in the capital city, total mean (millimetres)		633
Temperature in the capital city, mean °C (minimum and maximum)		2.3/9.9

a Official rate. **b** 2003. **c** 2004. **d** Excludes conscripts. **e** Age group 15 to 74 years. **f** European Labour Force Survey (Eurostat). **g** Non-resident departures. **h** 2009. **i** Age group 18 to 49 years. **j** 1995.

Lebanon

Region	Western Asia
Currency	Lebanese Pound (LBP)
Surface area (square kilometres)	10 452
Population in 2010 (estimated, 000)	4 228
Population density in 2010 (per square kilometre)	404.5
Capital city and population in 2011 (000)	Beirut (2 022)
United Nations membership date	24 October 1945

Economic indicators	2000	2005	2010
GDP: Gross domestic product (million current US$)	16 679	21 861	39 248
GDP: Growth rate at constant 2005 prices (annual %)	1.3	0.9	7.5
GDP per capita (current US$)	4 456.8	5 394.5	9 283.7
GNI: Gross national income per capita (current US$)	4 604.6	5 523.3	9 367.2
Gross fixed capital formation (% of GDP)	21.0	22.1	29.8
Exchange rates (national currency per US$) [a]	1 507.50	1 507.50	1 507.50
Balance of payments, current account (million US$)	−4 541[b]	−2 748	−9 415
CPI: Consumer price index (2000=100) [c]	...	...	105
Agricultural production index (2004-2006=100)	99	97	106
Food production index (2004-2006=100)	99	97	106
Labour force participation, adult female pop. (%)	19.3	21.1	22.5
Labour force participation, adult male pop. (%)	70.5	70.3	70.8
Tourist arrivals at national borders (000) [d]	742	1 140	2 168
Energy production, primary (000 mt oil equivalent)	39	90	53[e]
Telephone subscribers, total (per 100 inhabitants)	35.2	40.2	89.0
Internet users (per 100 inhabitants)	8.0	10.1	31.0

Total trade		Major trading partners			2010
	(million US$)	(% of exports)			(% of imports)
Exports	4 254.2	Switzerland	11.8	United States	10.7
Imports	17 969.7	United Arab Emirates	9.8	China	9.1
Balance	−13 715.5	France	8.2	Italy	7.8

Social indicators		
Population growth rate (average annual %)	2010-2015	0.7
Urban population growth rate (average annual %)	2010-2015	0.9
Rural population growth rate (average annual %)	2010-2015	−0.2
Urban population (%)	2011	87.3
Population aged 0-14 years (%)	2011	24.3
Population aged 60+ years (females and males, % of total)	2011	11.1/9.9
Sex ratio (males per 100 females)	2011	95.4
Life expectancy at birth (females and males, years)	2010-2015	75.1/70.7
Infant mortality rate (per 1 000 live births)	2010-2015	20.2
Fertility rate, total (live births per woman)	2010-2015	1.8
Contraceptive prevalence (ages 15-49, %)	2006-2010	58.0[f]
International migrant stock (000 and % of total population) [g]	mid-2010	758.2/17.8
Refugees and others of concern to UNHCR	end-2010	9 480
Education: Government expenditure (% of GDP)	2005-2011	1.8
Education: Primary-secondary gross enrolment ratio (f/m per 100)	2005-2011	94.4/90.9
Education: Female third-level students (% of total)	2005-2011	53.7
Seats held by women in national parliaments (%)	2011	3.1

Environmental indicators		
Threatened species	2011	56
Forested area (% of land area)	2009	13.4
CO_2 emission estimates (000 metric tons and metric tons per capita)	2008	17 085/4.1
Energy consumption per capita (kilograms oil equivalent)	2009	1 496.0
Rainfall in the capital city, total mean (millimetres)		826

a Market rate. b 2002. c Index base 2008=100. d Excludes Syrian nationals, Palestinians and students.
e 2009. f 2004. g Includes refugees.

Lesotho

Region	Southern Africa
Currency	Loti (LSL)
Surface area (square kilometres)	30 355
Population in 2010 (estimated, 000)	2 171
Population density in 2010 (per square kilometre)	71.5
Capital city and population in 2011 (000)	Maseru (239)
United Nations membership date	17 October 1966

Economic indicators	2000	2005	2010
GDP: Gross domestic product (million current US$)	771	1 355	2 129
GDP: Growth rate at constant 2005 prices (annual %)	5.1	2.5	2.4
GDP per capita (current US$)	392.7	656.0	980.7
GNI: Gross national income per capita (current US$)	629.6	898.6	1 316.8
Gross fixed capital formation (% of GDP)	43.2	23.4	29.9
Exchange rates (national currency per US$) [a]	7.57	6.32	6.63
Balance of payments, current account (million US$)	−71	−17	−421
CPI: Consumer price index (2000=100)	100	140	198
Agricultural production index (2004-2006=100)	107	108	112
Food production index (2004-2006=100)	109	108	113
Labour force participation, adult female pop. (%)	67.6	61.6	58.7
Labour force participation, adult male pop. (%)	80.1	75.3	73.3
Tourist arrivals at national borders (000) [b]	302	304	426
Energy production, primary (000 mt oil equivalent)	...	30	17[c]
Telephone subscribers, total (per 100 inhabitants)	2.2	14.4	47.3
Internet users (per 100 inhabitants)	0.2	2.6	3.9

Total trade		Major trading partners			2010
	(million US$)[d]	(% of exports)[d]		(% of imports)[d]	
Exports	244.7	South Africa	82.7	South Africa	95.2
Imports	1 066.2	United States	14.6	Japan	1.8
Balance	−821.5	Madagascar	0.7	Germany	1.4

Social indicators		
Population growth rate (average annual %)	2010-2015	1.0
Urban population growth rate (average annual %)	2010-2015	3.6
Rural population growth rate (average annual %)	2010-2015	<
Urban population (%)	2011	27.6
Population aged 0-14 years (%)	2011	37.0
Population aged 60+ years (females and males, % of total)	2011	7.4/5.2
Sex ratio (males per 100 females)	2011	97.0
Life expectancy at birth (females and males, years)	2010-2015	48.1/49.7
Infant mortality rate (per 1 000 live births)	2010-2015	62.1
Fertility rate, total (live births per woman)	2010-2015	3.1
Contraceptive prevalence (ages 15-49, %)	2006-2010	47.0
International migrant stock (000 and % of total population) [ef]	mid-2010	6.3/0.3
Refugees and others of concern to UNHCR	end-2010	0[g]
Education: Government expenditure (% of GDP)	2005-2011	13.1
Education: Primary-secondary gross enrolment ratio (f/m per 100)	2005-2011	82.1/77.4
Education: Female third-level students (% of total)	2005-2011	55.2
Seats held by women in national parliaments (%)	2011	24.2

Environmental indicators		
Threatened species	2011	16
Forested area (% of land area)	2009	1.4
Energy consumption per capita (kilograms oil equivalent)	2009	8.0

a Principal rate. **b** Arrivals of non-resident visitors at national borders. **c** 2009. **d** 2008. **e** Data refer to foreign citizens. **f** Includes refugees. **g** Value is zero, not available or not applicable.

Liberia

Region	Western Africa
Currency	Liberian Dollar (LRD)
Surface area (square kilometres)	111 369
Population in 2010 (estimated, 000)	3 994
Population density in 2010 (per square kilometre)	35.9
Capital city and population in 2011 (000)	Monrovia (750)
United Nations membership date	2 November 1945

Economic indicators	2000	2005	2010
GDP: Gross domestic product (million current US$)	528	578	873
GDP: Growth rate at constant 2005 prices (annual %)	22.4	5.3	5.2
GDP per capita (current US$)	185.4	181.6	218.6
GNI: Gross national income per capita (current US$)	128.4	142.9	166.5
Gross fixed capital formation (% of GDP)	7.3	16.4	20.0
Exchange rates (national currency per US$) [a]	42.75	56.50	71.50
Balance of payments, current account (million US$)	...	−208	−738
Agricultural production index (2004-2006=100)	100	105	102
Food production index (2004-2006=100)	101	104	122
Employment in industrial sector (% of employed)	...	2.5[bc]	9.2
Employment in agricultural sector (% of employed)	...	47.6[bc]	48.9
Labour force participation, adult female pop. (%)	58.2	58.3	57.8
Labour force participation, adult male pop. (%)	61.8	62.4	64.0
Telephone subscribers, total (per 100 inhabitants)	0.3	5.0[d]	39.5
Internet users (per 100 inhabitants)	<	0.6[b]	7.0

Social indicators		
Population growth rate (average annual %)	2010-2015	2.6
Urban population growth rate (average annual %)	2010-2015	3.4
Rural population growth rate (average annual %)	2010-2015	1.9
Urban population (%)	2011	48.2
Population aged 0-14 years (%)	2011	43.5
Population aged 60+ years (females and males, % of total)	2011	4.8/3.9
Sex ratio (males per 100 females)	2011	101.1
Life expectancy at birth (females and males, years)	2010-2015	58.6/56.4
Infant mortality rate (per 1 000 live births)	2010-2015	76.9
Fertility rate, total (live births per woman)	2010-2015	5.0
Contraceptive prevalence (ages 15-49, %)	2006-2010	11.4
International migrant stock (000 and % of total population)	mid-2010	96.3/2.4
Refugees and others of concern to UNHCR	end-2010	27 926
Education: Government expenditure (% of GDP)	2005-2011	2.8
Education: Primary-secondary gross enrolment ratio (f/m per 100)	2005-2011	64.0/87.4[e]
Education: Female third-level students (% of total)	2005-2011	35.3[e]
Seats held by women in national parliaments (%) [f]	2011	12.5

Environmental indicators		
Threatened species	2011	147
Forested area (% of land area)	2009	45.3
CO_2 emission estimates (000 metric tons and metric tons per capita)	2008	608/0.2
Energy consumption per capita (kilograms oil equivalent)	2009	41.0

a Principal rate. b 2007. c Core Welfare Indicators Questionnaire (World Bank). d Mobile cellular subscriptions only. e 2000. f As of 30 September 2011.

Libya

Region	Northern Africa
Currency	Libyan Dinar (LYD)
Surface area (square kilometres)	1 759 540
Population in 2010 (estimated, 000)	6 355
Population density in 2010 (per square kilometre)	3.6
Capital city and population in 2011 (000)	Tripoli (1 127)
United Nations membership date	14 December 1955

Economic indicators	2000	2005	2010
GDP: Gross domestic product (million current US$)	38 471	45 451	71 945
GDP: Growth rate at constant 2005 prices (annual %)	2.3	10.3	4.2
GDP per capita (current US$)	7 354.1	7 877.6	11 320.8
GNI: Gross national income per capita (current US$)	7 225.9	7 827.3	11 416.1
Gross fixed capital formation (% of GDP)	12.6	8.6	9.2
Exchange rates (national currency per US$)[a]	0.54	1.35	1.25
Balance of payments, current account (million US$)	6 270	14 945	16 801
Agricultural production index (2004-2006=100)	95	101	112
Food production index (2004-2006=100)	95	101	112
Labour force participation, adult female pop. (%)	27.4	30.2	30.4
Labour force participation, adult male pop. (%)	73.0	75.3	76.9
Tourist arrivals at national borders (000)	174	81[b]	34[bc]
Energy production, primary (000 mt oil equivalent)	72 223	94 019	87 287[d]
Telephone subscribers, total (per 100 inhabitants)	12.3	49.4	190.9
Internet users (per 100 inhabitants)	0.2	3.9	14.0

Social indicators		
Population growth rate (average annual %)	2010-2015	0.8
Urban population growth rate (average annual %)	2010-2015	1.0
Rural population growth rate (average annual %)	2010-2015	—<
Urban population (%)	2011	77.7
Population aged 0-14 years (%)	2011	30.7
Population aged 60+ years (females and males, % of total)	2011	6.8/6.6
Sex ratio (males per 100 females)	2011	101.5
Life expectancy at birth (females and males, years)	2010-2015	77.9/72.7
Infant mortality rate (per 1 000 live births)	2010-2015	13.3
Fertility rate, total (live births per woman)	2010-2015	2.4
Contraceptive prevalence (ages 15-49, %)	2006-2010	45.2[e]
International migrant stock (000 and % of total population)[f]	mid-2010	682.5/10.4
Refugees and others of concern to UNHCR	end-2010	11 117
Education: Government expenditure (% of GDP)	2005-2011	2.7[g]
Education: Primary-secondary gross enrolment ratio (f/m per 100)	2005-2011	115.6/109.0
Education: Female third-level students (% of total)[h]	2005-2011	51.4[i]

Environmental indicators		
Threatened species	2011	46
Forested area (% of land area)	2009	<
CO_2 emission estimates (000 metric tons and metric tons per capita)	2008	58 283/9.3
Energy consumption per capita (kilograms oil equivalent)	2009	2 920.0
Rainfall in the capital city, total mean (millimetres)		334
Temperature in the capital city, mean °C (minimum and maximum)		15.6/25.4

a Official rate. **b** Arrivals of non-resident tourists in hotels and similar establishments. **c** 2008. **d** 2009. **e** 1995. **f** Data refer to foreign citizens. **g** 1999. **h** UNESCO estimate. **i** 2003.

Liechtenstein

Region	Western Europe
Currency	Swiss Franc (CHF)
Surface area (square kilometres)	160
Population in 2010 (estimated, 000)	36
Population density in 2010 (per square kilometre)	225.2
Capital city and population in 2011 (000)	Vaduz (5)
United Nations membership date	18 September 1990

Economic indicators	2000	2005	2010
GDP: Gross domestic product (million current US$)	2 484	3 658	5 145
GDP: Growth rate at constant 2005 prices (annual %)	3.2	4.8	2.1
GDP per capita (current US$)	75 606.2	105 440.3	142 780.6
GNI: Gross national income per capita (current US$)	74 110.3	90 094.0	144 206.7
Gross fixed capital formation (% of GDP)	22.8	21.7	20.8
Exchange rates (national currency per US$) [a]	1.64	1.31	0.95
Agricultural production index (2004-2006=100)	97	101	99
Food production index (2004-2006=100)	97	101	99
Tourist arrivals at national borders (000) [b]	62	50	52[c]
Telephone subscribers, total (per 100 inhabitants)	91.5	136.9	152.9
Internet users (per 100 inhabitants)	36.5	63.4	80.0

Social indicators		
Population growth rate (average annual %)	2010-2015	0.8
Urban population growth rate (average annual %)	2010-2015	0.5
Rural population growth rate (average annual %)	2010-2015	0.8
Urban population (%)	2011	14.4
Population aged 0-14 years (%) [def]	2011	16.4[c]
Population aged 60+ years (females and males, % of total) [def]	2011	20.6/18.0[c]
Sex ratio (males per 100 females) [de]	2011	98.0[g]
Fertility rate, total (live births per woman) [e]	2010-2015	1.7[c]
International migrant stock (000 and % of total population) [h]	mid-2010	12.5/34.6
Refugees and others of concern to UNHCR	end-2010	142
Education: Government expenditure (% of GDP)	2005-2011	2.1
Education: Primary-secondary gross enrolment ratio (f/m per 100) [i]	2005-2011	85.1/84.0
Education: Female third-level students (% of total)	2005-2011	31.7
Seats held by women in national parliaments (%)	2011	24.0

Environmental indicators		
Threatened species	2011	4
Forested area (% of land area)	2009	43.1

a UN operational exchange rate. **b** Arrivals of non-resident tourists in hotels and similar establishments. **c** 2009. **d** De jure estimate. **e** Data compiled by the United Nations Demographic Yearbook system. **f** Data refer to the latest available census. **g** 2010. **h** Data refer to foreign citizens. **i** National estimate.

Lithuania

Region	Northern Europe
Currency	Litas (LTL)
Surface area (square kilometres)	65 300
Population in 2010 (estimated, 000)	3 324
Population density in 2010 (per square kilometre)	50.9
Capital city and population in 2011 (000)	Vilnius (546)
United Nations membership date	17 September 1991

Economic indicators	2000	2005	2010
GDP: Gross domestic product (million current US$)	11 501	26 100	36 478
GDP: Growth rate at constant 2005 prices (annual %)	3.3	7.8	1.4
GDP per capita (current US$)	3 285.9	7 641.1	10 975.5
GNI: Gross national income per capita (current US$)	3 228.8	7 524.9	10 835.3
Gross fixed capital formation (% of GDP)	18.9	22.9	16.4
Exchange rates (national currency per US$) [a]	4.00	2.91	2.61
Balance of payments, current account (million US$)	−675	−1 831	534
CPI: Consumer price index (2000=100)	100	104[b]	134
Industrial production index (2005=100)	84[c]	100	105
Agricultural production index (2004-2006=100)	102	106	99
Food production index (2004-2006=100)	102	106	99
Unemployment (% of labour force)	11.4[d]	8.3	17.8
Employment in industrial sector (% of employed)	26.8[e]	29.1[e]	24.4[f]
Employment in agricultural sector (% of employed)	18.7[e]	14.0[e]	9.0[f]
Labour force participation, adult female pop. (%)	54.8	51.1	53.9
Labour force participation, adult male pop. (%)	66.5	63.1	63.4
Tourist arrivals at national borders (000)	1 083	2 000	1 507
Energy production, primary (000 mt oil equivalent)	1 160	1 252	1 331[g]
Telephone subscribers, total (per 100 inhabitants)	48.9	150.9	169.2
Internet users (per 100 inhabitants)	6.4	36.2	62.1

Total trade		Major trading partners			2010
	(million US$)	(% of exports)			(% of imports)
Exports	20 813.9	Russian Federation	15.6	Russian Federation	32.7
Imports	23 378.0	Germany	9.8	Germany	10.9
Balance	−2 564.1	Latvia	9.6	Poland	8.8

Social indicators		
Population growth rate (average annual %)	2010-2015	−0.4
Urban population growth rate (average annual %)	2010-2015	−0.3
Rural population growth rate (average annual %)	2010-2015	−0.8
Urban population (%)	2011	67.1
Population aged 0-14 years (%)	2011	14.8
Population aged 60+ years (females and males, % of total)	2011	25.4/16.2
Sex ratio (males per 100 females)	2011	86.7
Life expectancy at birth (females and males, years)	2010-2015	78.3/67.2
Infant mortality rate (per 1 000 live births)	2010-2015	5.9
Fertility rate, total (live births per woman)	2010-2015	1.5
Contraceptive prevalence (ages 15-49, %) [h]	2006-2010	50.7[i]
International migrant stock (000 and % of total population)	mid-2010	128.9/4.0
Refugees and others of concern to UNHCR	end-2010	4 548
Education: Government expenditure (% of GDP)	2005-2011	4.9
Education: Primary-secondary gross enrolment ratio (f/m per 100)	2005-2011	97.5/98.0
Education: Female third-level students (% of total)	2005-2011	59.2
Deaths by assault (females and males, per 100 000)	2005-2008	4.0/11.3
Seats held by women in national parliaments (%)	2011	19.1

Environmental indicators		
Threatened species	2011	19
Forested area (% of land area)	2009	34.3
CO$_2$ emission estimates (000 metric tons and metric tons per capita)	2008	15 118/4.5
Energy consumption per capita (kilograms oil equivalent)	2009	1 776.0
Rainfall in the capital city, total mean (millimetres)		683
Temperature in the capital city, mean °C (minimum and maximum)		2.4/10.1

a Official rate. **b** Series linked to former series. **c** 2003. **d** 2004. **e** Excludes conscripts. **f** European Labour Force Survey (Eurostat). **g** 2009. **h** Age group 18 to 49 years. **i** 1994-1995.

Luxembourg

Region	Western Europe
Currency	Euro (EUR)
Surface area (square kilometres)	2 586
Population in 2010 (estimated, 000)	507
Population density in 2010 (per square kilometre)	196.2
Capital city and population in 2011 (000)	Luxembourg (94)
United Nations membership date	24 October 1945

Economic indicators	2000	2005	2010
GDP: Gross domestic product (million current US$)	20 270	37 659	53 330
GDP: Growth rate at constant 2005 prices (annual %)	8.4	5.4	2.7
GDP per capita (current US$)	46 544.2	82 369.7	105 095.4
GNI: Gross national income per capita (current US$)	40 556.6	70 739.9	74 733.1
Gross fixed capital formation (% of GDP)	21.9	22.0	18.0
Exchange rates (national currency per US$)[a]	1.07	0.85	0.75
Balance of payments, current account (million US$)	2 562	4 406	4 122
CPI: Consumer price index (2000=100)	100	112[b]	125
Industrial production index (2005=100)	93[c]	100	89
Agricultural production index (2004-2006=100)	114	100	97
Food production index (2004-2006=100)	114	100	97
Unemployment (% of labour force)	5.1[d]	4.5	4.4
Employment in industrial sector (% of employed)[e]	20.7[f]	17.2[f]	12.0
Employment in agricultural sector (% of employed)[e]	2.4	1.8	1.0
Labour force participation, adult female pop. (%)	41.5	45.5	48.9
Labour force participation, adult male pop. (%)	66.0	64.7	65.4
Tourist arrivals at national borders (000)[g]	852	913	849[h]
Energy production, primary (000 mt oil equivalent)	76	83	119[h]
Telephone subscribers, total (per 100 inhabitants)	126.8	165.0	197.0
Internet users (per 100 inhabitants)	22.9	70.0	90.0

Total trade		Major trading partners			2010
	(million US$)	(% of exports)			(% of imports)
Exports	13 911.3	Germany	28.4	Germany	25.6
Imports	20 400.0	France	16.2	Belgium	24.9
Balance	−6 488.7	Belgium	12.6	France	14.9

Social indicators		
Population growth rate (average annual %)	2010-2015	1.4
Urban population growth rate (average annual %)	2010-2015	1.6
Rural population growth rate (average annual %)	2010-2015	−0.2
Urban population (%)	2011	85.4
Population aged 0-14 years (%)	2011	17.6
Population aged 60+ years (females and males, % of total)	2011	20.8/17.2
Sex ratio (males per 100 females)	2011	99.0
Life expectancy at birth (females and males, years)	2010-2015	82.7/77.6
Infant mortality rate (per 1 000 live births)	2010-2015	2.3
Fertility rate, total (live births per woman)	2010-2015	1.7
International migrant stock (000 and % of total population)	mid-2010	173.2/35.2
Refugees and others of concern to UNHCR	end-2010	4 123
Education: Government expenditure (% of GDP)	2005-2011	3.7[i]
Education: Primary-secondary gross enrolment ratio (f/m per 100)	2005-2011	99.6/97.7
Education: Female third-level students (% of total)	2005-2011	48.3
Deaths by assault (females and males, per 100 000)	2005-2008	0.8/2.1[j]
Seats held by women in national parliaments (%)	2011	20.0

Environmental indicators		
Threatened species	2011	9
Forested area (% of land area)	2009	33.5
CO_2 emission estimates (000 metric tons and metric tons per capita)	2008	10 494/21.8
Energy consumption per capita (kilograms oil equivalent)	2009	8 091.0
Rainfall in the capital city, total mean (millimetres)		876
Temperature in the capital city, mean °C (minimum and maximum)		4.7/12.3

a Market rate. **b** Series linked to former series. **c** 2003. **d** 2004. **e** European Labour Force Survey (Eurostat). **f** Excludes mining and quarrying. **g** Arrivals of non-resident tourists in all types of accommodation establishments. **h** 2009. **i** 2001. **j** Rate based on 30 or fewer events.

Madagascar

Region	Eastern Africa
Currency	Malagasy Ariary (MGA) [a]
Surface area (square kilometres)	587 041
Population in 2010 (estimated, 000)	20 714
Population density in 2010 (per square kilometre)	35.3
Capital city and population in 2011 (000)	Antananarivo (1 987)
United Nations membership date	20 September 1960

Economic indicators	2000	2005	2010
GDP: Gross domestic product (million current US$)	3 878	5 039	8 739
GDP: Growth rate at constant 2005 prices (annual %)	4.7	4.6	0.5
GDP per capita (current US$)	252.4	281.7	421.9
GNI: Gross national income per capita (current US$)	247.8	277.3	417.4
Gross fixed capital formation (% of GDP)	16.2	22.2	18.8
Exchange rates (national currency per US$) [b]	1 310.09	2 159.82	2 146.12
Balance of payments, current account (million US$)	−283	−626	...
CPI: Consumer price index (2000=100)	100	166	264
Agricultural production index (2004-2006=100)	88	103	122
Food production index (2004-2006=100)	87	103	121
Employment in industrial sector (% of employed)	6.7 [cd]	3.7 [e]	...
Employment in agricultural sector (% of employed)	78.0 [cd]	80.4	...
Labour force participation, adult female pop. (%)	84.0	84.1	83.5
Labour force participation, adult male pop. (%)	89.7	89.2	88.7
Tourist arrivals at national borders (000) [f]	160	277	196
Energy production, primary (000 mt oil equivalent)	46	56	64 [g]
Telephone subscribers, total (per 100 inhabitants)	0.8	3.4	37.9
Internet users (per 100 inhabitants)	0.2	0.6	1.7

Total trade		Major trading partners			2010
(million US$)		(% of exports)			(% of imports)
Exports	1 082.2	France	33.1	France	14.4
Imports	2 545.8	Germany	7.3	China	12.2
Balance	−1 463.6	China	5.2	South Africa	7.7

Social indicators

Population growth rate (average annual %)	2010-2015	2.8
Urban population growth rate (average annual %)	2010-2015	4.7
Rural population growth rate (average annual %)	2010-2015	1.9
Urban population (%)	2011	32.6
Population aged 0-14 years (%)	2011	42.8
Population aged 60+ years (females and males, % of total)	2011	5.0/4.5
Sex ratio (males per 100 females)	2011	99.4
Life expectancy at birth (females and males, years)	2010-2015	68.6/65.2
Infant mortality rate (per 1 000 live births)	2010-2015	41.0
Fertility rate, total (live births per woman)	2010-2015	4.5
Contraceptive prevalence (ages 15-49, %)	2006-2010	39.9
International migrant stock (000 and % of total population) [h]	mid-2010	37.8/0.2
Refugees and others of concern to UNHCR	end-2010	0 [i]
Education: Government expenditure (% of GDP)	2005-2011	3.2
Education: Primary-secondary gross enrolment ratio (f/m per 100) [j]	2005-2011	86.4/89.1
Education: Female third-level students (% of total)	2005-2011	47.8
Seats held by women in national parliaments (%)	2011	12.5

Environmental indicators

Threatened species	2011	766
Forested area (% of land area)	2009	21.7
CO_2 emission estimates (000 metric tons and metric tons per capita)	2008	1 909/0.1
Energy consumption per capita (kilograms oil equivalent)	2009	31.0
Rainfall in the capital city, total mean (millimetres)		1 365
Temperature in the capital city, mean °C (minimum and maximum)		13.8/24.0

a Beginning 1 January 2005, the Malagasy Ariary replaced the Malagasy Franc, at a rate of 1 Ariary=5 Francs. **b** Official rate. **c** 2003. **d** Age group 6 years and over. **e** Excludes mining and quarrying. **f** Air arrivals of non-resident tourists. **g** 2009. **h** Data refer to foreign citizens. **i** Value is zero, not available or not applicable. **j** UNESCO estimate.

Malawi

Region	Eastern Africa
Currency	Kwacha (MWK)
Surface area (square kilometres)	118 484
Population in 2010 (estimated, 000)	14 901
Population density in 2010 (per square kilometre)	125.8
Capital city and population in 2011 (000)	Lilongwe (772)
United Nations membership date	1 December 1964

Economic indicators	2000	2005	2010
GDP: Gross domestic product (million current US$)	2 402	2 755	5 325
GDP: Growth rate at constant 2005 prices (annual %)	1.6	3.3	6.7
GDP per capita (current US$)	213.9	214.9	357.4
GNI: Gross national income per capita (current US$)	209.5	210.6	348.5
Gross fixed capital formation (% of GDP)	17.5	20.2	22.3
Exchange rates (national currency per US$)[a]	80.08	123.78	150.80
Balance of payments, current account (million US$)	−74	−620	−563[b]
CPI: Consumer price index (2000=100)	100	199	309
Agricultural production index (2004-2006=100)	98	85	166
Food production index (2004-2006=100)	98	85	165
Labour force participation, adult female pop. (%)	77.2	79.2	85.0
Labour force participation, adult male pop. (%)	81.2	86.3	81.2
Tourist arrivals at national borders (000)[c]	228	438	746
Energy production, primary (000 mt oil equivalent)	144[d]	145	167[bd]
Telephone subscribers, total (per 100 inhabitants)	0.9	4.1	21.5
Internet users (per 100 inhabitants)	0.1	0.4	2.3

Total trade		Major trading partners			2010
	(million US$)	(% of exports)			(% of imports)
Exports	1 066.2	Belgium	12.4	South Africa	30.1
Imports	2 173.0	Canada	11.0	China	9.1
Balance	−1 106.8	Egypt	9.2	India	7.6

Social indicators

Population growth rate (average annual %)	2010-2015	3.2
Urban population growth rate (average annual %)	2010-2015	4.2
Rural population growth rate (average annual %)	2010-2015	3.1
Urban population (%)	2011	15.7
Population aged 0-14 years (%)	2011	45.9
Population aged 60+ years (females and males, % of total)	2011	5.4/4.5
Sex ratio (males per 100 females)	2011	100.2
Life expectancy at birth (females and males, years)	2010-2015	55.2/54.9
Infant mortality rate (per 1 000 live births)	2010-2015	86.1
Fertility rate, total (live births per woman)	2010-2015	6.0
Contraceptive prevalence (ages 15-49, %)	2006-2010	41.0
International migrant stock (000 and % of total population)[e]	mid-2010	275.9/1.8
Refugees and others of concern to UNHCR	end-2010	15 102
Education: Government expenditure (% of GDP)	2005-2011	5.7
Education: Primary-secondary gross enrolment ratio (f/m per 100)	2005-2011	88.4/87.3
Education: Female third-level students (% of total)	2005-2011	38.0
Seats held by women in national parliaments (%)	2011	20.8

Environmental indicators

Threatened species	2011	159
Forested area (% of land area)	2009	34.7
CO_2 emission estimates (000 metric tons and metric tons per capita)	2008	1 227/0.1
Energy consumption per capita (kilograms oil equivalent)	2009	30.0
Rainfall in the capital city, total mean (millimetres)[f]		1 289
Temperature in the capital city, mean °C (minimum and maximum)[f]		12.2/24.1

a Official rate. b 2009. c Departures. d UNSD estimate. e Includes refugees. f Mzuzu.

Malaysia

Region	South-eastern Asia
Currency	Ringgit (MYR)
Surface area (square kilometres)	330 803
Population in 2010 (estimated, 000)	28 401 [a]
Population density in 2010 (per square kilometre)	85.9
Capital city and population in 2011 (000)	Kuala Lumpur (1 556) [b]
United Nations membership date	17 September 1957

Economic indicators	2000	2005	2010
GDP: Gross domestic product (million current US$)	93 790	137 954	237 797
GDP: Growth rate at constant 2005 prices (annual %)	8.9	5.3	7.2
GDP per capita (current US$)	4 005.6	5 285.6	8 372.8
GNI: Gross national income per capita (current US$)	3 680.7	5 043.3	8 083.0
Gross fixed capital formation (% of GDP)	25.3	20.5	20.3
Exchange rates (national currency per US$) [c]	3.80	3.78	3.08
Balance of payments, current account (million US$)	8 488	19 980	27 291
CPI: Consumer price index (2000=100)	100	109 [d]	124
Industrial production index (2005=100) [e]	86 [f]	100	107
Agricultural production index (2004-2006=100)	78	100	112
Food production index (2004-2006=100)	78	100	117
Unemployment (% of labour force)	...	3.3 [g]	3.3
Employment in industrial sector (% of employed) [h]	32.2	29.7	27.0 [i]
Employment in agricultural sector (% of employed) [h]	18.4	14.6	13.5 [i]
Labour force participation, adult female pop. (%)	44.6	44.1	43.7
Labour force participation, adult male pop. (%)	81.7	79.3	77.1
Tourist arrivals at national borders (000) [j]	10 222	16 431	24 577
Energy production, primary (000 mt oil equivalent)	77 124 [k]	96 488	91 705 [ik]
Telephone subscribers, total (per 100 inhabitants)	41.6	91.6	135.3
Internet users (per 100 inhabitants)	21.4	48.6	56.3

Total trade		Major trading partners			2010
	(million US$)	(% of exports)			(% of imports)
Exports	198 790.7	Singapore	13.4	Japan	12.6
Imports	164 586.3	China	12.6	China	12.6
Balance	34 204.4	Japan	10.4	Singapore	11.4

Social indicators		
Population growth rate (average annual %) [a]	2010-2015	1.6
Urban population growth rate (average annual %)	2010-2015	2.5
Rural population growth rate (average annual %)	2010-2015	−1.0
Urban population (%)	2011	72.8
Population aged 0-14 years (%) [a]	2011	29.9
Population aged 60+ years (females and males, % of total) [a]	2011	8.2/7.8
Sex ratio (males per 100 females) [a]	2011	102.9
Life expectancy at birth (females and males, years) [a]	2010-2015	76.9/72.5
Infant mortality rate (per 1 000 live births) [a]	2010-2015	6.9
Fertility rate, total (live births per woman) [a]	2010-2015	2.6
Contraceptive prevalence (ages 15-49, %)	2006-2010	54.5 [l]
International migrant stock (000 and % of total population) [m]	mid-2010	2 357.6/8.5
Refugees and others of concern to UNHCR	end-2010	212 856 [n]
Education: Government expenditure (% of GDP)	2005-2011	5.8
Education: Primary-secondary gross enrolment ratio (f/m per 100)	2005-2011	84.5/81.3
Education: Female third-level students (% of total)	2005-2011	55.6
Seats held by women in national parliaments (%)	2011	9.9

Environmental indicators		
Threatened species	2011	1 187
Forested area (% of land area)	2009	62.5
CO_2 emission estimates (000 metric tons and metric tons per capita)	2008	208 097/7.7
Energy consumption per capita (kilograms oil equivalent)	2009	2 477.0
Rainfall in the capital city, total mean (millimetres)		2 427
Temperature in the capital city, mean °C (minimum and maximum)		23.2/32.4

a Includes Sabah and Sarawak. **b** Kuala Lumpur is the financial capital, Putrajaya is the administrative capital. **c** Official rate. **d** Series linked to former series. **e** The indices are shown in terms of ISIC Rev. 3. **f** 2003. **g** 2006. **h** Age group 15 to 64 years. **i** 2009. **j** Includes residents of Singapore crossing the frontier by road through Johore Causeway. **k** UNSD estimate. **l** 1994. **m** Includes refugees. **n** According to UNHCR, and based on lists provided by refugee communities in Malaysia, there are 10,000 unregistered asylum-seekers in Malaysia who share the same profile as the current population of asylum-seekers and refugees and who are being progressively registered and having their refugee status determined.

Maldives

Region	South-central Asia
Currency	Rufiyaa (MVR)
Surface area (square kilometres)	300
Population in 2010 (estimated, 000)	316
Population density in 2010 (per square kilometre)	1 053.0
Capital city and population in 2011 (000)	Male (132)
United Nations membership date	21 September 1965

Economic indicators	2000	2005	2010
GDP: Gross domestic product (million current US$)	624	750	1 480
GDP: Growth rate at constant 2005 prices (annual %)	4.4	−5.0	11.6
GDP per capita (current US$)	2 285.0	2 539.5	4 684.5
GNI: Gross national income per capita (current US$)	2 175.1	2 417.5	4 446.4
Gross fixed capital formation (% of GDP)	26.3	61.1	56.7
Exchange rates (national currency per US$)[a]	11.77	12.80	12.80
Balance of payments, current account (million US$)	−51	−273	−463
CPI: Consumer price index (2000=100)[b]	100	108	146
Agricultural production index (2004-2006=100)	97	78	86
Food production index (2004-2006=100)	97	78	86
Employment in industrial sector (% of employed)[cd]	19.0[e]	24.3[f]	...
Employment in agricultural sector (% of employed)[cd]	13.7[e]	11.5[f]	...
Labour force participation, adult female pop. (%)	37.4	50.2	55.1
Labour force participation, adult male pop. (%)	71.4	74.6	76.4
Tourist arrivals at national borders (000)[g]	467	395	792
Telephone subscribers, total (per 100 inhabitants)	11.7	79.9	171.7
Internet users (per 100 inhabitants)	2.2	6.9	28.3

Total trade		Major trading partners			2010
	(million US$)		(% of exports)		(% of imports)
Exports	74.2	Thailand	29.9	United Arab Emirates	18.8
Imports	1 095.1	Sri Lanka	19.5	Singapore	17.9
Balance	−1 020.9	France	10.9	India	11.5

Social indicators		
Population growth rate (average annual %)	2010-2015	1.3
Urban population growth rate (average annual %)	2010-2015	3.9
Rural population growth rate (average annual %)	2010-2015	−0.7
Urban population (%)	2011	41.2
Population aged 0-14 years (%)	2011	25.8
Population aged 60+ years (females and males, % of total)	2011	6.6/7.3
Sex ratio (males per 100 females)	2011	101.6
Life expectancy at birth (females and males, years)	2010-2015	78.7/76.0
Infant mortality rate (per 1 000 live births)	2010-2015	8.1
Fertility rate, total (live births per woman)	2010-2015	1.7
Contraceptive prevalence (ages 15-49, %)	2006-2010	34.7
International migrant stock (000 and % of total population)[h]	mid-2010	3.3/1.0
Education: Government expenditure (% of GDP)	2005-2011	8.7
Education: Primary-secondary gross enrolment ratio (f/m per 100)[i]	2005-2011	103.2/101.4[j]
Education: Female third-level students (% of total)	2005-2011	69.9[j]
Seats held by women in national parliaments (%)	2011	6.5

Environmental indicators		
Threatened species	2011	62
Forested area (% of land area)	2009	3.0
CO_2 emission estimates (000 metric tons and metric tons per capita)	2008	920/3.0
Energy consumption per capita (kilograms oil equivalent)	2009	1 092.0
Rainfall in the capital city, total mean (millimetres)		1 901
Temperature in the capital city, mean °C (minimum and maximum)		25.8/30.6

a Market rate. b Male. c Population census. d Excludes conscripts. e Age group 12 years and over. f 2006. g Air arrivals. h Estimates. i UNESCO estimate. j 2004.

Mali

Region	Western Africa
Currency	CFA Franc (XOF)
Surface area (square kilometres)	1 240 192
Population in 2010 (estimated, 000)	15 370
Population density in 2010 (per square kilometre)	12.4
Capital city and population in 2011 (000)	Bamako (2 037)
United Nations membership date	28 September 1960

Economic indicators	2000	2005	2010
GDP: Gross domestic product (million current US$)	2 655	5 486	9 204
GDP: Growth rate at constant 2005 prices (annual %)	−3.3	6.1	4.5
GDP per capita (current US$)	235.1	416.4	598.8
GNI: Gross national income per capita (current US$)	232.2	400.2	598.8
Gross fixed capital formation (% of GDP)	18.9	15.4	21.2
Exchange rates (national currency per US$)[a]	704.95	556.04	490.91
Balance of payments, current account (million US$)	−255	−438	−655[b]
CPI: Consumer price index (2000=100)[c]	100	112	131[d]
Industrial production index (2005=100)[e]	89[f]	100	128
Agricultural production index (2004-2006=100)	75	103	148
Food production index (2004-2006=100)	77	103	161
Employment in industrial sector (% of employed)	...	5.6[g]	...
Employment in agricultural sector (% of employed)	...	66.0[g]	...
Labour force participation, adult female pop. (%)	37.2	36.4	36.8
Labour force participation, adult male pop. (%)	66.3	68.0	69.7
Tourist arrivals at national borders (000)[h]	86[i]	143[i]	169
Energy production, primary (000 mt oil equivalent)[j]	20	22	25[b]
Telephone subscribers, total (per 100 inhabitants)	0.4	6.4	49.2
Internet users (per 100 inhabitants)	0.1	0.5	2.7

Total trade		Major trading partners			2010
	(million US$)	(% of exports)			(% of imports)
Exports	1 996.3	South Africa	57.1	Senegal	13.6
Imports	4 703.5	Switzerland	12.1	France	13.4
Balance	−2 707.2	Italy	6.0	Benin	9.9

Social indicators

Population growth rate (average annual %)	2010-2015	3.0
Urban population growth rate (average annual %)	2010-2015	4.8
Rural population growth rate (average annual %)	2010-2015	1.9
Urban population (%)	2011	34.9
Population aged 0-14 years (%)	2011	47.2
Population aged 60+ years (females and males, % of total)	2011	4.1/2.9
Sex ratio (males per 100 females)	2011	100.0
Life expectancy at birth (females and males, years)	2010-2015	53.1/50.9
Infant mortality rate (per 1 000 live births)	2010-2015	92.2
Fertility rate, total (live births per woman)	2010-2015	6.1
Contraceptive prevalence (ages 15-49, %)	2006-2010	8.2
International migrant stock (000 and % of total population)[k]	mid-2010	162.7/1.2
Refugees and others of concern to UNHCR	end-2010	15 261
Education: Government expenditure (% of GDP)	2005-2011	4.5
Education: Primary-secondary gross enrolment ratio (f/m per 100)	2005-2011	56.9/68.6
Education: Female third-level students (% of total)	2005-2011	28.7
Seats held by women in national parliaments (%)	2011	10.2

Environmental indicators

Threatened species	2011	32
Forested area (% of land area)	2009	10.3
CO$_2$ emission estimates (000 metric tons and metric tons per capita)	2008	594/0.0
Energy consumption per capita (kilograms oil equivalent)	2009	15.0[j]
Rainfall in the capital city, total mean (millimetres)		991
Temperature in the capital city, mean °C (minimum and maximum)		21.3/35.0

a Official rate. **b** 2009. **c** Bamako. **d** Series linked to former series. **e** The indices are shown in terms of ISIC Rev. 3. **f** 2003. **g** 2006. **h** Arrivals of non-resident tourists in hotels and similar establishments. **i** Air arrivals. **j** UNSD estimate. **k** Includes refugees.

Malta

Region	Southern Europe
Currency	Euro (EUR)[a]
Surface area (square kilometres)	316
Population in 2010 (estimated, 000)	417
Population density in 2010 (per square kilometre)	1 318.1
Capital city and population in 2011 (000)	Valletta (198)
United Nations membership date	1 December 1964

Economic indicators	2000	2005	2010
GDP: Gross domestic product (million current US$)	3 957	5 981	8 163
GDP: Growth rate at constant 2005 prices (annual %)	6.8	3.7	2.7
GDP per capita (current US$)	9 957.8	14 612.4	19 599.2
GNI: Gross national income per capita (current US$)	9 708.0	13 951.5	17 988.6
Gross fixed capital formation (% of GDP)	22.6	22.0	16.6
Exchange rates (national currency per US$)	0.44[bc]	0.36[bc]	0.75[d]
Balance of payments, current account (million US$)	−480	−524	−342
CPI: Consumer price index (2000=100)	100	112	106
Industrial production index (2005=100)	...	100	99
Agricultural production index (2004-2006=100)	107	97	97
Food production index (2004-2006=100)	107	97	97
Unemployment (% of labour force)	7.2[e]	7.3	6.9
Employment in industrial sector (% of employed)[f]	32.3[g]	29.5[g]	24.6
Employment in agricultural sector (% of employed)[f]	1.7	1.7	1.3
Labour force participation, adult female pop. (%)	30.0	30.3	35.0
Labour force participation, adult male pop. (%)	71.0	68.7	67.8
Tourist arrivals at national borders (000)	1 216	1 171[h]	1 332[h]
Telephone subscribers, total (per 100 inhabitants)	80.2	128.5	169.0
Internet users (per 100 inhabitants)	13.1	41.2	63.0

Total trade		Major trading partners			2010
	(million US$)	(% of exports)		(% of imports)	
Exports	3 357.5	Singapore	14.7	Italy	23.2
Imports	4 245.8	United States	11.0	United Kingdom	8.3
Balance	−888.3	China, Hong Kong SAR	10.3	Germany	8.2

Social indicators		
Population growth rate (average annual %)	2010-2015	0.3
Urban population growth rate (average annual %)	2010-2015	0.5
Rural population growth rate (average annual %)	2010-2015	−2.8
Urban population (%)	2011	94.8
Population aged 0-14 years (%)	2011	14.7
Population aged 60+ years (females and males, % of total)	2011	24.0/20.0
Sex ratio (males per 100 females)	2011	98.5
Life expectancy at birth (females and males, years)	2010-2015	82.3/77.6
Infant mortality rate (per 1 000 live births)	2010-2015	5.4
Fertility rate, total (live births per woman)	2010-2015	1.3
Contraceptive prevalence (ages 15-49, %)[i]	2006-2010	85.8[j]
International migrant stock (000 and % of total population)[k]	mid-2010	15.5/3.8
Refugees and others of concern to UNHCR	end-2010	7 431
Education: Government expenditure (% of GDP)	2005-2011	5.8
Education: Primary-secondary gross enrolment ratio (f/m per 100)	2005-2011	97.1/104.8
Education: Female third-level students (% of total)	2005-2011	56.5
Deaths by assault (females and males, per 100 000)	2005-2008	</2.0[l]
Seats held by women in national parliaments (%)	2011	8.7

Environmental indicators		
Threatened species	2011	29
Forested area (% of land area)	2009	0.9
CO_2 emission estimates (000 metric tons and metric tons per capita)	2008	2 557/6.3
Energy consumption per capita (kilograms oil equivalent)	2009	1 967.0
Rainfall in the capital city, total mean (millimetres)[m]		553
Temperature in the capital city, mean °C (minimum and maximum)[m]		14.9/22.3

a Beginning 1 January 2008, the Maltese Liri (MTL) was replaced by the euro (1 EUR=0.42924 MTL). **b** Official rate. **c** Currency = Maltese Liri. **d** Market rate. **e** 2004. **f** European Labour Force Survey (Eurostat). **g** Excludes mining and quarrying. **h** Departures by air and by sea. **i** Age group 20 to 45 years. **j** 1993. **k** Data refer to foreign citizens. **l** Rate based on 30 or fewer events. **m** Luqa.

Marshall Islands

Region	Oceania-Micronesia
Currency	U.S. Dollar (USD)
Surface area (square kilometres)	181
Population in 2010 (estimated, 000)	54
Population density in 2010 (per square kilometre)	298.6
Capital city and population in 2011 (000)	Majuro (31)
United Nations membership date	17 September 1991

Economic indicators	2000	2005	2010
GDP: Gross domestic product (million current US$)	108	139	166
GDP: Growth rate at constant 2005 prices (annual %)	5.2	2.0	0.5
GDP per capita (current US$)	2 067.0	2 677.8	3 069.4
GNI: Gross national income per capita (current US$)	2 570.5	3 292.2	3 755.5
Gross fixed capital formation (% of GDP)	56.8	56.8	56.8
CPI: Consumer price index (2000=100)[a]	100	107	135[b]
Agricultural production index (2004-2006=100)	23	99	176
Food production index (2004-2006=100)	23	99	176
Tourist arrivals at national borders (000)	5[c]	9[d]	5
Telephone subscribers, total (per 100 inhabitants)	8.5	9.7	15.2
Internet users (per 100 inhabitants)	1.5	3.9	3.6[e]

Social indicators		
Population growth rate (average annual %)	2010-2015	1.6
Urban population growth rate (average annual %)	2010-2015	2.0
Rural population growth rate (average annual %)	2010-2015	0.5
Urban population (%)	2011	71.8
Population aged 0-14 years (%)[f]	2011	41.6
Population aged 60+ years (females and males, % of total)[f]	2011	4.6/4.3
Sex ratio (males per 100 females)[f]	2011	105.4
Life expectancy at birth (females and males, years)[g]	2010-2015	70.6/67.0[h]
Infant mortality rate (per 1 000 live births)[f]	2010-2015	21.0[i]
Fertility rate, total (live births per woman)[f]	2010-2015	4.4[j]
Contraceptive prevalence (ages 15-49, %)	2006-2010	44.6
International migrant stock (000 and % of total population)	mid-2010	1.7/2.7
Education: Government expenditure (% of GDP)[k]	2005-2011	12.2[h]
Education: Primary-secondary gross enrolment ratio (f/m per 100)	2005-2011	103.9/102.7
Education: Female third-level students (% of total)[k]	2005-2011	56.5[l]
Seats held by women in national parliaments (%)[m]	2011	3.0

Environmental indicators		
Threatened species	2011	86
Forested area (% of land area)	2009	70.2
CO_2 emission estimates (000 metric tons and metric tons per capita)	2008	99/1.6
Energy consumption per capita (kilograms oil equivalent)	2009	627.0[n]

a Majuro. **b** 2008. **c** Air arrivals. **d** Air and sea arrivals. **e** 2009. **f** Data compiled by the Secretariat of the Pacific Community Demography Programme. **g** Data compiled by the United Nations Demographic Yearbook system. **h** 2004. **i** 2003-2007. **j** 2002-2007. **k** UNESCO estimate. **l** 2003. **m** As of 31 October 2011. **n** UNSD estimate.

Martinique

Region	Caribbean
Currency	Euro (EUR)
Surface area (square kilometres)	1 128
Population in 2010 (estimated, 000)	406
Population density in 2010 (per square kilometre)	359.8
Capital city and population in 2011 (000)	Fort-de-France (87)

Economic indicators	2000	2005	2010
Exchange rates (national currency per US$)[a]	1.07	0.85	0.75
CPI: Consumer price index (2000=100)	100	111	121
Agricultural production index (2004-2006=100)	123	99	81
Food production index (2004-2006=100)	123	99	81
Labour force participation, adult female pop. (%)	54.9	51.0	48.4
Labour force participation, adult male pop. (%)	62.1	57.2	54.8
Tourist arrivals at national borders (000)	526	484	478
Energy production, primary (000 mt oil equivalent)	2	3	4[bc]
Telephone subscribers, total (per 100 inhabitants)	86.6	43.3[d]	42.4[d]
Internet users (per 100 inhabitants)	7.8	32.7	42.0[b]

Social indicators		
Population growth rate (average annual %)	2010-2015	0.3
Urban population growth rate (average annual %)	2010-2015	0.3
Rural population growth rate (average annual %)	2010-2015	0.4
Urban population (%)	2011	89.0
Population aged 0-14 years (%)	2011	19.1
Population aged 60+ years (females and males, % of total)	2011	21.8/18.7
Sex ratio (males per 100 females)	2011	87.8
Life expectancy at birth (females and males, years)	2010-2015	83.7/77.3
Infant mortality rate (per 1 000 live births)	2010-2015	7.2
Fertility rate, total (live births per woman)	2010-2015	1.8
Contraceptive prevalence (ages 15-49, %)	2006-2010	35.5[e]
International migrant stock (000 and % of total population)	mid-2010	71.5/17.6

Environmental indicators		
Threatened species	2011	33
Forested area (% of land area)	2009	45.8
CO$_2$ emission estimates (000 metric tons and metric tons per capita)	2008	1 916/4.8
Energy consumption per capita (kilograms oil equivalent)	2009	1 765.0[c]
Rainfall in the capital city, total mean (millimetres)[f]		2 030
Temperature in the capital city, mean °C (minimum and maximum)[f]		22.8/29.7

a Market rate. **b** 2009. **c** UNSD estimate. **d** Main telephone lines only. **e** 1976. **f** Le Lamentin.

Mauritania

Region	Western Africa
Currency	Ouguiya (MRO)
Surface area (square kilometres)	1 030 700
Population in 2010 (estimated, 000)	3 460
Population density in 2010 (per square kilometre)	3.4
Capital city and population in 2011 (000)	Nouakchott (786)
United Nations membership date	27 October 1961

Economic indicators	2000	2005	2010
GDP: Gross domestic product (million current US$)	1 294	2 184	3 913
GDP: Growth rate at constant 2005 prices (annual %)	−0.4	9.0	4.7
GDP per capita (current US$)	489.5	716.9	1 131.1
GNI: Gross national income per capita (current US$)	494.0	741.8	1 137.4
Gross fixed capital formation (% of GDP)	16.2	59.0	30.6
Exchange rates (national currency per US$) [a]	252.30	270.61	282.00
CPI: Consumer price index (2000=100)	100	139	170[b]
Agricultural production index (2004-2006=100)	89	100	113
Food production index (2004-2006=100)	89	100	113
Labour force participation, adult female pop. (%)	23.1	26.0	28.4
Labour force participation, adult male pop. (%)	78.1	78.6	79.1
Tourist arrivals at national borders (000)	30	...	...
Energy production, primary (000 mt oil equivalent)	...	0	567[c]
Telephone subscribers, total (per 100 inhabitants)	1.3	25.8	81.4
Internet users (per 100 inhabitants)	0.2	0.7	3.0

Total trade		Major trading partners			2010
	(million US$)	(% of exports)			(% of imports)
Exports	725.4	China	19.1	France	14.1
Imports	1 726.5	Switzerland	18.6	United Arab Emirates	12.1
Balance	−1 001.1	Japan	16.2	Netherlands	10.6

Social indicators		
Population growth rate (average annual %)	2010-2015	2.2
Urban population growth rate (average annual %)	2010-2015	2.9
Rural population growth rate (average annual %)	2010-2015	1.8
Urban population (%)	2011	41.5
Population aged 0-14 years (%)	2011	39.7
Population aged 60+ years (females and males, % of total)	2011	5.1/3.8
Sex ratio (males per 100 females)	2011	101.0
Life expectancy at birth (females and males, years)	2010-2015	61.0/57.4
Infant mortality rate (per 1 000 live births)	2010-2015	69.9
Fertility rate, total (live births per woman)	2010-2015	4.4
Contraceptive prevalence (ages 15-49, %)	2006-2010	9.3
International migrant stock (000 and % of total population) [de]	mid-2010	99.2/3.0
Refugees and others of concern to UNHCR	end-2010	28 349
Education: Government expenditure (% of GDP) [f]	2005-2011	4.3
Education: Primary-secondary gross enrolment ratio (f/m per 100) [f]	2005-2011	66.2/65.4
Education: Female third-level students (% of total)	2005-2011	28.2
Seats held by women in national parliaments (%)	2011	22.1

Environmental indicators		
Threatened species	2011	62
Forested area (% of land area)	2009	<
CO$_2$ emission estimates (000 metric tons and metric tons per capita)	2008	1 997/0.6
Energy consumption per capita (kilograms oil equivalent)	2009	180.0[g]

a Market rate. **b** 2008. **c** 2009. **d** Data refer to foreign citizens. **e** Includes refugees. **f** UNESCO estimate. **g** UNSD estimate.

Mauritius

Region	Eastern Africa
Currency	Mauritian Rupee (MUR)
Surface area (square kilometres)	1 969 [a]
Population in 2010 (estimated, 000)	1 299 [b]
Population density in 2010 (per square kilometre)	659.8 [c]
Capital city and population in 2011 (000)	Port Louis (151)
United Nations membership date	24 April 1968

Economic indicators	2000	2005	2010
GDP: Gross domestic product (million current US$)	4 663	6 489	9 729
GDP: Growth rate at constant 2005 prices (annual %)	8.2	1.5	4.0
GDP per capita (current US$)	3 899.0	5 163.1	7 488.3
GNI: Gross national income per capita (current US$)	3 882.4	5 131.3	7 624.0
Gross fixed capital formation (% of GDP)	22.5	21.5	24.6
Exchange rates (national currency per US$) [d]	27.88	30.67	30.39
Balance of payments, current account (million US$)	−37	−324	−800
CPI: Consumer price index (2000=100)	100	128	176
Industrial production index (2005=100) [e]	106 [f]	100	114
Agricultural production index (2004-2006=100)	95	98	97
Food production index (2004-2006=100)	95	99	97
Unemployment (% of labour force) [g]	8.4 [h]	9.5	7.7
Employment in industrial sector (% of employed)	38.8 [i]	32.4	28.2 [gj]
Employment in agricultural sector (% of employed)	12.1 [i]	10.0	8.7 [gj]
Labour force participation, adult female pop. (%)	41.2	41.4	43.9
Labour force participation, adult male pop. (%)	80.7	76.8	75.7
Tourist arrivals at national borders (000)	656	761	935
Energy production, primary (000 mt oil equivalent)	8	10	11 [k]
Telephone subscribers, total (per 100 inhabitants)	38.5	80.7	121.5
Internet users (per 100 inhabitants)	7.3	15.2	28.3

Total trade		Major trading partners				2010
	(million US$)	(% of exports)				(% of imports)
Exports	1 849.5	United Kingdom	23.7	India		22.3
Imports	4 402.3	France	16.2	China		13.3
Balance	−2 552.8	United States	10.9	France		8.8

Social indicators

Population growth rate (average annual %) [b]	2010-2015	0.5
Urban population growth rate (average annual %) [b]	2010-2015	0.6
Rural population growth rate (average annual %) [b]	2010-2015	0.5
Urban population (%) [b]	2011	41.8
Population aged 0-14 years (%) [b]	2011	21.3
Population aged 60+ years (females and males, % of total) [b]	2011	12.7/10.1
Sex ratio (males per 100 females) [b]	2011	97.5
Life expectancy at birth (females and males, years) [b]	2010-2015	76.9/70.4
Infant mortality rate (per 1 000 live births) [b]	2010-2015	12.1
Fertility rate, total (live births per woman) [b]	2010-2015	1.6
Contraceptive prevalence (ages 15-49, %)	2006-2010	75.8 [l]
International migrant stock (000 and % of total population) [b]	mid-2010	42.9/3.3
Refugees and others of concern to UNHCR	end-2010	0 [m]
Education: Government expenditure (% of GDP)	2005-2011	3.1
Education: Primary-secondary gross enrolment ratio (f/m per 100) [n]	2005-2011	93.9/93.8
Education: Female third-level students (% of total) [n]	2005-2011	54.8
Deaths by assault (females and males, per 100 000)	2005-2008	3.0/5.3 [o]
Seats held by women in national parliaments (%)	2011	18.8

Environmental indicators

Threatened species	2011	222
Forested area (% of land area)	2009	17.2
CO$_2$ emission estimates (000 metric tons and metric tons per capita)	2008	3 950/3.1
Energy consumption per capita (kilograms oil equivalent)	2009	909.0
Rainfall in the capital city, total mean (millimetres)		711
Temperature in the capital city, mean °C (minimum and maximum)		21.6/29.4

a Excludes the islands of Saint Brandon and Agalega. **b** Includes Agalega, Rodrigues and Saint Brandon. **c** Surface area excludes Agalega and Saint Brandon. **d** Market rate. **e** The indices are shown in terms of ISIC Rev. 3. **f** 2003. **g** Age group 16 years and over. **h** 2004. **i** Official estimates. **j** Average of quarterly estimates. **k** 2009. **l** 2002. **m** Value is zero, not available or not applicable. **n** UNESCO estimate. **o** Rate based on 30 or fewer events.

Mexico

Region	Central America
Currency	Mexican Peso (MXN)
Surface area (square kilometres)	1 964 375
Population in 2010 (estimated, 000)	113 423
Population density in 2010 (per square kilometre)	57.7
Capital city and population in 2011 (000)	Mexico City (20 446)
United Nations membership date	7 November 1945

Economic indicators	2000	2005	2010
GDP: Gross domestic product (million current US$)	636 731	846 095	1 032 220
GDP: Growth rate at constant 2005 prices (annual %)	6.6	3.3	5.8
GDP per capita (current US$)	6 369.9	7 945.8	9 100.7
GNI: Gross national income per capita (current US$)	6 220.8	7 807.3	8 958.5
Gross fixed capital formation (% of GDP)	21.4	20.3	20.4
Exchange rates (national currency per US$) [a]	9.57	10.78	12.36
Balance of payments, current account (million US$)	–18 767	–5 095	–5 679
CPI: Consumer price index (2000=100)	100	127	158
Industrial production index (2005=100) [b]	94[c]	100	106
Agricultural production index (2004-2006=100)	88	98	106
Food production index (2004-2006=100)	87	98	107
Unemployment (% of labour force) [d]	3.9[e]	3.6	5.4
Employment in industrial sector (% of employed) [d]	26.8[f]	25.5[f]	25.5
Employment in agricultural sector (% of employed) [d]	18.0[f]	14.9[f]	13.1
Labour force participation, adult female pop. (%)	38.8	41.0	43.9
Labour force participation, adult male pop. (%)	82.7	81.1	80.5
Tourist arrivals at national borders (000) [g]	20 641	21 915	22 260
Energy production, primary (000 mt oil equivalent)	210 947	233 572	199 414[h]
Telephone subscribers, total (per 100 inhabitants)	26.4	62.6	98.1
Internet users (per 100 inhabitants)	5.1	17.2	31.1

Total trade		Major trading partners			2010
	(million US$)	(% of exports)			(% of imports)
Exports	298 305.1	United States	80.1	United States	48.2
Imports	301 481.7	Canada	3.6	China	15.1
Balance	–3 176.6	China	1.4	Japan	5.0

Social indicators

Population growth rate (average annual %)	2010-2015	1.1
Urban population growth rate (average annual %)	2010-2015	1.5
Rural population growth rate (average annual %)	2010-2015	–0.2
Urban population (%)	2011	78.1
Population aged 0-14 years (%)	2011	28.7
Population aged 60+ years (females and males, % of total)	2011	9.8/8.7
Sex ratio (males per 100 females)	2011	97.3
Life expectancy at birth (females and males, years)	2010-2015	79.6/74.8
Infant mortality rate (per 1 000 live births)	2010-2015	14.2
Fertility rate, total (live births per woman)	2010-2015	2.2
Contraceptive prevalence (ages 15-49, %)	2006-2010	70.9
International migrant stock (000 and % of total population) [i]	mid-2010	725.7/0.7
Refugees and others of concern to UNHCR	end-2010	1 570
Education: Government expenditure (% of GDP)	2005-2011	4.9
Education: Primary-secondary gross enrolment ratio (f/m per 100)	2005-2011	101.9/99.6
Education: Female third-level students (% of total)	2005-2011	50.2
Deaths by assault (females and males, per 100 000)	2005-2008	2.0/14.2
Seats held by women in national parliaments (%)	2011	26.2

Environmental indicators

Threatened species	2011	946
Forested area (% of land area)	2009	33.4
CO_2 emission estimates (000 metric tons and metric tons per capita)	2008	475 444/4.4
Energy consumption per capita (kilograms oil equivalent)	2009	1 395.0
Rainfall in the capital city, total mean (millimetres)		816
Temperature in the capital city, mean °C (minimum and maximum)		9.6/23.4

a Principal rate. b The indices are shown in terms of ISIC Rev. 3. c 2003. d Age group 14 years and over. e 2004. f Second quarter. g Includes nationals residing abroad. h 2009. i Includes refugees.

Micronesia (Federated States of)

Region	Oceania-Micronesia
Currency	U.S. Dollar (USD)
Surface area (square kilometres)	702
Population in 2010 (estimated, 000)	111
Population density in 2010 (per square kilometre)	158.2
Capital city and population in 2011 (000)	Palikir (7)
United Nations membership date	17 September 1991

Economic indicators	2000	2005	2010
GDP: Gross domestic product (million current US$)	234	250	297
GDP: Growth rate at constant 2005 prices (annual %)	4.5	2.1	3.1
GDP per capita (current US$)	2 181.2	2 285.2	2 678.2
GNI: Gross national income per capita (current US$)	2 239.9	2 397.2	2 806.5
Gross fixed capital formation (% of GDP)	30.5	31.2	31.0
Exchange rates (national currency per US$)[a]	1.00	1.00	1.00
Agricultural production index (2004-2006=100)	89	101	105
Food production index (2004-2006=100)	89	101	105
Tourist arrivals at national borders (000)[bc]	21	19	26[d]
Telephone subscribers, total (per 100 inhabitants)	9.0[e]	24.3	32.4
Internet users (per 100 inhabitants)	3.7	11.9	20.0

Social indicators		
Population growth rate (average annual %)	2010-2015	0.6
Urban population growth rate (average annual %)	2010-2015	1.0
Rural population growth rate (average annual %)	2010-2015	0.4
Urban population (%)	2011	22.6
Population aged 0-14 years (%)	2011	36.1
Population aged 60+ years (females and males, % of total)	2011	6.7/5.7
Sex ratio (males per 100 females)	2011	104.2
Life expectancy at birth (females and males, years)	2010-2015	70.2/68.3
Infant mortality rate (per 1 000 live births)	2010-2015	31.5
Fertility rate, total (live births per woman)	2010-2015	3.3
International migrant stock (000 and % of total population)	mid-2010	2.7/2.4
Refugees and others of concern to UNHCR	end-2010	0[f]
Education: Government expenditure (% of GDP)[g]	2005-2011	6.7[h]
Education: Primary-secondary gross enrolment ratio (f/m per 100)	2005-2011	99.1/97.0
Seats held by women in national parliaments (%)	2011	0.0

Environmental indicators		
Threatened species	2011	150
Forested area (% of land area)	2009	91.6
CO_2 emission estimates (000 metric tons and metric tons per capita)	2008	62/0.6

a Official rate. **b** Arrivals in the States of Kosrae, Chuuk, Pohnpei and Yap. **c** Excludes citizens of the Federated States of Micronesia. **d** 2008. **e** Main telephone lines only. **f** Value is zero, not available or not applicable. **g** UNESCO estimate. **h** 2000.

Monaco

Region	Western Europe
Currency	Euro (EUR)
Surface area (square kilometres)	2
Population in 2010 (estimated, 000)	35
Population density in 2010 (per square kilometre)	17 703.5
Capital city and population in 2011 (000)	Monaco (35)
United Nations membership date	28 May 1993

Economic indicators	2000	2005	2010
GDP: Gross domestic product (million current US$)	2 657	4 280	5 424
GDP: Growth rate at constant 2005 prices (annual %)	3.7	1.8	1.5
GDP per capita (current US$)	75 641.6	121 386.0	153 176.7
GNI: Gross national income per capita (current US$)	75 641.6	121 386.0	153 176.7
Gross fixed capital formation (% of GDP)	19.0	19.4	19.3
Exchange rates (national currency per US$) [a]	1.07	0.85	0.75
Tourist arrivals at national borders (000) [b]	300	286	279
Telephone subscribers, total (per 100 inhabitants)	125.0	145.1	170.7
Internet users (per 100 inhabitants)	42.2	55.5	75.0

Social indicators		
Population growth rate (average annual %)	2010-2015	<
Urban population growth rate (average annual %)	2010-2015	<
Rural population growth rate (average annual %)	2010-2015	0.0
Urban population (%)	2011	100.0
Population aged 0-14 years (%) [cde]	2011	13.2 [f]
Population aged 60+ years (females and males, % of total) [cde]	2011	31.6/26.1 [f]
Sex ratio (males per 100 females) [cde]	2011	94.7 [g]
International migrant stock (000 and % of total population)	mid-2010	23.6/71.6
Refugees and others of concern to UNHCR	end-2010	1
Education: Government expenditure (% of GDP)	2005-2011	1.2
Seats held by women in national parliaments (%)	2011	26.1

Environmental indicators		
Threatened species	2011	14

a Market rate. b Arrivals of non-resident tourists in hotels and similar establishments. c De jure population count. d Data compiled by the United Nations Demographic Yearbook system. e Data refer to the latest available census. f 2000. g 2008.

Mongolia

Region	Eastern Asia
Currency	Tugrik (MNT)
Surface area (square kilometres)	1 564 100
Population in 2010 (estimated, 000)	2 756
Population density in 2010 (per square kilometre)	1.8
Capital city and population in 2011 (000)	Ulaanbaatar (1 184)
United Nations membership date	27 October 1961

Economic indicators	2000	2005	2010
GDP: Gross domestic product (million current US$)	1 137	2 523	6 192
GDP: Growth rate at constant 2005 prices (annual %)	1.1	7.3	6.4
GDP per capita (current US$)	471.5	990.6	2 246.7
GNI: Gross national income per capita (current US$)	449.5	938.0	2 084.7
Gross fixed capital formation (% of GDP)	25.4	28.0	35.6
Exchange rates (national currency per US$)[a]	1 097.00	1 221.00	1 256.47
Balance of payments, current account (million US$)	−156	−5	−887
CPI: Consumer price index (2000=100)[b]	...	100[c]	151[d]
Industrial production index (2005=100)[e]	94[f]	100	111
Agricultural production index (2004-2006=100)	144	97	117
Food production index (2004-2006=100)	144	97	116
Employment in industrial sector (% of employed)	14.1[ghi]	16.8[ghi]	14.9[dj]
Employment in agricultural sector (% of employed)	48.6[ghi]	39.9[ghi]	40.0[dj]
Labour force participation, adult female pop. (%)	55.7	55.2	53.9
Labour force participation, adult male pop. (%)	65.7	65.0	65.0
Tourist arrivals at national borders (000)[k]	137	338	457
Energy production, primary (000 mt oil equivalent)	1 548	2 311	6 191[d]
Telephone subscribers, total (per 100 inhabitants)	11.3	28.0	98.1
Internet users (per 100 inhabitants)	1.3	12.5[l]	12.9

Total trade		Major trading partners			2010
	(million US$)[m]	(% of exports)[m]		(% of imports)[m]	
Exports	1 886.6	China	74.2	Russian Federation	34.3
Imports	2 117.0	Canada	9.5	China	31.1
Balance	−230.4	United States	3.4	Republic of Korea	5.6

Social indicators		
Population growth rate (average annual %)	2010-2015	1.5
Urban population growth rate (average annual %)	2010-2015	2.8
Rural population growth rate (average annual %)	2010-2015	−1.4
Urban population (%)	2011	68.5
Population aged 0-14 years (%)	2011	27.8
Population aged 60+ years (females and males, % of total)	2011	6.7/5.2
Sex ratio (males per 100 females)	2011	97.5
Life expectancy at birth (females and males, years)	2010-2015	72.8/65.0
Infant mortality rate (per 1 000 live births)	2010-2015	30.7
Fertility rate, total (live births per woman)	2010-2015	2.5
Contraceptive prevalence (ages 15-49, %)	2006-2010	66.0[n]
International migrant stock (000 and % of total population)[o]	mid-2010	10.0/0.4
Refugees and others of concern to UNHCR	end-2010	273
Education: Government expenditure (% of GDP)	2005-2011	5.4
Education: Primary-secondary gross enrolment ratio (f/m per 100)	2005-2011	100.6/97.3
Education: Female third-level students (% of total)	2005-2011	60.3
Seats held by women in national parliaments (%)	2011	3.9

Environmental indicators		
Threatened species	2011	35
Forested area (% of land area)	2009	7.1
CO_2 emission estimates (000 metric tons and metric tons per capita)	2008	10 886/4.1
Energy consumption per capita (kilograms oil equivalent)	2009	1 454.0
Rainfall in the capital city, total mean (millimetres)		271
Temperature in the capital city, mean °C (minimum and maximum)		−14.5/15.4

a Market rate. **b** Index base 2006=100. **c** 2006. **d** 2009. **e** The indices are shown in terms of ISIC Rev. 3. **f** 2003. **g** December. **h** Official estimates. **i** Age group 16 years and over. **j** Data are derived from micro-sources. **k** Excludes diplomats and foreign residents in Mongolia. **l** 2008. **m** 2007. **n** 2005. **o** Data refer to foreign citizens.

Montenegro

Region	Southern Europe
Currency	Euro (EUR)
Surface area (square kilometres)	13 812
Population in 2010 (estimated, 000)	631
Population density in 2010 (per square kilometre)	45.7
Capital city and population in 2011 (000)	Podgorica (156)
United Nations membership date	28 June 2006

Economic indicators	2000	2005	2010
GDP: Gross domestic product (million current US$)	982	2 257	4 111
GDP: Growth rate at constant 2005 prices (annual %)	14.5	4.2	2.5
GDP per capita (current US$)	1 552.1	3 601.4	6 509.8
GNI: Gross national income per capita (current US$)	1 630.4	3 636.1	6 570.1
Gross fixed capital formation (% of GDP)	16.9	18.0	21.1
Exchange rates (national currency per US$)[a]	1.07	0.85	0.75
Balance of payments, current account (million US$)	...	−1 475[b]	−1 031
Industrial production index (2005=100)[c]	...	100	79
Agricultural production index (2004-2006=100)	83[d]	96[d]	104
Food production index (2004-2006=100)	83[d]	96[d]	104
Unemployment (% of labour force)	...	17.2[e]	19.6
Employment in industrial sector (% of employed)[f]	22.3[gh]	19.2[i]	...
Employment in agricultural sector (% of employed)[f]	9.0[gh]	8.6[i]	...
Labour force participation, adult female pop. (%)[d]	44.6	45.2	46.2
Labour force participation, adult male pop. (%)[d]	64.3	63.5	63.3
Tourist arrivals at national borders (000)[j]	136[k]	272	1 088
Energy production, primary (000 mt oil equivalent)	...	1 003	800[l]
Telephone subscribers, total (per 100 inhabitants)	...	113.9	212.1
Internet users (per 100 inhabitants)	...	28.8	52.0

Total trade		Major trading partners			2010
	(million US$)		(% of exports)		(% of imports)
Exports	436.6	Serbia	28.2	Serbia	26.2
Imports	2 181.9	Greece	17.1	Bosnia-Herzegovina	7.5
Balance	−1 745.3	Italy	14.8	Germany	7.1

Social indicators		
Population growth rate (average annual %)	2010-2015	0.1
Urban population growth rate (average annual %)	2010-2015	0.4
Rural population growth rate (average annual %)	2010-2015	−0.5
Urban population (%)	2011	63.3
Population aged 0-14 years (%)	2011	19.1
Population aged 60+ years (females and males, % of total)	2011	20.1/16.0
Sex ratio (males per 100 females)	2011	96.4
Life expectancy at birth (females and males, years)	2010-2015	77.4/72.5
Infant mortality rate (per 1 000 live births)	2010-2015	7.7
Fertility rate, total (live births per woman)	2010-2015	1.6
Contraceptive prevalence (ages 15-49, %)	2006-2010	39.4[m]
International migrant stock (000 and % of total population)	mid-2010	42.5/6.8
Refugees and others of concern to UNHCR	end-2010	18 042
Education: Primary-secondary gross enrolment ratio (f/m per 100)	2005-2011	105.0/104.8
Education: Female third-level students (% of total)	2005-2011	54.3
Seats held by women in national parliaments (%)	2011	11.1

Environmental indicators		
Threatened species	2011	78
Forested area (% of land area)	2009	40.4
CO₂ emission estimates (000 metric tons and metric tons per capita)	2008	1 949/3.1
Energy consumption per capita (kilograms oil equivalent)	2009	1 762.0
Rainfall in the capital city, total mean (millimetres)		1 661
Temperature in the capital city, mean °C (minimum and maximum)		10.7/20.5

a Market rate. b 2007. c The indices are shown in terms of ISIC Rev. 3. d Refers to Serbia and Montenegro. e 2008. f October. g 2003. h Population census. i Age group 15 to 64 years. j Arrivals of non-resident tourists in all types of accommodation establishments. k 2002. l 2009. m 2005-2006.

Morocco

Region	Northern Africa
Currency	Moroccan Dirham (MAD)
Surface area (square kilometres)	446 550
Population in 2010 (estimated, 000)	31 951
Population density in 2010 (per square kilometre)	71.6
Capital city and population in 2011 (000)	Rabat (1 843)
United Nations membership date	12 November 1956

Economic indicators	2000	2005	2010
GDP: Gross domestic product (million current US$)	37 022	59 524	91 542
GDP: Growth rate at constant 2005 prices (annual %)	1.6	3.0	3.3
GDP per capita (current US$)	1 285.8	1 958.5	2 865.0
GNI: Gross national income per capita (current US$)	1 252.2	1 933.4	2 910.1
Gross fixed capital formation (% of GDP)	26.0	27.5	31.0
Exchange rates (national currency per US$) [a]	10.62	9.25	8.36
Balance of payments, current account (million US$)	−501	949	−4 209
CPI: Consumer price index (2000=100)	100	107	117[b]
Agricultural production index (2004-2006=100)	72	93	126
Food production index (2004-2006=100)	72	93	126
Unemployment (% of labour force)	11.2[c]	11.2 ·	9.0
Employment in industrial sector (% of employed)	31.9[d]	19.5	21.7[b]
Employment in agricultural sector (% of employed)	5.1[d]	45.4	40.9[b]
Labour force participation, adult female pop. (%)	29.0	27.9	25.9
Labour force participation, adult male pop. (%)	78.9	77.4	74.7
Tourist arrivals at national borders (000) [e]	4 278	5 843	9 288
Energy production, primary (000 mt oil equivalent)	140	189	339[f]
Telephone subscribers, total (per 100 inhabitants)	13.1	45.2	111.8
Internet users (per 100 inhabitants)	0.7	15.1	49.0

Total trade		Major trading partners			2010
	(million US$)		(% of exports)		(% of imports)
Exports	17 764.8	France	22.5	France	15.6
Imports	35 378.9	Spain	16.9	Spain	10.6
Balance	−17 614.1	India	6.1	China	8.4

Social indicators

Population growth rate (average annual %)	2010-2015	1.0
Urban population growth rate (average annual %)	2010-2015	1.6
Rural population growth rate (average annual %)	2010-2015	0.1
Urban population (%)	2011	57.0
Population aged 0-14 years (%)	2011	27.7
Population aged 60+ years (females and males, % of total)	2011	8.8/8.0
Sex ratio (males per 100 females)	2011	96.1
Life expectancy at birth (females and males, years)	2010-2015	74.9/70.3
Infant mortality rate (per 1 000 live births)	2010-2015	28.5
Fertility rate, total (live births per woman)	2010-2015	2.2
Contraceptive prevalence (ages 15-49, %)	2006-2010	63.0[g]
International migrant stock (000 and % of total population) [h]	mid-2010	49.1/0.2
Refugees and others of concern to UNHCR	end-2010	1 072
Education: Government expenditure (% of GDP)	2005-2011	5.4
Education: Primary-secondary gross enrolment ratio (f/m per 100) [i]	2005-2011	76.2/85.9
Education: Female third-level students (% of total)	2005-2011	46.9
Seats held by women in national parliaments (%)	2011	16.7

Environmental indicators

Threatened species	2011	160
Forested area (% of land area)	2009	11.5
CO_2 emission estimates (000 metric tons and metric tons per capita)	2008	47 867/1.5
Energy consumption per capita (kilograms oil equivalent)	2009	445.0
Rainfall in the capital city, total mean (millimetres) [j]		300
Temperature in the capital city, mean °C (minimum and maximum) [j]		14.6/22.0

a Official rate. b 2008. c 2004. d Urban areas. e Includes nationals residing abroad. f 2009. g 2003-2004. h Data refer to foreign citizens. i UNESCO estimate. j Casablanca.

Mozambique

Region	Eastern Africa
Currency	(new) Metical (MZN) [a]
Surface area (square kilometres)	801 590
Population in 2010 (estimated, 000)	23 391
Population density in 2010 (per square kilometre)	29.2
Capital city and population in 2011 (000)	Maputo (1 150)
United Nations membership date	16 September 1975

Economic indicators	2000	2005	2010
GDP: Gross domestic product (million current US$)	4 310	6 579	9 533
GDP: Growth rate at constant 2005 prices (annual %)	1.5	8.4	7.0
GDP per capita (current US$)	236.8	316.7	407.6
GNI: Gross national income per capita (current US$)	206.5	300.0	383.3
Gross fixed capital formation (% of GDP)	31.0	18.7	21.9
Exchange rates (national currency per US$) [b]	17.14	24.18	32.58
Balance of payments, current account (million US$)	−764	−761	−1 113
CPI: Consumer price index (2000=100)	100	173	287
Agricultural production index (2004-2006=100)	84	95	115
Food production index (2004-2006=100)	91	94	113
Employment in industrial sector (% of employed)	3.4[cde]	...	...
Employment in agricultural sector (% of employed)	80.5[cde]	...	...
Labour force participation, adult female pop. (%)	87.7	87.4	86.3
Labour force participation, adult male pop. (%)	82.7	83.3	83.0
Tourist arrivals at national borders (000)	323[fg]	578[g]	2 224[h]
Energy production, primary (000 mt oil equivalent)	777	3 245	4 207[h]
Telephone subscribers, total (per 100 inhabitants)	0.8	7.6	31.3
Internet users (per 100 inhabitants)	0.1	0.9	4.2

Total trade		Major trading partners			2010
	(million US$)	(% of exports)			(% of imports)
Exports	2 243.1	Netherlands	52.7	South Africa	34.4
Imports	3 564.2	South Africa	20.8	Netherlands	18.0
Balance	−1 321.1	Portugal	4.8	India	5.7

Social indicators		
Population growth rate (average annual %)	2010-2015	2.2
Urban population growth rate (average annual %)	2010-2015	3.1
Rural population growth rate (average annual %)	2010-2015	1.9
Urban population (%)	2011	31.2
Population aged 0-14 years (%)	2011	43.9
Population aged 60+ years (females and males, % of total)	2011	5.7/4.6
Sex ratio (males per 100 females)	2011	95.0
Life expectancy at birth (females and males, years)	2010-2015	51.8/50.0
Infant mortality rate (per 1 000 live births)	2010-2015	77.9
Fertility rate, total (live births per woman)	2010-2015	4.7
Contraceptive prevalence (ages 15-49, %)	2006-2010	16.5[i]
International migrant stock (000 and % of total population) [j]	mid-2010	450.0/1.9
Refugees and others of concern to UNHCR	end-2010	9 996
Education: Government expenditure (% of GDP)	2005-2011	5.0
Education: Primary-secondary gross enrolment ratio (f/m per 100)	2005-2011	77.5/87.1
Education: Female third-level students (% of total)	2005-2011	33.1
Seats held by women in national parliaments (%)	2011	39.2

Environmental indicators		
Threatened species	2011	211
Forested area (% of land area)	2009	49.9
CO$_2$ emission estimates (000 metric tons and metric tons per capita)	2008	2 312/0.1
Energy consumption per capita (kilograms oil equivalent)	2009	78.0
Rainfall in the capital city, total mean (millimetres)		814
Temperature in the capital city, mean °C (minimum and maximum)		18.6/27.2

a Beginning 1 July 2006, 1 new Metical = 1000 old Meticais. b Principal rate. c 2003. d Household income and expenditure survey. e July of the preceding year to August of the current year. f 2001. g Data correspond to only 12 border posts. h 2009. i 2003-2004. j Includes refugees.

Myanmar

Region	South-eastern Asia
Currency	Kyat (MMK)
Surface area (square kilometres)	676 578
Population in 2010 (estimated, 000)	47 963
Population density in 2010 (per square kilometre)	70.9
Capital city and population in 2011 (000)	Nay Pyi Taw (1 060)
United Nations membership date	19 April 1948

Economic indicators	2000	2005	2010
GDP: Gross domestic product (million current US$)	7 275	11 931	42 027
GDP: Growth rate at constant 2005 prices (annual %)	13.8	13.6	10.4
GDP per capita (current US$)	161.8	257.6	876.2
GNI: Gross national income per capita (current US$)	161.8	257.6	876.2
Gross fixed capital formation (% of GDP)	11.8	12.7	22.8
Exchange rates (national currency per US$) [a]	6.53	5.95	5.52
Balance of payments, current account (million US$)	−212	588	1 527
CPI: Consumer price index (2000=100)	100	297	610[b]
Agricultural production index (2004-2006=100)	68	99	125
Food production index (2004-2006=100)	68	99	126
Labour force participation, adult female pop. (%)	74.0	74.5	75.0
Labour force participation, adult male pop. (%)	81.0	81.5	82.0
Tourist arrivals at national borders (000) [c]	208	232	311
Energy production, primary (000 mt oil equivalent)	6 844	14 235	13 005[d]
Telephone subscribers, total (per 100 inhabitants)	0.6	1.4	2.5
Internet users (per 100 inhabitants)	<[e]	0.1	0.2[d]

Total trade		Major trading partners			2010
	(million US$)	(% of exports)			(% of imports)
Exports	7 625.2	Thailand	41.7	China	27.1
Imports	4 164.3	China, Hong Kong SAR	21.1	Singapore	27.0
Balance	3 460.9	India	12.6	Thailand	11.4

Social indicators		
Population growth rate (average annual %)	2010-2015	0.8
Urban population growth rate (average annual %)	2010-2015	2.5
Rural population growth rate (average annual %)	2010-2015	−0.1
Urban population (%)	2011	32.6
Population aged 0-14 years (%)	2011	25.2
Population aged 60+ years (females and males, % of total)	2011	8.8/7.5
Sex ratio (males per 100 females)	2011	97.2
Life expectancy at birth (females and males, years)	2010-2015	67.9/64.1
Infant mortality rate (per 1 000 live births)	2010-2015	44.8
Fertility rate, total (live births per woman)	2010-2015	1.9
Contraceptive prevalence (ages 15-49, %)	2006-2010	41.0
International migrant stock (000 and % of total population) [f]	mid-2010	88.7/0.2
Refugees and others of concern to UNHCR	end-2010	859 403
Education: Government expenditure (% of GDP)	2005-2011	1.3[g]
Education: Primary-secondary gross enrolment ratio (f/m per 100)	2005-2011	86.4/84.5
Education: Female third-level students (% of total)	2005-2011	57.9
Seats held by women in national parliaments (%)	2011	4.3

Environmental indicators		
Threatened species	2011	260
Forested area (% of land area)	2009	49.1
CO_2 emission estimates (000 metric tons and metric tons per capita)	2008	12 765/0.3
Energy consumption per capita (kilograms oil equivalent)	2009	98.0
Rainfall in the capital city, total mean (millimetres) [h]		2 681
Temperature in the capital city, mean °C (minimum and maximum) [h]		22.6/32.3

a Official rate. b 2008. c Includes tourist arrivals through border entry points to Yangon. d 2009. e 2003.
f Data refer to foreign citizens. g 2001. h Yangon.

Namibia

Region	Southern Africa
Currency	Namibian Dollar (NAD)
Surface area (square kilometres)	824 268
Population in 2010 (estimated, 000)	2 283
Population density in 2010 (per square kilometre)	2.8
Capital city and population in 2011 (000)	Windhoek (380)
United Nations membership date	23 April 1990

Economic indicators	2000	2005	2010
GDP: Gross domestic product (million current US$)	3 909	7 261	11 701
GDP: Growth rate at constant 2005 prices (annual %)	3.5	2.5	4.4
GDP per capita (current US$)	2 061.7	3 491.1	5 124.7
GNI: Gross national income per capita (current US$)	2 079.2	3 437.1	5 086.2
Gross fixed capital formation (% of GDP)	16.6	18.6	24.0
Exchange rates (national currency per US$)[a]	7.57	6.32	6.63
Balance of payments, current account (million US$)	138	267	−314
CPI: Consumer price index (2000=100)[b]	100[c]	114	160
Agricultural production index (2004-2006=100)	85	104	93
Food production index (2004-2006=100)	85	104	94
Employment in industrial sector (% of employed)	12.2[d]	14.8[de]	17.7[fg]
Employment in agricultural sector (% of employed)	31.1[d]	29.9[de]	16.3[fg]
Labour force participation, adult female pop. (%)	48.8	55.2	58.4
Labour force participation, adult male pop. (%)	64.5	68.1	69.8
Tourist arrivals at national borders (000)	656	778	984
Energy production, primary (000 mt oil equivalent)	119	133	123[h]
Telephone subscribers, total (per 100 inhabitants)	10.1	28.3	73.9
Internet users (per 100 inhabitants)	1.6	4.0	6.5

Total trade		Major trading partners			2010
	(million US$)[f]	(% of exports)[f]			(% of imports)[f]
Exports	4 729.3	South Africa	31.8	South Africa	67.8
Imports	4 688.6	United Kingdom	15.0	United Kingdom	8.0
Balance	40.7	Angola	8.6	India	3.5

Social indicators		
Population growth rate (average annual %)	2010-2015	1.7
Urban population growth rate (average annual %)	2010-2015	3.1
Rural population growth rate (average annual %)	2010-2015	0.7
Urban population (%)	2011	38.4
Population aged 0-14 years (%)	2011	36.0
Population aged 60+ years (females and males, % of total)	2011	6.5/5.1
Sex ratio (males per 100 females)	2011	98.8
Life expectancy at birth (females and males, years)	2010-2015	63.0/62.1
Infant mortality rate (per 1 000 live births)	2010-2015	29.8
Fertility rate, total (live births per woman)	2010-2015	3.1
Contraceptive prevalence (ages 15-49, %)	2006-2010	55.1
International migrant stock (000 and % of total population)	mid-2010	138.9/6.3
Refugees and others of concern to UNHCR	end-2010	8 704
Education: Government expenditure (% of GDP)	2005-2011	8.1
Education: Primary-secondary gross enrolment ratio (f/m per 100)	2005-2011	93.3/89.4
Education: Female third-level students (% of total)	2005-2011	56.8
Seats held by women in national parliaments (%)	2011	24.4

Environmental indicators		
Threatened species	2011	95
Forested area (% of land area)	2009	8.9
CO$_2$ emission estimates (000 metric tons and metric tons per capita)	2008	3 964/1.9
Energy consumption per capita (kilograms oil equivalent)	2009	650.0

a Official rate. **b** Index base 2002=100. **c** 2002. **d** Age group 15 to 69 years. **e** 2004. **f** 2008. **g** Excludes regular military living in barracks. **h** 2009.

Nauru

Region	Oceania-Micronesia
Currency	Australian Dollar (AUD)
Surface area (square kilometres)	21
Population in 2010 (estimated, 000)	10
Population density in 2010 (per square kilometre)	488.3
Capital city and population in 2011 (000)	Nauru (10)
United Nations membership date	14 September 1999

Economic indicators	2000	2005	2010
GDP: Gross domestic product (million current US$)	21	26	63
GDP: Growth rate at constant 2005 prices (annual %)	−6.3	−9.8	0.0
GDP per capita (current US$)	2 098.6	2 599.7	6 190.1
GNI: Gross national income per capita (current US$)	2 227.1	2 720.6	6 084.0
Gross fixed capital formation (% of GDP)	33.2	60.6	58.6
Exchange rates (national currency per US$) [a]	1.80	1.37	0.99
Agricultural production index (2004-2006=100)	100	101	111
Food production index (2004-2006=100)	100	101	111
Telephone subscribers, total (per 100 inhabitants)	29.9	17.8[b]	60.5[c]
Internet users (per 100 inhabitants)	3.0[d]	...	6.0

Social indicators		
Population growth rate (average annual %)	2010-2015	0.6
Urban population growth rate (average annual %)	2010-2015	0.6
Rural population growth rate (average annual %)	2010-2015	0.0
Urban population (%)	2011	100.0
Population aged 0-14 years (%) [e]	2011	35.4
Population aged 60+ years (females and males, % of total) [e]	2011	3.0/2.8
Sex ratio (males per 100 females) [e]	2011	103.3
Life expectancy at birth (females and males, years) [f]	2010-2015	57.1/55.2[g]
Infant mortality rate (per 1 000 live births) [f]	2010-2015	45.8[h]
Fertility rate, total (live births per woman) [e]	2010-2015	3.3[h]
Contraceptive prevalence (ages 15-49, %)	2006-2010	35.6
International migrant stock (000 and % of total population) [i]	mid-2010	5.3/51.8
Education: Primary-secondary gross enrolment ratio (f/m per 100) [j]	2005-2011	82.8/74.0
Seats held by women in national parliaments (%)	2011	0.0

Environmental indicators		
Threatened species	2011	74
Forested area (% of land area)	2009	0.0
CO$_2$ emission estimates (000 metric tons and metric tons per capita)	2008	143/14.2
Energy consumption per capita (kilograms oil equivalent)	2009	4 738.0[k]

a UN operational exchange rate. b Main telephone lines only. c Mobile cellular subscriptions only. d 2001. e Data compiled by the Secretariat of the Pacific Community Demography Programme. f Data compiled by the United Nations Demographic Yearbook system. g 2006. h 2006-2007. i Data refer to foreign citizens. j National estimate. k UNSD estimate.

Nepal

Region	South-central Asia
Currency	Nepalese Rupee (NPR)
Surface area (square kilometres)	· 147 181
Population in 2010 (estimated, 000)	29 959
Population density in 2010 (per square kilometre)	203.6
Capital city and population in 2011 (000)	Kathmandu (1 015)
United Nations membership date	14 December 1955

Economic indicators	2000	2005	2010
GDP: Gross domestic product (million current US$)	5 730	8 259	16 020
GDP: Growth rate at constant 2005 prices (annual %)	6.1	3.1	4.6
GDP per capita (current US$)	234.9	302.7	534.7
GNI: Gross national income per capita (current US$)	234.7	303.6	538.9
Gross fixed capital formation (% of GDP)	19.6	19.9	20.2
Exchange rates (national currency per US$) [a]	74.30	74.05	71.95
Balance of payments, current account (million US$)	−299	1	−438
CPI: Consumer price index (2000=100)	100	123	175[b]
Agricultural production index (2004-2006=100)	86	100	114
Food production index (2004-2006=100)	86	100	114
Employment in industrial sector (% of employed)	13.4[cdef]	...	...
Employment in agricultural sector (% of employed)	65.7[cdef]	...	...
Labour force participation, adult female pop. (%)	81.9	80.9	80.3
Labour force participation, adult male pop. (%)	90.0	88.6	87.7
Tourist arrivals at national borders (000)	464	375	603
Energy production, primary (000 mt oil equivalent)	152	225	278[b]
Telephone subscribers, total (per 100 inhabitants)	1.1	2.6	33.5
Internet users (per 100 inhabitants)	0.2	0.8	7.9

Total trade		Major trading partners			2010
	(million US$)		(% of exports)		(% of imports)
Exports	834.0	India	65.5	India	57.0
Imports	5 127.5	United States	6.3	China	10.5
Balance	−4 293.5	Bangladesh	5.5	United Arab Emirates	8.9

Social indicators		
Population growth rate (average annual %)	2010-2015	1.7
Urban population growth rate (average annual %)	2010-2015	3.6
Rural population growth rate (average annual %)	2010-2015	1.3
Urban population (%)	2011	17.0
Population aged 0-14 years (%)	2011	35.5
Population aged 60+ years (females and males, % of total)	2011	7.0/5.7
Sex ratio (males per 100 females)	2011	98.4
Life expectancy at birth (females and males, years)	2010-2015	70.1/68.1
Infant mortality rate (per 1 000 live births)	2010-2015	32.0
Fertility rate, total (live births per woman)	2010-2015	2.6
Contraceptive prevalence (ages 15-49, %)	2006-2010	48.0
International migrant stock (000 and % of total population) [g]	mid-2010	945.9/3.2
Refugees and others of concern to UNHCR	end-2010	891 319
Education: Government expenditure (% of GDP)	2005-2011	4.7
Education: Primary-secondary gross enrolment ratio (f/m per 100)	2005-2011	67.5/82.0[h]
Education: Female third-level students (% of total)	2005-2011	40.7
Seats held by women in national parliaments (%)	2011	33.2

Environmental indicators		
Threatened species	2011	92
Forested area (% of land area)	2009	25.4
CO_2 emission estimates (000 metric tons and metric tons per capita)	2008	3 539/0.1
Energy consumption per capita (kilograms oil equivalent)	2009	47.0
Rainfall in the capital city, total mean (millimetres)		1 425
Temperature in the capital city, mean °C (minimum and maximum)		11.7/24.8

a Official rate. **b** 2009. **c** 2001. **d** June. **e** Population census. **f** Age group 10 years and over. **g** Includes refugees. **h** 2002.

Netherlands

Region	Western Europe
Currency	Euro (EUR)
Surface area (square kilometres)	37 354
Population in 2010 (estimated, 000)	16 613
Population density in 2010 (per square kilometre)	444.7
Capital city and population in 2011 (000)	Amsterdam (1 056) [a]
United Nations membership date	10 December 1945

Economic indicators	2000	2005	2010
GDP: Gross domestic product (million current US$)	385 074	638 471	779 310
GDP: Growth rate at constant 2005 prices (annual %)	3.9	2.1	1.7
GDP per capita (current US$)	24 275.3	39 156.9	46 909.7
GNI: Gross national income per capita (current US$)	24 799.2	39 345.9	46 511.9
Gross fixed capital formation (% of GDP)	22.0	18.9	18.3
Exchange rates (national currency per US$) [b]	1.07	0.85	0.75
Balance of payments, current account (million US$)	7 264	46 618	51 635
CPI: Consumer price index (2000=100)	100	113	122
Industrial production index (2005=100)	96 [c]	100	105
Agricultural production index (2004-2006=100)	105	100	110
Food production index (2004-2006=100)	105	100	110
Unemployment (% of labour force)	4.6 [d]	4.7	4.5
Employment in industrial sector (% of employed) [e]	20.2	19.6	15.9
Employment in agricultural sector (% of employed) [e]	3.0	3.2	2.8
Labour force participation, adult female pop. (%)	53.3	56.8	58.3
Labour force participation, adult male pop. (%)	72.9	72.6	71.5
Tourist arrivals at national borders (000) [f]	10 003	10 012	10 883
Energy production, primary (000 mt oil equivalent)	60 531	65 446	65 475 [g]
Telephone subscribers, total (per 100 inhabitants)	130.1	143.7	159.0
Internet users (per 100 inhabitants)	44.0	81.0	90.7

Total trade (million US$)	Major trading partners				2010
		(% of exports)		(% of imports)	
Exports	492 645.9	Germany	24.3	Germany	17.8
Imports	439 986.6	Belgium	11.1	Belgium	9.6
Balance	52 659.3	France	8.7	China	9.3

Social indicators		
Population growth rate (average annual %)	2010-2015	0.3
Urban population growth rate (average annual %)	2010-2015	0.7
Rural population growth rate (average annual %)	2010-2015	−2.1
Urban population (%)	2011	83.2
Population aged 0-14 years (%)	2011	17.5
Population aged 60+ years (females and males, % of total)	2011	24.0/20.6
Sex ratio (males per 100 females)	2011	98.6
Life expectancy at birth (females and males, years)	2010-2015	82.8/78.9
Infant mortality rate (per 1 000 live births)	2010-2015	4.2
Fertility rate, total (live births per woman)	2010-2015	1.8
Contraceptive prevalence (ages 15-49, %) [h]	2006-2010	69.0
International migrant stock (000 and % of total population)	mid-2010	1 752.9/10.5
Refugees and others of concern to UNHCR	end-2010	90 075
Education: Government expenditure (% of GDP)	2005-2011	5.5
Education: Primary-secondary gross enrolment ratio (f/m per 100)	2005-2011	113.4/115.1
Education: Female third-level students (% of total)	2005-2011	51.8
Deaths by assault (females and males, per 100 000)	2005-2008	0.6/1.3
Seats held by women in national parliaments (%)	2011	39.3

Environmental indicators		
Threatened species	2011	28
Forested area (% of land area)	2009	10.8
CO$_2$ emission estimates (000 metric tons and metric tons per capita)	2008	173 608/10.5
Energy consumption per capita (kilograms oil equivalent)	2009	3 723.0
Rainfall in the capital city, total mean (millimetres)		780
Temperature in the capital city, mean °C (minimum and maximum)		6.1/13.4

a Amsterdam is the capital, The Hague is the seat of government. b Market rate. c 2003. d 2004. e European Labour Force Survey (Eurostat). f Arrivals of non-resident tourists in all types of accommodation establishments. g 2009. h Age group 18 to 45 years.

Netherlands Antilles[a]

Region	Caribbean
Currency	Netherlands Antilles Guilder (ANG)
Surface area (square kilometres)	800
Population in 2010 (estimated, 000)	201
Population density in 2010 (per square kilometre)	250.9
Capital city and population in 2011 (000)	Willemstad (115)

Economic indicators	2000	2005	2010
GDP: Gross domestic product (million current US$)	2 857	3 277	4 078
GDP: Growth rate at constant 2005 prices (annual %)	−2.0	1.1	0.0
GDP per capita (current US$)	15 889.9	17 622.4	20 321.1
GNI: Gross national income per capita (current US$)	16 014.5	17 541.9	20 108.1
Gross fixed capital formation (% of GDP)	30.5	29.9	35.6
Exchange rates (national currency per US$)[b]	1.79	1.79	1.79[c]
Balance of payments, current account (million US$)	−48	−106	−827[c]
CPI: Consumer price index (2000=100)[d]	100	109	130
Agricultural production index (2004-2006=100)	91	100	106
Food production index (2004-2006=100)	91	100	106
Employment in industrial sector (% of employed)[de]	18.0	15.3	17.6[f]
Employment in agricultural sector (% of employed)[de]	1.1	0.9	1.1[f]
Labour force participation, adult female pop. (%)	54.6	56.3	57.1
Labour force participation, adult male pop. (%)	68.4	67.5	69.3
Telephone subscribers, total (per 100 inhabitants)[g]	44.5	45.7	44.9

Total trade	Major trading partners			2010
(million US$)[f]		(% of exports)[f]		(% of imports)[f]
Exports 146.2	Netherlands	34.2	United States	39.4
Imports 1 437.0	United States	23.0	Netherlands	23.1
Balance −1 290.8				

Social indicators		
Population growth rate (average annual %)	2010-2015	0.7
Urban population growth rate (average annual %)	2010-2015	0.9
Rural population growth rate (average annual %)	2010-2015	−2.2
Urban population (%)	2011	93.4
Population aged 0-14 years (%)	2011	20.3
Population aged 60+ years (females and males, % of total)	2011	16.7/14.8
Sex ratio (males per 100 females)	2011	86.4
Life expectancy at birth (females and males, years)	2010-2015	79.9/73.5
Infant mortality rate (per 1 000 live births)	2010-2015	12.3
Fertility rate, total (live births per woman)	2010-2015	1.9
International migrant stock (000 and % of total population)	mid-2010	53.0/26.4
Education: Primary-secondary gross enrolment ratio (f/m per 100)	2005-2011	109.3/106.6[h]
Education: Female third-level students (% of total)	2005-2011	59.7[h]

Environmental indicators		
Threatened species	2011	42
Forested area (% of land area)	2009	1.5
CO_2 emission estimates (000 metric tons and metric tons per capita)	2008	6 214/31.8
Energy consumption per capita (kilograms oil equivalent)	2009	10 551.0
Rainfall in the capital city, total mean (millimetres)[d]		552

a The Netherlands Antilles was dissolved on 10 October 2010. Unless otherwise indicated, the data refer to Curaçao, Sint Maarten (Dutch part), Bonaire, Saba and Sint Eustatius. b Official rate. c 2009. d Curaçao. e October. f 2008. g Main telephone lines only. h 2002.

New Caledonia

Region	Oceania-Melanesia		
Currency	CFP Franc (XPF)		
Surface area (square kilometres)	18 575		
Population in 2010 (estimated, 000)	251		
Population density in 2010 (per square kilometre)	13.5		
Capital city and population in 2011 (000)	Nouméa (157)		

Economic indicators	2000	2005	2010
GDP: Gross domestic product (million current US$)	3 412	6 236	8 861
GDP: Growth rate at constant 2005 prices (annual %)	2.1	3.6	3.5
GDP per capita (current US$)	16 094.8	26 987.0	35 319.5
GNI: Gross national income per capita (current US$)	16 094.8	26 987.0	35 319.5
Gross fixed capital formation (% of GDP)	21.8	28.5	39.2
Exchange rates (national currency per US$) [a]	128.17	100.84	90.81
CPI: Consumer price index (2000=100) [b]	100	108	119
Agricultural production index (2004-2006=100)	94	99	97
Food production index (2004-2006=100)	94	99	97
Employment in industrial sector (% of employed) [cd]	32.0	21.3	22.4[e]
Employment in agricultural sector (% of employed) [cd]	4.8	3.1	2.7[e]
Labour force participation, adult female pop. (%)	48.2	47.7	46.8
Labour force participation, adult male pop. (%)	70.8	70.1	68.6
Tourist arrivals at national borders (000) [f]	110	101	99
Energy production, primary (000 mt oil equivalent)	39	31	39[g]
Telephone subscribers, total (per 100 inhabitants)	47.6	82.0	116.8
Internet users (per 100 inhabitants)	13.9	32.4	34.0[g]

Total trade		Major trading partners			2010
	(million US$)	(% of exports)			(% of imports)
Exports	1 267.6	France	21.4	France	22.3
Imports	3 303.2	Japan	18.8	China	17.6
Balance	−2 035.6			Singapore	12.9

Social indicators

Population growth rate (average annual %)	2010-2015	1.5
Urban population growth rate (average annual %)	2010-2015	1.2
Rural population growth rate (average annual %)	2010-2015	1.9
Urban population (%)	2011	61.7
Population aged 0-14 years (%)	2011	24.9
Population aged 60+ years (females and males, % of total)	2011	12.6/11.7
Sex ratio (males per 100 females)	2011	100.0
Life expectancy at birth (females and males, years)	2010-2015	80.5/73.8
Infant mortality rate (per 1 000 live births)	2010-2015	4.7
Fertility rate, total (live births per woman)	2010-2015	2.1
International migrant stock (000 and % of total population)	mid-2010	59.8/23.6

Environmental indicators

Threatened species	2011	473
Forested area (% of land area)	2009	45.9
CO_2 emission estimates (000 metric tons and metric tons per capita)	2008	3 147/12.8
Energy consumption per capita (kilograms oil equivalent)	2009	3 837.0
Rainfall in the capital city, total mean (millimetres)		1 072
Temperature in the capital city, mean °C (minimum and maximum)		20.2/26.0

a UN operational exchange rate. b Nouméa. c Population census. d Age group 14 years and over. e 2008. f Includes nationals residing abroad. g 2009.

New Zealand

Region	Oceania
Currency	New Zealand Dollar (NZD)
Surface area (square kilometres)	270 467
Population in 2010 (estimated, 000)	4 368
Population density in 2010 (per square kilometre)	16.2
Capital city and population in 2011 (000)	Wellington (410)
United Nations membership date	24 October 1945

Economic indicators	2000	2005	2010
GDP: Gross domestic product (million current US$)	53 385	113 058	141 406
GDP: Growth rate at constant 2005 prices (annual %)	2.5	3.3	2.3
GDP per capita (current US$)	13 837.3	27 347.6	32 372.1
GNI: Gross national income per capita (current US$)	13 032.6	25 559.1	31 032.1
Gross fixed capital formation (% of GDP)	20.1	24.0	19.0
Exchange rates (national currency per US$) [a]	2.27	1.47	1.30
Balance of payments, current account (million US$)	−2 407	−8 777	−4 994
CPI: Consumer price index (2000=100)	100	113	130
Industrial production index (2005=100) [b]	95[c]	100	89
Agricultural production index (2004-2006=100)	88	99	103
Food production index (2004-2006=100)	87	99	104
Unemployment (% of labour force)	4.0[d]	3.8	6.5
Employment in industrial sector (% of employed) [e]	23.2[f]	22.0[f]	20.9[g]
Employment in agricultural sector (% of employed) [e]	8.7[f]	7.1[f]	6.6[g]
Labour force participation, adult female pop. (%)	56.8	60.3	61.5
Labour force participation, adult male pop. (%)	73.3	74.8	74.2
Tourist arrivals at national borders (000)	1 780	2 353	2 492
Energy production, primary (000 mt oil equivalent)	12 000	10 051	11 845[g]
Telephone subscribers, total (per 100 inhabitants)	87.4	127.2	157.7
Internet users (per 100 inhabitants)	47.4	62.7	83.0

Total trade		Major trading partners			2010
	(million US$)	(% of exports)			(% of imports)
Exports	30 931.9	Australia	23.0	Australia	18.2
Imports	30 157.8	China	11.1	China	16.0
Balance	774.1	United States	8.6	United States	10.4

Social indicators		
Population growth rate (average annual %)	2010-2015	1.0
Urban population growth rate (average annual %)	2010-2015	1.1
Rural population growth rate (average annual %)	2010-2015	0.7
Urban population (%)	2011	86.2
Population aged 0-14 years (%)	2011	20.5
Population aged 60+ years (females and males, % of total)	2011	19.5/17.7
Sex ratio (males per 100 females)	2011	96.6
Life expectancy at birth (females and males, years)	2010-2015	82.8/78.9
Infant mortality rate (per 1 000 live births)	2010-2015	4.8
Fertility rate, total (live births per woman)	2010-2015	2.1
Contraceptive prevalence (ages 15-49, %) [h]	2006-2010	75.0[i]
International migrant stock (000 and % of total population)	mid-2010	962.1/22.4
Refugees and others of concern to UNHCR	end-2010	2 523
Education: Government expenditure (% of GDP)	2005-2011	7.2
Education: Primary-secondary gross enrolment ratio (f/m per 100)	2005-2011	112.7/109.6
Education: Female third-level students (% of total)	2005-2011	58.1
Deaths by assault (females and males, per 100 000)	2005-2008	1.1/2.0[j]
Seats held by women in national parliaments (%)	2011	32.2

Environmental indicators		
Threatened species	2011	155
Forested area (% of land area)	2009	31.4
CO$_2$ emission estimates (000 metric tons and metric tons per capita)	2008	33 068/7.8
Energy consumption per capita (kilograms oil equivalent)	2009	3 257.0
Rainfall in the capital city, total mean (millimetres)		944
Temperature in the capital city, mean °C (minimum and maximum)		10.2/16.3

a Market rate. **b** The indices are shown in terms of ISIC Rev. 3. **c** 2003. **d** 2004. **e** Average of quarterly estimates. **f** Excludes Chathams, Antarctic Territory and other minor offshore islands. **g** 2009. **h** Age group 20 to 49 years. **i** 1995. **j** Rate based on 30 or fewer events.

Nicaragua

Region	Central America
Currency	Cordoba Oro (NIO)
Surface area (square kilometres)	130 373
Population in 2010 (estimated, 000)	5 788
Population density in 2010 (per square kilometre)	44.4
Capital city and population in 2011 (000)	Managua (970)
United Nations membership date	24 October 1945

Economic indicators	2000	2005	2010
GDP: Gross domestic product (million current US$)	3 938	4 872	6 551
GDP: Growth rate at constant 2005 prices (annual %)	4.1	4.3	4.5
GDP per capita (current US$)	776.2	898.2	1 131.9
GNI: Gross national income per capita (current US$)	736.4	870.5	1 083.8
Gross fixed capital formation (% of GDP)	28.7	28.5	27.4
Exchange rates (national currency per US$)[a]	13.06	17.15	21.88
Balance of payments, current account (million US$)	–936	–784	–963
CPI: Consumer price index (2000=100)[b]	100[c]	147	234
Agricultural production index (2004-2006=100)	84	104	116
Food production index (2004-2006=100)	82	102	117
Employment in industrial sector (% of employed)[d]	14.7[e]	19.7[f]	...
Employment in agricultural sector (% of employed)[d]	43.5[e]	28.9[f]	...
Labour force participation, adult female pop. (%)	38.2	43.5	46.2
Labour force participation, adult male pop. (%)	82.5	80.5	80.0
Tourist arrivals at national borders (000)	486	712[g]	1 011[g]
Energy production, primary (000 mt oil equivalent)	30	61	61[h]
Telephone subscribers, total (per 100 inhabitants)	5.0	24.7	69.6
Internet users (per 100 inhabitants)	1.0	2.6	10.0

Total trade		Major trading partners			2010
	(million US$)	(% of exports)			(% of imports)
Exports	1 847.6	United States	32.8	United States	20.7
Imports	4 190.8	Venezuela	13.5	Venezuela	17.7
Balance	–2 343.2	El Salvador	10.7	China	8.7

Social indicators

Population growth rate (average annual %)	2010-2015	1.4
Urban population growth rate (average annual %)	2010-2015	1.9
Rural population growth rate (average annual %)	2010-2015	0.7
Urban population (%)	2011	57.5
Population aged 0-14 years (%)	2011	33.9
Population aged 60+ years (females and males, % of total)	2011	6.8/6.0
Sex ratio (males per 100 females)	2011	97.9
Life expectancy at birth (females and males, years)	2010-2015	77.5/71.4
Infant mortality rate (per 1 000 live births)	2010-2015	18.3
Fertility rate, total (live births per woman)	2010-2015	2.5
Contraceptive prevalence (ages 15-49, %)	2006-2010	72.4
International migrant stock (000 and % of total population)[i]	mid-2010	40.1/0.7
Refugees and others of concern to UNHCR	end-2010	96
Education: Government expenditure (% of GDP)[j]	2005-2011	3.1[k]
Education: Primary-secondary gross enrolment ratio (f/m per 100)	2005-2011	96.2/94.7
Education: Female third-level students (% of total)[j]	2005-2011	52.1[k]
Seats held by women in national parliaments (%)	2011	40.2

Environmental indicators

Threatened species	2011	126
Forested area (% of land area)	2009	26.5
CO_2 emission estimates (000 metric tons and metric tons per capita)	2008	4 327/0.8
Energy consumption per capita (kilograms oil equivalent)	2009	249.0
Rainfall in the capital city, total mean (millimetres)[l]		1 989
Temperature in the capital city, mean °C (minimum and maximum)[lm]		26.9/26.9

a Principal rate. **b** Index base 1999=100. **c** 1999. **d** Age group 10 years and over. **e** Official estimates. **f** November. **g** Includes nationals residing abroad. **h** 2009. **i** Includes refugees. **j** UNESCO estimate. **k** 2003. **l** Chinandega. **m** Refers to average temperature.

Niger

Region	Western Africa
Currency	CFA Franc (XOF)
Surface area (square kilometres)	1 267 000
Population in 2010 (estimated, 000)	15 512
Population density in 2010 (per square kilometre)	12.2
Capital city and population in 2011 (000)	Niamey (1 297)
United Nations membership date	20 September 1960

Economic indicators	2000	2005	2010
GDP: Gross domestic product (million current US$)	1 727	3 369	5 549
GDP: Growth rate at constant 2005 prices (annual %)	−2.6	7.4	7.5
GDP per capita (current US$)	158.1	259.3	357.7
GNI: Gross national income per capita (current US$)	156.6	258.6	355.9
Gross fixed capital formation (% of GDP)	15.1	21.6	40.2
Exchange rates (national currency per US$) [a]	704.95	556.04	490.91
Balance of payments, current account (million US$)	−104	−312	−1 320[b]
CPI: Consumer price index (2000=100) [c]	100	114	132[b]
Agricultural production index (2004-2006=100)	72	102	155
Food production index (2004-2006=100)	72	102	155
Employment in industrial sector (% of employed)	...	11.1[de]	...
Employment in agricultural sector (% of employed)	...	56.9[de]	...
Labour force participation, adult female pop. (%)	38.0	39.2	39.8
Labour force participation, adult male pop. (%)	88.4	90.6	90.1
Tourist arrivals at national borders (000)	50	58	66[b]
Energy production, primary (000 mt oil equivalent)	87	100	124[b]
Telephone subscribers, total (per 100 inhabitants)	0.2	2.7	25.1
Internet users (per 100 inhabitants)	<	0.2	0.8

Total trade		Major trading partners			2010
	(million US$)	(% of exports)			(% of imports)
Exports	483.5	United States	16.7	China	43.8
Imports	2 290.0	Japan	16.5	France	11.0
Balance	−1 806.5	Switzerland	15.6	United States	6.1

Social indicators		
Population growth rate (average annual %)	2010-2015	3.5
Urban population growth rate (average annual %)	2010-2015	4.9
Rural population growth rate (average annual %)	2010-2015	3.2
Urban population (%)	2011	17.8
Population aged 0-14 years (%)	2011	49.0
Population aged 60+ years (females and males, % of total)	2011	4.0/3.7
Sex ratio (males per 100 females)	2011	101.3
Life expectancy at birth (females and males, years)	2010-2015	55.8/54.8
Infant mortality rate (per 1 000 live births)	2010-2015	85.8
Fertility rate, total (live births per woman)	2010-2015	6.9
Contraceptive prevalence (ages 15-49, %)	2006-2010	11.2
International migrant stock (000 and % of total population) [f]	mid-2010	202.2/1.3
Refugees and others of concern to UNHCR	end-2010	332
Education: Government expenditure (% of GDP)	2005-2011	3.9
Education: Primary-secondary gross enrolment ratio (f/m per 100)	2005-2011	36.5/46.6
Education: Female third-level students (% of total)	2005-2011	29.8
Seats held by women in national parliaments (%)	2011	13.3

Environmental indicators		
Threatened species	2011	27
Forested area (% of land area)	2009	1.0
CO_2 emission estimates (000 metric tons and metric tons per capita)	2008	850/0.1
Energy consumption per capita (kilograms oil equivalent)	2009	26.0
Rainfall in the capital city, total mean (millimetres)		541
Temperature in the capital city, mean °C (minimum and maximum)		22.4/36.2

a Official rate. **b** 2009. **c** Niamey. **d** Core Welfare Indicators Questionnaire (World Bank). **e** April to July.
f Includes refugees.

Nigeria

Region	Western Africa
Currency	Naira (NGN)
Surface area (square kilometres)	923 768
Population in 2010 (estimated, 000)	158 423
Population density in 2010 (per square kilometre)	171.5
Capital city and population in 2011 (000)	Abuja (2 153)
United Nations membership date	7 October 1960

Economic indicators	2000	2005	2010
GDP: Gross domestic product (million current US$)	46 386	112 248	196 410
GDP: Growth rate at constant 2005 prices (annual %)	5.3	3.4	2.8
GDP per capita (current US$)	375.0	802.8	1 239.8
GNI: Gross national income per capita (current US$)	346.0	771.3	1 145.2
Gross fixed capital formation (% of GDP)	7.0	5.5	13.6
Exchange rates (national currency per US$) [a]	109.55	129.00	150.66
Balance of payments, current account (million US$)	7 427	36 529	2 476
CPI: Consumer price index (2000=100)	100	207	338[b]
Agricultural production index (2004-2006=100)	81	100	89
Food production index (2004-2006=100)	81	100	89
Employment in industrial sector (% of employed)	...	11.5[cde]	...
Employment in agricultural sector (% of employed)	...	44.6[cde]	...
Labour force participation, adult female pop. (%)	44.8	47.5	47.8
Labour force participation, adult male pop. (%)	66.8	61.9	63.0
Tourist arrivals at national borders (000)	813	1 010	1 414[f]
Energy production, primary (000 mt oil equivalent)	126 114	151 084	138 459[f]
Telephone subscribers, total (per 100 inhabitants)	0.5	14.2	55.8
Internet users (per 100 inhabitants)	0.1	3.6	28.4

Total trade		Major trading partners			2010
	(million US$)		(% of exports)		(% of imports)
Exports	86 567.9	United States	34.4	United States	17.9
Imports	44 235.3	India	10.5	China	16.6
Balance	42 332.6	Brazil	7.0	France	5.9

Social indicators

Population growth rate (average annual %)	2010-2015	2.5
Urban population growth rate (average annual %)	2010-2015	3.8
Rural population growth rate (average annual %)	2010-2015	1.3
Urban population (%)	2011	49.6
Population aged 0-14 years (%)	2011	42.8
Population aged 60+ years (females and males, % of total)	2011	5.7/4.9
Sex ratio (males per 100 females)	2011	102.6
Life expectancy at birth (females and males, years)	2010-2015	53.4/51.7
Infant mortality rate (per 1 000 live births)	2010-2015	87.6
Fertility rate, total (live births per woman)	2010-2015	5.4
Contraceptive prevalence (ages 15-49, %)	2006-2010	14.6
International migrant stock (000 and % of total population) [gh]	mid-2010	1 127.7/0.7
Refugees and others of concern to UNHCR	end-2010	10 562
Education: Primary-secondary gross enrolment ratio (f/m per 100)	2005-2011	62.0/68.9
Education: Female third-level students (% of total)	2005-2011	40.7
Seats held by women in national parliaments (%)	2011	3.7

Environmental indicators

Threatened species	2011	300
Forested area (% of land area)	2009	10.4
CO_2 emission estimates (000 metric tons and metric tons per capita)	2008	95 678/0.6
Energy consumption per capita (kilograms oil equivalent)	2009	107.0
Rainfall in the capital city, total mean (millimetres)		1 220
Temperature in the capital city, mean °C (minimum and maximum)		20.6/32.9

a Principal rate. **b** Series linked to former series. **c** 2004. **d** Living standards survey. **e** September of the preceding year to August of the current year. **f** 2009. **g** Data refer to foreign citizens. **h** Includes refugees.

Niue

Region	Oceania-Polynesia
Currency	New Zealand Dollar (NZD)
Surface area (square kilometres)	260
Population in 2010 (estimated, 000)	1
Population density in 2010 (per square kilometre)	5.7
Capital city and population in 2011 (000)	Alofi (1)

Economic indicators	2000	2005	2010
Exchange rates (national currency per US$) [a]	2.26	1.46	1.31
CPI: Consumer price index (2000=100)	100	117	139[b]
Agricultural production index (2004-2006=100)	95	101	104
Food production index (2004-2006=100)	95	101	104
Employment in industrial sector (% of employed)	20.4[cd]	...	...
Employment in agricultural sector (% of employed)	9.0[cd]	...	...
Tourist arrivals at national borders (000) [e]	2	3	6
Telephone subscribers, total (per 100 inhabitants)	76.8	62.3[f]	68.1[f]
Internet users (per 100 inhabitants)	26.5	51.7	74.5[g]

Social indicators		
Population growth rate (average annual %)	2010-2015	-2.8
Urban population growth rate (average annual %)	2010-2015	-1.6
Rural population growth rate (average annual %)	2010-2015	-3.5
Urban population (%)	2011	37.9
Population aged 0-14 years (%) [h]	2011	24.5
Population aged 60+ years (females and males, % of total) [h]	2011	18.6/14.2
Sex ratio (males per 100 females) [h]	2011	96.0
Life expectancy at birth (females and males, years) [i]	2010-2015	76.0/67.0[j]
Infant mortality rate (per 1 000 live births) [i]	2010-2015	7.8[k]
Fertility rate, total (live births per woman) [h]	2010-2015	2.6[k]
International migrant stock (000 and % of total population)	mid-2010	0.4/25.6
Education: Primary-secondary gross enrolment ratio (f/m per 100) [l]	2005-2011	124.3/96.1

Environmental indicators		
Threatened species	2011	44
Forested area (% of land area)	2009	71.9
CO_2 emission estimates (000 metric tons and metric tons per capita)	2008	4/2.0
Energy consumption per capita (kilograms oil equivalent)	2009	734.0[m]

a UN operational exchange rate. b 2008. c 2001. d Population census. e Includes Niueans residing usually in New Zealand. f Main telephone lines only. g 2009. h Data compiled by the Secretariat of the Pacific Community Demography Programme. i Data compiled by the United Nations Demographic Yearbook system. j 2006. k 2001-2006. l National estimate. m UNSD estimate.

Northern Mariana Islands

Region	Oceania-Micronesia
Currency	U.S. Dollar (USD)
Surface area (square kilometres)	457
Population in 2010 (estimated, 000)	61
Population density in 2010 (per square kilometre)	133.3
Capital city and population in 2011 (000)	Garapan (...) [a]

Economic indicators	2000	2005	2010
CPI: Consumer price index (2000=100) [b]	100	100	120[c]
Employment in industrial sector (% of employed)	47.2[de]	...	...
Employment in agricultural sector (% of employed)	1.5[d]	...	...
Tourist arrivals at national borders (000) [f]	517	498	345[c]
Telephone subscribers, total (per 100 inhabitants)	35.1	34.6[g]	41.9[g]

Social indicators		
Population growth rate (average annual %)	2010-2015	1.8
Urban population growth rate (average annual %)	2010-2015	1.9
Rural population growth rate (average annual %)	2010-2015	0.4
Urban population (%)	2011	91.5
Population aged 0-14 years (%) [h]	2011	26.2
Population aged 60+ years (females and males, % of total) [h]	2011	7.0/6.4
Sex ratio (males per 100 females) [h]	2011	102.3
Life expectancy at birth (females and males, years) [i]	2010-2015	79.9/74.5[c]
Infant mortality rate (per 1 000 live births) [i]	2010-2015	4.9[j]
Fertility rate, total (live births per woman) [h]	2010-2015	1.6[k]
Contraceptive prevalence (ages 15-49, %)	2006-2010	20.5[l]
International migrant stock (000 and % of total population)	mid-2010	54.8/62.0

Environmental indicators		
Threatened species	2011	88
Forested area (% of land area)	2009	66.3

a The population of Garapan was estimated at 3,588 in the year 2000. Garapan is located on the island of Saipan, the population of which is 55,950. b Saipan. c 2009. d Age group 16 years and over. e Excludes electricity, gas and water. f Air arrivals. g Main telephone lines only. h Data compiled by the Secretariat of the Pacific Community Demography Programme. i Data compiled by the United Nations Demographic Yearbook system. j 2006-2008. k 1999-2001. l 1970.

Norway

Region	Northern Europe
Currency	Norwegian Krone (NOK)
Surface area (square kilometres)	386 204 [a]
Population in 2010 (estimated, 000)	4 883 [a]
Population density in 2010 (per square kilometre)	12.6 [a]
Capital city and population in 2011 (000)	Oslo (915)
United Nations membership date	27 November 1945

Economic indicators	2000	2005	2010
GDP: Gross domestic product (million current US$)	168 288	302 013	413 056
GDP: Growth rate at constant 2005 prices (annual %)	3.3	2.7	0.4
GDP per capita (current US$)	37 473.4	65 324.1	84 588.7
GNI: Gross national income per capita (current US$)	36 967.9	65 775.6	84 791.5
Gross fixed capital formation (% of GDP)	18.4	18.8	20.3
Exchange rates (national currency per US$) [b]	8.85	6.77	5.86
Balance of payments, current account (million US$)	25 079	49 003	51 444
CPI: Consumer price index (2000=100)	100	109	122
Industrial production index (2005=100)	100 [c]	100	88
Agricultural production index (2004-2006=100)	100	99	101
Food production index (2004-2006=100)	100	99	101
Unemployment (% of labour force) [d]	4.2 [e]	4.4	3.5
Employment in industrial sector (% of employed) [f]	21.8	20.8	19.7
Employment in agricultural sector (% of employed) [f]	4.3	3.3	2.5
Labour force participation, adult female pop. (%)	60.3	60.4	61.5
Labour force participation, adult male pop. (%)	72.2	70.5	70.2
Tourist arrivals at national borders (000)	3 104	3 824	4 767
Energy production, primary (000 mt oil equivalent) [a]	226 188	230 931	223 412 [g]
Telephone subscribers, total (per 100 inhabitants)	125.3	148.5	149.5
Internet users (per 100 inhabitants)	26.8	82.0	93.4

Total trade		Major trading partners			2010
	(million US$) [a]	(% of exports) [a]			(% of imports) [a]
Exports	131 395.4	United Kingdom	27.0	Sweden	14.1
Imports	77 251.7	Netherlands	12.0	Germany	12.3
Balance	54 143.7	Germany	11.3	China	8.5

Social indicators		
Population growth rate (average annual %) [a]	2010-2015	0.7
Urban population growth rate (average annual %) [a]	2010-2015	1.0
Rural population growth rate (average annual %) [a]	2010-2015	−0.7
Urban population (%) [a]	2011	79.4
Population aged 0-14 years (%) [a]	2011	18.6
Population aged 60+ years (females and males, % of total) [a]	2011	23.2/19.7
Sex ratio (males per 100 females) [a]	2011	100.3
Life expectancy at birth (females and males, years) [a]	2010-2015	83.5/79.1
Infant mortality rate (per 1 000 live births) [a]	2010-2015	2.9
Fertility rate, total (live births per woman) [a]	2010-2015	2.0
Contraceptive prevalence (ages 15-49, %) [h]	2006-2010	88.4 [i]
International migrant stock (000 and % of total population) [a]	mid-2010	485.4/10.0
Refugees and others of concern to UNHCR	end-2010	55 851
Education: Government expenditure (% of GDP)	2005-2011	6.5
Education: Primary-secondary gross enrolment ratio (f/m per 100)	2005-2011	103.7/104.8
Education: Female third-level students (% of total)	2005-2011	61.1
Deaths by assault (females and males, per 100 000)	2005-2008	0.7/0.7 [j]
Seats held by women in national parliaments (%)	2011	39.6

Environmental indicators		
Threatened species	2011	42
Forested area (% of land area)	2009	32.7
CO_2 emission estimates (000 metric tons and metric tons per capita)	2008	49 951/10.5
Energy consumption per capita (kilograms oil equivalent) [a]	2009	5 685.0
Rainfall in the capital city, total mean (millimetres)		763
Temperature in the capital city, mean °C (minimum and maximum)		2.4/9.6

a Includes Svalbard and Jan Mayen Islands. **b** Official rate. **c** 2003. **d** Age group 16 years and over. **e** 2004. **f** European Labour Force Survey (Eurostat). **g** 2009. **h** Age group 20 to 44 years. **i** 2005. **j** Rate based on 30 or fewer events.

Occupied Palestinian Territory

Region	Western Asia
Currency	Shekel (ILS)
Surface area (square kilometres)	6 020
Population in 2010 (estimated, 000)	4 039[a]
Population density in 2010 (per square kilometre)	671.0
Capital city and population in 2011 (000)	Ramallah (75)

Economic indicators	2000	2005	2010
GDP: Gross domestic product (million current US$)	4 195	4 634	7 349
GDP: Growth rate at constant 2005 prices (annual %)	-8.7	8.6	6.5
GDP per capita (current US$)	1 311.4	1 303.4	1 819.5
GNI: Gross national income per capita (current US$)	1 520.7	1 404.1	1 984.8
Gross fixed capital formation (% of GDP)	32.9	27.1	26.1
Exchange rates (national currency per US$)[b]	4.04	4.60	3.55
Balance of payments, current account (million US$)	-990	-1 152	-737[c]
CPI: Consumer price index (2000=100)	100	119	148
Agricultural production index (2004-2006=100)	88	107	103
Food production index (2004-2006=100)	88	107	103
Unemployment (% of labour force)	26.8[d]	23.5	23.7
Employment in industrial sector (% of employed)	34.4[e]	26.3	25.7[f]
Employment in agricultural sector (% of employed)	13.7[e]	14.6	13.4[f]
Labour force participation, adult female pop. (%)	10.5	14.2	14.7
Labour force participation, adult male pop. (%)	67.0	67.2	66.3
Tourist arrivals at national borders (000)[g]	310	88	522
Telephone subscribers, total (per 100 inhabitants)	8.7	25.4	...
Internet users (per 100 inhabitants)	1.1	16.0	37.4

Total trade		Major trading partners				2010
	(million US$)	(% of exports)				(% of imports)
Exports	575.5	Israel	84.9	Israel		72.6
Imports	3 958.5	Jordan	5.4	China		4.6
Balance	-3 383.0	United Arab Emirates	2.0	Turkey		4.5

Social indicators		
Population growth rate (average annual %)[a]	2010-2015	2.8
Urban population growth rate (average annual %)	2010-2015	3.1
Rural population growth rate (average annual %)	2010-2015	1.9
Urban population (%)	2011	74.4
Population aged 0-14 years (%)	2011	42.0
Population aged 60+ years (females and males, % of total)	2011	4.6/4.2
Sex ratio (males per 100 females)	2011	103.1
Life expectancy at birth (females and males, years)[a]	2010-2015	74.8/71.5
Infant mortality rate (per 1 000 live births)[a]	2010-2015	19.5
Fertility rate, total (live births per woman)[a]	2010-2015	4.3
Contraceptive prevalence (ages 15-49, %)	2006-2010	50.2
International migrant stock (000 and % of total population)	mid-2010	1 923.8/43.6
Refugees and others of concern to UNHCR	end-2010	13
Education: Government expenditure (% of GDP)	2005-2011	5.6
Education: Primary-secondary gross enrolment ratio (f/m per 100)	2005-2011	89.6/85.8
Education: Female third-level students (% of total)	2005-2011	56.3

Environmental indicators		
Threatened species	2011	19
Forested area (% of land area)	2009	1.5
CO$_2$ emission estimates (000 metric tons and metric tons per capita)	2008	2 052/0.5
Energy consumption per capita (kilograms oil equivalent)	2009	272.0

a Includes East Jerusalem. b Market rate. c 2009. d 2004. e Age group 10 years and over. f 2008. g Arrivals of non-resident tourists in hotels and similar establishments. h Main telephone lines only.

Oman

Region	Western Asia
Currency	Omani Rial (OMR)
Surface area (square kilometres)	309 500
Population in 2010 (estimated, 000)	2 782
Population density in 2010 (per square kilometre)	9.0
Capital city and population in 2011 (000)	Muscat (743)
United Nations membership date	7 October 1971

Economic indicators	2000	2005	2010
GDP: Gross domestic product (million current US$)	19 450	30 905	57 850
GDP: Growth rate at constant 2005 prices (annual %)	4.6	4.0	4.2
GDP per capita (current US$)	8 590.4	12 720.6	20 791.0
GNI: Gross national income per capita (current US$)	8 220.5	12 299.9	19 544.9
Gross fixed capital formation (% of GDP)	15.6	23.2	28.7
Exchange rates (national currency per US$) [a]	0.38	0.38	0.38
Balance of payments, current account (million US$)	3 129	5 178	5 096
CPI: Consumer price index (2000=100) [b]	100	100	128[c]
Agricultural production index (2004-2006=100)	90	112	118
Food production index (2004-2006=100)	90	112	118
Employment in industrial sector (% of employed)	11.2[de]	...	...
Employment in agricultural sector (% of employed)	6.4[de]	...	...
Labour force participation, adult female pop. (%)	22.7	25.1	28.0
Labour force participation, adult male pop. (%)	77.6	76.4	79.9
Tourist arrivals at national borders (000)	829[f]	896	1 524[c]
Energy production, primary (000 mt oil equivalent)	57 304	58 091	64 017[c]
Telephone subscribers, total (per 100 inhabitants)	17.0	65.8	175.7
Internet users (per 100 inhabitants)	3.5	6.7	62.0

Total trade		Major trading partners	2010
	(million US$)	(% of exports)	(% of imports)
Exports	36 599.7		
Imports	19 972.7		
Balance	16 627.0		

Social indicators		
Population growth rate (average annual %)	2010-2015	1.9
Urban population growth rate (average annual %)	2010-2015	2.2
Rural population growth rate (average annual %)	2010-2015	0.9
Urban population (%)	2011	73.4
Population aged 0-14 years (%)	2011	27.1
Population aged 60+ years (females and males, % of total)	2011	4.6/4.1
Sex ratio (males per 100 females)	2011	143.9
Life expectancy at birth (females and males, years)	2010-2015	76.4/71.4
Infant mortality rate (per 1 000 live births)	2010-2015	8.4
Fertility rate, total (live births per woman)	2010-2015	2.2
Contraceptive prevalence (ages 15-49, %)	2006-2010	31.7[g]
International migrant stock (000 and % of total population) [h]	mid-2010	826.1/28.4
Refugees and others of concern to UNHCR	end-2010	91
Education: Government expenditure (% of GDP)	2005-2011	4.4
Education: Primary-secondary gross enrolment ratio (f/m per 100)	2005-2011	101.6/103.6
Education: Female third-level students (% of total)	2005-2011	50.0
Seats held by women in national parliaments (%)	2011	1.2

Environmental indicators		
Threatened species	2011	83
Forested area (% of land area)	2009	<
CO$_2$ emission estimates (000 metric tons and metric tons per capita)	2008	45 712/16.4
Energy consumption per capita (kilograms oil equivalent)	2009	6 573.0
Rainfall in the capital city, total mean (millimetres)		98
Temperature in the capital city, mean °C (minimum and maximum)		24.0/33.2

a Official rate. **b** Muscat. **c** 2009. **d** Age group 12 years and over. **e** Omani nationals only. **f** 2001. **g** 2000. **h** Data refer to foreign citizens.

Pakistan

Region	South-central Asia
Currency	Pakistani Rupee (PKR)
Surface area (square kilometres)	796 095
Population in 2010 (estimated, 000)	173 593
Population density in 2010 (per square kilometre)	218.1
Capital city and population in 2011 (000)	Islamabad (919)
United Nations membership date	30 September 1947

Economic indicators	2000	2005	2010
GDP: Gross domestic product (million current US$)	71 319	109 213	174 150
GDP: Growth rate at constant 2005 prices (annual %)	4.3	7.7	4.1
GDP per capita (current US$)	493.5	688.4	1 003.2
GNI: Gross national income per capita (current US$)	487.3	702.7	1 041.5
Gross fixed capital formation (% of GDP)	15.9	17.5	13.8
Exchange rates (national currency per US$)[a]	58.03	59.83	85.71
Balance of payments, current account (million US$)	−85	−3 606	−1 490
CPI: Consumer price index (2000=100)	100	129	234
Agricultural production index (2004-2006=100)	88	100	111
Food production index (2004-2006=100)	88	101	113
Employment in industrial sector (% of employed)[b]	18.0[c]	20.3[c]	20.1[de]
Employment in agricultural sector (% of employed)[b]	48.4[c]	43.0[c]	44.7[de]
Labour force participation, adult female pop. (%)	16.0	19.3	22.4
Labour force participation, adult male pop. (%)	83.7	84.1	83.3
Tourist arrivals at national borders (000)	557	798	855[f]
Energy production, primary (000 mt oil equivalent)	23 767	39 619	40 375[f]
Telephone subscribers, total (per 100 inhabitants)	2.3	11.4	59.1
Internet users (per 100 inhabitants)	1.3[g]	6.3	16.8

Total trade	Major trading partners				2010
(million US$)		(% of exports)		(% of imports)	
Exports	21 413.1	United States	17.2	United Arab Emirates	14.0
Imports	37 537.0	United Arab Emirates	8.6	China	14.0
Balance	−16 123.9	Afghanistan	7.9	Saudi Arabia	10.2

Social indicators		
Population growth rate (average annual %)	2010-2015	1.8
Urban population growth rate (average annual %)	2010-2015	2.7
Rural population growth rate (average annual %)	2010-2015	1.2
Urban population (%)	2011	36.2
Population aged 0-14 years (%)	2011	35.0
Population aged 60+ years (females and males, % of total)	2011	6.4/6.5
Sex ratio (males per 100 females)	2011	103.3
Life expectancy at birth (females and males, years)	2010-2015	66.9/64.9
Infant mortality rate (per 1 000 live births)	2010-2015	65.7
Fertility rate, total (live births per woman)	2010-2015	3.2
Contraceptive prevalence (ages 15-49, %)	2006-2010	27.0
International migrant stock (000 and % of total population)[h]	mid-2010	4 233.6/2.3
Refugees and others of concern to UNHCR	end-2010	4 041 642[i]
Education: Government expenditure (% of GDP)	2005-2011	2.4
Education: Primary-secondary gross enrolment ratio (f/m per 100)	2005-2011	52.4/65.8
Education: Female third-level students (% of total)[j]	2005-2011	44.5
Seats held by women in national parliaments (%)	2011	22.2

Environmental indicators		
Threatened species	2011	113
Forested area (% of land area)	2009	2.2
CO_2 emission estimates (000 metric tons and metric tons per capita)	2008	163 044/0.9
Energy consumption per capita (kilograms oil equivalent)	2009	347.0
Rainfall in the capital city, total mean (millimetres)		1 142
Temperature in the capital city, mean °C (minimum and maximum)		14.1/28.6

a Market rate. **b** Age group 10 years and over. **c** July. **d** January. **e** 2008. **f** 2009. **g** 2001. **h** Includes refugees. **i** The refugee population is an estimated number of Afghan refugees registered with the Government of Pakistan, and is subject to change after completion of the verfication exercise ongoing at the time of reporting. **j** National estimate.

Palau

Region	Oceania-Micronesia
Currency	U.S. Dollar (USD)
Surface area (square kilometres)	459
Population in 2010 (estimated, 000)	20
Population density in 2010 (per square kilometre)	44.6
Capital city and population in 2011 (000)	Melekeok (1)
United Nations membership date	15 December 1994

Economic indicators	2000	2005	2010
GDP: Gross domestic product (million current US$)	120	145	222
GDP: Growth rate at constant 2005 prices (annual %)	0.3	5.5	2.5
GDP per capita (current US$)	6 252.0	7 267.4	10 821.8
GNI: Gross national income per capita (current US$)	6 538.9	7 481.9	10 073.2
Gross fixed capital formation (% of GDP)	25.4	14.5	18.7
Tourist arrivals at national borders (000)[a]	58	86	84[b]
Energy production, primary (000 mt oil equivalent)[c]	2	2	2[b]
Telephone subscribers, total (per 100 inhabitants)	...	70.5	105.0
Internet users (per 100 inhabitants)	20.2[d]	...	...

Social indicators		
Population growth rate (average annual %)	2010-2015	0.8
Urban population growth rate (average annual %)	2010-2015	1.7
Rural population growth rate (average annual %)	2010-2015	−4.3
Urban population (%)	2011	84.3
Population aged 0-14 years (%)[e]	2011	20.0
Population aged 60+ years (females and males, % of total)[e]	2011	10.8/8.4
Sex ratio (males per 100 females)[e]	2011	115.3
Life expectancy at birth (females and males, years)[e]	2010-2015	72.1/66.3[f]
Infant mortality rate (per 1 000 live births)[e]	2010-2015	20.1[g]
Fertility rate, total (live births per woman)[e]	2010-2015	2.0[h]
Contraceptive prevalence (ages 15-49, %)[i]	2006-2010	32.8[d]
International migrant stock (000 and % of total population)	mid-2010	5.8/28.1
Refugees and others of concern to UNHCR	end-2010	0[j]
Education: Government expenditure (% of GDP)[k]	2005-2011	10.3[l]
Education: Primary-secondary gross enrolment ratio (f/m per 100)[m]	2005-2011	100.4/100.7[n]
Education: Female third-level students (% of total)[k]	2005-2011	63.4[l]
Seats held by women in national parliaments (%)	2011	0.0

Environmental indicators		
Threatened species	2011	130
Forested area (% of land area)	2009	87.6
CO$_2$ emission estimates (000 metric tons and metric tons per capita)	2008	235/5.1
Energy consumption per capita (kilograms oil equivalent)	2009	3 479.0[c]

a Air arrivals (Palau International Airport). **b** 2009. **c** UNSD estimate. **d** 2003. **e** Data compiled by the Secretariat of the Pacific Community Demography Programme. **f** 2005. **g** 2004-2006. **h** 2003-2005. **i** Age group 15 to 44 years. **j** Value is zero, not available or not applicable. **k** UNESCO estimate. **l** 2002. **m** National estimate. **n** 2004.

Panama

Region	Central America
Currency	Balboa (PAB)
Surface area (square kilometres)	75 417
Population in 2010 (estimated, 000)	3 517
Population density in 2010 (per square kilometre)	46.6
Capital city and population in 2011 (000)	Panama City (1 426)
United Nations membership date	13 November 1945

Economic indicators	2000	2005	2010
GDP: Gross domestic product (million current US$)	11 621	15 465	26 777
GDP: Growth rate at constant 2005 prices (annual %)	2.7	7.2	7.5
GDP per capita (current US$)	3 931.0	4 775.5	7 614.0
GNI: Gross national income per capita (current US$)	3 647.3	4 331.9	6 950.4
Gross fixed capital formation (% of GDP)	21.2	16.8	26.8
Exchange rates (national currency per US$) [a]	1.00	1.00	1.00
Balance of payments, current account (million US$)	–673	–1 022	–2 953
CPI: Consumer price index (2000=100) [bc]	100[d]	103	127
Agricultural production index (2004-2006=100)	96	99	108
Food production index (2004-2006=100)	97	99	108
Unemployment (% of labour force)	...	6.0[e]	6.4[f]
Employment in industrial sector (% of employed)	17.4[g]	17.0[g]	19.1[f]
Employment in agricultural sector (% of employed)	17.0[g]	19.3[g]	17.9[f]
Labour force participation, adult female pop. (%)	45.2	48.1	49.3
Labour force participation, adult male pop. (%)	81.8	81.2	82.6
Tourist arrivals at national borders (000)	484	702	1 324
Energy production, primary (000 mt oil equivalent)	294	320	335[f]
Telephone subscribers, total (per 100 inhabitants)	28.4	68.5	200.5
Internet users (per 100 inhabitants)	6.6	11.5	42.8

Total trade		Major trading partners			2010
	(million US$)	(% of exports)			(% of imports)
Exports	10 986.6	United States	19.8	China	24.9
Imports	16 737.1	Venezuela	16.1	United States	20.5
Balance	–5 750.5	Colombia	15.6	Singapore	10.4

Social indicators		
Population growth rate (average annual %)	2010-2015	1.5
Urban population growth rate (average annual %)	2010-2015	2.2
Rural population growth rate (average annual %)	2010-2015	–1.0
Urban population (%)	2011	75.3
Population aged 0-14 years (%)	2011	28.6
Population aged 60+ years (females and males, % of total)	2011	10.3/9.4
Sex ratio (males per 100 females)	2011	101.5
Life expectancy at birth (females and males, years)	2010-2015	79.1/73.9
Infant mortality rate (per 1 000 live births)	2010-2015	16.2
Fertility rate, total (live births per woman)	2010-2015	2.4
Contraceptive prevalence (ages 15-49, %) [h]	2006-2010	58.2[i]
International migrant stock (000 and % of total population)	mid-2010	121.0/3.5
Refugees and others of concern to UNHCR	end-2010	17 555
Education: Government expenditure (% of GDP)	2005-2011	3.8
Education: Primary-secondary gross enrolment ratio (f/m per 100)	2005-2011	91.8/91.2
Education: Female third-level students (% of total)	2005-2011	59.6
Seats held by women in national parliaments (%)	2011	8.5

Environmental indicators		
Threatened species	2011	352
Forested area (% of land area)	2009	43.9
CO$_2$ emission estimates (000 metric tons and metric tons per capita)	2008	6 907/2.0
Energy consumption per capita (kilograms oil equivalent)	2009	759.0
Rainfall in the capital city, total mean (millimetres)		1 907
Temperature in the capital city, mean °C (minimum and maximum)		20.0/33.8

a Official rate. b Urban areas. c Index base 2003=100. d 2003. e 2008. f 2009. g August. h Age group 15 to 44 years. i 1984-1985.

Papua New Guinea

Region	Oceania-Melanesia		
Currency	Kina (PGK)		
Surface area (square kilometres)	462 840		
Population in 2010 (estimated, 000)	6 858		
Population density in 2010 (per square kilometre)	14.8		
Capital city and population in 2011 (000)	Port Moresby (343)		
United Nations membership date	10 October 1975		

Economic indicators	2000	2005	2010
GDP: Gross domestic product (million current US$)	3 499	4 866	9 796
GDP: Growth rate at constant 2005 prices (annual %)	−2.5	3.9	7.1
GDP per capita (current US$)	650.6	798.3	1 428.4
GNI: Gross national income per capita (current US$)	624.4	710.0	1 330.2
Gross fixed capital formation (% of GDP)	20.4	16.5	13.6
Exchange rates (national currency per US$)[a]	3.07	3.10	2.64
Balance of payments, current account (million US$)	345	539	−914
CPI: Consumer price index (2000=100)	100	146	189
Agricultural production index (2004-2006=100)	92	100	106
Food production index (2004-2006=100)	91	99	105
Employment in industrial sector (% of employed)	3.6[bcd]	...	...
Employment in agricultural sector (% of employed)	72.3[bcd]	...	...
Labour force participation, adult female pop. (%)	70.8	71.3	70.6
Labour force participation, adult male pop. (%)	73.5	74.4	74.1
Tourist arrivals at national borders (000)	58	69	114[e]
Energy production, primary (000 mt oil equivalent)	3 907	2 805	2 341[f]
Telephone subscribers, total (per 100 inhabitants)	1.4	2.3	29.6
Internet users (per 100 inhabitants)	0.8	1.7	1.3

Social indicators		
Population growth rate (average annual %)	2010-2015	2.2
Urban population growth rate (average annual %)	2010-2015	2.7
Rural population growth rate (average annual %)	2010-2015	2.1
Urban population (%)	2011	12.5
Population aged 0-14 years (%)	2011	38.8
Population aged 60+ years (females and males, % of total)	2011	5.3/4.1
Sex ratio (males per 100 females)	2011	104.1
Life expectancy at birth (females and males, years)	2010-2015	65.5/61.2
Infant mortality rate (per 1 000 live births)	2010-2015	44.5
Fertility rate, total (live births per woman)	2010-2015	3.8
Contraceptive prevalence (ages 15-49, %)	2006-2010	35.7
International migrant stock (000 and % of total population)[gh]	mid-2010	24.6/0.4
Refugees and others of concern to UNHCR	end-2010	9 699
Education: Primary-secondary gross enrolment ratio (f/m per 100)	2005-2011	45.1/53.9[i]
Education: Female third-level students (% of total)[i]	2005-2011	35.2[k]
Seats held by women in national parliaments (%)	2011	0.9

Environmental indicators		
Threatened species	2011	454
Forested area (% of land area)	2009	63.8
CO_2 emission estimates (000 metric tons and metric tons per capita)	2008	2 107/0.3
Energy consumption per capita (kilograms oil equivalent)	2009	179.0
Rainfall in the capital city, total mean (millimetres)		899
Temperature in the capital city, mean °C (minimum and maximum)		23.3/31.3

a Official rate. **b** July. **c** Population census. **d** Age group 10 years and over. **e** 2008. **f** 2009. **g** Data refer to foreign citizens. **h** Includes refugees. **i** 1998. **j** UNESCO estimate. **k** 1999.

Paraguay

Region	South America
Currency	Guarani (PYG)
Surface area (square kilometres)	406 752
Population in 2010 (estimated, 000)	6 455
Population density in 2010 (per square kilometre)	15.9
Capital city and population in 2011 (000)	Asunción (2 139)
United Nations membership date	24 October 1945

Economic indicators	2000	2005	2010
GDP: Gross domestic product (million current US$)	7 095	7 473	17 886
GDP: Growth rate at constant 2005 prices (annual %)	–3.3	2.9	15.3
GDP per capita (current US$)	1 327.8	1 267.1	2 771.1
GNI: Gross national income per capita (current US$)	1 327.5	1 257.3	2 735.8
Gross fixed capital formation (% of GDP)	17.5	19.3	16.5
Exchange rates (national currency per US$)[a]	3 526.90	6 120.00	4 573.75
Balance of payments, current account (million US$)	–163	16	–641
CPI: Consumer price index (2000=100)[b]	100	150	212
Agricultural production index (2004-2006=100)	76	97	141
Food production index (2004-2006=100)	75	98	146
Unemployment (% of labour force)[c]	...	...	7.2
Employment in industrial sector (% of employed)[c]	16.9[d]	15.7[e]	18.9[f]
Employment in agricultural sector (% of employed)[c]	31.9[d]	32.4[e]	26.5[f]
Labour force participation, adult female pop. (%)	51.0	54.7	57.4
Labour force participation, adult male pop. (%)	86.7	85.7	86.4
Tourist arrivals at national borders (000)[g]	289	341	465
Energy production, primary (000 mt oil equivalent)	4 600	4 403	4 739[h]
Telephone subscribers, total (per 100 inhabitants)	20.7	37.4	97.3
Internet users (per 100 inhabitants)	0.8	7.9	19.8

Total trade		Major trading partners			2010
	(million US$)	(% of exports)			(% of imports)
Exports	4 533.8	Uruguay	22.0	China	34.2
Imports	10 040.2	Brazil	14.6	Brazil	24.1
Balance	–5 506.4	Chile	12.1	Argentina	15.7

Social indicators		
Population growth rate (average annual %)	2010-2015	1.7
Urban population growth rate (average annual %)	2010-2015	2.6
Rural population growth rate (average annual %)	2010-2015	0.3
Urban population (%)	2011	61.9
Population aged 0-14 years (%)	2011	33.1
Population aged 60+ years (females and males, % of total)	2011	8.1/7.5
Sex ratio (males per 100 females)	2011	101.7
Life expectancy at birth (females and males, years)	2010-2015	74.9/70.8
Infant mortality rate (per 1 000 live births)	2010-2015	27.4
Fertility rate, total (live births per woman)	2010-2015	2.9
Contraceptive prevalence (ages 15-49, %)[i]	2006-2010	79.4
International migrant stock (000 and % of total population)	mid-2010	161.3/2.5
Refugees and others of concern to UNHCR	end-2010	115
Education: Government expenditure (% of GDP)	2005-2011	4.0
Education: Primary-secondary gross enrolment ratio (f/m per 100)	2005-2011	83.4/83.7
Education: Female third-level students (% of total)	2005-2011	58.3
Seats held by women in national parliaments (%)	2011	12.5

Environmental indicators		
Threatened species	2011	48
Forested area (% of land area)	2009	44.7
CO_2 emission estimates (000 metric tons and metric tons per capita)	2008	4 115/0.7
Energy consumption per capita (kilograms oil equivalent)	2009	358.0
Rainfall in the capital city, total mean (millimetres)		1 401
Temperature in the capital city, mean °C (minimum and maximum)		18.2/28.4

a Market rate. **b** Asunción. **c** Age group 10 years and over. **d** September of the current year to August of the following year. **e** October to December. **f** 2008. **g** Excludes nationals residing abroad and crew members. **h** 2009. **i** Age group 15 to 44 years.

Peru

Region	South America
Currency	Nuevo Sol (PEN)
Surface area (square kilometres)	1 285 216
Population in 2010 (estimated, 000)	29 077
Population density in 2010 (per square kilometre)	22.6
Capital city and population in 2011 (000)	Lima (9 130)
United Nations membership date	31 October 1945

Economic indicators	2000	2005	2010
GDP: Gross domestic product (million current US$)	53 336	79 389	157 324
GDP: Growth rate at constant 2005 prices (annual %)	3.0	6.8	8.8
GDP per capita (current US$)	2 062.3	2 880.7	5 410.7
GNI: Gross national income per capita (current US$)	2 007.7	2 690.4	5 026.2
Gross fixed capital formation (% of GDP)	20.2	18.3	26.3
Exchange rates (national currency per US$)[a]	3.53	3.43	2.81
Balance of payments, current account (million US$)	−1 546	1 148	−2 315
CPI: Consumer price index (2000=100)[b]	100	110	126[c]
Industrial production index (2005=100)[d]	87[e]	100	130
Agricultural production index (2004-2006=100)	86	99	127
Food production index (2004-2006=100)	85	100	129
Unemployment (% of labour force)[bf]	9.4[g]	9.6	7.9
Employment in industrial sector (% of employed)[fh]	21.2[i]	23.8[i]	24.4[i]
Employment in agricultural sector (% of employed)[fh]	0.6[i]	0.7[i]	0.8[i]
Labour force participation, adult female pop. (%)	57.6	57.5	67.4
Labour force participation, adult male pop. (%)	82.8	79.1	84.7
Tourist arrivals at national borders (000)[k]	800	1 571[l]	2 299
Energy production, primary (000 mt oil equivalent)	7 471	8 787	13 274[j]
Telephone subscribers, total (per 100 inhabitants)	11.6	29.0	111.0
Internet users (per 100 inhabitants)	3.1	17.1	34.3

Total trade		Major trading partners			2010
	(million US$)	(% of exports)		(% of imports)	
Exports	35 205.1	United States	16.6	United States	19.5
Imports	30 030.5	China	15.4	China	17.1
Balance	5 174.6	Switzerland	10.9	Brazil	7.3

Social indicators		
Population growth rate (average annual %)	2010-2015	1.1
Urban population growth rate (average annual %)	2010-2015	1.6
Rural population growth rate (average annual %)	2010-2015	−0.4
Urban population (%)	2011	77.3
Population aged 0-14 years (%)	2011	29.6
Population aged 60+ years (females and males, % of total)	2011	9.6/8.4
Sex ratio (males per 100 females)	2011	100.5
Life expectancy at birth (females and males, years)	2010-2015	76.9/71.7
Infant mortality rate (per 1 000 live births)	2010-2015	18.3
Fertility rate, total (live births per woman)	2010-2015	2.4
Contraceptive prevalence (ages 15-49, %)	2006-2010	73.2
International migrant stock (000 and % of total population)	mid-2010	37.6/0.1
Refugees and others of concern to UNHCR	end-2010	1 411
Education: Government expenditure (% of GDP)	2005-2011	2.6
Education: Primary-secondary gross enrolment ratio (f/m per 100)	2005-2011	100.3/101.4
Education: Female third-level students (% of total)[m]	2005-2011	50.9
Seats held by women in national parliaments (%)	2011	21.5

Environmental indicators		
Threatened species	2011	562
Forested area (% of land area)	2009	53.2
CO_2 emission estimates (000 metric tons and metric tons per capita)	2008	40 502/1.4
Energy consumption per capita (kilograms oil equivalent)	2009	524.0
Rainfall in the capital city, total mean (millimetres)		13
Temperature in the capital city, mean °C (minimum and maximum)		16.7/22.1

a Market rate. **b** Lima. **c** Series linked to former series. **d** The indices are shown in terms of ISIC Rev. 3. **e** 2003. **f** Age group 14 years and over. **g** 2004. **h** Metropolitan Lima. **i** Third quarter. **j** 2009. **k** Includes nationals residing abroad. **l** Preliminary data. **m** UNESCO estimate.

Philippines

Region	South-eastern Asia
Currency	Philippine Peso (PHP)
Surface area (square kilometres)	300 000
Population in 2010 (estimated, 000)	93 261
Population density in 2010 (per square kilometre)	310.9
Capital city and population in 2011 (000)	Manila (11 862)
United Nations membership date	24 October 1945

Economic indicators	2000	2005	2010
GDP: Gross domestic product (million current US$)	81 026	103 072	199 591
GDP: Growth rate at constant 2005 prices (annual %)	4.4	4.8	7.6
GDP per capita (current US$)	1 048.1	1 204.9	2 140.1
GNI: Gross national income per capita (current US$)	1 228.4	1 517.4	2 851.5
Gross fixed capital formation (% of GDP)	22.1	19.9	20.5
Exchange rates (national currency per US$)[a]	50.00	53.07	43.88
Balance of payments, current account (million US$)	−2 228	1 980	8 924
CPI: Consumer price index (2000=100)	100	130	160[b]
Agricultural production index (2004-2006=100)	83	100	112
Food production index (2004-2006=100)	84	100	112
Unemployment (% of labour force)	11.8[c]	8.7	7.4
Employment in industrial sector (% of employed)	16.2[de]	15.6[de]	14.6[bf]
Employment in agricultural sector (% of employed)	37.1[de]	36.0[de]	35.2[bf]
Labour force participation, adult female pop. (%)	48.7	49.8	49.5
Labour force participation, adult male pop. (%)	81.7	80.0	79.4
Tourist arrivals at national borders (000)[g]	1 992	2 623	3 520
Energy production, primary (000 mt oil equivalent)	2 368	6 560	8 663[b]
Telephone subscribers, total (per 100 inhabitants)	12.3	44.6	92.9
Internet users (per 100 inhabitants)	2.0	5.4	25.0

Total trade		Major trading partners			2010
	(million US$)	(% of exports)			(% of imports)
Exports	51 431.7	Japan	15.2	Japan	12.5
Imports	58 228.6	United States	14.7	United States	10.8
Balance	−6 796.9	Singapore	14.3	Singapore	9.3

Social indicators

Population growth rate (average annual %)	2010-2015	1.7
Urban population growth rate (average annual %)	2010-2015	2.2
Rural population growth rate (average annual %)	2010-2015	1.2
Urban population (%)	2011	48.8
Population aged 0-14 years (%)	2011	35.0
Population aged 60+ years (females and males, % of total)	2011	6.7/5.2
Sex ratio (males per 100 females)	2011	100.6
Life expectancy at birth (females and males, years)	2010-2015	72.6/66.0
Infant mortality rate (per 1 000 live births)	2010-2015	20.9
Fertility rate, total (live births per woman)	2010-2015	3.1
Contraceptive prevalence (ages 15-49, %)	2006-2010	50.7
International migrant stock (000 and % of total population)[hi]	mid-2010	435.4/0.5
Refugees and others of concern to UNHCR	end-2010	139 893
Education: Government expenditure (% of GDP)	2005-2011	2.7
Education: Primary-secondary gross enrolment ratio (f/m per 100)	2005-2011	98.4/97.3
Education: Female third-level students (% of total)	2005-2011	54.5
Seats held by women in national parliaments (%)	2011	22.1

Environmental indicators

Threatened species	2011	705
Forested area (% of land area)	2009	25.5
CO$_2$ emission estimates (000 metric tons and metric tons per capita)	2008	83 089/0.9
Energy consumption per capita (kilograms oil equivalent)	2009	232.0
Rainfall in the capital city, total mean (millimetres)		2 201
Temperature in the capital city, mean °C (minimum and maximum)		25.2/31.2

a Market rate. **b** 2009. **c** 2004. **d** October. **e** Excludes regular military living in barracks. **f** April. **g** Includes nationals residing abroad. **h** Data refer to foreign citizens. **i** Includes refugees.

Poland

Region	Eastern Europe
Currency	Zloty (PLN)
Surface area (square kilometres)	312 679 [a]
Population in 2010 (estimated, 000)	38 277
Population density in 2010 (per square kilometre)	122.4
Capital city and population in 2011 (000)	Warsaw (1 723)
United Nations membership date	24 October 1945

Economic indicators	2000	2005	2010
GDP: Gross domestic product (million current US$)	171 276	303 912	469 393
GDP: Growth rate at constant 2005 prices (annual %)	4.3	3.6	3.9
GDP per capita (current US$)	4 471.7	7 963.1	12 263.2
GNI: Gross national income per capita (current US$)	4 455.5	7 811.1	11 814.8
Gross fixed capital formation (% of GDP)	23.8	18.3	19.9
Exchange rates (national currency per US$) [b]	4.14	3.26	2.96
Balance of payments, current account (million US$)	−10 343	−7 242	−21 873
CPI: Consumer price index (2000=100)	100	115	131
Industrial production index (2005=100)	...	100	134
Agricultural production index (2004-2006=100)	102	99	100
Food production index (2004-2006=100)	102	99	100
Unemployment (% of labour force)	19.0 [c]	17.7	9.6
Employment in industrial sector (% of employed)	30.8 [d]	29.2 [d]	30.2 [e]
Employment in agricultural sector (% of employed)	18.8 [d]	17.4 [d]	12.8 [e]
Labour force participation, adult female pop. (%)	49.2	47.5	48.2
Labour force participation, adult male pop. (%)	63.5	62.5	64.3
Tourist arrivals at national borders (000)	17 400	15 200	12 470
Energy production, primary (000 mt oil equivalent)	76 023	74 494	61 943 [f]
Telephone subscribers, total (per 100 inhabitants)	46.2	107.4	142.7
Internet users (per 100 inhabitants)	7.3	38.8	62.3

Total trade		Major trading partners			2010
	(million US$)	(% of exports)		(% of imports)	
Exports	157 064.9	Germany	26.0	Germany	21.7
Imports	174 127.6	France	6.8	Russian Federation	10.5
Balance	−17 062.7	United Kingdom	6.3	China	9.5

Social indicators

Population growth rate (average annual %)	2010-2015	<
Urban population growth rate (average annual %)	2010-2015	−<
Rural population growth rate (average annual %)	2010-2015	0.2
Urban population (%)	2011	60.9
Population aged 0-14 years (%)	2011	14.8
Population aged 60+ years (females and males, % of total)	2011	22.9/16.5
Sex ratio (males per 100 females)	2011	93.2
Life expectancy at birth (females and males, years)	2010-2015	80.6/72.2
Infant mortality rate (per 1 000 live births)	2010-2015	5.6
Fertility rate, total (live births per woman)	2010-2015	1.4
Contraceptive prevalence (ages 15-49, %) [g]	2006-2010	72.7 [h]
International migrant stock (000 and % of total population)	mid-2010	827.5/2.2
Refugees and others of concern to UNHCR	end-2010	18 444
Education: Government expenditure (% of GDP)	2005-2011	5.1
Education: Primary-secondary gross enrolment ratio (f/m per 100)	2005-2011	96.7/97.7
Education: Female third-level students (% of total)	2005-2011	57.9
Deaths by assault (females and males, per 100 000)	2005-2008	0.7/1.9
Seats held by women in national parliaments (%)	2011	23.9

Environmental indicators

Threatened species	2011	50
Forested area (% of land area)	2009	30.6
CO_2 emission estimates (000 metric tons and metric tons per capita)	2008	315 808/8.3
Energy consumption per capita (kilograms oil equivalent)	2009	2 319.0
Rainfall in the capital city, total mean (millimetres)		520
Temperature in the capital city, mean °C (minimum and maximum)		4.0/12.3

a Includes inland waters as well as part of internal waters. **b** Official rate. **c** 2004. **d** Excludes conscripts and regular military living in barracks. **e** European Labour Force Survey (Eurostat). **f** 2009. **g** Age group 20 to 49 years. **h** 1991.

Portugal

Region	Southern Europe
Currency	Euro (EUR)
Surface area (square kilometres)	92 207
Population in 2010 (estimated, 000)	10 676
Population density in 2010 (per square kilometre)	115.8
Capital city and population in 2011 (000)	Lisbon (2 843)
United Nations membership date	14 December 1955

Economic indicators	2000	2005	2010
GDP: Gross domestic product (million current US$)	117 014	191 176	228 859
GDP: Growth rate at constant 2005 prices (annual %)	3.9	0.8	1.4
GDP per capita (current US$)	11 320.8	18 131.8	21 437.6
GNI: Gross national income per capita (current US$)	11 085.9	17 862.0	20 708.7
Gross fixed capital formation (% of GDP)	27.9	23.1	19.1
Exchange rates (national currency per US$) [a]	1.07	0.85	0.75
Balance of payments, current account (million US$)	−12 189	−19 821	−22 851
CPI: Consumer price index (2000=100) [b]	100	117	127
Industrial production index (2005=100)	108[c]	100	92
Agricultural production index (2004-2006=100)	101	97	101
Food production index (2004-2006=100)	101	97	101
Unemployment (% of labour force)	6.7[d]	7.6	10.8
Employment in industrial sector (% of employed) [e]	34.4	30.6	27.7
Employment in agricultural sector (% of employed) [e]	12.5	11.8	10.9
Labour force participation, adult female pop. (%)	52.8	55.5	56.4
Labour force participation, adult male pop. (%)	69.7	69.3	68.0
Tourist arrivals at national borders (000)	12 097[f]	10 612[g]	6 756[h]
Energy production, primary (000 mt oil equivalent)	1 029	599	1 684[i]
Telephone subscribers, total (per 100 inhabitants)	106.3	148.7	184.3
Internet users (per 100 inhabitants)	16.4	35.0	51.1

Total trade		Major trading partners			2010
	(million US$)	(% of exports)			(% of imports)
Exports	48 743.6	Spain	26.5	Spain	31.2
Imports	75 572.5	Germany	12.8	Germany	13.8
Balance	−26 828.9	France	11.8	France	7.2

Social indicators		
Population growth rate (average annual %)	2010-2015	0.1
Urban population growth rate (average annual %)	2010-2015	0.9
Rural population growth rate (average annual %)	2010-2015	−1.4
Urban population (%)	2011	61.1
Population aged 0-14 years (%)	2011	15.0
Population aged 60+ years (females and males, % of total)	2011	26.5/21.4
Sex ratio (males per 100 females)	2011	94.0
Life expectancy at birth (females and males, years)	2010-2015	82.8/76.8
Infant mortality rate (per 1 000 live births)	2010-2015	4.2
Fertility rate, total (live births per woman)	2010-2015	1.3
Contraceptive prevalence (ages 15-49, %)	2006-2010	86.8[j]
International migrant stock (000 and % of total population)	mid-2010	918.6/8.6
Refugees and others of concern to UNHCR	end-2010	487
Education: Government expenditure (% of GDP)	2005-2011	4.9
Education: Primary-secondary gross enrolment ratio (f/m per 100)	2005-2011	110.3/110.2
Education: Female third-level students (% of total)	2005-2011	53.4
Seats held by women in national parliaments (%)	2011	26.5

Environmental indicators		
Threatened species	2011	245
Forested area (% of land area)	2009	37.7
CO_2 emission estimates (000 metric tons and metric tons per capita)	2008	56 264/5.3
Energy consumption per capita (kilograms oil equivalent)	2009	1 827.0
Rainfall in the capital city, total mean (millimetres)		751
Temperature in the capital city, mean °C (minimum and maximum)		12.8/20.8

a Market rate. b Excludes rent. c 2003. d 2004. e European Labour Force Survey (Eurostat). f Excludes nationals residing abroad. g Includes nationals residing abroad. h Arrivals of non-resident tourists in all types of accommodation establishments. i 2009. j 2005-2006.

Puerto Rico

Region	Caribbean
Currency	U.S. Dollar (USD)
Surface area (square kilometres)	8 870
Population in 2010 (estimated; 000)	3 749
Population density in 2010 (per square kilometre)	422.7
Capital city and population in 2011 (000)	San Juan (2 475)

Economic indicators	2000	2005	2010
GDP: Gross domestic product (million current US$)	69 208	86 157	99 202
GDP: Growth rate at constant 2005 prices (annual %)	6.3	−0.2	−1.8
GDP per capita (current US$)	18 144.1	22 780.9	26 461.0
GNI: Gross national income per capita (current US$)	11 460.1	14 911.7	17 433.0
Gross fixed capital formation (% of GDP)	16.9	13.7	10.4
CPI: Consumer price index (2000=100)	100	156	131
Agricultural production index (2004-2006=100)	110	97	104
Food production index (2004-2006=100)	111	97	105
Unemployment (% of labour force) [ab]	10.6[c]	11.3	16.1
Employment in industrial sector (% of employed) [b]	22.3	19.0	18.1[d]
Employment in agricultural sector (% of employed) [b]	1.9	2.1	1.5[d]
Labour force participation, adult female pop. (%)	34.8	38.1	35.4
Labour force participation, adult male pop. (%)	59.6	61.0	54.4
Tourist arrivals at national borders (000) [e]	3 341	3 686	3 679
Energy production, primary (000 mt oil equivalent)	14	12	13[f]
Telephone subscribers, total (per 100 inhabitants)	68.6	80.2	102.0
Internet users (per 100 inhabitants)	10.5	23.4	45.3

Social indicators		
Population growth rate (average annual %)	2010-2015	−<
Urban population growth rate (average annual %)	2010-2015	0.1
Rural population growth rate (average annual %)	2010-2015	−9.6
Urban population (%)	2011	98.9
Population aged 0-14 years (%)	2011	20.8
Population aged 60+ years (females and males, % of total)	2011	19.9/16.4
Sex ratio (males per 100 females)	2011	92.7
Life expectancy at birth (females and males, years)	2010-2015	83.2/75.4
Infant mortality rate (per 1 000 live births)	2010-2015	7.2
Fertility rate, total (live births per woman)	2010-2015	1.8
Contraceptive prevalence (ages 15-49, %) [g]	2006-2010	84.1[h]
International migrant stock (000 and % of total population)	mid-2010	324.0/8.1
Education: Primary-secondary gross enrolment ratio (f/m per 100)	2005-2011	89.2/85.5
Education: Female third-level students (% of total)	2005-2011	59.1

Environmental indicators		
Threatened species	2011	108
Forested area (% of land area)	2009	61.2
Energy consumption per capita (kilograms oil equivalent)	2009	192.0
Rainfall in the capital city, total mean (millimetres)		1 329
Temperature in the capital city, mean °C (minimum and maximum)		23.3/30.2

a Official estimates. b Age group 16 years and over. c 2004. d 2008. e Air arrivals of non-resident tourists.
f 2009. g Age group 18 to 44 years. h 2002.

Qatar

Region	Western Asia
Currency	Qatari Rial (QAR)
Surface area (square kilometres)	11 607
Population in 2010 (estimated, 000)	1 759
Population density in 2010 (per square kilometre)	151.5
Capital city and population in 2011 (000)	Doha (567)
United Nations membership date	21 September 1971

Economic indicators	2000	2005	2010
GDP: Gross domestic product (million current US$)	17 760	44 530	127 333
GDP: Growth rate at constant 2005 prices (annual %)	9.1	7.5	19.4
GDP per capita (current US$)	30 052.8	54 240.3	72 397.9
GNI: Gross national income per capita (current US$)	29 448.9	53 280.4	71 116.7
Gross fixed capital formation (% of GDP)	19.5	32.0	35.0
Exchange rates (national currency per US$)[a]	3.64	3.64	3.64
CPI: Consumer price index (2000=100)	100	121	164
Agricultural production index (2004-2006=100)	112	96	138
Food production index (2004-2006=100)	112	96	138
Employment in industrial sector (% of employed)[b]	38.2[c]	41.6[d]	...
Employment in agricultural sector (% of employed)[b]	2.3[c]	3.0[d]	...
Labour force participation, adult female pop. (%)	39.1	46.4	52.1
Labour force participation, adult male pop. (%)	92.2	94.7	95.2
Tourist arrivals at national borders (000)[ef]	378	913	1 866
Energy production, primary (000 mt oil equivalent)	61 143	97 843	149 538[g]
Telephone subscribers, total (per 100 inhabitants)	47.6	112.3	149.4
Internet users (per 100 inhabitants)	4.9	24.7	81.6

Total trade	Major trading partners		2010
(million US$)	(% of exports)		(% of imports)
Imports 23 239.5		United States	11.8
		China	9.1
		Japan	7.5

Social indicators		
Population growth rate (average annual %)	2010-2015	2.9
Urban population growth rate (average annual %)	2010-2015	3.0
Rural population growth rate (average annual %)	2010-2015	−8.6
Urban population (%)	2011	98.8
Population aged 0-14 years (%)	2011	14.0
Population aged 60+ years (females and males, % of total)	2011	2.4/1.9
Sex ratio (males per 100 females)	2011	315.0
Life expectancy at birth (females and males, years)	2010-2015	78.2/78.7
Infant mortality rate (per 1 000 live births)	2010-2015	8.2
Fertility rate, total (live births per woman)	2010-2015	2.2
Contraceptive prevalence (ages 15-49, %)	2006-2010	43.2[h]
International migrant stock (000 and % of total population)[i]	mid-2010	1 305.4/86.6
Refugees and others of concern to UNHCR	end-2010	1 267
Education: Government expenditure (% of GDP)	2005-2011	2.4
Education: Primary-secondary gross enrolment ratio (f/m per 100)	2005-2011	103.1/94.8
Education: Female third-level students (% of total)	2005-2011	63.0
Seats held by women in national parliaments (%)	2011	0.0

Environmental indicators		
Threatened species	2011	33
Forested area (% of land area)	2009	0.0
CO_2 emission estimates (000 metric tons and metric tons per capita)	2008	68 422/53.4
Energy consumption per capita (kilograms oil equivalent)	2009	16 034.0
Rainfall in the capital city, total mean (millimetres)		75
Temperature in the capital city, mean °C (minimum and maximum)		21.6/32.7

a Official rate. **b** March. **c** 2001. **d** 2006. **e** Arrivals in hotels only. **f** Arrivals of non-resident tourists in hotels and similar establishments. **g** 2009. **h** 1998. **i** Data refer to foreign citizens.

Republic of Korea

Region	Eastern Asia
Currency	South Korean Won (KRW)
Surface area (square kilometres)	99 897
Population in 2010 (estimated, 000)	48 184
Population density in 2010 (per square kilometre)	482.3
Capital city and population in 2011 (000)	Seoul (9 736)
United Nations membership date	17 September 1991

Economic indicators	2000	2005	2010
GDP: Gross domestic product (million current US$)	533 385	844 866	1 014 370
GDP: Growth rate at constant 2005 prices (annual %)	8.8	4.0	6.2
GDP per capita (current US$)	11 598.5	17 959.0	21 052.2
GNI: Gross national income per capita (current US$)	11 539.3	17 942.1	21 057.9
Gross fixed capital formation (% of GDP)	30.0	28.9	28.6
Exchange rates (national currency per US$)[a]	1 264.50	1 011.60	1 134.80
Balance of payments, current account (million US$)	14 803	18 607	28 214
CPI: Consumer price index (2000=100)	100	118	137
Industrial production index (2005=100)	85[b]	100	139
Agricultural production index (2004-2006=100)	104	100	101
Food production index (2004-2006=100)	103	100	101
Unemployment (% of labour force)	3.7[c]	3.7	3.7
Employment in industrial sector (% of employed)	28.1[d]	26.8	17.0
Employment in agricultural sector (% of employed)	10.6[d]	7.9	6.6
Labour force participation, adult female pop. (%)	48.9	50.0	49.2
Labour force participation, adult male pop. (%)	73.4	73.4	71.6
Tourist arrivals at national borders (000)[ef]	5 322	6 023	8 798
Energy production, primary (000 mt oil equivalent)	13 434	14 848	15 454[g]
Telephone subscribers, total (per 100 inhabitants)	114.6	132.3	164.6
Internet users (per 100 inhabitants)	44.7	73.5	83.7

Total trade		Major trading partners			2010
	(million US$)	(% of exports)			(% of imports)
Exports	466 380.6	China	25.1	China	16.8
Imports	425 208.0	United States	10.7	Japan	15.1
Balance	41 172.6	Japan	6.0	United States	9.5

Social indicators		
Population growth rate (average annual %)	2010-2015	0.4
Urban population growth rate (average annual %)	2010-2015	0.7
Rural population growth rate (average annual %)	2010-2015	−1.3
Urban population (%)	2011	83.2
Population aged 0-14 years (%)	2011	16.1
Population aged 60+ years (females and males, % of total)	2011	18.3/14.1
Sex ratio (males per 100 females)	2011	99.4
Life expectancy at birth (females and males, years)	2010-2015	84.0/77.3
Infant mortality rate (per 1 000 live births)	2010-2015	3.7
Fertility rate, total (live births per woman)	2010-2015	1.4
Contraceptive prevalence (ages 15-49, %)[h]	2006-2010	80.0
International migrant stock (000 and % of total population)	mid-2010	534.8/1.1
Refugees and others of concern to UNHCR	end-2010	1 249
Education: Government expenditure (% of GDP)	2005-2011	4.8
Education: Primary-secondary gross enrolment ratio (f/m per 100)	2005-2011	99.7/100.8
Education: Female third-level students (% of total)	2005-2011	38.9
Seats held by women in national parliaments (%)	2011	14.7

Environmental indicators		
Threatened species	2011	68
Forested area (% of land area)	2009	64.2
CO_2 emission estimates (000 metric tons and metric tons per capita)	2008	508 754/10.6
Energy consumption per capita (kilograms oil equivalent)	2009	3 466.0
Rainfall in the capital city, total mean (millimetres)		1 344
Temperature in the capital city, mean °C (minimum and maximum)		8.2/16.9

a Market rate. b 2003. c 2004. d Estimates based on 2000 population census results. e Includes nationals residing abroad and crew members. f Arrivals of non-resident visitors at national borders. g 2009. h Age group 15 to 44 years.

Republic of Moldova

Region	Eastern Europe
Currency	Moldovan Leu (MDL)
Surface area (square kilometres)	33 846
Population in 2010 (estimated, 000)	3 573 [a]
Population density in 2010 (per square kilometre)	105.6
Capital city and population in 2011 (000)	Chisinau (677)
United Nations membership date	2 March 1992

Economic indicators	2000	2005	2010
GDP: Gross domestic product (million current US$)	1 288	2 988	5 809
GDP: Growth rate at constant 2005 prices (annual %)	2.1	7.5	7.0
GDP per capita (current US$)	313.7	793.3	1 625.8
GNI: Gross national income per capita (current US$)	329.3	900.5	1 788.6
Gross fixed capital formation (% of GDP)	15.4	24.6	22.7
Exchange rates (national currency per US$) [b]	12.38	12.83	12.15
Balance of payments, current account (million US$)	−108	−248	−592
CPI: Consumer price index (2000=100)	100	163	232 [c]
Agricultural production index (2004-2006=100)	91	100	92
Food production index (2004-2006=100)	89	100	92
Unemployment (% of labour force)	8.1 [d]	7.3	6.4 [c]
Employment in industrial sector (% of employed)	13.9	16.0	19.7 [e]
Employment in agricultural sector (% of employed)	50.9	40.6	31.1 [e]
Labour force participation, adult female pop. (%)	55.4	46.9	37.9
Labour force participation, adult male pop. (%)	63.7	51.0	44.5
Tourist arrivals at national borders (000) [f]	18	23	8
Energy production, primary (000 mt oil equivalent)	5	13	22 [c]
Telephone subscribers, total (per 100 inhabitants)	17.6	53.6	121.1
Internet users (per 100 inhabitants)	1.3	14.6	40.0

Total trade		Major trading partners			2010
	(million US$)	(% of exports)			(% of imports)
Exports	1 541.5	Russian Federation	26.2	Russian Federation	15.2
Imports	3 855.3	Romania	16.0	Ukraine	13.7
Balance	−2 313.8	Italy	9.6	Romania	10.0

Social indicators		
Population growth rate (average annual %) [a]	2010-2015	−0.7
Urban population growth rate (average annual %)	2010-2015	0.8
Rural population growth rate (average annual %)	2010-2015	−2.1
Urban population (%)	2011	47.7
Population aged 0-14 years (%)	2011	16.7
Population aged 60+ years (females and males, % of total)	2011	18.7/13.7
Sex ratio (males per 100 females) [a]	2011	90.3
Life expectancy at birth (females and males, years) [a]	2010-2015	73.5/66.2
Infant mortality rate (per 1 000 live births) [a]	2010-2015	14.3
Fertility rate, total (live births per woman) [a]	2010-2015	1.5
Contraceptive prevalence (ages 15-49, %)	2006-2010	67.8 [g]
International migrant stock (000 and % of total population)	mid-2010	408.3/11.4
Refugees and others of concern to UNHCR	end-2010	2 260
Education: Government expenditure (% of GDP)	2005-2011	9.1
Education: Primary-secondary gross enrolment ratio (f/m per 100) [h]	2005-2011	90.3/89.0
Education: Female third-level students (% of total)	2005-2011	56.4
Seats held by women in national parliaments (%)	2011	18.8

Environmental indicators		
Threatened species	2011	29
Forested area (% of land area)	2009	11.6
CO_2 emission estimates (000 metric tons and metric tons per capita)	2008	4 771/1.3
Energy consumption per capita (kilograms oil equivalent)	2009	540.0
Rainfall in the capital city, total mean (millimetres)		547
Temperature in the capital city, mean °C (minimum and maximum)		5.6/14.3

a Includes Transnistria. b Official rate. c 2009. d 2004. e 2008. f Excludes the regions of the left bank of the Dniester river and the municipality of Bender. g 2005. h National estimate.

Réunion

Region	Eastern Africa
Currency	Euro (EUR)
Surface area (square kilometres)	2 513
Population in 2010 (estimated, 000)	846
Population density in 2010 (per square kilometre)	336.7
Capital city and population in 2011 (000)	Saint-Denis (145)

Economic indicators	2000	2005	2010
Exchange rates (national currency per US$) [a]	1.07	0.85	0.75
CPI: Consumer price index (2000=100)	100	110	121
Agricultural production index (2004-2006=100)	95	99	103
Food production index (2004-2006=100)	95	99	103
Labour force participation, adult female pop. (%)	51.0	50.8	51.7
Labour force participation, adult male pop. (%)	66.6	64.6	64.0
Tourist arrivals at national borders (000)	430	409	420
Energy production, primary (000 mt oil equivalent) [b]	48	50	65[c]
Telephone subscribers, total (per 100 inhabitants)	75.3	47.8[d]	56.8[d]
Internet users (per 100 inhabitants)	13.8	28.1	36.3[c]

Social indicators		
Population growth rate (average annual %)	2010-2015	1.1
Urban population growth rate (average annual %)	2010-2015	1.3
Rural population growth rate (average annual %)	2010-2015	−2.7
Urban population (%)	2011	94.3
Population aged 0-14 years (%)	2011	25.4
Population aged 60+ years (females and males, % of total)	2011	12.9/11.0
Sex ratio (males per 100 females)	2011	96.0
Life expectancy at birth (females and males, years)	2010-2015	81.5/74.2
Infant mortality rate (per 1 000 live births)	2010-2015	5.9
Fertility rate, total (live births per woman)	2010-2015	2.3
Contraceptive prevalence (ages 15-49, %) [e]	2006-2010	66.6[f]
International migrant stock (000 and % of total population)	mid-2010	174.9/20.9

Environmental indicators		
Threatened species	2011	105
Forested area (% of land area)	2009	35.0
CO_2 emission estimates (000 metric tons and metric tons per capita)	2008	2 814/3.4
Energy consumption per capita (kilograms oil equivalent)	2009	1 076.0[b]

a Market rate. **b** UNSD estimate. **c** 2009. **d** Main telephone lines only. **e** Age group 20 to 44 years. **f** 1997.

Romania

Region	Eastern Europe
Currency	(new) Leu (RON)[a]
Surface area (square kilometres)	238 391
Population in 2010 (estimated, 000)	21 486
Population density in 2010 (per square kilometre)	90.1
Capital city and population in 2011 (000)	Bucharest (1 937)
United Nations membership date	14 December 1955

Economic indicators	2000	2005	2010
GDP: Gross domestic product (million current US$)	37 305	99 173	161 629
GDP: Growth rate at constant 2005 prices (annual %)	2.4	4.2	−1.9
GDP per capita (current US$)	1 681.0	4 555.1	7 522.4
GNI: Gross national income per capita (current US$)	1 667.0	4 421.3	7 429.8
Gross fixed capital formation (% of GDP)	18.8	23.7	22.7
Exchange rates (national currency per US$)[b]	2.59	3.11	3.20
Balance of payments, current account (million US$)	−1 355	−8 621	−6 480
CPI: Consumer price index (2000=100)	100	232	295[c]
Industrial production index (2005=100)	101[d]	100	123
Agricultural production index (2004-2006=100)	79	95	91
Food production index (2004-2006=100)	78	95	91
Unemployment (% of labour force)	8.1[e]	7.2	7.3
Employment in industrial sector (% of employed)	26.2	30.3	28.7[f]
Employment in agricultural sector (% of employed)	42.8	32.1	30.1[f]
Labour force participation, adult female pop. (%)	58.3	48.0	48.2
Labour force participation, adult male pop. (%)	71.4	62.6	64.5
Tourist arrivals at national borders (000)[g]	5 264	5 839	7 575[c]
Energy production, primary (000 mt oil equivalent)	25 899	24 645	23 480[c]
Telephone subscribers, total (per 100 inhabitants)	28.8	81.5	135.6
Internet users (per 100 inhabitants)	3.6	21.5	39.9

Total trade		Major trading partners			2010
	(million US$)	(% of exports)			(% of imports)
Exports	49 413.4	Germany	18.1	Germany	16.7
Imports	62 006.6	Italy	13.8	Italy	11.6
Balance	−12 593.2	France	8.3	Hungary	8.7

Social indicators		
Population growth rate (average annual %)	2010-2015	−0.2
Urban population growth rate (average annual %)	2010-2015	−0.2
Rural population growth rate (average annual %)	2010-2015	−0.3
Urban population (%)	2011	52.8
Population aged 0-14 years (%)	2011	15.2
Population aged 60+ years (females and males, % of total)	2011	23.5/17.7
Sex ratio (males per 100 females)	2011	94.2
Life expectancy at birth (females and males, years)	2010-2015	78.0/70.6
Infant mortality rate (per 1 000 live births)	2010-2015	12.2
Fertility rate, total (live births per woman)	2010-2015	1.4
Contraceptive prevalence (ages 15-49, %)[h]	2006-2010	70.3[e]
International migrant stock (000 and % of total population)	mid-2010	132.8/0.6
Refugees and others of concern to UNHCR	end-2010	1 730
Education: Government expenditure (% of GDP)	2005-2011	4.3
Education: Primary-secondary gross enrolment ratio (f/m per 100)	2005-2011	94.9/95.6
Education: Female third-level students (% of total)	2005-2011	56.3
Deaths by assault (females and males, per 100 000)	2005-2008	1.6/3.4
Seats held by women in national parliaments (%)	2011	11.4

Environmental indicators		
Threatened species	2011	77
Forested area (% of land area)	2009	28.4
CO$_2$ emission estimates (000 metric tons and metric tons per capita)	2008	94 583/4.4
Energy consumption per capita (kilograms oil equivalent)	2009	1 384.0
Rainfall in the capital city, total mean (millimetres)		595
Temperature in the capital city, mean °C (minimum and maximum)		5.7/16.5

a Beginning 1 July 2005, 1 new Leu = 10000 old Lei. **b** Principal rate. **c** 2009. **d** 2003. **e** 2004. **f** European Labour Force Survey (Eurostat). **g** Arrivals of non-resident visitors at national borders. **h** Age group 15 to 44 years.

Russian Federation

Region	Eastern Europe
Currency	Russian Rouble (RUB)
Surface area (square kilometres)	17 098 240
Population in 2010 (estimated, 000)	142 958
Population density in 2010 (per square kilometre)	8.4
Capital city and population in 2011 (000)	Moscow (11 621)
United Nations membership date	24 October 1945

Economic indicators	2000	2005	2010
GDP: Gross domestic product (million current US$)	259 446	764 016	1 479 820
GDP: Growth rate at constant 2005 prices (annual %)	10.1	6.4	4.0
GDP per capita (current US$)	1 767.9	5 311.5	10 351.4
GNI: Gross national income per capita (current US$)	1 716.5	5 160.4	10 012.7
Gross fixed capital formation (% of GDP)	16.9	17.8	21.9
Exchange rates (national currency per US$) [a]	28.16	28.78	30.48
Balance of payments, current account (million US$)	46 839	84 602	70 253
CPI: Consumer price index (2000=100)	100	200	325
Industrial production index (2005=100) [b]	88 [c]	100	112
Agricultural production index (2004-2006=100)	89	100	93
Food production index (2004-2006=100)	89	100	93
Unemployment (% of labour force) [d]	8.1 [e]	7.2	7.5
Employment in industrial sector (% of employed) [d]	28.4	29.8	27.9 [f]
Employment in agricultural sector (% of employed) [d]	14.5	10.2	9.7 [f]
Labour force participation, adult female pop. (%)	54.8	54.6	56.1
Labour force participation, adult male pop. (%)	68.9	67.4	70.7
Tourist arrivals at national borders (000) [g]	21 169	22 201	22 281
Energy production, primary (000 mt oil equivalent)	1 003 106	1 231 227	1 202 411 [f]
Telephone subscribers, total (per 100 inhabitants)	24.1	111.3	197.7
Internet users (per 100 inhabitants)	2.0	15.2	43.0

Total trade		Major trading partners			2010
	(million US$)	(% of exports)			(% of imports)
Exports	400 100.0	Netherlands	13.5	China	15.7
Imports	248 700.0	Italy	6.8	Germany	10.7
Balance	151 400.0	Germany	6.3		

Social indicators		
Population growth rate (average annual %)	2010-2015	−0.1
Urban population growth rate (average annual %)	2010-2015	0.1
Rural population growth rate (average annual %)	2010-2015	−0.8
Urban population (%)	2011	73.8
Population aged 0-14 years (%)	2011	15.3
Population aged 60+ years (females and males, % of total)	2011	22.2/13.5
Sex ratio (males per 100 females)	2011	86.1
Life expectancy at birth (females and males, years)	2010-2015	75.0/63.3
Infant mortality rate (per 1 000 live births)	2010-2015	10.5
Fertility rate, total (live births per woman)	2010-2015	1.5
Contraceptive prevalence (ages 15-49, %) [h]	2006-2010	79.5
International migrant stock (000 and % of total population)	mid-2010	12 270.4/8.7
Refugees and others of concern to UNHCR	end-2010	132 552
Education: Government expenditure (% of GDP)	2005-2011	4.1
Education: Primary-secondary gross enrolment ratio (f/m per 100)	2005-2011	91.1/92.5
Education: Female third-level students (% of total)	2005-2011	56.6
Deaths by assault (females and males, per 100 000)	2005-2008	9.4/32.8
Seats held by women in national parliaments (%)	2011	14.0

Environmental indicators		
Threatened species	2011	169
Forested area (% of land area)	2009	49.4
CO_2 emission estimates (000 metric tons and metric tons per capita)	2008	1 707 256/12.1
Energy consumption per capita (kilograms oil equivalent)	2009	4 364.0
Rainfall in the capital city, total mean (millimetres)		691
Temperature in the capital city, mean °C (minimum and maximum)		1.2/8.9

a Official rate. **b** The indices are shown in terms of ISIC Rev. 3. **c** 2003. **d** Age group 15 to 72 years. **e** 2004. **f** 2009. **g** Arrivals of non-resident visitors at national borders. **h** Age group less than 50 years.

Rwanda

Region	Eastern Africa
Currency	Rwanda Franc (RWF)
Surface area (square kilometres)	26 338
Population in 2010 (estimated, 000)	10 624
Population density in 2010 (per square kilometre)	403.4
Capital city and population in 2011 (000)	Kigali (1 004)
United Nations membership date	18 September 1962

Economic indicators	2000	2005	2010
GDP: Gross domestic product (million current US$)	1 772	2 581	5 655
GDP: Growth rate at constant 2005 prices (annual %)	6.3	9.3	7.5
GDP per capita (current US$)	218.8	280.5	532.3
GNI: Gross national income per capita (current US$)	212.3	277.6	528.0
Gross fixed capital formation (% of GDP)	14.2	15.8	21.0
Exchange rates (national currency per US$)[a]	430.49	553.72	594.45
Balance of payments, current account (million US$)	−94	−84	−421
CPI: Consumer price index (2000=100)[b]	100	138	214
Agricultural production index (2004-2006=100)	82	100	137
Food production index (2004-2006=100)	82	101	137
Employment in industrial sector (% of employed)	...	3.8	...
Employment in agricultural sector (% of employed)	...	78.8	...
Labour force participation, adult female pop. (%)	86.4	85.7	86.3
Labour force participation, adult male pop. (%)	85.4	83.8	85.2
Tourist arrivals at national borders (000)	104	...	666[c]
Energy production, primary (000 mt oil equivalent)	11	6	9[d]
Telephone subscribers, total (per 100 inhabitants)	0.7	2.7	33.8
Internet users (per 100 inhabitants)	0.1	0.6	13.0

Total trade		Major trading partners			2010
	(million US$)	(% of exports)			(% of imports)
Exports	237.8	Switzerland	22.9	Sweden	9.4
Imports	1 273.8	Kenya	16.5	United Arab Emirates	7.0
Balance	−1 036.0	Belgium	11.2	Kenya	6.2

Social indicators		
Population growth rate (average annual %)	2010-2015	2.9
Urban population growth rate (average annual %)	2010-2015	4.5
Rural population growth rate (average annual %)	2010-2015	2.5
Urban population (%)	2011	19.1
Population aged 0-14 years (%)	2011	42.9
Population aged 60+ years (females and males, % of total)	2011	4.7/4.1
Sex ratio (males per 100 females)	2011	96.5
Life expectancy at birth (females and males, years)	2010-2015	57.1/54.5
Infant mortality rate (per 1 000 live births)	2010-2015	92.9
Fertility rate, total (live births per woman)	2010-2015	5.3
Contraceptive prevalence (ages 15-49, %)	2006-2010	36.4
International migrant stock (000 and % of total population)[e]	mid-2010	465.5/4.5
Refugees and others of concern to UNHCR	end-2010	66 594
Education: Government expenditure (% of GDP)	2005-2011	4.7
Education: Primary-secondary gross enrolment ratio (f/m per 100)	2005-2011	93.7/91.9
Education: Female third-level students (% of total)	2005-2011	43.8
Seats held by women in national parliaments (%)	2011	56.3

Environmental indicators		
Threatened species	2011	55
Forested area (% of land area)	2009	17.2
CO$_2$ emission estimates (000 metric tons and metric tons per capita)	2008	703/0.1
Energy consumption per capita (kilograms oil equivalent)	2009	18.0[f]
Rainfall in the capital city, total mean (millimetres)		1 028

a Official rate. b Kigali. c Arrivals of non-resident visitors at national borders. d 2009. e Includes refugees.
f UNSD estimate.

Saint Kitts and Nevis

Region	Caribbean
Currency	E.C. Dollar (XCD)
Surface area (square kilometres)	261
Population in 2010 (estimated, 000)	52
Population density in 2010 (per square kilometre)	200.8
Capital city and population in 2011 (000)	Basseterre (13)
United Nations membership date	23 September 1983

Economic indicators	2000	2005	2010
GDP: Gross domestic product (million current US$)	329	439	550
GDP: Growth rate at constant 2005 prices (annual %)	4.3	5.6	−1.5
GDP per capita (current US$)	7 143.9	8 921.9	10 493.8
GNI: Gross national income per capita (current US$)	6 490.4	8 207.2	9 857.8
Gross fixed capital formation (% of GDP)	49.6	42.3	38.1
Exchange rates (national currency per US$)[a]	2.70	2.70	2.70
Balance of payments, current account (million US$)	−66	−65	−96
CPI: Consumer price index (2000=100)[b]	100[c]	111	136
Agricultural production index (2004-2006=100)	144	91	29
Food production index (2004-2006=100)	144	91	29
Employment in industrial sector (% of employed)	48.9[c]	...	...
Employment in agricultural sector (% of employed)	0.2[c]	...	...
Tourist arrivals at national borders (000)[d]	73	141	92
Telephone subscribers, total (per 100 inhabitants)	50.1	145.0	190.5
Internet users (per 100 inhabitants)	5.9	34.0	76.0

Total trade		Major trading partners			2010
	(million US$)[e]	(% of exports)[e]		(% of imports)[e]	
Exports	51.2	United States	84.6	United States	61.0
Imports	324.8	United Kingdom	4.5	Trinidad and Tobago	11.5
Balance	−273.6	Netherlands Antilles	2.3	United Kingdom	4.5

Social indicators		
Population growth rate (average annual %)	2010-2015	1.2
Urban population growth rate (average annual %)	2010-2015	1.4
Rural population growth rate (average annual %)	2010-2015	1.1
Urban population (%)	2011	32.0
Population aged 0-14 years (%)[fgh]	2011	30.7[i]
Population aged 60+ years (females and males, % of total)[fgh]	2011	11.6/10.2[i]
Sex ratio (males per 100 females)[gjk]	2011	98.8[l]
Life expectancy at birth (females and males, years)[g]	2010-2015	70.7/68.2[m]
Contraceptive prevalence (ages 15-49, %)[n]	2006-2010	40.6[o]
International migrant stock (000 and % of total population)	mid-2010	5.1/9.6
Refugees and others of concern to UNHCR	end-2010	0[p]
Education: Government expenditure (% of GDP)	2005-2011	4.5
Education: Primary-secondary gross enrolment ratio (f/m per 100)	2005-2011	95.0/95.2
Education: Female third-level students (% of total)	2005-2011	67.3
Seats held by women in national parliaments (%)	2011	6.7

Environmental indicators		
Threatened species	2011	39
Forested area (% of land area)	2009	42.3
CO$_2$ emission estimates (000 metric tons and metric tons per capita)	2008	249/4.9
Energy consumption per capita (kilograms oil equivalent)	2009	1 680.0[q]

a Official rate. b Index base 2001=100. c 2001. d Air arrivals of non-resident tourists. e 2008. f De facto estimate. g Data compiled by the United Nations Demographic Yearbook system. h Data refer to the latest available census. i 2000. j The distribution between males and females was extrapolated from previous years. k De facto national estimate. l 2005. m 1998. n Age group 15 to 44 years. o 1984. p Value is zero, not available or not applicable. q UNSD estimate.

Saint Lucia

Region	Caribbean
Currency	E.C. Dollar (XCD)
Surface area (square kilometres)	539 [ab]
Population in 2010 (estimated, 000)	174
Population density in 2010 (per square kilometre)	323.3
Capital city and population in 2011 (000)	Castries (21)
United Nations membership date	18 September 1979

Economic indicators	2000	2005	2010
GDP: Gross domestic product (million current US$)	700	847	1 164
GDP: Growth rate at constant 2005 prices (annual %)	−0.4	8.5	0.4
GDP per capita (current US$)	4 455.5	5 124.7	6 677.1
GNI: Gross national income per capita (current US$)	4 220.2	4 881.5	5 485.8
Gross fixed capital formation (% of GDP)	29.8	31.9	34.5
Exchange rates (national currency per US$) [c]	2.70	2.70	2.70
Balance of payments, current account (million US$)	−95	−129	−150
CPI: Consumer price index (2000=100)	100	112	...
Agricultural production index (2004-2006=100)	118	92	111
Food production index (2004-2006=100)	118	92	111
Employment in industrial sector (% of employed) [d]	20.3	16.1 [e]	...
Employment in agricultural sector (% of employed)	20.8	14.8 [e]	...
Labour force participation, adult female pop. (%)	62.1	63.4	63.9
Labour force participation, adult male pop. (%)	75.5	77.6	77.0
Tourist arrivals at national borders (000) [f]	270	318	306
Telephone subscribers, total (per 100 inhabitants)	32.7	87.5	135.7
Internet users (per 100 inhabitants)	5.1	21.6	40.0

Total trade		Major trading partners			2010
	(million US$) [g]	(% of exports) [g]		(% of imports) [g]	
Exports	164.0	United States	34.0	United States	42.6
Imports	655.7	Trinidad and Tobago	23.2	Trinidad and Tobago	23.8
Balance	−491.7	United Kingdom	15.1	Japan	4.3

Social indicators		
Population growth rate (average annual %)	2010-2015	1.0
Urban population growth rate (average annual %)	2010-2015	−3.1
Rural population growth rate (average annual %)	2010-2015	1.8
Urban population (%)	2011	17.5
Population aged 0-14 years (%)	2011	25.5
Population aged 60+ years (females and males, % of total)	2011	10.4/8.5
Sex ratio (males per 100 females)	2011	94.8
Life expectancy at birth (females and males, years)	2010-2015	77.5/72.2
Infant mortality rate (per 1 000 live births)	2010-2015	12.3
Fertility rate, total (live births per woman)	2010-2015	1.9
Contraceptive prevalence (ages 15-49, %) [h]	2006-2010	47.3 [i]
International migrant stock (000 and % of total population)	mid-2010	10.2/5.9
Refugees and others of concern to UNHCR	end-2010	6
Education: Government expenditure (% of GDP)	2005-2011	5.8
Education: Primary-secondary gross enrolment ratio (f/m per 100)	2005-2011	93.8/96.4
Education: Female third-level students (% of total)	2005-2011	72.3
Seats held by women in national parliaments (%) [j]	2011	11.1

Environmental indicators		
Threatened species	2011	49
Forested area (% of land area)	2009	77.1
CO$_2$ emission estimates (000 metric tons and metric tons per capita)	2008	396/2.3
Energy consumption per capita (kilograms oil equivalent)	2009	747.0
Rainfall in the capital city, total mean (millimetres) [k]		1 399
Temperature in the capital city, mean °C (minimum and maximum) [k]		24.5/30.0

a Refers to habitable area. b Excludes St. Lucia's Forest Reserve. c Official rate. d Excludes mining and quarrying. e 2004. f Excludes nationals residing abroad. g 2008. h Age group 15 to 44 years. i 1988. j As of 31 October 2011. k Vieux-Fort.

Saint Vincent and the Grenadines

Region	Caribbean
Currency	E.C. Dollar (XCD)
Surface area (square kilometres)	389
Population in 2010 (estimated, 000)	109
Population density in 2010 (per square kilometre)	281.1
Capital city and population in 2011 (000)	Kingstown (31)
United Nations membership date	16 September 1980

Economic indicators	2000	2005	2010
GDP: Gross domestic product (million current US$)	397	551	675
GDP: Growth rate at constant 2005 prices (annual %)	1.8	2.0	-2.8
GDP per capita (current US$)	3 683.8	5 070.4	6 171.7
GNI: Gross national income per capita (current US$)	3 506.1	4 798.2	6 323.0
Gross fixed capital formation (% of GDP)	23.3	26.6	25.5
Exchange rates (national currency per US$) [a]	2.70	2.70	2.70
Balance of payments, current account (million US$)	-24	-102	-206
CPI: Consumer price index (2000=100) [b]	100	109	134
Agricultural production index (2004-2006=100)	91	102	124
Food production index (2004-2006=100)	91	102	124
Employment in industrial sector (% of employed)	19.6[cd]	...	...
Employment in agricultural sector (% of employed)	15.4[cd]	...	...
Labour force participation, adult female pop. (%)	50.2	53.3	55.5
Labour force participation, adult male pop. (%)	79.5	79.1	78.5
Tourist arrivals at national borders (000) [e]	73	96	72
Energy production, primary (000 mt oil equivalent)	2	2	2[fg]
Telephone subscribers, total (per 100 inhabitants)	25.3	85.6	140.4
Internet users (per 100 inhabitants)	3.3	9.2	69.6[f]

Total trade		Major trading partners			2010
	(million US$)	(% of exports)			(% of imports)
Exports	41.5	Saint Lucia	20.7	United States	33.0
Imports	379.5	Trinidad and Tobago	16.1	Trinidad and Tobago	27.1
Balance	-338.0	Barbados	11.3	United Kingdom	5.7

Social indicators		
Population growth rate (average annual %)	2010-2015	0.0
Urban population growth rate (average annual %)	2010-2015	0.8
Rural population growth rate (average annual %)	2010-2015	-0.8
Urban population (%)	2011	49.3
Population aged 0-14 years (%)	2011	26.1
Population aged 60+ years (females and males, % of total)	2011	10.5/8.9
Sex ratio (males per 100 females)	2011	101.9
Life expectancy at birth (females and males, years)	2010-2015	74.7/70.5
Infant mortality rate (per 1 000 live births)	2010-2015	21.0
Fertility rate, total (live births per woman)	2010-2015	2.0
Contraceptive prevalence (ages 15-49, %) [h]	2006-2010	58.3[i]
International migrant stock (000 and % of total population)	mid-2010	8.6/7.9
Refugees and others of concern to UNHCR	end-2010	0[j]
Education: Government expenditure (% of GDP)	2005-2011	4.9
Education: Primary-secondary gross enrolment ratio (f/m per 100)	2005-2011	104.5/107.7
Seats held by women in national parliaments (%)	2011	17.4

Environmental indicators		
Threatened species	2011	44
Forested area (% of land area)	2009	68.3
CO$_2$ emission estimates (000 metric tons and metric tons per capita)	2008	202/1.9
Energy consumption per capita (kilograms oil equivalent)	2009	633.0[g]

a Official rate. b St. Vincent. c 2001. d Population census. e Air arrivals of non-resident tourists. f 2009.
g UNSD estimate. h Age group 15 to 44 years. i 1988. j Value is zero, not available or not applicable.

Samoa

Region	Oceania-Polynesia		
Currency	Tala (WST)		
Surface area (square kilometres)	2 842		
Population in 2010 (estimated, 000)	183		
Population density in 2010 (per square kilometre)	64.4		
Capital city and population in 2011 (000)	Apia (37)		
United Nations membership date	15 December 1976		

Economic indicators	2000	2005	2010
GDP: Gross domestic product (million current US$)	231	435	612
GDP: Growth rate at constant 2005 prices (annual %)	7.1	5.3	1.5
GDP per capita (current US$)	1 308.4	2 414.6	3 343.3
GNI: Gross national income per capita (current US$)	1 308.5	2 273.9	3 231.8
Gross fixed capital formation (% of GDP)	13.9	10.2	8.8
Exchange rates (national currency per US$) [a]	3.34	2.76	2.34
Balance of payments, current account (million US$)	...	−25	−58
CPI: Consumer price index (2000=100) [b]	100	133	162[c]
Agricultural production index (2004-2006=100)	92	102	122
Food production index (2004-2006=100)	92	102	122
Employment in industrial sector (% of employed)	19.7[def]	...	...
Employment in agricultural sector (% of employed)	39.9[de]	...	...
Labour force participation, adult female pop. (%)	42.5	43.0	42.9
Labour force participation, adult male pop. (%)	79.6	79.2	78.2
Tourist arrivals at national borders (000)	88	102	130
Energy production, primary (000 mt oil equivalent)	4	4	5[gh]
Telephone subscribers, total (per 100 inhabitants)	6.3	24.1	110.7
Internet users (per 100 inhabitants)	0.6	3.4	7.0

Total trade		Major trading partners			2010
	(million US$)	(% of exports)			(% of imports)
Exports	59.5	Australia	77.1	New Zealand	30.7
Imports	309.8	New Zealand	10.9	Australia	23.3
Balance	−250.3	American Samoa	5.2	United States	11.5

Social indicators

Population growth rate (average annual %)	2010-2015	0.5
Urban population growth rate (average annual %)	2010-2015	−0.5
Rural population growth rate (average annual %)	2010-2015	0.7
Urban population (%)	2011	19.9
Population aged 0-14 years (%)	2011	37.4
Population aged 60+ years (females and males, % of total)	2011	8.4/6.5
Sex ratio (males per 100 females)	2011	106.8
Life expectancy at birth (females and males, years)	2010-2015	76.0/69.9
Infant mortality rate (per 1 000 live births)	2010-2015	19.9
Fertility rate, total (live births per woman)	2010-2015	3.8
Contraceptive prevalence (ages 15-49, %)	2006-2010	28.7
International migrant stock (000 and % of total population)	mid-2010	9.0/5.0
Education: Government expenditure (% of GDP)	2005-2011	5.4
Education: Primary-secondary gross enrolment ratio (f/m per 100)	2005-2011	99.4/92.4
Education: Female third-level students (% of total) [i]	2005-2011	44.4[d]
Seats held by women in national parliaments (%)	2011	4.1

Environmental indicators

Threatened species	2011	78
Forested area (% of land area)	2009	60.4
CO_2 emission estimates (000 metric tons and metric tons per capita)	2008	161/0.9
Energy consumption per capita (kilograms oil equivalent)	2009	326.0[h]
Rainfall in the capital city, total mean (millimetres)		2 965
Temperature in the capital city, mean °C (minimum and maximum)		23.5/30.2

a Official rate. b Excludes rent. c 2008. d 2001. e Population census. f Excludes mining and quarrying.
g 2009. h UNSD estimate. i UNESCO estimate.

San Marino

Region	Southern Europe
Currency	Euro (EUR)
Surface area (square kilometres)	61
Population in 2010 (estimated, 000)	32
Population density in 2010 (per square kilometre)	517.0
Capital city and population in 2011 (000)	San Marino (4)
United Nations membership date	2 March 1992

Economic indicators	2000	2005	2010
GDP: Gross domestic product (million current US$)	774	1 375	1 487
GDP: Growth rate at constant 2005 prices (annual %)	2.2	2.3	1.3
GDP per capita (current US$)	28 698.3	45 391.8	47 170.6
GNI: Gross national income per capita (current US$)	25 111.0	39 810.2	41 255.8
Gross fixed capital formation (% of GDP)	42.9	53.0	35.1
Exchange rates (national currency per US$) [a]	1.07	0.85	0.75
CPI: Consumer price index (2000=100) [b]	100	103	118
Employment in industrial sector (% of employed) [cde]	41.2[f]	39.3	36.9[g]
Employment in agricultural sector (% of employed) [cd]	0.5[f]	0.5	0.3[g]
Tourist arrivals at national borders (000) [hi]	43	50	120
Telephone subscribers, total (per 100 inhabitants)	129.1	125.4	144.9
Internet users (per 100 inhabitants)	48.8	50.3	54.2[j]

Social indicators		
Population growth rate (average annual %)	2010-2015	0.6
Urban population growth rate (average annual %)	2010-2015	0.7
Rural population growth rate (average annual %)	2010-2015	0.2
Urban population (%)	2011	94.1
Population aged 0-14 years (%) [klm]	2011	15.2[n]
Population aged 60+ years (females and males, % of total) [klm]	2011	23.2/19.7[n]
Sex ratio (males per 100 females) [lo]	2011	94.6[p]
Life expectancy at birth (females and males, years) [l]	2010-2015	84.6/78.0[q]
International migrant stock (000 and % of total population)	mid-2010	11.7/37.1
Education: Primary-secondary gross enrolment ratio (f/m per 100) [r]	2005-2011	99.2/93.2
Education: Female third-level students (% of total)	2005-2011	58.2
Seats held by women in national parliaments (%)	2011	16.7

Environmental indicators		
Forested area (% of land area)	2009	0.0

a Market rate. b Index base 2003=100. c December. d Official estimates. e Manufacturing and construction only. f 2001. g 2008. h Arrivals of non-resident tourists in hotels and similar establishments. i Includes Italian tourists. j 2009. k De facto estimate. l Data compiled by the United Nations Demographic Yearbook system. m Data refer to the latest available census. n 2004. o De facto national estimate. p 2010. q 2000. r UNESCO estimate.

Sao Tome and Principe

Region	Middle Africa
Currency	Dobra (STD)
Surface area (square kilometres)	964
Population in 2010 (estimated, 000)	165
Population density in 2010 (per square kilometre)	171.6
Capital city and population in 2011 (000)	São Tomé (64)
United Nations membership date	16 September 1975

Economic indicators	2000	2005	2010
GDP: Gross domestic product (million current US$)	77	123	212
GDP: Growth rate at constant 2005 prices (annual %)	0.5	3.1	4.5
GDP per capita (current US$)	544.7	807.6	1 283.3
GNI: Gross national income per capita (current US$)	497.6	785.3	1 302.1
Gross fixed capital formation (% of GDP)	35.8	26.8	26.1
Exchange rates (national currency per US$) [a]	8 610.65	11 929.70	18 335.60
Balance of payments, current account (million US$)	−20	−36	−107
CPI: Consumer price index (2000=100) [b]	321 [c]	561	1 264 [d]
Agricultural production index (2004-2006=100)	97	98	110
Food production index (2004-2006=100)	97	98	110
Employment in industrial sector (% of employed)	19.2 [e]	...	...
Employment in agricultural sector (% of employed)	27.9 [e]	...	...
Labour force participation, adult female pop. (%)	38.4	40.9	43.2
Labour force participation, adult male pop. (%)	73.8	75.6	76.4
Tourist arrivals at national borders (000)	7	16	8
Telephone subscribers, total (per 100 inhabitants)	3.3 [f]	12.5	66.6
Internet users (per 100 inhabitants)	4.6	13.8	18.8

Total trade		Major trading partners			2010
	(million US$)		(% of exports)		(% of imports)
Exports	6.4	Portugal	42.2	Portugal	62.3
Imports	112.2	Belgium	21.9	Angola	15.6
Balance	−105.8	Netherlands	15.6	Gabon	5.2

Social indicators

Population growth rate (average annual %)	2010-2015	2.0
Urban population growth rate (average annual %)	2010-2015	3.0
Rural population growth rate (average annual %)	2010-2015	0.1
Urban population (%)	2011	62.7
Population aged 0-14 years (%)	2011	39.9
Population aged 60+ years (females and males, % of total)	2011	5.9/4.5
Sex ratio (males per 100 females)	2011	98.2
Life expectancy at birth (females and males, years)	2010-2015	66.5/63.5
Infant mortality rate (per 1 000 live births)	2010-2015	47.5
Fertility rate, total (live births per woman)	2010-2015	3.5
Contraceptive prevalence (ages 15-49, %)	2006-2010	38.4
International migrant stock (000 and % of total population) [g]	mid-2010	5.3/3.2
Refugees and others of concern to UNHCR	end-2010	0 [h]
Education: Primary-secondary gross enrolment ratio (f/m per 100)	2005-2011	102.3/100.8
Education: Female third-level students (% of total)	2005-2011	48.8
Seats held by women in national parliaments (%)	2011	18.2

Environmental indicators

Threatened species	2011	73
Forested area (% of land area)	2009	28.1
CO$_2$ emission estimates (000 metric tons and metric tons per capita)	2008	128/0.8
Energy consumption per capita (kilograms oil equivalent)	2009	271.0 [i]

a Official rate. **b** Index base 1996=100. **c** 10 months' average. **d** 2009. **e** Age group 10 years and over. **f** Main telephone lines only. **g** Data refer to foreign citizens. **h** Value is zero, not available or not applicable. **i** UNSD estimate.

Saudi Arabia

Region	Western Asia
Currency	Saudi Riyal (SAR)
Surface area (square kilometres)	2 149 690
Population in 2010 (estimated, 000)	27 448
Population density in 2010 (per square kilometre)	12.8
Capital city and population in 2011 (000)	Riyadh (5 451)
United Nations membership date	24 October 1945

Economic indicators	2000	2005	2010
GDP: Gross domestic product (million current US$)	188 442	315 583	434 666
GDP: Growth rate at constant 2005 prices (annual %)	4.9	5.6	3.8
GDP per capita (current US$)	9 400.8	13 126.8	15 835.9
GNI: Gross national income per capita (current US$)	9 445.3	13 144.8	16 061.1
Gross fixed capital formation (% of GDP)	17.5	16.5	21.1
Exchange rates (national currency per US$) [a]	3.75	3.74	3.75
Balance of payments, current account (million US$)	14 317	90 061	66 751
CPI: Consumer price index (2000=100) [b]	100	100	130
Agricultural production index (2004-2006=100)	81	101	106
Food production index (2004-2006=100)	81	101	106
Employment in industrial sector (% of employed)	19.9	20.3[c]	20.4[d]
Employment in agricultural sector (% of employed)	6.1	4.0[c]	4.1[d]
Labour force participation, adult female pop. (%)	16.2	17.6	17.4
Labour force participation, adult male pop. (%)	74.0	74.1	74.2
Tourist arrivals at national borders (000)	6 585	8 037	10 850
Energy production, primary (000 mt oil equivalent)	489 492	584 410	533 208[d]
Telephone subscribers, total (per 100 inhabitants)	21.7	74.9	203.0
Internet users (per 100 inhabitants)	2.2	12.7	41.0

Total trade		Major trading partners		2010
	(million US$)	(% of exports)		(% of imports)
Exports	251 143.0		United States	13.1
Imports	106 863.0		China	11.6
Balance	144 280.0		Germany	7.7

Social indicators		
Population growth rate (average annual %)	2010-2015	2.1
Urban population growth rate (average annual %)	2010-2015	2.4
Rural population growth rate (average annual %)	2010-2015	1.0
Urban population (%)	2011	82.3
Population aged 0-14 years (%)	2011	30.1
Population aged 60+ years (females and males, % of total)	2011	5.0/4.4
Sex ratio (males per 100 females)	2011	123.3
Life expectancy at birth (females and males, years)	2010-2015	75.6/73.2
Infant mortality rate (per 1 000 live births)	2010-2015	16.2
Fertility rate, total (live births per woman)	2010-2015	2.6
Contraceptive prevalence (ages 15-49, %)	2006-2010	23.8
International migrant stock (000 and % of total population) [ef]	mid-2010	7 288.9/27.8
Refugees and others of concern to UNHCR	end-2010	70 669
Education: Government expenditure (% of GDP)	2005-2011	5.6
Education: Primary-secondary gross enrolment ratio (f/m per 100)	2005-2011	101.8/104.8
Education: Female third-level students (% of total)	2005-2011	52.4
Seats held by women in national parliaments (%)	2011	0.0

Environmental indicators		
Threatened species	2011	106
Forested area (% of land area)	2009	<
CO_2 emission estimates (000 metric tons and metric tons per capita)	2008	433 202/17.2
Energy consumption per capita (kilograms oil equivalent)	2009	6 046.0
Rainfall in the capital city, total mean (millimetres)		99
Temperature in the capital city, mean °C (minimum and maximum)		19.7/32.9

a Official rate. **b** All cities. **c** 2006. **d** 2009. **e** Data refer to foreign citizens. **f** Includes refugees.

Senegal

Region	Western Africa
Currency	CFA Franc (XOF)
Surface area (square kilometres)	196 712 [a]
Population in 2010 (estimated, 000)	12 434
Population density in 2010 (per square kilometre)	63.2
Capital city and population in 2011 (000)	Dakar (3 035)
United Nations membership date	28 September 1960

Economic indicators	2000	2005	2010
GDP: Gross domestic product (million current US$)	4 680	8 708	12 841
GDP: Growth rate at constant 2005 prices (annual %)	3.2	5.6	4.2
GDP per capita (current US$)	492.3	801.0	1 032.7
GNI: Gross national income per capita (current US$)	488.1	796.0	1 011.3
Gross fixed capital formation (% of GDP)	22.4	23.3	27.3
Exchange rates (national currency per US$) [b]	704.95	556.04	490.91
Balance of payments, current account (million US$)	−332	−676	−865
CPI: Consumer price index (2000=100) [c]	100	108	122 [d]
Industrial production index (2005=100) [e]	88 [f]	100	104
Agricultural production index (2004-2006=100)	106	107	152
Food production index (2004-2006=100)	107	107	154
Employment in industrial sector (% of employed)	12.4 [g]	14.8 [h]	...
Employment in agricultural sector (% of employed)	45.6 [g]	33.7 [h]	...
Labour force participation, adult female pop. (%)	64.1	64.9	66.0
Labour force participation, adult male pop. (%)	88.5	88.3	88.3
Tourist arrivals at national borders (000)	389 [i]	769	875 [j]
Energy production, primary (000 mt oil equivalent)	2	13	16 [d]
Telephone subscribers, total (per 100 inhabitants)	4.8	18.4	69.9
Internet users (per 100 inhabitants)	0.4	4.8	16.0

Total trade		Major trading partners			2010
	(million US$)	(% of exports)			(% of imports)
Exports	2 088.1	Mali	26.1	France	19.7
Imports	4 782.2	India	10.0	Nigeria	10.2
Balance	−2 694.1	Switzerland	7.9	China	8.3

Social indicators		
Population growth rate (average annual %)	2010-2015	2.6
Urban population growth rate (average annual %)	2010-2015	3.3
Rural population growth rate (average annual %)	2010-2015	2.1
Urban population (%)	2011	42.5
Population aged 0-14 years (%)	2011	43.5
Population aged 60+ years (females and males, % of total)	2011	4.1/3.7
Sex ratio (males per 100 females)	2011	98.4
Life expectancy at birth (females and males, years)	2010-2015	60.9/58.6
Infant mortality rate (per 1 000 live births)	2010-2015	49.8
Fertility rate, total (live births per woman)	2010-2015	4.6
Contraceptive prevalence (ages 15-49, %)	2006-2010	11.8 [k]
International migrant stock (000 and % of total population) [l]	mid-2010	210.1/1.6
Refugees and others of concern to UNHCR	end-2010	22 849
Education: Government expenditure (% of GDP)	2005-2011	5.6
Education: Primary-secondary gross enrolment ratio (f/m per 100)	2005-2011	62.2/62.2
Education: Female third-level students (% of total) [m]	2005-2011	37.3
Seats held by women in national parliaments (%)	2011	22.7

Environmental indicators		
Threatened species	2011	87
Forested area (% of land area)	2009	44.2
CO_2 emission estimates (000 metric tons and metric tons per capita)	2008	4 972/0.4
Energy consumption per capita (kilograms oil equivalent)	2009	91.0
Rainfall in the capital city, total mean (millimetres)		514
Temperature in the capital city, mean °C (minimum and maximum)		21.7/27.6

a Surface area is based on 2002 population and housing census. **b** Official rate. **c** Dakar. **d** 2009. **e** The indices are shown in terms of ISIC Rev. 3. **f** 2003. **g** 2001. **h** 2006. **i** Arrivals of non-resident tourists in hotels and similar establishments. **j** 2007. **k** 2005. **l** Includes refugees. **m** UNESCO estimate.

Serbia

Region	Southern Europe
Currency	Dinar (RSD)
Surface area (square kilometres)	88 361
Population in 2010 (estimated, 000)	9 856 [a]
Population density in 2010 (per square kilometre)	111.5
Capital city and population in 2011 (000)	Belgrade (1 135)
United Nations membership date	1 November 2000

Economic indicators	2000	2005	2010
GDP: Gross domestic product (million current US$)	8 728	25 231	37 713
GDP: Growth rate at constant 2005 prices (annual %)	5.3	5.6	1.8
GDP per capita (current US$)	1 161.3	3 391.0	5 123.2
GNI: Gross national income per capita (current US$)	1 161.2	3 354.2	5 042.6
Gross fixed capital formation (% of GDP)	12.7	19.0	18.6
Exchange rates (national currency per US$) [b]	63.17	72.22	79.28
Balance of payments, current account (million US$)	...	−7 154 [c]	−3 115
CPI: Consumer price index (2000=100)	100	330	137 [d]
Industrial production index (2005=100)	93 [e]	100	99
Agricultural production index (2004-2006=100)	83 [f]	96 [f]	102
Food production index (2004-2006=100)	83 [f]	96 [f]	102
Unemployment (% of labour force)	...	13.6 [g]	19.2
Employment in industrial sector (% of employed) [h]	...	27.6	25.1 [i]
Employment in agricultural sector (% of employed) [h]	...	23.3	24.0 [i]
Labour force participation, adult female pop. (%) [f]	44.6	45.2	46.2
Labour force participation, adult male pop. (%) [f]	64.3	63.5	63.3
Tourist arrivals at national borders (000) [j]	312 [k]	453	683
Energy production, primary (000 mt oil equivalent)	...	9 405	9 200 [i]
Telephone subscribers, total (per 100 inhabitants)	...	104.7	169.7
Internet users (per 100 inhabitants)	...	26.3	40.9

Total trade		Major trading partners			2010
	(million US$)	(% of exports)		(% of imports)	
Exports	9 794.5	Italy	11.4	Russian Federation	12.9
Imports	16 734.5	Bosnia-Herzegovina	11.1	Germany	10.6
Balance	−6 940.0	Germany	10.3	Italy	8.6

Social indicators		
Population growth rate (average annual %) [a]	2010-2015	−0.1
Urban population growth rate (average annual %)	2010-2015	0.5
Rural population growth rate (average annual %)	2010-2015	−0.9
Urban population (%)	2011	56.4
Population aged 0-14 years (%) [a]	2011	17.5
Population aged 60+ years (females and males, % of total) [a]	2011	22.1/18.0
Sex ratio (males per 100 females) [a]	2011	98.0
Life expectancy at birth (females and males, years) [a]	2010-2015	77.1/72.5
Infant mortality rate (per 1 000 live births) [a]	2010-2015	10.6
Fertility rate, total (live births per woman) [a]	2010-2015	1.6 [l]
Contraceptive prevalence (ages 15-49, %)	2006-2010	41.2 [m]
International migrant stock (000 and % of total population)	mid-2010	525.4/5.3
Refugees and others of concern to UNHCR	end-2010	312 961
Education: Government expenditure (% of GDP)	2005-2011	5.0
Education: Primary-secondary gross enrolment ratio (f/m per 100) [n]	2005-2011	93.4/92.3
Education: Female third-level students (% of total)	2005-2011	55.3
Seats held by women in national parliaments (%)	2011	21.6

Environmental indicators		
Threatened species	2011	51
Forested area (% of land area)	2009	30.5
CO$_2$ emission estimates (000 metric tons and metric tons per capita)	2008	49 893/5.1
Energy consumption per capita (kilograms oil equivalent)	2009	1 376.0
Rainfall in the capital city, total mean (millimetres)		683
Temperature in the capital city, mean °C (minimum and maximum)		7.8/16.7

a Includes Kosovo. **b** Official rate. **c** 2007. **d** Index base 2006=100. **e** 2003. **f** Refers to Serbia and Montenegro. **g** 2008. **h** October. **i** 2009. **j** Arrivals of non-resident tourists in all types of accommodation establishments. **k** 2002. **l** 2010. **m** 2005. **n** National estimate.

Seychelles

Region	Eastern Africa		
Currency	Seychelles Rupee (SCR)		
Surface area (square kilometres)	452		
Population in 2010 (estimated, 000)	87		
Population density in 2010 (per square kilometre)	191.6		
Capital city and population in 2011 (000)	Victoria (27)		
United Nations membership date	21 September 1976		

Economic indicators	2000	2005	2010
GDP: Gross domestic product (million current US$)	769	928	991
GDP: Growth rate at constant 2005 prices (annual %)	−0.1	6.7	9.6
GDP per capita (current US$)	9 775.4	11 113.4	11 450.6
GNI: Gross national income per capita (current US$)	9 217.8	10 633.5	10 534.1
Gross fixed capital formation (% of GDP)	27.6	32.7	52.4
Exchange rates (national currency per US$) [a]	6.27	5.50	12.15
Balance of payments, current account (million US$)	−54	−188	−225
CPI: Consumer price index (2000=100)	100	115	215
Agricultural production index (2004-2006=100)	147	96	77
Food production index (2004-2006=100)	148	96	79
Tourist arrivals at national borders (000)	130	129	175
Telephone subscribers, total (per 100 inhabitants)	59.2	96.1	161.4
Internet users (per 100 inhabitants)	7.4	25.4	41.0

Total trade		Major trading partners		2010
	(million US$)[b]	(% of exports)[b]		(% of imports)[b]
Exports	340.6		United Arab Emirates	16.7
Imports	1 021.9		Saudi Arabia	14.5
Balance	−681.3		Singapore	8.2

Social indicators

Population growth rate (average annual %)	2010-2015	0.3
Urban population growth rate (average annual %)	2010-2015	1.1
Rural population growth rate (average annual %)	2010-2015	−0.5
Urban population (%)	2011	53.6
Population aged 0-14 years (%) [cde]	2011	22.8[f]
Population aged 60+ years (females and males, % of total) [cde]	2011	13.8/8.9[f]
Sex ratio (males per 100 females) [dg]	2011	104.7[f]
Life expectancy at birth (females and males, years) [d]	2010-2015	78.0/68.4[b]
Fertility rate, total (live births per woman) [d]	2010-2015	2.3[h]
International migrant stock (000 and % of total population)	mid-2010	10.8/12.8
Education: Government expenditure (% of GDP)	2005-2011	5.0
Education: Primary-secondary gross enrolment ratio (f/m per 100)	2005-2011	120.5/115.9
Seats held by women in national parliaments (%)	2011	43.8

Environmental indicators

Threatened species	2011	209
Forested area (% of land area)	2009	88.5
CO$_2$ emission estimates (000 metric tons and metric tons per capita)	2008	682/8.1
Energy consumption per capita (kilograms oil equivalent)	2009	2 808.0
Rainfall in the capital city, total mean (millimetres)		2 172
Temperature in the capital city, mean °C (minimum and maximum)		24.4/29.8

a Official rate. b 2008. c De facto estimate. d Data compiled by the United Nations Demographic Yearbook system. e Data refer to the latest available census. f 2010. g De facto national estimate. h 2009.

Sierra Leone

Region	Western Africa	
Currency	Leone (SLL)	
Surface area (square kilometres)	72 300	
Population in 2010 (estimated, 000)	5 868	
Population density in 2010 (per square kilometre)	81.2	
Capital city and population in 2011 (000)	Freetown (941)	
United Nations membership date	27 September 1961	

Economic indicators	2000	2005	2010
GDP: Gross domestic product (million current US$)	926	1 491	2 064
GDP: Growth rate at constant 2005 prices (annual %)	3.8	7.5	4.9
GDP per capita (current US$)	223.4	289.2	351.7
GNI: Gross national income per capita (current US$)	221.6	279.4	338.7
Gross fixed capital formation (% of GDP)	6.9	8.3	8.1
Exchange rates (national currency per US$) [a]	1 666.67	2 932.52	4 198.01
Balance of payments, current account (million US$)	−112	−171	−483
CPI: Consumer price index (2000=100)	100[b]	132	239
Agricultural production index (2004-2006=100)	52	98	114
Food production index (2004-2006=100)	51	97	116
Employment in industrial sector (% of employed)	4.2[b]	6.5[cdef]	...
Employment in agricultural sector (% of employed)	67.3[b]	68.5[cdef]	...
Labour force participation, adult female pop. (%)	67.3	66.6	66.4
Labour force participation, adult male pop. (%)	63.3	67.8	68.9
Tourist arrivals at national borders (000) [g]	16	40	39
Energy production, primary (000 mt oil equivalent)	1	2	2[hi]
Telephone subscribers, total (per 100 inhabitants)	0.8	0.5[j]	34.3
Internet users (per 100 inhabitants)	0.1	0.2	0.3[h]

Social indicators		
Population growth rate (average annual %)	2010-2015	2.1
Urban population growth rate (average annual %)	2010-2015	3.0
Rural population growth rate (average annual %)	2010-2015	1.5
Urban population (%)	2011	39.2
Population aged 0-14 years (%)	2011	42.9
Population aged 60+ years (females and males, % of total)	2011	3.6/3.7
Sex ratio (males per 100 females)	2011	95.6
Life expectancy at birth (females and males, years)	2010-2015	48.9/47.5
Infant mortality rate (per 1 000 live births)	2010-2015	103.5
Fertility rate, total (live births per woman)	2010-2015	4.7
Contraceptive prevalence (ages 15-49, %)	2006-2010	8.2
International migrant stock (000 and % of total population) [k]	mid-2010	106.8/1.8
Refugees and others of concern to UNHCR	end-2010	8 573
Education: Government expenditure (% of GDP)	2005-2011	4.3
Education: Primary-secondary gross enrolment ratio (f/m per 100) [l]	2005-2011	47.6/70.3[m]
Education: Female third-level students (% of total) [l]	2005-2011	28.8[n]
Seats held by women in national parliaments (%)	2011	13.2

Environmental indicators		
Threatened species	2011	133
Forested area (% of land area)	2009	38.3
CO$_2$ emission estimates (000 metric tons and metric tons per capita)	2008	1 334/0.3
Energy consumption per capita (kilograms oil equivalent)	2009	76.0[i]
Rainfall in the capital city, total mean (millimetres)		2 946
Temperature in the capital city, mean °C (minimum and maximum)		23.8/29.9

a Market rate. **b** 2003. **c** 2004. **d** December. **e** Population census. **f** Age group 10 years and over. **g** Air arrivals. **h** 2009. **i** UNSD estimate. **j** Main telephone lines only. **k** Includes refugees. **l** UNESCO estimate. **m** 2001. **n** 2002.

Singapore

Region	South-eastern Asia
Currency	Singaporean Dollar (SGD)
Surface area (square kilometres)	712
Population in 2010 (estimated, 000)	5 086
Population density in 2010 (per square kilometre)	7 143.9
Capital city and population in 2011 (000)	Singapore (5 188)
United Nations membership date	21 September 1965

Economic indicators	2000	2005	2010
GDP: Gross domestic product (million current US$)	94 308	125 429	222 699
GDP: Growth rate at constant 2005 prices (annual %)	9.1	7.4	14.5
GDP per capita (current US$)	24 062.5	29 402.0	43 783.1
GNI: Gross national income per capita (current US$)	23 862.5	27 357.9	42 165.1
Gross fixed capital formation (% of GDP)	30.3	21.1	25.0
Exchange rates (national currency per US$) [a]	1.73	1.66	1.29
Balance of payments, current account (million US$)	10 244	26 429	49 558
CPI: Consumer price index (2000=100)	100	103	117
Agricultural production index (2004-2006=100)	66	88	97
Food production index (2004-2006=100)	66	88	97
Unemployment (% of labour force)	3.6[b]	3.3	2.1
Employment in industrial sector (% of employed) [cde]	25.8[f]	21.7	21.8[g]
Employment in agricultural sector (% of employed)	0.9[fh]	1.1[h]	1.1[gi]
Labour force participation, adult female pop. (%)	52.6	53.5	56.7
Labour force participation, adult male pop. (%)	78.4	77.3	77.0
Tourist arrivals at national borders (000)	6 062	7 079	9 161
Telephone subscribers, total (per 100 inhabitants)	119.8	146.0	184.4
Internet users (per 100 inhabitants)	36.0	61.0	71.0

Total trade		Major trading partners			2010
	(million US$)	(% of exports)			(% of imports)
Exports	351 867.2	Malaysia	11.9	Malaysia	11.7
Imports	310 791.1	China, Hong Kong SAR	11.7	United States	11.5
Balance	41 076.1	China	10.3	China	10.8

Social indicators		
Population growth rate (average annual %)	2010-2015	1.1
Urban population growth rate (average annual %)	2010-2015	1.1
Rural population growth rate (average annual %)	2010-2015	0.0
Urban population (%)	2011	100.0
Population aged 0-14 years (%)	2011	16.8
Population aged 60+ years (females and males, % of total)	2011	15.7/13.8
Sex ratio (males per 100 females)	2011	101.7
Life expectancy at birth (females and males, years)	2010-2015	83.7/78.9
Infant mortality rate (per 1 000 live births)	2010-2015	1.9
Fertility rate, total (live births per woman)	2010-2015	1.4
Contraceptive prevalence (ages 15-49, %) [j]	2006-2010	62.0[k]
International migrant stock (000 and % of total population)	mid-2010	1 966.9/40.7
Refugees and others of concern to UNHCR	end-2010	7
Education: Government expenditure (% of GDP)	2005-2011	3.3
Education: Female third-level students (% of total)	2005-2011	49.6
Seats held by women in national parliaments (%)	2011	22.2

Environmental indicators		
Threatened species	2011	275
Forested area (% of land area)	2009	3.3
CO_2 emission estimates (000 metric tons and metric tons per capita)	2008	32 269/7.0
Energy consumption per capita (kilograms oil equivalent)	2009	4 344.0
Rainfall in the capital city, total mean (millimetres)		2 150
Temperature in the capital city, mean °C (minimum and maximum)		23.9/30.9

a Market rate. b 2004. c June. d Manufacturing and construction only. e Permanent residents only. f 2001. g 2009. h Includes mining and quarrying, electricity, gas and water supply and activities not classifiable by economic activity. i Includes mining and quarrying, electricity, gas, steam and air conditioning supply. j Age group 15 to 44 years. k 1997.

Slovakia

Region	Eastern Europe
Currency	Euro (EUR)[a]
Surface area (square kilometres)	49 037
Population in 2010 (estimated, 000)	5 462
Population density in 2010 (per square kilometre)	111.4
Capital city and population in 2011 (000)	Bratislava (434)
United Nations membership date	19 January 1993

Economic indicators	2000	2005	2010
GDP: Gross domestic product (million current US$)	20 403	47 895	87 263
GDP: Growth rate at constant 2005 prices (annual %)	1.4	6.7	4.2
GDP per capita (current US$)	3 774.9	8 844.2	15 976.0
GNI: Gross national income per capita (current US$)	3 753.8	8 594.2	15 758.0
Gross fixed capital formation (% of GDP)	25.9	26.6	22.2
Exchange rates (national currency per US$)	47.39[bc]	31.95[bc]	0.75[d]
Balance of payments, current account (million US$)	−694	−4 005	−3 009
CPI: Consumer price index (2000=100)	100	133	153
Industrial production index (2005=100)	96[e]	100	143
Agricultural production index (2004-2006=100)	92	102	82
Food production index (2004-2006=100)	92	102	82
Unemployment (% of labour force)	18.2[f]	16.3	14.4
Employment in industrial sector (% of employed)	37.3[gh]	38.8[gh]	37.1[i]
Employment in agricultural sector (% of employed)	6.7[gh]	4.7[gh]	3.2[i]
Labour force participation, adult female pop. (%)	52.8	51.4	50.9
Labour force participation, adult male pop. (%)	68.2	68.5	68.0
Tourist arrivals at national borders (000)	1 053[j]	6 184	6 643[k]
Energy production, primary (000 mt oil equivalent)	3 084	2 832	2 586[l]
Telephone subscribers, total (per 100 inhabitants)	54.4	105.9	128.6
Internet users (per 100 inhabitants)	9.4	55.2	79.4

Total trade		Major trading partners			2010
	(million US$)	(% of exports)			(% of imports)
Exports	63 998.6	Germany	19.2	Germany	16.1
Imports	64 382.0	Czech Republic	13.7		
Balance	−383.4	Poland	7.3		

Social indicators		
Population growth rate (average annual %)	2010-2015	0.2
Urban population growth rate (average annual %)	2010-2015	0.1
Rural population growth rate (average annual %)	2010-2015	0.3
Urban population (%)	2011	54.7
Population aged 0-14 years (%)	2011	15.0
Population aged 60+ years (females and males, % of total)	2011	20.8/14.7
Sex ratio (males per 100 females)	2011	94.7
Life expectancy at birth (females and males, years)	2010-2015	79.5/71.9
Infant mortality rate (per 1 000 live births)	2010-2015	5.7
Fertility rate, total (live births per woman)	2010-2015	1.4
Contraceptive prevalence (ages 15-49, %)[m]	2006-2010	79.8[n]
International migrant stock (000 and % of total population)[o]	mid-2010	130.7/2.4
Refugees and others of concern to UNHCR	end-2010	1 639
Education: Government expenditure (% of GDP)	2005-2011	3.6
Education: Primary-secondary gross enrolment ratio (f/m per 100)	2005-2011	93.0/92.3
Education: Female third-level students (% of total)	2005-2011	60.5
Deaths by assault (females and males, per 100 000)	2005-2008	1.1/2.3[p]
Seats held by women in national parliaments (%)	2011	16.0

Environmental indicators		
Threatened species	2011	40
Forested area (% of land area)	2009	40.2
CO_2 emission estimates (000 metric tons and metric tons per capita)	2008	37 527/7.0
Energy consumption per capita (kilograms oil equivalent)	2009	2 508.0
Rainfall in the capital city, total mean (millimetres)		557
Temperature in the capital city, mean °C (minimum and maximum)		5.7/15.2

a Beginning 1 January 2009, the Slovak Koruna (SKK) was replaced by the euro (1 EUR=30.126 SKK). **b** Official rate. **c** Currency = Slovak Koruna. **d** Market rate. **e** 2003. **f** 2004. **g** Excludes persons on child-care leave. **h** Excludes conscripts. **i** European Labour Force Survey (Eurostat). **j** Non-resident tourists staying in commercial accommodation only (representing approximately 25% of all tourists). **k** 2008. **l** 2009. **m** Age group 15 to 44 years. **n** 1997. **o** Includes refugees. **p** Rate based on 30 or fewer events.

Slovenia

Region	Southern Europe
Currency	Euro (EUR)[a]
Surface area (square kilometres)	20 273
Population in 2010 (estimated, 000)	2 030
Population density in 2010 (per square kilometre)	100.1
Capital city and population in 2011 (000)	Ljubljana (273)
United Nations membership date	22 May 1992

Economic indicators	2000	2005	2010
GDP: Gross domestic product (million current US$)	19 982	35 718	46 906
GDP: Growth rate at constant 2005 prices (annual %)	4.3	4.0	1.4
GDP per capita (current US$)	10 064.4	17 840.3	23 109.8
GNI: Gross national income per capita (current US$)	10 070.7	17 689.0	22 769.1
Gross fixed capital formation (% of GDP)	26.3	25.4	21.6
Exchange rates (national currency per US$)	227.38[bc]	202.43[bc]	0.75[d]
Balance of payments, current account (million US$)	−548	−681	−388
CPI: Consumer price index (2000=100)[e]	100	131[f]	148[g]
Industrial production index (2005=100)	92[h]	100	102
Agricultural production index (2004-2006=100)	96	99	92
Food production index (2004-2006=100)	96	99	92
Unemployment (% of labour force)	6.3[i]	6.5	7.2
Employment in industrial sector (% of employed)	37.4[jk]	37.2[il]	32.5[m]
Employment in agricultural sector (% of employed)	9.5[jk]	8.8[il]	8.8[m]
Labour force participation, adult female pop. (%)	51.4	52.8	53.1
Labour force participation, adult male pop. (%)	64.1	66.1	65.2
Tourist arrivals at national borders (000)[n]	1 090	1 555	1 869
Energy production, primary (000 mt oil equivalent)	1 809	1 991	2 068[g]
Telephone subscribers, total (per 100 inhabitants)	100.8	138.8	149.4
Internet users (per 100 inhabitants)	15.1	46.8	70.0

Total trade		Major trading partners			2010
	(million US$)	(% of exports)			(% of imports)
Exports	24 188.0	Germany	19.8	Germany	16.2
Imports	26 360.4	Italy	12.2	Italy	15.8
Balance	−2 172.4	Austria	8.2	Austria	7.9

Social indicators		
Population growth rate (average annual %)	2010-2015	0.2
Urban population growth rate (average annual %)	2010-2015	0.2
Rural population growth rate (average annual %)	2010-2015	0.3
Urban population (%)	2011	49.9
Population aged 0-14 years (%)	2011	14.0
Population aged 60+ years (females and males, % of total)	2011	26.1/19.6
Sex ratio (males per 100 females)	2011	95.8
Life expectancy at birth (females and males, years)	2010-2015	82.8/76.1
Infant mortality rate (per 1 000 live births)	2010-2015	3.3
Fertility rate, total (live births per woman)	2010-2015	1.5
Contraceptive prevalence (ages 15-49, %)[o]	2006-2010	78.9[p]
International migrant stock (000 and % of total population)	mid-2010	163.9/8.1
Refugees and others of concern to UNHCR	end-2010	4 525
Education: Government expenditure (% of GDP)	2005-2011	5.2
Education: Primary-secondary gross enrolment ratio (f/m per 100)	2005-2011	97.0/97.6
Education: Female third-level students (% of total)	2005-2011	58.0
Deaths by assault (females and males, per 100 000)	2005-2008	</0.8[q]
Seats held by women in national parliaments (%)	2011	14.4

Environmental indicators		
Threatened species	2011	116
Forested area (% of land area)	2009	62.1
CO_2 emission estimates (000 metric tons and metric tons per capita)	2008	17 144/8.5
Energy consumption per capita (kilograms oil equivalent)	2009	2 687.0
Rainfall in the capital city, total mean (millimetres)		1 368
Temperature in the capital city, mean °C (minimum and maximum)		5.9/15.0

a Beginning 1 January 2007, the Slovenian tolar (SIT) was replaced by the euro (1 EUR=239.64 SIT). **b** Official rate. **c** Currency = Slovenian tolar. **d** Market rate. **e** Urban areas. **f** Series linked to former series. **g** 2009. **h** 2003. **i** 2004. **j** Second quarter. **k** Excludes regular military living in barracks. **l** Excludes conscripts and regular military living in barracks. **m** European Labour Force Survey (Eurostat). **n** Arrivals of non-resident tourists in all types of accommodation establishments. **o** Age group 15 to 44 years. **p** 1994-1995. **q** Rate based on 30 or fewer events.

Solomon Islands

Region	Oceania-Melanesia
Currency	Solomon Is. Dollar (SBD)
Surface area (square kilometres)	28 896
Population in 2010 (estimated, 000)	538
Population density in 2010 (per square kilometre)	18.6
Capital city and population in 2011 (000)	Honiara (68)
United Nations membership date	19 September 1978

Economic indicators	2000	2005	2010
GDP: Gross domestic product (million current US$)	338	429	642
GDP: Growth rate at constant 2005 prices (annual %)	−14.2	12.9	7.1
GDP per capita (current US$)	827.4	914.2	1 193.5
GNI: Gross national income per capita (current US$)	828.2	917.7	1 082.6
Gross fixed capital formation (% of GDP)	18.3	16.0	19.3
Exchange rates (national currency per US$)[a]	5.10	7.58	8.06
Balance of payments, current account (million US$)	−41	−90	−373
CPI: Consumer price index (2000=100)[b]	100	149	209[c]
Agricultural production index (2004-2006=100)	82	103	119
Food production index (2004-2006=100)	82	103	119
Labour force participation, adult female pop. (%)	53.0	53.6	53.1
Labour force participation, adult male pop. (%)	78.6	79.4	79.9
Tourist arrivals at national borders (000)	5	9	21
Telephone subscribers, total (per 100 inhabitants)	2.2	2.9	7.1
Internet users (per 100 inhabitants)	0.5	0.8	5.0

Total trade		Major trading partners			2010
	(million US$)[d]	(% of exports)[d]			(% of imports)[d]
Exports	158.5	China	46.6	Australia	31.2
Imports	285.0	Thailand	7.2	Singapore	27.1
Balance	−126.5	Philippines	7.1	Japan	8.2

Social indicators		
Population growth rate (average annual %)	2010-2015	2.5
Urban population growth rate (average annual %)	2010-2015	4.7
Rural population growth rate (average annual %)	2010-2015	1.9
Urban population (%)	2011	20.5
Population aged 0-14 years (%)	2011	39.5
Population aged 60+ years (females and males, % of total)	2011	5.4/4.7
Sex ratio (males per 100 females)[e]	2011	107.5
Life expectancy at birth (females and males, years)	2010-2015	70.0/67.0
Infant mortality rate (per 1 000 live births)	2010-2015	34.6
Fertility rate, total (live births per woman)	2010-2015	4.0
Contraceptive prevalence (ages 15-49, %)	2006-2010	34.6
International migrant stock (000 and % of total population)	mid-2010	7.0/1.3
Education: Government expenditure (% of GDP)[f]	2005-2011	2.3[g]
Education: Primary-secondary gross enrolment ratio (f/m per 100)	2005-2011	69.7/74.5
Seats held by women in national parliaments (%)	2011	0.0

Environmental indicators		
Threatened species	2011	221
Forested area (% of land area)	2009	79.3
CO_2 emission estimates (000 metric tons and metric tons per capita)	2008	198/0.4
Energy consumption per capita (kilograms oil equivalent)	2009	122.0[h]
Rainfall in the capital city, total mean (millimetres)[i]		3 290
Temperature in the capital city, mean °C (minimum and maximum)[i]		23.2/30.1

a Official rate. **b** Honiara. **c** 2008. **d** 2007. **e** Data compiled by the Secretariat of the Pacific Community Demography Programme. **f** UNESCO estimate. **g** 1999. **h** UNSD estimate. **i** Auki.

Somalia

Region	Eastern Africa
Currency	Somali Shilling (SOS)
Surface area (square kilometres)	637 657
Population in 2010 (estimated, 000)	9 331
Population density in 2010 (per square kilometre)	14.6
Capital city and population in 2011 (000)	Mogadishu (1 554)
United Nations membership date	20 September 1960

Economic indicators	2000	2005	2010
GDP: Gross domestic product (million current US$)	2 052	2 316	1 071
GDP: Growth rate at constant 2005 prices (annual %)	3.0	3.0	2.6
GDP per capita (current US$)	277.3	277.0	114.8
GNI: Gross national income per capita (current US$)	266.1	265.8	110.2
Gross fixed capital formation (% of GDP)	20.4	20.3	19.9
Exchange rates (national currency per US$) [a]	10 460.00	15 141.00	31 900.00
Agricultural production index (2004-2006=100)	93	100	114
Food production index (2004-2006=100)	93	100	114
Labour force participation, adult female pop. (%)	36.6	37.1	37.6
Labour force participation, adult male pop. (%)	77.8	77.6	77.0
Telephone subscribers, total (per 100 inhabitants)	1.4	7.2	8.0
Internet users (per 100 inhabitants)	<	1.1	1.2 [b]

Social indicators		
Population growth rate (average annual %)	2010-2015	2.6
Urban population growth rate (average annual %)	2010-2015	3.8
Rural population growth rate (average annual %)	2010-2015	1.8
Urban population (%)	2011	37.7
Population aged 0-14 years (%)	2011	45.0
Population aged 60+ years (females and males, % of total)	2011	4.7/4.1
Sex ratio (males per 100 females)	2011	98.4
Life expectancy at birth (females and males, years)	2010-2015	53.4/50.1
Infant mortality rate (per 1 000 live births)	2010-2015	100.0
Fertility rate, total (live births per woman)	2010-2015	6.3
Contraceptive prevalence (ages 15-49, %)	2006-2010	14.6 [c]
International migrant stock (000 and % of total population) [de]	mid-2010	22.8/0.2
Refugees and others of concern to UNHCR	end-2010	1 489 862
Education: Primary-secondary gross enrolment ratio (f/m per 100) [f]	2005-2011	15.0/28.1
Seats held by women in national parliaments (%)	2011	6.8

Environmental indicators		
Threatened species	2011	130
Forested area (% of land area)	2009	10.9
CO_2 emission estimates (000 metric tons and metric tons per capita)	2008	649/0.1
Energy consumption per capita (kilograms oil equivalent)	2009	22.0 [g]

a UN operational exchange rate. b 2009. c 2005-2006. d Estimates. e Includes refugees. f UNESCO estimate. g UNSD estimate.

South Africa

Region	Southern Africa
Currency	Rand (ZAR)
Surface area (square kilometres)	1 221 037
Population in 2010 (estimated, 000)	50 133
Population density in 2010 (per square kilometre)	41.1
Capital city and population in 2011 (000)	Pretoria (1 501)[a]
United Nations membership date	7 November 1945

Economic indicators	2000	2005	2010
GDP: Gross domestic product (million current US$)	132 878	247 052	363 704
GDP: Growth rate at constant 2005 prices (annual %)	4.2	5.3	2.8
GDP per capita (current US$)	2 968.6	5 169.2	7 254.8
GNI: Gross national income per capita (current US$)	2 897.7	5 065.8	7 110.6
Gross fixed capital formation (% of GDP)	14.9	16.8	19.6
Exchange rates (national currency per US$)[b]	7.57	6.32	6.63
Balance of payments, current account (million US$)	−191	−8 518	−10 117
CPI: Consumer price index (2000=100)	100	128	179
Agricultural production index (2004-2006=100)	97	102	120
Food production index (2004-2006=100)	96	102	121
Unemployment (% of labour force)[c]	24.7[d]	23.8	24.9
Employment in industrial sector (% of employed)	24.2[c]	25.6[c]	25.0[ef]
Employment in agricultural sector (% of employed)	15.6[c]	7.5[c]	5.1[ef]
Labour force participation, adult female pop. (%)	43.8	45.7	43.8
Labour force participation, adult male pop. (%)	61.0	61.5	60.4
Tourist arrivals at national borders (000)	5 872[g]	7 369[g]	8 074
Energy production, primary (000 mt oil equivalent)	127 161	132 694	134 151[f]
Telephone subscribers, total (per 100 inhabitants)	29.7	81.0	108.9
Internet users (per 100 inhabitants)	5.4	7.5	12.3

Total trade		Major trading partners			2010
	(million US$)	(% of exports)		(% of imports)	
Exports	71 484.3	China	11.4	China	14.3
Imports	80 139.3	United States	9.9	Germany	11.3
Balance	−8 655.0	Japan	9.0	United States	7.3

Social indicators		
Population growth rate (average annual %)	2010-2015	0.5
Urban population growth rate (average annual %)	2010-2015	1.2
Rural population growth rate (average annual %)	2010-2015	−0.7
Urban population (%)	2011	62.0
Population aged 0-14 years (%)	2011	29.9
Population aged 60+ years (females and males, % of total)	2011	8.9/6.2
Sex ratio (males per 100 females)	2011	98.2
Life expectancy at birth (females and males, years)	2010-2015	54.1/53.1
Infant mortality rate (per 1 000 live births)	2010-2015	45.9
Fertility rate, total (live births per woman)	2010-2015	2.4
Contraceptive prevalence (ages 15-49, %)	2006-2010	59.9[h]
International migrant stock (000 and % of total population)[i]	mid-2010	1 862.9/3.7
Refugees and others of concern to UNHCR	end-2010	229 601
Education: Government expenditure (% of GDP)	2005-2011	6.0
Education: Primary-secondary gross enrolment ratio (f/m per 100)	2005-2011	98.1/98.8
Seats held by women in national parliaments (%)[j]	2011	44.5

Environmental indicators		
Threatened species	2011	444
Forested area (% of land area)	2009	7.6
CO$_2$ emission estimates (000 metric tons and metric tons per capita)	2008	435 521/8.8
Energy consumption per capita (kilograms oil equivalent)	2009	2 698.0
Rainfall in the capital city, total mean (millimetres)[k]		713
Temperature in the capital city, mean °C (minimum and maximum)[k]		10.1/21.9

a Pretoria is the administrative capital, Cape Town is the legislative capital and Bloemfontein is the judicial capital. b Principal rate. c Age group 15 to 64 years. d 2004. e Average of quarterly estimates. f 2009. g Excludes arrivals by work and contract workers. h 2003-2004. i Includes refugees. j The figures on the distribution of seats do not include the 36 special rotating delegates appointed on an ad hoc basis and the percentages are therefore calculated on the basis of the 54 permanent seats. k Johannesburg.

Spain

Region	Southern Europe
Currency	Euro (EUR)
Surface area (square kilometres)	505 992
Population in 2010 (estimated, 000)	46 077 [a]
Population density in 2010 (per square kilometre)	91.1
Capital city and population in 2011 (000)	Madrid (6 574)
United Nations membership date	14 December 1955

Economic indicators	2000	2005	2010
GDP: Gross domestic product (million current US$)	580 673	1 130 170	1 407 320
GDP: Growth rate at constant 2005 prices (annual %)	5.1	3.6	−0.1
GDP per capita (current US$)	14 412.9	26 043.5	30 542.8
GNI: Gross national income per capita (current US$)	14 291.5	25 676.2	30 137.9
Gross fixed capital formation (% of GDP)	25.8	29.4	22.5
Exchange rates (national currency per US$) [b]	1.07	0.85	0.75
Balance of payments, current account (million US$)	−23 185	−83 388	−64 342
CPI: Consumer price index (2000=100) [c]	100	114	128
Industrial production index (2005=100)	98 [d]	100	83
Agricultural production index (2004-2006=100)	100	95	104
Food production index (2004-2006=100)	100	94	104
Unemployment (% of labour force) [e]	11.0 [f]	9.2	20.1
Employment in industrial sector (% of employed) [eg]	30.8	29.7	23.1
Employment in agricultural sector (% of employed) [eg]	6.7	5.3	4.3
Labour force participation, adult female pop. (%)	40.7	45.8	51.5
Labour force participation, adult male pop. (%)	66.1	68.0	67.4
Tourist arrivals at national borders (000)	46 403	55 914	52 677
Energy production, primary (000 mt oil equivalent)	16 922	15 604	15 443 [h]
Telephone subscribers, total (per 100 inhabitants)	102.7	143.2	155.8
Internet users (per 100 inhabitants)	13.6	47.9	65.8

Total trade		Major trading partners			2010
	(million US$)	(% of exports)			(% of imports)
Exports	246 265.3	France	18.3	Germany	11.7
Imports	315 547.2	Germany	10.5	France	10.7
Balance	−69 281.9	Portugal	8.9	China	7.9

Social indicators

Population growth rate (average annual %) [a]	2010-2015	0.6
Urban population growth rate (average annual %)	2010-2015	0.8
Rural population growth rate (average annual %)	2010-2015	−<
Urban population (%)	2011	77.4
Population aged 0-14 years (%) [a]	2011	15.1
Population aged 60+ years (females and males, % of total) [a]	2011	24.9/20.0
Sex ratio (males per 100 females) [a]	2011	97.6
Life expectancy at birth (females and males, years) [a]	2010-2015	84.8/78.8
Infant mortality rate (per 1 000 live births) [a]	2010-2015	3.6
Fertility rate, total (live births per woman) [a]	2010-2015	1.5
Contraceptive prevalence (ages 15-49, %)	2006-2010	65.7
International migrant stock (000 and % of total population)	mid-2010	6 377.5/14.1
Refugees and others of concern to UNHCR	end-2010	6 566
Education: Government expenditure (% of GDP)	2005-2011	4.6
Education: Primary-secondary gross enrolment ratio (f/m per 100)	2005-2011	114.0/111.9
Education: Female third-level students (% of total)	2005-2011	54.1
Deaths by assault (females and males, per 100 000)	2005-2008	</1.4
Seats held by women in national parliaments (%)	2011	36.0

Environmental indicators

Threatened species	2011	514
Forested area (% of land area)	2009	36.1
CO$_2$ emission estimates (000 metric tons and metric tons per capita)	2008	329 016/7.4
Energy consumption per capita (kilograms oil equivalent)	2009	2 537.0
Rainfall in the capital city, total mean (millimetres)		436
Temperature in the capital city, mean °C (minimum and maximum)		9.7/19.5

a Includes Canary Islands, Ceuta and Melilla. **b** Market rate. **c** Index base 2001=100. **d** 2003. **e** Age group 16 years and over. **f** 2004. **g** European Labour Force Survey (Eurostat). **h** 2009.

Sri Lanka

Region	South-central Asia
Currency	Sri Lanka Rupee (LKR)
Surface area (square kilometres)	65 610
Population in 2010 (estimated, 000)	20 860
Population density in 2010 (per square kilometre)	317.9
Capital city and population in 2011 (000)	Colombo (693) [a]
United Nations membership date	14 December 1955

Economic indicators	2000	2005	2010
GDP: Gross domestic product (million current US$)	16 717	24 406	49 549
GDP: Growth rate at constant 2005 prices (annual %)	6.0	6.2	8.0
GDP per capita (current US$)	891.8	1 230.0	2 375.3
GNI: Gross national income per capita (current US$)	875.9	1 214.9	2 341.0
Gross fixed capital formation (% of GDP)	24.8	23.4	25.9
Exchange rates (national currency per US$) [b]	82.58	102.12	110.95
Balance of payments, current account (million US$)	−1 044	−743	−1 471
CPI: Consumer price index (2000=100) [cd]	100	160	219
Agricultural production index (2004-2006=100)	95	103	121
Food production index (2004-2006=100)	95	103	125
Unemployment (% of labour force) [ef]	8.5 [g]	6.5 [h]	4.9
Employment in industrial sector (% of employed) [e]	22.4 [fi]	25.6	25.1 [ik]
Employment in agricultural sector (% of employed) [e]	34.5 [fi]	30.7	32.6 [ik]
Labour force participation, adult female pop. (%)	37.2	34.3	34.6
Labour force participation, adult male pop. (%)	76.8	76.1	76.2
Tourist arrivals at national borders (000) [l]	400	549	654
Energy production, primary (000 mt oil equivalent)	275	297	336 [k]
Telephone subscribers, total (per 100 inhabitants)	6.4	23.2	100.4
Internet users (per 100 inhabitants)	0.7	1.8	12.0

Total trade		Major trading partners			2010
	(million US$)	(% of exports)			(% of imports)
Exports	8 304.1	United States	21.3	India	20.6
Imports	12 353.7	United Kingdom	12.3	Singapore	13.1
Balance	−4 049.6	India	5.6	China	10.1

Social indicators		
Population growth rate (average annual %)	2010-2015	0.8
Urban population growth rate (average annual %)	2010-2015	1.4
Rural population growth rate (average annual %)	2010-2015	0.7
Urban population (%)	2011	15.1
Population aged 0-14 years (%)	2011	24.9
Population aged 60+ years (females and males, % of total)	2011	13.5/11.7
Sex ratio (males per 100 females)	2011	97.4
Life expectancy at birth (females and males, years)	2010-2015	78.4/72.1
Infant mortality rate (per 1 000 live births)	2010-2015	11.2
Fertility rate, total (live births per woman)	2010-2015	2.2
Contraceptive prevalence (ages 15-49, %)	2006-2010	68.0
International migrant stock (000 and % of total population) [m]	mid-2010	339.9/1.7
Refugees and others of concern to UNHCR	end-2010	440 323
Education: Government expenditure (% of GDP)	2005-2011	2.1
Education: Primary-secondary gross enrolment ratio (f/m per 100) [n]	2005-2011	95.0/92.0 [o]
Education: Female third-level students (% of total)	2005-2011	65.1
Seats held by women in national parliaments (%)	2011	5.8

Environmental indicators		
Threatened species	2011	559
Forested area (% of land area)	2009	29.9
CO$_2$ emission estimates (000 metric tons and metric tons per capita)	2008	11 754/0.6
Energy consumption per capita (kilograms oil equivalent)	2009	198.0
Rainfall in the capital city, total mean (millimetres)		2 524
Temperature in the capital city, mean °C (minimum and maximum)		24.1/30.6

a Colombo is the commercial capital, Sri Jayewardenepura Kotte is the administrative and legislative capital. **b** Market rate. **c** Colombo. **d** Index base 2002=100. **e** Age group 10 years and over. **f** Excludes the Northern and Eastern provinces. **g** 2004. **h** 2006. **i** 2002. **j** Excludes the Northern Province. **k** 2009. **l** Excludes nationals residing abroad. **m** Data refer to foreign citizens. **n** UNESCO estimate. **o** 2003.

Sudan[a]

Region	Northern Africa
Currency	Sudanese Pound (SDG)[b]
Surface area (square kilometres)	2 505 813
Population in 2010 (estimated, 000)	43 552
Population density in 2010 (per square kilometre)	17.4
Capital city and population in 2011 (000)	Khartoum (4 632)
United Nations membership date	12 November 1956

Economic indicators	2000	2005	2010
GDP: Gross domestic product (million current US$)	13 092	35 183	79 480
GDP: Growth rate at constant 2005 prices (annual %)	8.4	6.1	5.1
GDP per capita (current US$)	383.0	916.0	1 824.9
GNI: Gross national income per capita (current US$)	366.2	880.9	1 758.6
Gross fixed capital formation (% of GDP)	9.7	20.7	18.5
Exchange rates (national currency per US$)[c]	2.57	2.31	2.48
Balance of payments, current account (million US$)	−557	−3 013	157
Agricultural production index (2004-2006=100)	72	100	119
Food production index (2004-2006=100)	72	100	120
Labour force participation, adult female pop. (%)	29.1	29.9	30.8
Labour force participation, adult male pop. (%)	75.7	76.1	76.5
Tourist arrivals at national borders (000)	38	246[d]	420[de]
Energy production, primary (000 mt oil equivalent)	9 050	15 540	24 260[e]
Telephone subscribers, total (per 100 inhabitants)	1.2	6.2	41.4
Internet users (per 100 inhabitants)	<	1.3	...

Total trade		Major trading partners			2010
	(million US$)[e]	(% of exports)[e]			(% of imports)[e]
Exports	9 079.5	China	65.3	China	16.6
Imports	8 589.9	United Arab Emirates	10.5	Japan	9.5
Balance	489.6	Canada	8.8	Saudi Arabia	7.6

Social indicators		
Population growth rate (average annual %)	2010-2015	2.4
Urban population growth rate (average annual %)[f]	2010-2015	2.6
Rural population growth rate (average annual %)[f]	2010-2015	1.9
Urban population (%)[f]	2011	33.2
Population aged 0-14 years (%)	2011	39.8
Population aged 60+ years (females and males, % of total)	2011	6.1/5.3
Sex ratio (males per 100 females)	2011	101.6
Life expectancy at birth (females and males, years)	2010-2015	63.8/60.2
Infant mortality rate (per 1 000 live births)	2010-2015	57.3
Fertility rate, total (live births per woman)	2010-2015	4.2
Contraceptive prevalence (ages 15-49, %)	2006-2010	7.6
International migrant stock (000 and % of total population)[g]	mid-2010	753.5/1.7
Refugees and others of concern to UNHCR	end-2010	1 958 524
Education: Primary-secondary gross enrolment ratio (f/m per 100)	2005-2011	55.3/61.7
Education: Female third-level students (% of total)[h]	2005-2011	47.2[i]
Seats held by women in national parliaments (%)	2011	25.1

Environmental indicators		
Threatened species	2011	113
Forested area (% of land area)	2009	29.5
CO$_2$ emission estimates (000 metric tons and metric tons per capita)	2008	14 040/0.3
Energy consumption per capita (kilograms oil equivalent)	2009	99.0
Rainfall in the capital city, total mean (millimetres)		162
Temperature in the capital city, mean °C (minimum and maximum)		22.7/37.1

a Unless otherwise indicated, the data include those for South Sudan. **b** Beginning 1 July 2007, 1 new Sudanese Pound = 100 dinars. **c** Principal rate. **d** Includes nationals residing abroad. **e** 2009. **f** Excludes South Sudan. **g** Includes refugees. **h** UNESCO estimate. **i** 2000.

Suriname

Region	South America
Currency	Surinamese Dollar (SRD)
Surface area (square kilometres)	163 820
Population in 2010 (estimated, 000)	525
Population density in 2010 (per square kilometre)	3.2
Capital city and population in 2011 (000)	Paramaribo (278)
United Nations membership date	4 December 1975

Economic indicators	2000	2005	2010
GDP: Gross domestic product (million current US$)[a]	946	1 785	3 682
GDP: Growth rate at constant 2005 prices (annual %)[a]	2.1	3.9	4.4
GDP per capita (current US$)[a]	2 026.1	3 574.4	7 018.0
GNI: Gross national income per capita (current US$)	1 923.5	3 491.7	7 047.1
Gross fixed capital formation (% of GDP)	56.2	87.9	68.3
Exchange rates (national currency per US$)[b]	2.18	2.74	2.74
Balance of payments, current account (million US$)	32	−144	653
CPI: Consumer price index (2000=100)[cd]	77	171	249
Agricultural production index (2004-2006=100)	95	99	137
Food production index (2004-2006=100)	95	99	137
Employment in industrial sector (% of employed)	...	23.0[efg]	...
Employment in agricultural sector (% of employed)	...	8.0[efg]	...
Labour force participation, adult female pop. (%)	36.3	37.8	40.1
Labour force participation, adult male pop. (%)	66.3	67.3	68.7
Tourist arrivals at national borders (000)	57[h]	161	205
Energy production, primary (000 mt oil equivalent)	670	715	744[i]
Telephone subscribers, total (per 100 inhabitants)	24.9	62.9	185.8
Internet users (per 100 inhabitants)	2.5	6.4	31.6

Total trade		Major trading partners			2010
	(million US$)	(% of exports)			(% of imports)
Exports	2 025.6	Canada	28.5	United States	24.6
Imports	1 397.5	United Arab Emirates	13.7	Trinidad and Tobago	23.7
Balance	628.1	Belgium	10.1	Netherlands	17.5

Social indicators		
Population growth rate (average annual %)	2010-2015	0.9
Urban population growth rate (average annual %)	2010-2015	1.4
Rural population growth rate (average annual %)	2010-2015	−0.5
Urban population (%)	2011	69.7
Population aged 0-14 years (%)	2011	28.1
Population aged 60+ years (females and males, % of total)	2011	10.6/8.3
Sex ratio (males per 100 females)	2011	100.5
Life expectancy at birth (females and males, years)	2010-2015	74.2/67.8
Infant mortality rate (per 1 000 live births)	2010-2015	19.8
Fertility rate, total (live births per woman)	2010-2015	2.3
Contraceptive prevalence (ages 15-49, %)	2006-2010	45.6
International migrant stock (000 and % of total population)[i]	mid-2010	39.5/7.5
Refugees and others of concern to UNHCR	end-2010	8
Education: Primary-secondary gross enrolment ratio (f/m per 100)	2005-2011	96.6/91.6
Education: Female third-level students (% of total)	2005-2011	62.0[k]
Seats held by women in national parliaments (%)	2011	9.8

Environmental indicators		
Threatened species	2011	67
Forested area (% of land area)	2009	94.6
CO_2 emission estimates (000 metric tons and metric tons per capita)	2008	2 437/4.7
Energy consumption per capita (kilograms oil equivalent)	2009	1 357.0

a Excludes the informal sector. b Market rate. c Index base 2001=100. d Paramaribo. e 2004. f August.
g Population census. h Arrivals at Zanderij airport. i 2009. j Data refer to foreign citizens. k 2002.

Swaziland

Region	Southern Africa
Currency	Lilangeni (SZL)
Surface area (square kilometres)	17 364
Population in 2010 (estimated, 000)	1 186
Population density in 2010 (per square kilometre)	68.3
Capital city and population in 2011 (000)	Mbabane (66) [a]
United Nations membership date	24 September 1968

Economic indicators	2000	2005	2010
GDP: Gross domestic product (million current US$)	1 536	2 596	3 927
GDP: Growth rate at constant 2005 prices (annual %)	2.7	2.3	2.0
GDP per capita (current US$)	1 443.6	2 349.4	3 311.2
GNI: Gross national income per capita (current US$)	1 437.2	2 503.4	3 341.3
Gross fixed capital formation (% of GDP)	18.1	15.0	8.9
Exchange rates (national currency per US$) [b]	7.57	6.32	6.63
Balance of payments, current account (million US$)	−46	−103	−389
CPI: Consumer price index (2000=100)	100	140	193[c]
Agricultural production index (2004-2006=100)	89	103	104
Food production index (2004-2006=100)	87	103	104
Labour force participation, adult female pop. (%)	42.7	42.9	43.5
Labour force participation, adult male pop. (%)	71.7	70.8	70.7
Tourist arrivals at national borders (000)	281[d]	837[e]	868[e]
Energy production, primary (000 mt oil equivalent)	260	329	358[cf]
Telephone subscribers, total (per 100 inhabitants)	6.1	21.3	65.5
Internet users (per 100 inhabitants)	0.9	3.7	8.0

Total trade		Major trading partners			2010
	(million US$)[g]	(% of exports)[g]		(% of imports)[g]	
Exports	1 113.3	South Africa	79.8	South Africa	81.3
Imports	1 270.1	Italy	13.8	China	4.0
Balance	−156.8	Namibia	2.8	Japan	2.4

Social indicators		
Population growth rate (average annual %)	2010-2015	1.4
Urban population growth rate (average annual %)	2010-2015	1.2
Rural population growth rate (average annual %)	2010-2015	1.4
Urban population (%)	2011	21.3
Population aged 0-14 years (%)	2011	37.9
Population aged 60+ years (females and males, % of total)	2011	5.9/4.7
Sex ratio (males per 100 females)	2011	96.9
Life expectancy at birth (females and males, years)	2010-2015	48.5/49.7
Infant mortality rate (per 1 000 live births)	2010-2015	64.6
Fertility rate, total (live births per woman)	2010-2015	3.2
Contraceptive prevalence (ages 15-49, %)	2006-2010	50.6
International migrant stock (000 and % of total population) [h]	mid-2010	40.4/3.4
Refugees and others of concern to UNHCR	end-2010	759
Education: Government expenditure (% of GDP)	2005-2011	7.4
Education: Primary-secondary gross enrolment ratio (f/m per 100)	2005-2011	88.6/94.2
Education: Female third-level students (% of total)	2005-2011	49.8
Seats held by women in national parliaments (%)	2011	13.6

Environmental indicators		
Threatened species	2011	31
Forested area (% of land area)	2009	32.5
CO_2 emission estimates (000 metric tons and metric tons per capita)	2008	1 092/1.0
Energy consumption per capita (kilograms oil equivalent)	2009	359.0[f]
Rainfall in the capital city, total mean (millimetres)		1 442
Temperature in the capital city, mean °C (minimum and maximum)		10.5/22.5

a Mbabane is the administrative capital, Lobamba is the legislative capital. b Official rate. c 2009. d Arrivals in hotels only. e Arrivals of non-resident tourists in hotels and similar establishments. f UNSD estimate. g 2007. h Includes refugees.

Sweden

Region	Northern Europe
Currency	Swedish Krona (SEK)
Surface area (square kilometres)	450 295
Population in 2010 (estimated, 000)	9 380
Population density in 2010 (per square kilometre)	20.8
Capital city and population in 2011 (000)	Stockholm (1 385)
United Nations membership date	19 November 1946

Economic indicators	2000	2005	2010
GDP: Gross domestic product (million current US$)	247 259	370 580	458 725
GDP: Growth rate at constant 2005 prices (annual %)	4.5	3.2	5.7
GDP per capita (current US$)	27 906.9	41 041.7	48 906.2
GNI: Gross national income per capita (current US$)	27 672.2	41 336.6	49 803.0
Gross fixed capital formation (% of GDP)	18.0	17.9	17.9
Exchange rates (national currency per US$) [a]	9.54	7.96	6.71
Balance of payments, current account (million US$)	9 860	24 260	30 408
CPI: Consumer price index (2000=100)	100	108	116
Industrial production index (2005=100)	92[b]	100	93
Agricultural production index (2004-2006=100)	104	100	95
Food production index (2004-2006=100)	104	100	95
Unemployment (% of labour force) [c]	5.5[d]	7.1	8.4
Employment in industrial sector (% of employed)	24.5[ef]	22.0[efg]	19.9[hi]
Employment in agricultural sector (% of employed)	2.4[ef]	2.0[efg]	2.1[hi]
Labour force participation, adult female pop. (%)	58.1	59.3	59.3
Labour force participation, adult male pop. (%)	67.9	68.1	68.2
Tourist arrivals at national borders (000) [j]	3 828	4 883	4 951
Energy production, primary (000 mt oil equivalent)	11 889	12 975	11 076[k]
Telephone subscribers, total (per 100 inhabitants)	136.8	163.2	168.5
Internet users (per 100 inhabitants)	45.7	84.8	90.0

Total trade		Major trading partners			2010
	(million US$)	(% of exports)			(% of imports)
Exports	158 079.2	Norway	10.0	Germany	18.2
Imports	148 421.2	Germany	10.0	Norway	9.0
Balance	9 658.0	United Kingdom	7.4	Denmark	8.3

Social indicators		
Population growth rate (average annual %)	2010-2015	0.6
Urban population growth rate (average annual %)	2010-2015	0.7
Rural population growth rate (average annual %)	2010-2015	−0.5
Urban population (%)	2011	85.2
Population aged 0-14 years (%)	2011	16.6
Population aged 60+ years (females and males, % of total)	2011	26.9/23.4
Sex ratio (males per 100 females)	2011	99.3
Life expectancy at birth (females and males, years)	2010-2015	83.7/79.7
Infant mortality rate (per 1 000 live births)	2010-2015	2.5
Fertility rate, total (live births per woman)	2010-2015	1.9
Contraceptive prevalence (ages 15-49, %) [l]	2006-2010	75.2[m]
International migrant stock (000 and % of total population)	mid-2010	1 306.0/14.1
Refugees and others of concern to UNHCR	end-2010	110 608
Education: Government expenditure (% of GDP)	2005-2011	6.8
Education: Primary-secondary gross enrolment ratio (f/m per 100)	2005-2011	99.8/100.5
Education: Female third-level students (% of total)	2005-2011	60.1
Deaths by assault (females and males, per 100 000)	2005-2008	0.7/1.7
Seats held by women in national parliaments (%)	2011	45.0

Environmental indicators		
Threatened species	2011	34
Forested area (% of land area)	2009	68.7
CO_2 emission estimates (000 metric tons and metric tons per capita)	2008	49 010/5.3
Energy consumption per capita (kilograms oil equivalent)	2009	2 709.0
Rainfall in the capital city, total mean (millimetres)		539
Temperature in the capital city, mean °C (minimum and maximum)		3.6/10.0

a Official rate. **b** 2003. **c** Age group 15 to 74 years. **d** 2004. **e** Excludes conscripts. **f** Age group 16 to 64 years. **g** Change in methodology, therefore data are not strictly comparable with those of previous years. **h** Age group 16 to 74 years. **i** European Labour Force Survey (Eurostat). **j** Arrivals of non-resident tourists in all types of accommodation establishments. **k** 2009. **l** Age group 18 to 44 years. **m** 1996.

Switzerland

Region	Western Europe
Currency	Swiss Franc (CHF)
Surface area (square kilometres)	41 285
Population in 2010 (estimated, 000)	7 664
Population density in 2010 (per square kilometre)	185.6
Capital city and population in 2011 (000)	Bern (353)
United Nations membership date	10 September 2002

Economic indicators	2000	2005	2010
GDP: Gross domestic product (million current US$)	249 912	372 477	527 920
GDP: Growth rate at constant 2005 prices (annual %)	3.6	2.6	2.7
GDP per capita (current US$)	34 865.5	50 232.8	68 880.2
GNI: Gross national income per capita (current US$)	37 427.9	54 967.4	72 220.3
Gross fixed capital formation (% of GDP)	22.8	21.7	20.8
Exchange rates (national currency per US$) [a]	1.64	1.31	0.94
Balance of payments, current account (million US$)	32 830	53 149	76 901
CPI: Consumer price index (2000=100)	100	104	109
Industrial production index (2005=100) [b]	93[c]	100	117
Agricultural production index (2004-2006=100)	102	99	103
Food production index (2004-2006=100)	102	99	103
Unemployment (% of labour force)	...	...	4.5
Employment in industrial sector (% of employed)	25.7[d]	23.7[d]	21.1[e]
Employment in agricultural sector (% of employed)	4.5[d]	3.8[d]	3.3[e]
Labour force participation, adult female pop. (%)	57.8	59.4	60.6
Labour force participation, adult male pop. (%)	77.7	75.1	75.4
Tourist arrivals at national borders (000) [f]	7 821	7 229	8 628
Energy production, primary (000 mt oil equivalent) [g]	5 589	4 887	5 648[h]
Telephone subscribers, total (per 100 inhabitants)	137.8	161.6	181.4
Internet users (per 100 inhabitants)	47.1	70.1	83.9

Total trade		Major trading partners			2010
	(million US$)[g]	(% of exports)[g]			(% of imports)[g]
Exports	195 609.3	Germany	19.3	Germany	31.9
Imports	176 280.6	United States	10.1	Italy	10.2
Balance	19 328.7	Italy	7.9	France	8.5

Social indicators		
Population growth rate (average annual %)	2010-2015	0.4
Urban population growth rate (average annual %)	2010-2015	0.5
Rural population growth rate (average annual %)	2010-2015	0.1
Urban population (%)	2011	73.7
Population aged 0-14 years (%)	2011	15.1
Population aged 60+ years (females and males, % of total)	2011	25.2/20.9
Sex ratio (males per 100 females)	2011	96.8
Life expectancy at birth (females and males, years)	2010-2015	84.7/80.2
Infant mortality rate (per 1 000 live births)	2010-2015	3.5
Fertility rate, total (live births per woman)	2010-2015	1.5
Contraceptive prevalence (ages 15-49, %) [i]	2006-2010	82.0[j]
International migrant stock (000 and % of total population)	mid-2010	1 762.8/23.2
Refugees and others of concern to UNHCR	end-2010	61 791
Education: Government expenditure (% of GDP)	2005-2011	5.4
Education: Primary-secondary gross enrqlment ratio (f/m per 100)	2005-2011	97.1/99.5
Education: Female third-level students (% of total)	2005-2011	49.7
Deaths by assault (females and males, per 100 000)	2005-2008	0.6/0.6[k]
Seats held by women in national parliaments (%)	2011	28.5

Environmental indicators		
Threatened species	2011	55
Forested area (% of land area)	2009	30.9
CO_2 emission estimates (000 metric tons and metric tons per capita)	2008	40 359/5.3
Energy consumption per capita (kilograms oil equivalent) [g]	2009	2 567.0
Rainfall in the capital city, total mean (millimetres) [l]		1 086
Temperature in the capital city, mean °C (minimum and maximum) [l]		4.9/12.7

a Official rate. **b** The indices are shown in terms of ISIC Rev. 3. **c** 2003. **d** Official estimates. **e** European Labour Force Survey (Eurostat). **f** Arrivals of non-resident tourists in hotels and similar establishments. **g** Includes Liechtenstein. **h** 2009. **i** Age group 20 to 49 years. **j** 1994-1995. **k** Rate based on 30 or fewer events. **l** Zurich.

Syrian Arab Republic

Region	Western Asia
Currency	Syrian Pound (SYP)
Surface area (square kilometres)	185 180
Population in 2010 (estimated, 000)	20 411
Population density in 2010 (per square kilometre)	110.2
Capital city and population in 2011 (000)	Damascus (2 650)
United Nations membership date	24 October 1945

Economic indicators	2000	2005	2010
GDP: Gross domestic product (million current US$)	19 666	28 397	59 834
GDP: Growth rate at constant 2005 prices (annual %)	0.7	6.2	3.2
GDP per capita (current US$)	1 230.0	1 536.3	2 931.5
GNI: Gross national income per capita (current US$)	1 168.7	1 470.0	2 818.5
Gross fixed capital formation (% of GDP)	17.3	23.0	19.7
Exchange rates (national currency per US$) [a]	46.00	52.00	46.58
Balance of payments, current account (million US$)	1 061	295	−367
CPI: Consumer price index (2000=100)	100	122	173
Agricultural production index (2004-2006=100)	80	100	94
Food production index (2004-2006=100)	78	100	96
Unemployment (% of labour force)	...	10.9[b]	8.6
Employment in industrial sector (% of employed)	26.1[c]	28.3[d]	32.2[e]
Employment in agricultural sector (% of employed)	32.9[c]	19.6[d]	14.9[e]
Labour force participation, adult female pop. (%)	20.4	16.0	12.9
Labour force participation, adult male pop. (%)	80.3	76.1	71.6
Tourist arrivals at national borders (000) [fg]	2 100[h]	3 571[h]	8 546[i]
Energy production, primary (000 mt oil equivalent)	34 402	28 521	24 664[j]
Telephone subscribers, total (per 100 inhabitants)	10.7	31.7	77.8
Internet users (per 100 inhabitants)	0.2	5.7	20.7

Total trade	Major trading partners				2010
(million US$)	(% of exports)				(% of imports)
Exports	11 352.9	Iraq	20.2	Turkey	9.5
Imports	17 561.6	Italy	13.4	China	8.8
Balance	−6 208.7	Germany	13.0	Italy	7.4

Social indicators		
Population growth rate (average annual %)	2010-2015	1.7
Urban population growth rate (average annual %)	2010-2015	2.4
Rural population growth rate (average annual %)	2010-2015	0.8
Urban population (%)	2011	56.1
Population aged 0-14 years (%)	2011	36.2
Population aged 60+ years (females and males, % of total)	2011	6.3/5.8
Sex ratio (males per 100 females)	2011	102.4
Life expectancy at birth (females and males, years)	2010-2015	77.7/74.5
Infant mortality rate (per 1 000 live births)	2010-2015	13.8
Fertility rate, total (live births per woman)	2010-2015	2.8
Contraceptive prevalence (ages 15-49, %)	2006-2010	58.3
International migrant stock (000 and % of total population) [kl]	mid-2010	2 205.9/9.8
Refugees and others of concern to UNHCR	end-2010	1 307 918[m]
Education: Government expenditure (% of GDP)	2005-2011	4.9
Education: Primary-secondary gross enrolment ratio (f/m per 100)	2005-2011	88.1/88.8
Seats held by women in national parliaments (%)	2011	12.4

Environmental indicators		
Threatened species	2011	81
Forested area (% of land area)	2009	2.6
CO_2 emission estimates (000 metric tons and metric tons per capita)	2008	71 540/3.4
Energy consumption per capita (kilograms oil equivalent)	2009	1 104.0
Rainfall in the capital city, total mean (millimetres)		108
Temperature in the capital city, mean °C (minimum and maximum)		8.8/26.3

a UN operational exchange rate. **b** 2008. **c** Official estimates. **d** 2006. **e** January to June. **f** Arrivals of non-resident tourists in all types of accommodation establishments. **g** Includes nationals residing abroad. **h** Excludes Iraqi nationals. **i** Includes Iraqi nationals. **j** 2009. **k** Data refer to foreign citizens. **l** Includes refugees. **m** Refugee figures for Iraqis in the Syrian Arab Republic are government estimates.

Tajikistan

Region	South-central Asia
Currency	Somoni (TJS)[a]
Surface area (square kilometres)	143 100
Population in 2010 (estimated, 000)	6 879
Population density in 2010 (per square kilometre)	48.1
Capital city and population in 2011 (000)	Dushanbe (739)
United Nations membership date	2 March 1992

Economic indicators	2000	2005	2010
GDP: Gross domestic product (million current US$)	861	2 312	5 613
GDP: Growth rate at constant 2005 prices (annual %)	8.3	6.7	6.5
GDP per capita (current US$)	139.4	358.3	816.0
GNI: Gross national income per capita (current US$)	171.5	458.1	1 080.9
Gross fixed capital formation (% of GDP)	7.4	11.1	18.4
Exchange rates (national currency per US$)[b]	2.20	3.20	4.40
Balance of payments, current account (million US$)	−15[c]	−19	−383
Agricultural production index (2004-2006=100)	64	99	126
Food production index (2004-2006=100)	64	99	140
Employment in industrial sector (% of employed)	...	17.9[d]	...
Employment in agricultural sector (% of employed)	...	55.5[d]	...
Labour force participation, adult female pop. (%)	58.4	57.1	57.3
Labour force participation, adult male pop. (%)	75.2	73.8	74.8
Tourist arrivals at national borders (000)	4	...	...
Energy production, primary (000 mt oil equivalent)	1 258	1 547	1 503[e]
Telephone subscribers, total (per 100 inhabitants)	3.6	8.5	91.7
Internet users (per 100 inhabitants)	0.1	0.3	11.6

Social indicators		
Population growth rate (average annual %)	2010-2015	1.5
Urban population growth rate (average annual %)	2010-2015	1.7
Rural population growth rate (average annual %)	2010-2015	1.4
Urban population (%)	2011	26.5
Population aged 0-14 years (%)	2011	36.5
Population aged 60+ years (females and males, % of total)	2011	5.4/4.4
Sex ratio (males per 100 females)	2011	96.7
Life expectancy at birth (females and males, years)	2010-2015	71.2/64.8
Infant mortality rate (per 1 000 live births)	2010-2015	51.0
Fertility rate, total (live births per woman)	2010-2015	3.2
Contraceptive prevalence (ages 15-49, %)	2006-2010	37.1
International migrant stock (000 and % of total population)	mid-2010	284.3/4.0
Refugees and others of concern to UNHCR	end-2010	7 087
Education: Government expenditure (% of GDP)	2005-2011	4.0
Education: Primary-secondary gross enrolment ratio (f/m per 100)	2005-2011	87.8/97.1
Education: Female third-level students (% of total)	2005-2011	29.1
Seats held by women in national parliaments (%)	2011	19.0

Environmental indicators		
Threatened species	2011	42
Forested area (% of land area)	2009	2.9
CO_2 emission estimates (000 metric tons and metric tons per capita)	2008	3 144/0.5
Energy consumption per capita (kilograms oil equivalent)	2009	343.0
Rainfall in the capital city, total mean (millimetres)		653
Temperature in the capital city, mean °C (minimum and maximum)		8.1/22.0

a Beginning November 2000, 1 Somoni = 1000 Rubles. b Official rate. c 2002. d 2004. e 2009.

Thailand

Region	South-eastern Asia
Currency	Baht (THB)
Surface area (square kilometres)	513 120
Population in 2010 (estimated, 000)	69 122
Population density in 2010 (per square kilometre)	134.7
Capital city and population in 2011 (000)	Bangkok (8 426)
United Nations membership date	16 December 1946

Economic indicators

	2000	2005	2010
GDP: Gross domestic product (million current US$)	122 725	176 352	318 850
GDP: Growth rate at constant 2005 prices (annual %)	4.8	4.6	7.8
GDP per capita (current US$)	1 943.2	2 644.0	4 612.8
GNI: Gross national income per capita (current US$)	1 912.9	2 515.8	4 413.8
Gross fixed capital formation (% of GDP)	22.0	28.9	24.7
Exchange rates (national currency per US$) [a]	43.27	41.03	30.15
Balance of payments, current account (million US$)	9 313	−7 647	14 754
CPI: Consumer price index (2000=100)	100	112	129
Agricultural production index (2004-2006=100)	91	98	110
Food production index (2004-2006=100)	94	98	112
Unemployment (% of labour force) [b]	2.1[c]	1.8	1.0
Employment in industrial sector (% of employed) [d]	19.0[be]	20.2	19.5[f]
Employment in agricultural sector (% of employed) [d]	48.8[b]	42.6	41.5[f]
Labour force participation, adult female pop. (%)	65.0	65.7	63.8
Labour force participation, adult male pop. (%)	80.5	81.0	80.2
Tourist arrivals at national borders (000)	9 579[g]	11 567[g]	15 936
Energy production, primary (000 mt oil equivalent)	30 915	39 651	49 027[f]
Telephone subscribers, total (per 100 inhabitants)	13.7	57.2	113.6
Internet users (per 100 inhabitants)	3.7	15.0	21.2

Total trade

Total trade (million US$)		Major trading partners			2010	
		(% of exports)			(% of imports)	
Exports	195 311.5	China	11.0	Japan	20.8	
Imports	182 393.4	Japan	10.5	China	13.3	
Balance	12 918.1	United States	10.4	United States	5.9	

Social indicators

Population growth rate (average annual %)	2010-2015	0.5
Urban population growth rate (average annual %)	2010-2015	1.6
Rural population growth rate (average annual %)	2010-2015	−0.1
Urban population (%)	2011	34.1
Population aged 0-14 years (%)	2011	20.2
Population aged 60+ years (females and males, % of total)	2011	14.3/12.3
Sex ratio (males per 100 females)	2011	96.6
Life expectancy at birth (females and males, years)	2010-2015	77.8/71.1
Infant mortality rate (per 1 000 live births)	2010-2015	11.4
Fertility rate, total (live births per woman)	2010-2015	1.5
Contraceptive prevalence (ages 15-49, %)	2006-2010	81.1
International migrant stock (000 and % of total population) [h]	mid-2010	1 157.3/1.7
Refugees and others of concern to UNHCR	end-2010	649 430[i]
Education: Government expenditure (% of GDP)	2005-2011	3.8
Education: Primary-secondary gross enrolment ratio (f/m per 100)	2005-2011	84.6/81.8
Education: Female third-level students (% of total)	2005-2011	55.7
Seats held by women in national parliaments (%)	2011	15.8

Environmental indicators

Threatened species	2011	518
Forested area (% of land area)	2009	37.1
CO_2 emission estimates (000 metric tons and metric tons per capita)	2008	285 499/4.3
Energy consumption per capita (kilograms oil equivalent)	2009	1 254.0
Rainfall in the capital city, total mean (millimetres)		1 498
Temperature in the capital city, mean °C (minimum and maximum)		24.1/32.7

a Official rate. **b** Age group 13 years and over. **c** 2004. **d** Third quarter. **e** Includes repair and installation services and sanitary services. **f** 2009. **g** Includes arrivals of nationals residing abroad. **h** Includes refugees. **i** Figures for stateless persons are based on ongoing discussions between the Thai authorities and UNHCR and will be further verified.

The former Yugoslav Republic of Macedonia

Region	Southern Europe
Currency	Denar (MKD)
Surface area (square kilometres)	25 713
Population in 2010 (estimated, 000)	2 061
Population density in 2010 (per square kilometre)	80.1
Capital city and population in 2011 (000)	Skopje (499)
United Nations membership date	8 April 1993

Economic indicators	2000	2005	2010
GDP: Gross domestic product (million current US$)	3 587	5 987	9 138
GDP: Growth rate at constant 2005 prices (annual %)	4.6	4.4	1.8
GDP per capita (current US$)	1 785.3	2 937.4	4 434.5
GNI: Gross national income per capita (current US$)	1 762.6	2 881.0	4 351.4
Gross fixed capital formation (% of GDP)	22.3	21.3	19.5
Exchange rates (national currency per US$) [a]	66.33	51.86	46.31
Balance of payments, current account (million US$)	−103	−159	−262
CPI: Consumer price index (2000=100)	100	109	123[b]
Industrial production index (2005=100)	...	100	101
Agricultural production index (2004-2006=100)	97	99	116
Food production index (2004-2006=100)	98	99	116
Unemployment (% of labour force)	37.2[c]	37.2	32.0
Employment in industrial sector (% of employed)	33.3[de]	32.3	31.3[f]
Employment in agricultural sector (% of employed)	23.9[de]	19.5	19.7[f]
Labour force participation, adult female pop. (%)	41.0	42.0	42.7
Labour force participation, adult male pop. (%)	65.6	64.0	68.9
Tourist arrivals at national borders (000) [g]	224	197	262
Energy production, primary (000 mt oil equivalent)	2 126	1 983	2 111[b]
Telephone subscribers, total (per 100 inhabitants)	31.0	81.7	124.6
Internet users (per 100 inhabitants)	2.5	26.5	51.9

Total trade		Major trading partners			2010
	(million US$)[b]		(% of exports)[b]		(% of imports)[b]
Exports	2 691.5	Serbia	24.2	Germany	10.3
Imports	5 043.1	Germany	16.7	Russian Federation	9.8
Balance	−2 351.6	Greece	10.8	Greece	8.7

Social indicators

Population growth rate (average annual %)	2010-2015	0.1
Urban population growth rate (average annual %)	2010-2015	0.3
Rural population growth rate (average annual %)	2010-2015	−0.2
Urban population (%)	2011	59.3
Population aged 0-14 years (%)	2011	17.3
Population aged 60+ years (females and males, % of total)	2011	19.0/15.2
Sex ratio (males per 100 females)	2011	100.4
Life expectancy at birth (females and males, years)	2010-2015	77.1/73.0
Infant mortality rate (per 1 000 live births)	2010-2015	13.1
Fertility rate, total (live births per woman)	2010-2015	1.4
Contraceptive prevalence (ages 15-49, %)	2006-2010	13.5[h]
International migrant stock (000 and % of total population)[i]	mid-2010	129.7/6.4
Refugees and others of concern to UNHCR	end-2010	3 132
Education: Government expenditure (% of GDP)	2005-2011	3.5[d]
Education: Primary-secondary gross enrolment ratio (f/m per 100)	2005-2011	84.6/85.4
Education: Female third-level students (% of total)	2005-2011	53.0
Seats held by women in national parliaments (%)	2011	30.9

Environmental indicators

Threatened species	2011	95
Forested area (% of land area)	2009	39.4
CO_2 emission estimates (000 metric tons and metric tons per capita)	2008	11 805/5.8
Energy consumption per capita (kilograms oil equivalent)	2009	1 568.0
Rainfall in the capital city, total mean (millimetres)		504
Temperature in the capital city, mean °C (minimum and maximum)		6.0/18.2

a Market rate. **b** 2009. **c** 2004. **d** 2002. **e** April. **f** 2008. **g** Arrivals of non-resident tourists in all types of accommodation establishments. **h** 2005-2006. **i** Includes refugees.

Timor-Leste

Region	South-eastern Asia
Currency	U.S. Dollar (USD)
Surface area (square kilometres)	14 919
Population in 2010 (estimated, 000)	1 124
Population density in 2010 (per square kilometre)	75.4
Capital city and population in 2011 (000)	Dili (180)
United Nations membership date	27 September 2002

Economic indicators	2000	2005	2010
GDP: Gross domestic product (million current US$) [a]	316	350	794
GDP: Growth rate at constant 2005 prices (annual %) [a]	13.7	6.2	6.1
GDP per capita (current US$) [a]	380.9	346.3	706.1
GNI: Gross national income per capita (current US$)	389.4	687.9	2 404.9
Gross fixed capital formation (% of GDP)	37.6	29.4	21.9
Balance of payments, current account (million US$)	...	541 [b]	1 717
Agricultural production index (2004-2006=100)	90	98	125
Food production index (2004-2006=100)	90	98	131
Labour force participation, adult female pop. (%)	38.2	39.0	38.4
Labour force participation, adult male pop. (%)	74.8	76.1	74.4
Tourist arrivals at national borders (000) [c]	...	14 [b]	40
Energy production, primary (000 mt oil equivalent) [d]	...	7 395	7 418 [e]
Telephone subscribers, total (per 100 inhabitants)	...	3.5	53.7
Internet users (per 100 inhabitants)	...	0.1	0.2

Social indicators		
Population growth rate (average annual %)	2010-2015	2.9
Urban population growth rate (average annual %)	2010-2015	4.3
Rural population growth rate (average annual %)	2010-2015	2.4
Urban population (%)	2011	28.3
Population aged 0-14 years (%)	2011	45.8
Population aged 60+ years (females and males, % of total)	2011	5.2/4.5
Sex ratio (males per 100 females)	2011	104.0
Life expectancy at birth (females and males, years)	2010-2015	64.2/62.1
Infant mortality rate (per 1 000 live births)	2010-2015	56.5
Fertility rate, total (live births per woman)	2010-2015	5.9
Contraceptive prevalence (ages 15-49, %)	2006-2010	22.3
International migrant stock (000 and % of total population)	mid-2010	13.8/1.2
Refugees and others of concern to UNHCR	end-2010	5
Education: Government expenditure (% of GDP)	2005-2011	14.0
Education: Primary-secondary gross enrolment ratio (f/m per 100)	2005-2011	86.8/89.0
Education: Female third-level students (% of total)	2005-2011	40.0
Seats held by women in national parliaments (%)	2011	29.2

Environmental indicators		
Threatened species	2011	18
Forested area (% of land area)	2009	50.7
CO$_2$ emission estimates (000 metric tons and metric tons per capita)	2008	191/0.2
Energy consumption per capita (kilograms oil equivalent)	2009	56.0 [d]

a Refers to non-oil GDP. b 2006. c Air arrivals at Dili Airport. d UNSD estimate. e 2009.

Togo

Region	Western Africa
Currency	CFA Franc (XOF)
Surface area (square kilometres)	56 785
Population in 2010 (estimated, 000)	6 028
Population density in 2010 (per square kilometre)	106.2
Capital city and population in 2011 (000)	Lomé (1 524)
United Nations membership date	20 September 1960

Economic indicators

	2000	2005	2010
GDP: Gross domestic product (million current US$)	1 294	2 110	3 162
GDP: Growth rate at constant 2005 prices (annual %)	−1.0	1.2	3.7
GDP per capita (current US$)	270.0	390.2	524.6
GNI: Gross national income per capita (current US$)	264.1	383.6	523.7
Gross fixed capital formation (% of GDP)	15.1	16.5	17.7
Exchange rates (national currency per US$) [a]	704.95	556.04	490.91
Balance of payments, current account (million US$)	−140	−204	−177
CPI: Consumer price index (2000=100) [b]	100	114	134[c]
Industrial production index (2005=100)	100[d]	100	124
Agricultural production index (2004-2006=100)	90	97	120
Food production index (2004-2006=100)	85	99	127
Employment in industrial sector (% of employed)	...	6.8[ef]	...
Employment in agricultural sector (% of employed)	...	54.1[ef]	...
Labour force participation, adult female pop. (%)	76.0	79.6	80.3
Labour force participation, adult male pop. (%)	82.0	80.9	81.2
Tourist arrivals at national borders (000) [g]	60	81	150[h]
Energy production, primary (000 mt oil equivalent)	17	6	8[h]
Telephone subscribers, total (per 100 inhabitants)	1.9	9.2	44.2
Internet users (per 100 inhabitants)	1.9	4.0	5.4

Total trade

	Total trade (million US$)	Major trading partners		2010	
		(% of exports)		(% of imports)	
Exports	667.2	Benin	13.4	France	17.7
Imports	989.5	Burkina Faso	11.5	China	16.4
Balance	−322.3	Ghana	9.9	Belgium	6.8

Social indicators

Population growth rate (average annual %)	2010-2015	2.0
Urban population growth rate (average annual %)	2010-2015	3.3
Rural population growth rate (average annual %)	2010-2015	1.2
Urban population (%)	2011	38.0
Population aged 0-14 years (%)	2011	39.3
Population aged 60+ years (females and males, % of total)	2011	5.7/4.9
Sex ratio (males per 100 females)	2011	98.1
Life expectancy at birth (females and males, years)	2010-2015	59.4/56.2
Infant mortality rate (per 1 000 live births)	2010-2015	67.3
Fertility rate, total (live births per woman)	2010-2015	3.9
Contraceptive prevalence (ages 15-49, %)	2006-2010	16.8
International migrant stock (000 and % of total population) [i]	mid-2010	185.4/2.7
Refugees and others of concern to UNHCR	end-2010	14 231
Education: Government expenditure (% of GDP)	2005-2011	4.5
Education: Primary-secondary gross enrolment ratio (f/m per 100) [j]	2005-2011	69.0/91.8
Education: Female third-level students (% of total)	2005-2011	17.0[k]
Seats held by women in national parliaments (%)	2011	11.1

Environmental indicators

Threatened species	2011	56
Forested area (% of land area)	2009	5.6
CO$_2$ emission estimates (000 metric tons and metric tons per capita)	2008	1 418/0.2
Energy consumption per capita (kilograms oil equivalent)	2009	73.0
Rainfall in the capital city, total mean (millimetres)		877
Temperature in the capital city, mean °C (minimum and maximum)		23.1/30.7

a Official rate. **b** Lomé. **c** Series linked to former series. **d** 2004. **e** 2006. **f** Core Welfare Indicators Questionnaire (World Bank). **g** Arrivals of non-resident tourists in hotels and similar establishments. **h** 2009. **i** Includes refugees. **j** UNESCO estimate. **k** 1998.

Tonga

Region	Oceania-Polynesia
Currency	Pa'anga (TOP)
Surface area (square kilometres)	747
Population in 2010 (estimated, 000)	104
Population density in 2010 (per square kilometre)	139.3
Capital city and population in 2011 (000)	Nuku'alofa (25)
United Nations membership date	14 September 1999

Economic indicators	2000	2005	2010
GDP: Gross domestic product (million current US$)	189	259	369
GDP: Growth rate at constant 2005 prices (annual %)	3.1	−0.8	0.3
GDP per capita (current US$)	1 926.0	2 566.5	3 543.1
GNI: Gross national income per capita (current US$)	1 950.7	2 565.6	3 583.3
Gross fixed capital formation (% of GDP)	21.1	21.8	24.7
Exchange rates (national currency per US$)[a]	1.98	2.06	1.81
Balance of payments, current account (million US$)	−11[b]	−21	−54
CPI: Consumer price index (2000=100)[c]	100	160	203[d]
Agricultural production index (2004-2006=100)	97	99	109
Food production index (2004-2006=100)	97	99	109
Employment in industrial sector (% of employed)	30.6[e]	...	...
Employment in agricultural sector (% of employed)	31.8[e]	...	...
Labour force participation, adult female pop. (%)	49.2	53.3	53.6
Labour force participation, adult male pop. (%)	73.3	75.2	75.2
Tourist arrivals at national borders (000)[f]	35	42	45
Telephone subscribers, total (per 100 inhabitants)	10.1	43.2	82.0
Internet users (per 100 inhabitants)	2.4	4.9	12.0

Total trade		Major trading partners			2010
	(million US$)	(% of exports)			(% of imports)
Exports	8.3	China, Hong Kong SAR	43.4	New Zealand	31.9
Imports	158.8	New Zealand	16.9	Singapore	20.5
Balance	−150.5	United States	15.7	United States	13.0

Social indicators		
Population growth rate (average annual %)	2010-2015	0.4
Urban population growth rate (average annual %)	2010-2015	0.8
Rural population growth rate (average annual %)	2010-2015	0.3
Urban population (%)	2011	23.4
Population aged 0-14 years (%)	2011	37.4
Population aged 60+ years (females and males, % of total)	2011	9.1/6.9
Sex ratio (males per 100 females)	2011	100.4
Life expectancy at birth (females and males, years)	2010-2015	75.4/69.7
Infant mortality rate (per 1 000 live births)	2010-2015	20.6
Fertility rate, total (live births per woman)	2010-2015	3.8
International migrant stock (000 and % of total population)	mid-2010	0.9/0.8
Refugees and others of concern to UNHCR	end-2010	3
Education: Government expenditure (% of GDP)	2005-2011	3.9[g]
Education: Primary-secondary gross enrolment ratio (f/m per 100)	2005-2011	105.5/107.5
Education: Female third-level students (% of total)[h]	2005-2011	59.8[g]
Seats held by women in national parliaments (%)[i]	2011	3.6

Environmental indicators		
Threatened species	2011	59
Forested area (% of land area)	2009	12.5
CO$_2$ emission estimates (000 metric tons and metric tons per capita)	2008	176/1.7
Energy consumption per capita (kilograms oil equivalent)	2009	561.0[j]

a Official rate. **b** 2001. **c** Excludes rent. **d** 2009. **e** 2003. **f** Air arrivals. **g** 2004. **h** UNESCO estimate. **i** No women were elected in 2008, however one woman was appointed to the Cabinet. As cabinet ministers also sit in parliament, there is one woman out of a total of 32 members. **j** UNSD estimate.

Trinidad and Tobago

Region	Caribbean
Currency	Trinidad and Tobago Dollar (TTD)
Surface area (square kilometres)	5 130
Population in 2010 (estimated, 000)	1 341
Population density in 2010 (per square kilometre)	261.5
Capital city and population in 2011 (000)	Port of Spain (66)
United Nations membership date	18 September 1962

Economic indicators	2000	2005	2010
GDP: Gross domestic product (million current US$)	8 154	15 982	20 397
GDP: Growth rate at constant 2005 prices (annual %)	6.9	6.2	2.5
GDP per capita (current US$)	6 311.2	12 150.3	15 205.1
GNI: Gross national income per capita (current US$)	5 826.3	11 576.3	15 640.9
Gross fixed capital formation (% of GDP)	15.6	28.7	11.2
Exchange rates (national currency per US$) [a]	6.30	6.31	6.42
Balance of payments, current account (million US$)	544	3 594	1 614
CPI: Consumer price index (2000=100)	100	126	196
Industrial production index (2005=100) [b]	86[c]	100	159
Agricultural production index (2004-2006=100)	94	96	89
Food production index (2004-2006=100)	93	96	89
Unemployment (% of labour force)	8.3[d]	8.0	5.3[e]
Employment in industrial sector (% of employed)	28.0	31.0	32.2[f]
Employment in agricultural sector (% of employed)	7.2	4.3	3.8[f]
Labour force participation, adult female pop. (%)	47.2	54.2	54.6
Labour force participation, adult male pop. (%)	76.9	77.1	78.0
Tourist arrivals at national borders (000) [g]	399	463	413[e]
Energy production, primary (000 mt oil equivalent)	19 170	34 428	47 999[e]
Telephone subscribers, total (per 100 inhabitants)	37.1	94.8	163.1
Internet users (per 100 inhabitants)	7.7	29.0	48.5

Total trade	Major trading partners			2010
(million US$)	(% of exports)		(% of imports)	
Exports 10 981.7	United States	48.1	United States	28.0
Imports 6 479.6	Jamaica	6.5	Gabon	12.9
Balance 4 502.1	Barbados	3.4	Colombia	9.5

Social indicators		
Population growth rate (average annual %)	2010-2015	0.3
Urban population growth rate (average annual %)	2010-2015	2.2
Rural population growth rate (average annual %)	2010-2015	0.0
Urban population (%)	2011	13.7
Population aged 0-14 years (%)	2011	20.5
Population aged 60+ years (females and males, % of total)	2011	12.6/9.2
Sex ratio (males per 100 females)	2011	93.9
Life expectancy at birth (females and males, years)	2010-2015	73.8/66.9
Infant mortality rate (per 1 000 live births)	2010-2015	24.5
Fertility rate, total (live births per woman)	2010-2015	1.6
Contraceptive prevalence (ages 15-49, %)	2006-2010	42.5
International migrant stock (000 and % of total population)	mid-2010	34.4/2.6
Refugees and others of concern to UNHCR	end-2010	131
Education: Government expenditure (% of GDP) [h]	2005-2011	4.2[i]
Education: Primary-secondary gross enrolment ratio (f/m per 100) [h]	2005-2011	97.5/96.8
Education: Female third-level students (% of total) [h]	2005-2011	55.6
Seats held by women in national parliaments (%)	2011	28.6

Environmental indicators		
Threatened species	2011	53
Forested area (% of land area)	2009	44.3
CO$_2$ emission estimates (000 metric tons and metric tons per capita)	2008	49 731/37.3
Energy consumption per capita (kilograms oil equivalent)	2009	16 476.0
Rainfall in the capital city, total mean (millimetres)		1 408
Temperature in the capital city, mean °C (minimum and maximum)		22.0/31.9

a Official rate. b The indices are shown in terms of ISIC Rev. 3. c 2003. d 2004. e 2009. f 2008. g Air arrivals. h UNESCO estimate. i 2002.

Tunisia

Region	Northern Africa
Currency	Tunisian Dinar (TND)
Surface area (square kilometres)	163 610
Population in 2010 (estimated, 000)	10 481
Population density in 2010 (per square kilometre)	64.1
Capital city and population in 2011 (000)	Tunis (790)
United Nations membership date	12 November 1956

Economic indicators	2000	2005	2010
GDP: Gross domestic product (million current US$)	21 473	32 272	44 252
GDP: Growth rate at constant 2005 prices (annual %)	4.3	4.0	3.7
GDP per capita (current US$)	2 270.9	3 255.8	4 222.1
GNI: Gross national income per capita (current US$)	2 171.2	3 088.1	4 007.7
Gross fixed capital formation (% of GDP)	25.2	21.5	24.7
Exchange rates (national currency per US$) [a]	1.39	1.36	1.44
Balance of payments, current account (million US$)	−821	−299	−2 104
CPI: Consumer price index (2000=100)	100	114	139
Industrial production index (2005=100) [b]	95[c]	100	120
Agricultural production index (2004-2006=100)	84	101	103
Food production index (2004-2006=100)	84	101	103
Labour force participation, adult female pop. (%)	23.7	24.3	25.3
Labour force participation, adult male pop. (%)	71.6	68.3	69.7
Tourist arrivals at national borders (000) [d]	5 058	6 378	6 903
Energy production, primary (000 mt oil equivalent)	5 596	5 634	6 553[e]
Telephone subscribers, total (per 100 inhabitants)	11.4	70.0	118.3
Internet users (per 100 inhabitants)	2.8	9.7	36.8

Total trade		Major trading partners			2010
(million US$)		(% of exports)			(% of imports)
Exports	16 426.6	France	28.7	France	18.9
Imports	22 215.4	Italy	19.9	Italy	17.6
Balance	−5 788.8	Germany	8.5	Germany	7.6

Social indicators		
Population growth rate (average annual %)	2010-2015	1.0
Urban population growth rate (average annual %)	2010-2015	1.3
Rural population growth rate (average annual %)	2010-2015	0.4
Urban population (%)	2011	66.3
Population aged 0-14 years (%)	2011	23.3
Population aged 60+ years (females and males, % of total)	2011	10.5/9.8
Sex ratio (males per 100 females)	2011	99.9
Life expectancy at birth (females and males, years)	2010-2015	77.1/72.6
Infant mortality rate (per 1 000 live births)	2010-2015	18.4
Fertility rate, total (live births per woman)	2010-2015	1.9
Contraceptive prevalence (ages 15-49, %)	2006-2010	60.2
International migrant stock (000 and % of total population) [f]	mid-2010	33.6/0.3
Refugees and others of concern to UNHCR	end-2010	112
Education: Government expenditure (% of GDP)	2005-2011	6.3
Education: Primary-secondary gross enrolment ratio (f/m per 100) [g]	2005-2011	98.7/97.5
Education: Female third-level students (% of total)	2005-2011	59.5
Seats held by women in national parliaments (%)	2011	26.3

Environmental indicators		
Threatened species	2011	78
Forested area (% of land area)	2009	6.1
CO₂ emission estimates (000 metric tons and metric tons per capita)	2008	24 992/2.5
Energy consumption per capita (kilograms oil equivalent)	2009	789.0
Rainfall in the capital city, total mean (millimetres)		466
Temperature in the capital city, mean °C (minimum and maximum)		13.3/23.5

a Market rate. **b** The indices are shown in terms of ISIC Rev. 3. **c** 2003. **d** Excludes nationals residing abroad. **e** 2009. **f** Data refer to foreign citizens. **g** UNESCO estimate.

Turkey

Region	Western Asia/Southern Europe
Currency	Turkish Lira (TRY)
Surface area (square kilometres)	783 562
Population in 2010 (estimated, 000)	72 752
Population density in 2010 (per square kilometre)	92.9
Capital city and population in 2011 (000)	Ankara (4 194)
United Nations membership date	24 October 1945

Economic indicators

	2000	2005	2010
GDP: Gross domestic product (million current US$)	266 560	482 986	734 440
GDP: Growth rate at constant 2005 prices (annual %)	6.8	8.4	9.0
GDP per capita (current US$)	4 189.4	7 087.8	10 095.1
GNI: Gross national income per capita (current US$)	4 223.4	7 076.2	10 097.3
Gross fixed capital formation (% of GDP)	20.4	21.0	18.7
Exchange rates (national currency per US$) [a]	0.67	1.35	1.54
Balance of payments, current account (million US$)	−9 920	−22 197	−47 695
CPI: Consumer price index (2000=100)	100	329	500
Industrial production index (2005=100)		100	116
Agricultural production index (2004-2006=100)	...	100	106
Food production index (2004-2006=100)	95	101	109
Unemployment (% of labour force)	10.3[b]	10.6	11.9
Employment in industrial sector (% of employed)	24.0	24.8	26.2[c]
Employment in agricultural sector (% of employed)	36.0	29.5	23.7[c]
Labour force participation, adult female pop. (%)	26.6	23.8	28.1
Labour force participation, adult male pop. (%)	73.5	71.2	71.4
Tourist arrivals at national borders (000)	9 586	20 273	27 000
Energy production, primary (000 mt oil equivalent)	18 525	17 323	23 720[d]
Telephone subscribers, total (per 100 inhabitants)	54.3	91.9	107.2
Internet users (per 100 inhabitants)	3.8	15.5	39.8

Total trade

	(million US$)
Exports	113 979.5
Imports	185 541.0
Balance	−71 561.5

Major trading partners
2010

(% of exports)		(% of imports)	
Germany	10.1	Russian Federation	11.6
United Kingdom	6.4	Germany	9.5
Italy	5.7	China	9.3

Social indicators

Population growth rate (average annual %)	2010-2015	1.1
Urban population growth rate (average annual %)	2010-2015	2.4
Rural population growth rate (average annual %)	2010-2015	−2.3
Urban population (%)	2011	71.5
Population aged 0-14 years (%)	2011	26.0
Population aged 60+ years (females and males, % of total)	2011	10.1/8.5
Sex ratio (males per 100 females)	2011	99.5
Life expectancy at birth (females and males, years)	2010-2015	76.6/72.0
Infant mortality rate (per 1 000 live births)	2010-2015	19.9
Fertility rate, total (live births per woman)	2010-2015	2.0
Contraceptive prevalence (ages 15-49, %)	2006-2010	73.0
International migrant stock (000 and % of total population) [e]	mid-2010	1 411.0/1.9
Refugees and others of concern to UNHCR	end-2010	18 088
Education: Government expenditure (% of GDP)	2005-2011	3.6
Education: Primary-secondary gross enrolment ratio (f/m per 100)	2005-2011	85.4/90.2
Education: Female third-level students (% of total)	2005-2011	43.6
Seats held by women in national parliaments (%)	2011	14.2

Environmental indicators

Threatened species	2011	171
Forested area (% of land area)	2009	14.6
CO$_2$ emission estimates (000 metric tons and metric tons per capita)	2008	283 748/3.9
Energy consumption per capita (kilograms oil equivalent)	2009	1 254.0
Rainfall in the capital city, total mean (millimetres)		337
Temperature in the capital city, mean °C (minimum and maximum)		6.6/18.7

a Market rate. b 2004. c European Labour Force Survey (Eurostat). d 2009. e Includes refugees.

Turkmenistan

Region	South-central Asia		
Currency	Turkmen (new) Manat (TMT)[a]		
Surface area (square kilometres)	488 100		
Population in 2010 (estimated, 000)	5 042		
Population density in 2010 (per square kilometre)	10.3		
Capital city and population in 2011 (000)	Ashgabat (683)		
United Nations membership date	2 March 1992		

Economic indicators	2000	2005	2010
GDP: Gross domestic product (million current US$)	4 932	12 436	23 130
GDP: Growth rate at constant 2005 prices (annual %)	5.5	13.0	9.2
GDP per capita (current US$)	1 095.7	2 619.2	4 587.5
GNI: Gross national income per capita (current US$)	1 028.9	2 437.3	4 424.4
Gross fixed capital formation (% of GDP)	34.7	22.9	14.4
Exchange rates (national currency per US$)	5 200.00[b]	5 200.00[c]	2.85[c]
Agricultural production index (2004-2006=100)	71	107	124
Food production index (2004-2006=100)	69	106	125
Labour force participation, adult female pop. (%)	47.8	47.0	46.4
Labour force participation, adult male pop. (%)	74.0	74.8	75.7
Tourist arrivals at national borders (000)	3	12	8[d]
Energy production, primary (000 mt oil equivalent)	50 306	66 956	44 469[e]
Telephone subscribers, total (per 100 inhabitants)	8.3	10.6	73.7
Internet users (per 100 inhabitants)	0.1	1.0	2.2

Social indicators		
Population growth rate (average annual %)	2010-2015	1.2
Urban population growth rate (average annual %)	2010-2015	1.9
Rural population growth rate (average annual %)	2010-2015	0.6
Urban population (%)	2011	48.7
Population aged 0-14 years (%)	2011	28.8
Population aged 60+ years (females and males, % of total)	2011	7.1/5.3
Sex ratio (males per 100 females)	2011	96.9
Life expectancy at birth (females and males, years)	2010-2015	69.4/61.2
Infant mortality rate (per 1 000 live births)	2010-2015	48.8
Fertility rate, total (live births per woman)	2010-2015	2.3
Contraceptive prevalence (ages 15-49, %)	2006-2010	61.8[f]
International migrant stock (000 and % of total population)	mid-2010	207.7/4.0
Refugees and others of concern to UNHCR	end-2010	20 062
Seats held by women in national parliaments (%)	2011	16.8

Environmental indicators		
Threatened species	2011	47
Forested area (% of land area)	2009	8.8
CO_2 emission estimates (000 metric tons and metric tons per capita)	2008	47 801/9.5
Energy consumption per capita (kilograms oil equivalent)	2009	4 043.0
Rainfall in the capital city, total mean (millimetres)		227
Temperature in the capital city, mean °C (minimum and maximum)		10.4/23.2

a Beginning 1 January 2009, 1 new Manat = 5000 old Manat. **b** Official rate. **c** UN operational exchange rate. **d** 2007. **e** 2009. **f** 2000.

Tuvalu

Region	Oceania-Polynesia
Currency	Australian Dollar (AUD)
Surface area (square kilometres)	26
Population in 2010 (estimated, 000)	10
Population density in 2010 (per square kilometre)	378.0
Capital city and population in 2011 (000)	Funafuti (5)
United Nations membership date	5 September 2000

Economic indicators	2000	2005	2010
GDP: Gross domestic product (million current US$)	12	22	31
GDP: Growth rate at constant 2005 prices (annual %)	13.4	–4.1	1.6
GDP per capita (current US$)	1 301.9	2 288.7	3 187.2
GNI: Gross national income per capita (current US$)	2 090.0	3 612.8	4 606.8
Gross fixed capital formation (% of GDP)	11.7	73.4	77.4
Exchange rates (national currency per US$) [a]	1.80	1.37	0.99
CPI: Consumer price index (2000=100) [b]	100	117	122[c]
Agricultural production index (2004-2006=100)	94	101	113
Food production index (2004-2006=100)	94	101	113
Tourist arrivals at national borders (000)	1	1	2
Telephone subscribers, total (per 100 inhabitants)	7.0[d]	22.6	41.9
Internet users (per 100 inhabitants)	5.2	10.0[c]	25.0

Total trade		Major trading partners	2010
	(million US$)	(% of exports)	(% of imports)[e]
Imports	26.5[e]	Fiji	23.8
		Australia	18.1
		New Zealand	17.4

Social indicators		
Population growth rate (average annual %)	2010-2015	0.2
Urban population growth rate (average annual %)	2010-2015	1.0
Rural population growth rate (average annual %)	2010-2015	–0.6
Urban population (%)	2011	50.6
Population aged 0-14 years (%) [f]	2011	31.7
Population aged 60+ years (females and males, % of total) [f]	2011	10.1/7.0
Sex ratio (males per 100 females) [f]	2011	99.2
Life expectancy at birth (females and males, years) [g]	2010-2015	65.1/61.7[h]
Infant mortality rate (per 1 000 live births) [g]	2010-2015	17.3[i]
Fertility rate, total (live births per woman) [f]	2010-2015	3.7[j]
Contraceptive prevalence (ages 15-49, %)	2006-2010	30.5
International migrant stock (000 and % of total population) [k]	mid-2010	0.2/1.5
Education: Primary-secondary gross enrolment ratio (f/m per 100) [l]	2005-2011	96.9/86.3[m]
Seats held by women in national parliaments (%)	2011	6.7

Environmental indicators		
Threatened species	2011	86
Forested area (% of land area)	2009	33.3

a UN operational exchange rate. **b** Funafuti. **c** 2007. **d** Main telephone lines only. **e** 2008. **f** Data compiled by the Secretariat of the Pacific Community Demography Programme. **g** Data compiled by the United Nations Demographic Yearbook system. **h** 1997-2002. **i** 2006-2008. **j** 2002-2007. **k** Data refer to foreign citizens. **l** National estimate. **m** 2001.

Uganda

Region	Eastern Africa
Currency	Ugandan Shilling (UGX)
Surface area (square kilometres)	241 550
Population in 2010 (estimated, 000)	33 425
Population density in 2010 (per square kilometre)	138.4
Capital city and population in 2011 (000)	Kampala (1 659)
United Nations membership date	25 October 1962

Economic indicators	2000	2005	2010
GDP: Gross domestic product (million current US$)	6 341	10 040	17 015
GDP: Growth rate at constant 2005 prices (annual %)	4.4	10.0	2.5
GDP per capita (current US$)	261.9	353.1	509.1
GNI: Gross national income per capita (current US$)	257.5	344.3	498.8
Gross fixed capital formation (% of GDP)	17.8	21.3	21.4
Exchange rates (national currency per US$) [a]	1 766.68	1 816.86	2 308.30
Balance of payments, current account (million US$)	−825	−26	−1 740
CPI: Consumer price index (2000=100)	100	124	186
Agricultural production index (2004-2006=100)	90	100	108
Food production index (2004-2006=100)	90	100	108
Employment in industrial sector (% of employed) [bcd]	6.5[e]	4.5	6.0[f]
Employment in agricultural sector (% of employed) [bc]	65.5[e]	71.6	65.6[f]
Labour force participation, adult female pop. (%)	80.7	77.1	76.2
Labour force participation, adult male pop. (%)	82.6	80.0	79.6
Tourist arrivals at national borders (000)	193	468	946
Energy production, primary (000 mt oil equivalent)	136	156	110[f]
Telephone subscribers, total (per 100 inhabitants)	0.8	4.9	39.4
Internet users (per 100 inhabitants)	0.2	1.7	12.5

Total trade		Major trading partners			2010
	(million US$)	(% of exports)			(% of imports)
Exports	1 618.6	Sudan	12.9	India	14.7
Imports	4 664.3	Kenya	11.8	Kenya	11.0
Balance	−3 045.7	Dem. Rep. of Congo	11.4	China	8.9

Social indicators		
Population growth rate (average annual %)	2010-2015	3.1
Urban population growth rate (average annual %)	2010-2015	5.7
Rural population growth rate (average annual %)	2010-2015	2.6
Urban population (%)	2011	15.6
Population aged 0-14 years (%)	2011	48.4
Population aged 60+ years (females and males, % of total)	2011	4.2/3.5
Sex ratio (males per 100 females)	2011	100.0
Life expectancy at birth (females and males, years)	2010-2015	55.4/53.8
Infant mortality rate (per 1 000 live births)	2010-2015	72.3
Fertility rate, total (live births per woman)	2010-2015	5.9
Contraceptive prevalence (ages 15-49, %)	2006-2010	23.7
International migrant stock (000 and % of total population) [g]	mid-2010	646.6/1.9
Refugees and others of concern to UNHCR	end-2010	585 253
Education: Government expenditure (% of GDP)	2005-2011	3.2
Education: Primary-secondary gross enrolment ratio (f/m per 100) [h]	2005-2011	83.1/84.4
Education: Female third-level students (% of total)	2005-2011	44.3
Seats held by women in national parliaments (%)	2011	34.9

Environmental indicators		
Threatened species	2011	167
Forested area (% of land area)	2009	15.4
CO$_2$ emission estimates (000 metric tons and metric tons per capita)	2008	3 745/0.1
Energy consumption per capita (kilograms oil equivalent)	2009	36.0
Rainfall in the capital city, total mean (millimetres)		1 180
Temperature in the capital city, mean °C (minimum and maximum)		17.3/26.7

a Principal rate. **b** May of the current year to April of the following year. **c** Age group 14 to 64 years. **d** Manufacturing only. **e** 2002. **f** 2009. **g** Includes refugees. **h** UNESCO estimate.

Ukraine

Region	Eastern Europe
Currency	Hryvnia (UAH)
Surface area (square kilometres)	603 500
Population in 2010 (estimated, 000)	45 448
Population density in 2010 (per square kilometre)	75.3
Capital city and population in 2011 (000)	Kiev (2 829)
United Nations membership date	24 October 1945

Economic indicators	2000	2005	2010
GDP: Gross domestic product (million current US$)	31 262	86 142	137 936
GDP: Growth rate at constant 2005 prices (annual %)	5.9	2.7	4.2
GDP per capita (current US$)	639.4	1 835.8	3 035.0
GNI: Gross national income per capita (current US$)	620.1	1 814.8	2 997.3
Gross fixed capital formation (% of GDP)	19.7	22.0	19.1
Exchange rates (national currency per US$) [a]	5.43	5.05	7.96
Balance of payments, current account (million US$)	1 481	2 531	−3 018
CPI: Consumer price index (2000=100)	100	147	262[b]
Industrial production index (2005=100) [c]	87[d]	100	94
Agricultural production index (2004-2006=100)	85	100	107
Food production index (2004-2006=100)	85	100	107
Unemployment (% of labour force) [e]	8.6[f]	7.2	8.1
Employment in industrial sector (% of employed)	20.8[ghi]	24.2[e]	...
Employment in agricultural sector (% of employed)	23.4[gh]	19.4[e]	15.8[ei]
Labour force participation, adult female pop. (%)	51.8	51.7	53.0
Labour force participation, adult male pop. (%)	64.7	65.0	66.2
Tourist arrivals at national borders (000)	6 431	17 631	21 203
Energy production, primary (000 mt oil equivalent)	64 676	67 304	61 497[b]
Telephone subscribers, total (per 100 inhabitants)	23.0	88.8	147.1
Internet users (per 100 inhabitants)	0.7	3.8	45.0

Total trade		Major trading partners			2010
	(million US$)	(% of exports)			(% of imports)
Exports	51 430.3	Russian Federation	26.1	Russian Federation	36.5
Imports	60 737.1	Turkey	5.9	China	7.7
Balance	−9 306.8	Italy	4.7	Germany	7.6

Social indicators		
Population growth rate (average annual %)	2010-2015	−0.6
Urban population growth rate (average annual %)	2010-2015	−0.3
Rural population growth rate (average annual %)	2010-2015	−1.2
Urban population (%)	2011	68.9
Population aged 0-14 years (%)	2011	14.4
Population aged 60+ years (females and males, % of total)	2011	25.1/16.0
Sex ratio (males per 100 females)	2011	85.2
Life expectancy at birth (females and males, years)	2010-2015	74.6/63.5
Infant mortality rate (per 1 000 live births)	2010-2015	11.8
Fertility rate, total (live births per woman)	2010-2015	1.5
Contraceptive prevalence (ages 15-49, %)	2006-2010	66.7
International migrant stock (000 and % of total population)	mid-2010	5 257.5/11.6
Refugees and others of concern to UNHCR	end-2010	46 356
Education: Government expenditure (% of GDP)	2005-2011	2.6
Education: Primary-secondary gross enrolment ratio (f/m per 100) [k]	2005-2011	96.1/97.4
Education: Female third-level students (% of total)	2005-2011	54.5
Deaths by assault (females and males, per 100 000)	2005-2008	5.1/13.4
Seats held by women in national parliaments (%)	2011	8.0

Environmental indicators		
Threatened species	2011	80
Forested area (% of land area)	2009	16.7
CO_2 emission estimates (000 metric tons and metric tons per capita)	2008	323 267/7.0
Energy consumption per capita (kilograms oil equivalent)	2009	2 236.0
Rainfall in the capital city, total mean (millimetres)		648
Temperature in the capital city, mean °C (minimum and maximum)		4.3/11.9

a Official rate. b 2009. c The indices are shown in terms of ISIC Rev. 3. d 2003. e Age group 15 to 70 years. f 2004. g Official estimates. h Excludes self-employed persons. i Excludes electricity, gas and water. j 2008. k National estimate.

United Arab Emirates

Region	Western Asia
Currency	United Arab Emirates Dirham (AED)
Surface area (square kilometres)	83 600
Population in 2010 (estimated, 000)	7 512
Population density in 2010 (per square kilometre)	89.9
Capital city and population in 2011 (000)	Abu Dhabi (942)
United Nations membership date	9 December 1971

Economic indicators	2000	2005	2010
GDP: Gross domestic product (million current US$)	104 337	180 617	297 648
GDP: Growth rate at constant 2005 prices (annual %)	12.2	4.9	1.4
GDP per capita (current US$)	34 395.2	44 384.8	39 624.7
GNI: Gross national income per capita (current US$)	35 085.8	45 094.0	40 367.4
Gross fixed capital formation (% of GDP)	22.2	18.4	23.8
Exchange rates (national currency per US$) [a]	3.67	3.67	3.67
CPI: Consumer price index (2000=100)	100	122	166[b]
Agricultural production index (2004-2006=100)	192	105	101
Food production index (2004-2006=100)	193	105	101
Employment in industrial sector (% of employed)	33.4[c]	39.8[de]	24.3[bf]
Employment in agricultural sector (% of employed)	7.9[c]	4.9[de]	4.2[bf]
Labour force participation, adult female pop. (%)	33.8	37.7	43.7
Labour force participation, adult male pop. (%)	91.9	92.4	92.0
Tourist arrivals at national borders (000) [gh]	3 907	7 126	...
Energy production, primary (000 mt oil equivalent)	160 741	179 085	173 711[i]
Telephone subscribers, total (per 100 inhabitants)	80.7	141.8	165.2
Internet users (per 100 inhabitants)	23.6	40.0	78.0

Total trade		Major trading partners	2010
	(million US$)	(% of exports)	(% of imports)
Exports	198 362.0		
Imports	180 726.0		
Balance	17 636.0		

Social indicators		
Population growth rate (average annual %)	2010-2015	2.2
Urban population growth rate (average annual %)	2010-2015	2.5
Rural population growth rate (average annual %)	2010-2015	0.3
Urban population (%)	2011	84.4
Population aged 0-14 years (%)	2011	16.9
Population aged 60+ years (females and males, % of total)	2011	1.0/1.3
Sex ratio (males per 100 females)	2011	227.5
Life expectancy at birth (females and males, years)	2010-2015	78.0/76.0
Infant mortality rate (per 1 000 live births)	2010-2015	6.6
Fertility rate, total (live births per woman)	2010-2015	1.7
Contraceptive prevalence (ages 15-49, %)	2006-2010	27.5[j]
International migrant stock (000 and % of total population) [kl]	mid-2010	3 293.3/70.0
Refugees and others of concern to UNHCR	end-2010	624
Education: Government expenditure (% of GDP)	2005-2011	1.0
Education: Primary-secondary gross enrolment ratio (f/m per 100)	2005-2011	98.8/96.6
Education: Female third-level students (% of total)	2005-2011	59.7
Seats held by women in national parliaments (%)	2011	17.5

Environmental indicators		
Threatened species	2011	48
Forested area (% of land area)	2009	3.8
CO$_2$ emission estimates (000 metric tons and metric tons per capita)	2008	154 940/34.6
Energy consumption per capita (kilograms oil equivalent)	2009	9 481.0
Rainfall in the capital city, total mean (millimetres)		80
Temperature in the capital city, mean °C (minimum and maximum)		20.8/34.4

a Official rate. **b** 2008. **c** Official estimates. **d** December. **e** Population census. **f** February. **g** Arrivals of non-resident tourists in hotels only. **h** Includes domestic tourism and nationals residing abroad. **i** 2009. **j** 1995. **k** Data refer to foreign citizens. **l** Includes refugees.

United Kingdom

Region	Northern Europe
Currency	Pound Sterling (GBP)
Surface area (square kilometres)	242 900 [a]
Population in 2010 (estimated, 000)	62 036
Population density in 2010 (per square kilometre)	255.4 [a]
Capital city and population in 2011 (000)	London (9 005)
United Nations membership date	24 October 1945

Economic indicators	2000	2005	2010
GDP: Gross domestic product (million current US$)	1 477 130	2 280 540	2 253 550
GDP: Growth rate at constant 2005 prices (annual %)	4.5	2.1	1.8
GDP per capita (current US$)	25 089.7	37 881.0	36 326.8
GNI: Gross national income per capita (current US$)	25 043.5	38 516.1	36 847.0
Gross fixed capital formation (% of GDP)	17.1	16.7	14.9
Exchange rates (national currency per US$) [b]	0.67	0.58	0.64
Balance of payments, current account (million US$)	−38 800	−59 410	−71 600
CPI: Consumer price index (2000=100)	100	113	131
Industrial production index (2005=100) [c]	100 [d]	100	90
Agricultural production index (2004-2006=100)	103	100	100
Food production index (2004-2006=100)	103	100	100
Unemployment (% of labour force) [e]	4.7 [f]	4.8	7.8
Employment in industrial sector (% of employed) [e]	25.1 [g]	22.2 [g]	19.1 [h]
Employment in agricultural sector (% of employed) [e]	1.5 [g]	1.3 [g]	1.2 [h]
Labour force participation, adult female pop. (%)	54.0	55.0	55.5
Labour force participation, adult male pop. (%)	70.4	69.3	68.6
Tourist arrivals at national borders (000)	23 212	28 039	28 295
Energy production, primary (000 mt oil equivalent)	263 242	194 374	147 423 [i]
Telephone subscribers, total (per 100 inhabitants)	133.6	165.3	184.6
Internet users (per 100 inhabitants)	26.8	70.0	85.0

Total trade		Major trading partners			2010
	(million US$)	(% of exports)			(% of imports)
Exports	405 868.9	United States	14.3	Germany	12.7
Imports	562 501.1	Germany	10.9	China	9.3
Balance	−156 632.2	Netherlands	7.8	United States	8.9

Social indicators		
Population growth rate (average annual %)	2010-2015	0.6
Urban population growth rate (average annual %)	2010-2015	0.8
Rural population growth rate (average annual %)	2010-2015	−<
Urban population (%)	2011	79.6
Population aged 0-14 years (%)	2011	17.4
Population aged 60+ years (females and males, % of total)	2011	24.6/21.1
Sex ratio (males per 100 females)	2011	97.0
Life expectancy at birth (females and males, years)	2010-2015	82.4/78.3
Infant mortality rate (per 1 000 live births)	2010-2015	4.7
Fertility rate, total (live births per woman)	2010-2015	1.9
Contraceptive prevalence (ages 15-49, %) [j]	2006-2010	84.0
International migrant stock (000 and % of total population)	mid-2010	6 451.7/10.4
Refugees and others of concern to UNHCR	end-2010	253 235
Education: Government expenditure (% of GDP)	2005-2011	4.5
Education: Primary-secondary gross enrolment ratio (f/m per 100)	2005-2011	104.3/103.2
Education: Female third-level students (% of total)	2005-2011	57.0
Deaths by assault (females and males, per 100 000)	2005-2008	</0.5
Seats held by women in national parliaments (%)	2011	22.0

Environmental indicators		
Threatened species	2011	79
Forested area (% of land area)	2009	11.9
CO$_2$ emission estimates (000 metric tons and metric tons per capita)	2008	522 428/8.5
Energy consumption per capita (kilograms oil equivalent)	2009	3 036.0
Rainfall in the capital city, total mean (millimetres)		611
Temperature in the capital city, mean °C (minimum and maximum)		7.5/14.4

a Excludes Channel Islands and Isle of Man. b Market rate. c The indices are shown in terms of ISIC Rev. 3. d 2003. e Age group 16 years and over. f 2004. g Second quarter. h European Labour Force Survey (Eurostat). i 2009. j Age group 16 to 49 years.

United Republic of Tanzania

Region	Eastern Africa
Currency	Tanzanian Shilling (TZS)
Surface area (square kilometres)	945 087
Population in 2010 (estimated, 000)	44 841
Population density in 2010 (per square kilometre)	47.5
Capital city and population in 2011 (000)	Dodoma (226)
United Nations membership date	14 December 1961

Economic indicators	2000	2005	2010
GDP: Gross domestic product (million current US$) [a]	10 186	14 142	22 502
GDP: Growth rate at constant 2005 prices (annual %) [a]	4.9	7.4	6.8
GDP per capita (current US$) [a]	307.5	374.5	516.2
GNI: Gross national income per capita (current US$) [a]	305.0	369.6	514.4
Gross fixed capital formation (% of GDP) [a]	16.4	24.7	27.9
Exchange rates (national currency per US$) [b]	803.26	1 165.51	1 455.15
Balance of payments, current account (million US$)	−428	−1 105	−1 978
CPI: Consumer price index (2000=100)	100	127	181[c]
Agricultural production index (2004-2006=100)	67	100	110
Food production index (2004-2006=100)	67	100	110
Employment in industrial sector (% of employed) [a]	2.6[def]	4.3[g]	...
Employment in agricultural sector (% of employed) [a]	82.1[def]	76.5[g]	...
Labour force participation, adult female pop. (%)	87.0	88.6	88.3
Labour force participation, adult male pop. (%)	90.8	90.5	90.3
Tourist arrivals at national borders (000)	459	590	783
Energy production, primary (000 mt oil equivalent)	240	534	909[c]
Telephone subscribers, total (per 100 inhabitants)	0.8	8.0	47.2
Internet users (per 100 inhabitants)	0.1	4.3	11.0

Total trade		Major trading partners			2010
	(million US$)	(% of exports)			(% of imports)
Exports	4 050.5	Switzerland	17.5	India	11.2
Imports	8 012.9	China	16.2	China	10.9
Balance	−3 962.4	South Africa	10.7	South Africa	9.6

Social indicators		
Population growth rate (average annual %)	2010-2015	3.1
Urban population growth rate (average annual %)	2010-2015	4.8
Rural population growth rate (average annual %)	2010-2015	2.4
Urban population (%)	2011	26.7
Population aged 0-14 years (%)	2011	44.8
Population aged 60+ years (females and males, % of total)	2011	5.4/4.4
Sex ratio (males per 100 females)	2011	99.9
Life expectancy at birth (females and males, years)	2010-2015	60.3/58.2
Infant mortality rate (per 1 000 live births)	2010-2015	53.7
Fertility rate, total (live births per woman)	2010-2015	5.5
Contraceptive prevalence (ages 15-49, %)	2006-2010	34.4
International migrant stock (000 and % of total population) [h]	mid-2010	659.2/1.5
Refugees and others of concern to UNHCR	end-2010	272 789
Education: Government expenditure (% of GDP)	2005-2011	6.2
Education: Female third-level students (% of total)	2005-2011	45.1
Seats held by women in national parliaments (%)	2011	36.0

Environmental indicators		
Threatened species	2011	695
Forested area (% of land area)	2009	38.2
CO_2 emission estimates (000 metric tons and metric tons per capita)	2008	6 460/0.2
Energy consumption per capita (kilograms oil equivalent)	2009	56.0
Rainfall in the capital city, total mean (millimetres)		484
Temperature in the capital city, mean °C (minimum and maximum)		16.6/28.6

a Excludes Zanzibar. **b** Official rate. **c** 2009. **d** 2001. **e** March. **f** Age group 10 years and over. **g** 2006. **h** Includes refugees.

United States of America

Region	Northern America
Currency	U.S. Dollar (USD)
Surface area (square kilometres)	9 629 091
Population in 2010 (estimated, 000)	310 384
Population density in 2010 (per square kilometre)	32.2
Capital city and population in 2011 (000)	Washington, D.C. (4 705)
United Nations membership date	24 October 1945

Economic indicators	2000	2005	2010
GDP: Gross domestic product (million current US$)	9 898 800	12 564 300	14 447 100
GDP: Growth rate at constant 2005 prices (annual %)	4.2	3.1	3.0
GDP per capita (current US$)	35 040.5	42 329.7	46 545.9
GNI: Gross national income per capita (current US$)	35 648.3	42 977.2	47 153.2
Gross fixed capital formation (% of GDP)	20.0	19.5	14.7
Balance of payments, current account (million US$)	–416 340	–745 780	–470 900
CPI: Consumer price index (2000=100)[a]	100	113	127
Industrial production index (2005=100)	95[b]	100	96
Agricultural production index (2004-2006=100)	96	100	105
Food production index (2004-2006=100)	96	100	106
Unemployment (% of labour force)[c]	5.5[d]	5.1	9.6
Employment in industrial sector (% of employed)[c]	23.2[ef]	20.6	16.7[g]
Employment in agricultural sector (% of employed)[c]	2.6[f]	1.6	1.6
Labour force participation, adult female pop. (%)	59.0	58.3	57.5
Labour force participation, adult male pop. (%)	74.1	72.4	70.2
Tourist arrivals at national borders (000)[h]	51 238	49 206	59 791
Energy production, primary (000 mt oil equivalent)[ijk]	1 492 235	1 455 431	1 524 724[l]
Telephone subscribers, total (per 100 inhabitants)	106.9	127.6	138.6
Internet users (per 100 inhabitants)	43.1	68.0	74.0

Total trade		Major trading partners			2010
	(million US$)[i]	(% of exports)[i]			(% of imports)[i]
Exports	1 277 109.0	Canada	19.4	China	19.5
Imports	1 966 497.0	Mexico	12.8	Canada	14.2
Balance	–689 387.5	China	7.2	Mexico	11.8

Social indicators

Population growth rate (average annual %)	2010-2015	0.9
Urban population growth rate (average annual %)	2010-2015	1.1
Rural population growth rate (average annual %)	2010-2015	–0.6
Urban population (%)	2011	82.4
Population aged 0-14 years (%)	2011	20.1
Population aged 60+ years (females and males, % of total)	2011	20.6/16.9
Sex ratio (males per 100 females)	2011	97.5
Life expectancy at birth (females and males, years)	2010-2015	81.3/76.2
Infant mortality rate (per 1 000 live births)	2010-2015	6.5
Fertility rate, total (live births per woman)	2010-2015	2.1
Contraceptive prevalence (ages 15-49, %)[m]	2006-2010	78.6
International migrant stock (000 and % of total population)[n]	mid-2010	42 813.3/13.5
Refugees and others of concern to UNHCR	end-2010	270 859
Education: Government expenditure (% of GDP)	2005-2011	5.5
Education: Primary-secondary gross enrolment ratio (f/m per 100)	2005-2011	98.8/98.7
Education: Female third-level students (% of total)	2005-2011	57.1
Deaths by assault (females and males, per 100 000)	2005-2008	2.5/9.7
Seats held by women in national parliaments (%)	2011	16.8

Environmental indicators

Threatened species	2011	1 157
Forested area (% of land area)	2009	33.2
CO$_2$ emission estimates (000 metric tons and metric tons per capita)[ijk]	2008	5 667 853/18.0
Energy consumption per capita (kilograms oil equivalent)[ijk]	2009	6 486.0
Rainfall in the capital city, total mean (millimetres)		902
Temperature in the capital city, mean °C (minimum and maximum)		10.4/20.4

a All urban consumers. **b** 2003. **c** Age group 16 years and over. **d** 2004. **e** Includes sanitary services. **f** Estimates based on 1990 population census results. **g** Excludes electricity, gas, steam and air conditioning supply and water supply. **h** Includes Mexicans staying one or more nights in the US. **i** Includes Puerto Rico and US Virgin Islands. **j** Includes American Samoa, Guam and Northern Mariana Islands. **k** Includes Johnston Atoll, Midway Islands and Wake Island. **l** 2009. **m** Age group 15 to 44 years. **n** Estimates include persons born in other United States territories and American citizens at birth who were born abroad and reside in the United States.

United States Virgin Islands

Region	Caribbean		
Currency	U.S. Dollar (USD)		
Surface area (square kilometres)	347		
Population in 2010 (estimated, 000)	109		
Population density in 2010 (per square kilometre)	314.3		
Capital city and population in 2011 (000)	Charlotte Amalie (60)		

Economic indicators	2000	2005	2010
Exchange rates (national currency per US$)[a]	1.00	1.00	1.00
Agricultural production index (2004-2006=100)	94	98	118
Food production index (2004-2006=100)	94	98	118
Labour force participation, adult female pop. (%)	52.9	54.3	53.8
Labour force participation, adult male pop. (%)	77.3	75.4	72.5
Tourist arrivals at national borders (000)	546	593	590
Telephone subscribers, total (per 100 inhabitants)	95.2	139.0	69.5[b]
Internet users (per 100 inhabitants)	13.8	27.3	27.4[c]

Social indicators		
Population growth rate (average annual %)	2010-2015	-0.3
Urban population growth rate (average annual %)	2010-2015	-0.1
Rural population growth rate (average annual %)	2010-2015	-3.6
Urban population (%)	2011	95.5
Population aged 0-14 years (%)	2011	19.9
Population aged 60+ years (females and males, % of total)	2011	22.9/20.8
Sex ratio (males per 100 females)	2011	89.9
Life expectancy at birth (females and males, years)	2010-2015	82.6/76.5
Infant mortality rate (per 1 000 live births)	2010-2015	10.0
Fertility rate, total (live births per woman)	2010-2015	1.9
Contraceptive prevalence (ages 15-49, %)[d]	2006-2010	78.4[e]
International migrant stock (000 and % of total population)	mid-2010	61.8/56.5

Environmental indicators		
Threatened species	2011	36
Forested area (% of land area)	2009	58.3

a UN operational exchange rate. **b** Main telephone lines only. **c** 2009. **d** Age group 18 to 44 years. **e** 2002.

Uruguay

Region	South America
Currency	Uruguayan Peso (UYU)
Surface area (square kilometres)	176 215
Population in 2010 (estimated, 000)	3 369
Population density in 2010 (per square kilometre)	19.1
Capital city and population in 2011 (000)	Montevideo (1 672)
United Nations membership date	18 December 1945

Economic indicators	2000	2005	2010
GDP: Gross domestic product (million current US$)	22 823	17 363	40 265
GDP: Growth rate at constant 2005 prices (annual %)	−1.9	7.5	8.5
GDP per capita (current US$)	6 876.4	5 225.8	11 952.4
GNI: Gross national income per capita (current US$)	6 856.5	5 075.4	11 624.7
Gross fixed capital formation (% of GDP)	14.3	16.6	18.8
Exchange rates (national currency per US$) [a]	12.52	24.10	20.09
Balance of payments, current account (million US$)	−566	24	−160
CPI: Consumer price index (2000=100) [b]	100	162	230
Agricultural production index (2004-2006=100)	84	101	116
Food production index (2004-2006=100)	83	101	117
Unemployment (% of labour force) [cd]	...	10.9[e]	6.8
Employment in industrial sector (% of employed) [cdf]	24.7	21.9	...
Employment in agricultural sector (% of employed) [cdf]	4.1	4.6[g]	...
Labour force participation, adult female pop. (%)	52.1	52.8	55.4
Labour force participation, adult male pop. (%)	75.8	74.1	76.6
Tourist arrivals at national borders (000)	1 968	1 808	2 353
Energy production, primary (000 mt oil equivalent)	606	575	455[h]
Telephone subscribers, total (per 100 inhabitants)	40.4	65.0	160.3
Internet users (per 100 inhabitants)	10.5	20.1	47.7

Total trade

Total trade	(million US$)[h]	Major trading partners		2010
		(% of exports)[h]		(% of imports)[h]
Exports	5 385.5	Brazil	20.4	Argentina 23.6
Imports	6 906.7			Brazil 21.1
Balance	−1 521.2			China 11.9

Social indicators

Population growth rate (average annual %)	2010-2015	0.4
Urban population growth rate (average annual %)	2010-2015	0.5
Rural population growth rate (average annual %)	2010-2015	−0.9
Urban population (%)	2011	92.6
Population aged 0-14 years (%)	2011	22.3
Population aged 60+ years (females and males, % of total)	2011	21.0/15.6
Sex ratio (males per 100 females)	2011	93.3
Life expectancy at birth (females and males, years)	2010-2015	80.7/73.7
Infant mortality rate (per 1 000 live births)	2010-2015	11.8
Fertility rate, total (live births per woman)	2010-2015	2.0
Contraceptive prevalence (ages 15-49, %) [i]	2006-2010	77.0[j]
International migrant stock (000 and % of total population)	mid-2010	79.9/2.4
Refugees and others of concern to UNHCR	end-2010	229
Education: Government expenditure (% of GDP)	2005-2011	2.9
Education: Primary-secondary gross enrolment ratio (f/m per 100)	2005-2011	102.7/98.8
Education: Female third-level students (% of total)	2005-2011	62.7
Deaths by assault (females and males, per 100 000) [i]	2005-2008	2.6/6.6
Seats held by women in national parliaments (%)	2011	15.2

Environmental indicators

Threatened species	2011	82
Forested area (% of land area)	2009	9.7
CO$_2$ emission estimates (000 metric tons and metric tons per capita)	2008	8 321/2.5
Energy consumption per capita (kilograms oil equivalent)	2009	907.0
Rainfall in the capital city, total mean (millimetres)		1 101
Temperature in the capital city, mean °C (minimum and maximum)		12.4/21.4

a Market rate. b Montevideo. c Urban areas. d Age group 14 years and over. e 2006. f Excludes conscripts.
g Includes mining and quarrying. h 2009. i Age group 15 to 50 years. j 2004.

Uzbekistan

Region	South-central Asia
Currency	Uzbekistan Sum (UZS)
Surface area (square kilometres)	447 400
Population in 2010 (estimated, 000)	27 445
Population density in 2010 (per square kilometre)	61.3
Capital city and population in 2011 (000)	Tashkent (2 227)
United Nations membership date	2 March 1992

Economic indicators	2000	2005	2010
GDP: Gross domestic product (million current US$)	13 759	14 396	39 173
GDP: Growth rate at constant 2005 prices (annual %)	4.0	7.0	8.5
GDP per capita (current US$)	555.4	554.8	1 427.3
GNI: Gross national income per capita (current US$)	546.5	553.9	1 446.1
Gross fixed capital formation (% of GDP)	24.0	22.0	23.9
Exchange rates (national currency per US$) [a]	690.00	1 177.00	1 640.00
Agricultural production index (2004-2006=100)	77	100	127
Food production index (2004-2006=100)	76	99	135
Labour force participation, adult female pop. (%)	47.5	47.5	47.6
Labour force participation, adult male pop. (%)	72.1	72.5	74.4
Tourist arrivals at national borders (000)	302	242	975
Energy production, primary (000 mt oil equivalent)	60 069	61 736	66 545[b]
Telephone subscribers, total (per 100 inhabitants)	6.9	9.7	83.1
Internet users (per 100 inhabitants)	0.5	3.3	20.0

Social indicators		
Population growth rate (average annual %)	2010-2015	1.1
Urban population growth rate (average annual %)	2010-2015	1.3
Rural population growth rate (average annual %)	2010-2015	1.1
Urban population (%)	2011	36.2
Population aged 0-14 years (%)	2011	28.9
Population aged 60+ years (females and males, % of total)	2011	7.0/5.6
Sex ratio (males per 100 females)	2011	98.8
Life expectancy at birth (females and males, years)	2010-2015	71.9/65.7
Infant mortality rate (per 1 000 live births)	2010-2015	44.5
Fertility rate, total (live births per woman)	2010-2015	2.3
Contraceptive prevalence (ages 15-49, %)	2006-2010	64.9
International migrant stock (000 and % of total population)	mid-2010	1 175.9/4.2
Refugees and others of concern to UNHCR	end-2010	311
Education: Primary-secondary gross enrolment ratio (f/m per 100)	2005-2011	100.7/103.2
Education: Female third-level students (% of total)	2005-2011	38.6
Seats held by women in national parliaments (%)	2011	22.0

Environmental indicators		
Threatened species	2011	51
Forested area (% of land area)	2009	7.7
CO_2 emission estimates (000 metric tons and metric tons per capita)	2008	124 803/4.6
Energy consumption per capita (kilograms oil equivalent)	2009	1 934.0
Rainfall in the capital city, total mean (millimetres)		419
Temperature in the capital city, mean °C (minimum and maximum)		8.3/21.0

a UN operational exchange rate. b 2009.

Vanuatu

Region	Oceania-Melanesia
Currency	Vatu (VUV)
Surface area (square kilometres)	12 189
Population in 2010 (estimated, 000)	240
Population density in 2010 (per square kilometre)	19.7
Capital city and population in 2011 (000)	Port Vila (47)
United Nations membership date	15 September 1981

Economic indicators

	2000	2005	2010
GDP: Gross domestic product (million current US$)	272	393	710
GDP: Growth rate at constant 2005 prices (annual %)	5.9	5.3	5.0
GDP per capita (current US$)	1 469.8	1 862.4	2 963.5
GNI: Gross national income per capita (current US$)	1 212.1	1 731.3	2 792.9
Gross fixed capital formation (% of GDP)	24.6	19.7	27.8
Exchange rates (national currency per US$) [a]	142.81	112.33	93.15
Balance of payments, current account (million US$)	−14	−53	−54
CPI: Consumer price index (2000=100)	100	112	133
Agricultural production index (2004-2006=100)	92	99	110
Food production index (2004-2006=100)	92	99	110
Employment in industrial sector (% of employed)	...	...	7.0[bcd]
Employment in agricultural sector (% of employed)	...	...	60.5[bcd]
Labour force participation, adult female pop. (%)	70.0	65.3	61.3
Labour force participation, adult male pop. (%)	83.8	81.6	79.7
Tourist arrivals at national borders (000)	58	62	97
Telephone subscribers, total (per 100 inhabitants)	3.8	9.3	121.1
Internet users (per 100 inhabitants)	2.1	5.1	8.0

Total trade		Major trading partners		2010
	(million US$)[e]	(% of exports)[e]		(% of imports)[e]
Exports	29.9		Australia	31.1
Imports	201.7		New Zealand	16.8
Balance	−171.8		Singapore	12.4

Social indicators

Population growth rate (average annual %)	2010-2015	2.4
Urban population growth rate (average annual %)	2010-2015	3.6
Rural population growth rate (average annual %)	2010-2015	2.0
Urban population (%)	2011	24.9
Population aged 0-14 years (%)	2011	37.9
Population aged 60+ years (females and males, % of total)	2011	5.5/5.5
Sex ratio (males per 100 females)	2011	103.8
Life expectancy at birth (females and males, years)	2010-2015	73.6/69.5
Infant mortality rate (per 1 000 live births)	2010-2015	24.1
Fertility rate, total (live births per woman)	2010-2015	3.8
Contraceptive prevalence (ages 15-49, %)	2006-2010	38.4
International migrant stock (000 and % of total population)	mid-2010	0.8/0.3
Refugees and others of concern to UNHCR	end-2010	4
Education: Government expenditure (% of GDP)	2005-2011	5.2
Education: Primary-secondary gross enrolment ratio (f/m per 100)	2005-2011	84.2/86.5
Education: Female third-level students (% of total) [f]	2005-2011	36.1[g]
Seats held by women in national parliaments (%)	2011	1.9

Environmental indicators

Threatened species	2011	123
Forested area (% of land area)	2009	36.1
CO$_2$ emission estimates (000 metric tons and metric tons per capita)	2008	92/0.4
Energy consumption per capita (kilograms oil equivalent)	2009	172.0
Rainfall in the capital city, total mean (millimetres)		2 222
Temperature in the capital city, mean °C (minimum and maximum)		21.5/28.2

a Official rate. b Population census. c November. d 2009. e 2007. f UNESCO estimate. g 2004.

Venezuela (Bolivarian Republic of)

Region	South America
Currency	Bolivar Fuerte (VEF)[a]
Surface area (square kilometres)	912 050
Population in 2010 (estimated, 000)	28 980
Population density in 2010 (per square kilometre)	31.8
Capital city and population in 2011 (000)	Caracas (3 242)
United Nations membership date	15 November 1945

Economic indicators	2000	2005	2010
GDP: Gross domestic product (million current US$)	117 146	145 513	391 307
GDP: Growth rate at constant 2005 prices (annual %)	3.7	10.3	-1.4
GDP per capita (current US$)	4 811.3	5 457.3	13 502.7
GNI: Gross national income per capita (current US$)	4 754.1	5 374.8	13 459.7
Gross fixed capital formation (% of GDP)	21.0	20.3	17.5
Exchange rates (national currency per US$)[b]	0.70	2.15	2.59
Balance of payments, current account (million US$)	11 853	25 110	14 378
CPI: Consumer price index (2000=100)[c]	100	255	581[d]
Agricultural production index (2004-2006=100)	98	101	112
Food production index (2004-2006=100)	97	101	112
Unemployment (% of labour force)	15.1[e]	12.2	8.5
Employment in industrial sector (% of employed)[f]	22.8	20.8	23.0[g]
Employment in agricultural sector (% of employed)[f]	10.6	9.7	8.5[g]
Labour force participation, adult female pop. (%)	48.4	51.5	51.6
Labour force participation, adult male pop. (%)	82.0	81.5	80.2
Tourist arrivals at national borders (000)	469	706	615[d]
Energy production, primary (000 mt oil equivalent)	209 808	200 168	196 711[d]
Telephone subscribers, total (per 100 inhabitants)	32.8	60.6	120.6
Internet users (per 100 inhabitants)	3.4	12.6	35.7

Total trade		Major trading partners	2010
	(million US$)	(% of exports)	(% of imports)
Exports	66 962.7	United States	30.5
Imports	32 342.9	China	11.1
Balance	34 619.8	Brazil	9.8

Social indicators		
Population growth rate (average annual %)	2010-2015	1.5
Urban population growth rate (average annual %)	2010-2015	1.7
Rural population growth rate (average annual %)	2010-2015	-1.6
Urban population (%)	2011	93.5
Population aged 0-14 years (%)	2011	29.1
Population aged 60+ years (females and males, % of total)	2011	9.4/8.3
Sex ratio (males per 100 females)	2011	100.7
Life expectancy at birth (females and males, years)	2010-2015	77.7/71.8
Infant mortality rate (per 1 000 live births)	2010-2015	15.3
Fertility rate, total (live births per woman)	2010-2015	2.4
Contraceptive prevalence (ages 15-49, %)	2006-2010	70.3[h]
International migrant stock (000 and % of total population)	mid-2010	1 007.4/3.5
Refugees and others of concern to UNHCR	end-2010	217 406
Education: Government expenditure (% of GDP)	2005-2011	3.7
Education: Primary-secondary gross enrolment ratio (f/m per 100)	2005-2011	94.6/92.9
Education: Female third-level students (% of total)[i]	2005-2011	62.1
Deaths by assault (females and males, per 100 000)	2005-2008	3.5/65.2
Seats held by women in national parliaments (%)	2011	17.0

Environmental indicators		
Threatened species	2011	274
Forested area (% of land area)	2009	52.8
CO$_2$ emission estimates (000 metric tons and metric tons per capita)	2008	169 394/6.0
Energy consumption per capita (kilograms oil equivalent)	2009	2 514.0
Rainfall in the capital city, total mean (millimetres)		913
Temperature in the capital city, mean °C (minimum and maximum)		16.0/30.3

a Beginning 1 January 2008, 1 Bolivar Fuerte = 1000 Bolivares. b Official rate. c Caracas. d 2009. e 2004.
f Second semester. g 2008. h 1998. i National estimate.

Viet Nam

Region	South-eastern Asia
Currency	Dong (VND)
Surface area (square kilometres)	349 340
Population in 2010 (estimated, 000)	87 848
Population density in 2010 (per square kilometre)	251.5
Capital city and population in 2011 (000)	Hanoi (2 955)
United Nations membership date	20 September 1977

Economic indicators

	2000	2005	2010
GDP: Gross domestic product (million current US$)	31 173	52 917	103 902
GDP: Growth rate at constant 2005 prices (annual %)	6.8	8.4	6.8
GDP per capita (current US$)	395.8	636.3	1 182.7
GNI: Gross national income per capita (current US$)	390.1	623.6	1 144.6
Gross fixed capital formation (% of GDP)	27.7	32.9	35.6
Exchange rates (national currency per US$)[a]	14 514.00	15 916.00	18 932.00
Balance of payments, current account (million US$)	1 106	−560	−4 287
CPI: Consumer price index (2000=100)	100	126[b]	189[c]
Industrial production index (2005=100)[d]	...	100	156
Agricultural production index (2004-2006=100)	78	100	119
Food production index (2004-2006=100)	78	100	117
Employment in industrial sector (% of employed)	12.4[e]	20.2[fg]	...
Employment in agricultural sector (% of employed)	65.3[e]	51.7[fg]	...
Labour force participation, adult female pop. (%)	74.3	73.5	73.1
Labour force participation, adult male pop. (%)	82.7	81.7	81.1
Tourist arrivals at national borders (000)[h]	2 140	3 477	3 747[c]
Energy production, primary (000 mt oil equivalent)	27 394	51 098	58 316[c]
Telephone subscribers, total (per 100 inhabitants)	4.2	11.5[i]	194.0
Internet users (per 100 inhabitants)	0.3	12.7	27.6

Total trade

Total trade	(million US$)	Major trading partners			2010
		(% of exports)			(% of imports)
Exports	72 236.7	United States	19.7	China	23.8
Imports	84 838.6	China	10.7	Republic of Korea	11.5
Balance	−12 601.9	Japan	10.7	Japan	10.6

Social indicators

Population growth rate (average annual %)	2010-2015	1.0
Urban population growth rate (average annual %)	2010-2015	3.0
Rural population growth rate (average annual %)	2010-2015	0.1
Urban population (%)	2011	31.0
Population aged 0-14 years (%)	2011	23.2
Population aged 60+ years (females and males, % of total)	2011	9.8/7.4
Sex ratio (males per 100 females)	2011	97.8
Life expectancy at birth (females and males, years)	2010-2015	77.4/73.4
Infant mortality rate (per 1 000 live births)	2010-2015	18.3
Fertility rate, total (live births per woman)	2010-2015	1.8
Contraceptive prevalence (ages 15-49, %)	2006-2010	79.5
International migrant stock (000 and % of total population)[ik]	mid-2010	69.3/0.1
Refugees and others of concern to UNHCR	end-2010	12 128
Education: Government expenditure (% of GDP)	2005-2011	5.3
Education: Primary-secondary gross enrolment ratio (f/m per 100)	2005-2011	88.7/86.9
Education: Female third-level students (% of total)	2005-2011	49.2
Seats held by women in national parliaments (%)	2011	24.4

Environmental indicators

Threatened species	2011	469
Forested area (% of land area)	2009	44.0
CO$_2$ emission estimates (000 metric tons and metric tons per capita)	2008	127 280/0.4
Energy consumption per capita (kilograms oil equivalent)	2009	465.0
Rainfall in the capital city, total mean (millimetres)		1 653
Temperature in the capital city, mean °C (minimum and maximum)		21.4/27.5

a Market rate. **b** Series linked to former series. **c** 2009. **d** The indices are shown in terms of ISIC Rev. 3. **e** July. **f** 2006. **g** Living standards survey. **h** Arrivals of non-resident visitors at national borders. **i** Mobile cellular subscriptions only. **j** Data refer to foreign citizens. **k** Includes refugees.

Western Sahara

Region	Northern Africa	
Currency	Moroccan Dirham (MAD)	
Surface area (square kilometres)	266 000 [a]	
Population in 2010 (estimated, 000)	531	
Population density in 2010 (per square kilometre)	2.0	
Capital city and population in 2011 (000)	El Aaiún (237)	

Economic indicators	2000	2005	2010
Exchange rates (national currency per US$) [b]	10.62	9.25	8.36
Agricultural production index (2004-2006=100)	96	100	99
Food production index (2004-2006=100)	96	100	99

Social indicators		
Population growth rate (average annual %)	2010-2015	3.2
Urban population growth rate (average annual %)	2010-2015	3.5
Rural population growth rate (average annual %)	2010-2015	2.1
Urban population (%)	2011	82.0
Population aged 0-14 years (%)	2011	28.2
Population aged 60+ years (females and males, % of total)	2011	3.9/4.5
Sex ratio (males per 100 females)	2011	111.9
Life expectancy at birth (females and males, years)	2010-2015	70.1/66.1
Infant mortality rate (per 1 000 live births)	2010-2015	36.4
Fertility rate, total (live births per woman)	2010-2015	2.5
International migrant stock (000 and % of total population) [c]	mid-2010	4.4/0.8

Environmental indicators		
Threatened species	2011	41
Forested area (% of land area)	2009	2.7
CO$_2$ emission estimates (000 metric tons and metric tons per capita)	2008	238/0.5
Energy consumption per capita (kilograms oil equivalent)	2009	154.0 [d]

a Comprises the Northern Region (former Saguia el Hamra) and Southern Region (former Rio de Oro). b Official rate. c Estimates. d UNSD estimate.

Yemen

Region	Western Asia
Currency	Yemeni Rial (YER)
Surface area (square kilometres)	527 968
Population in 2010 (estimated, 000)	24 053
Population density in 2010 (per square kilometre)	45.6
Capital city and population in 2011 (000)	Sana'a (2 419)
United Nations membership date	30 September 1947

Economic indicators	2000	2005	2010
GDP: Gross domestic product (million current US$)	10 039	17 872	34 569
GDP: Growth rate at constant 2005 prices (annual %)	7.6	5.9	8.0
GDP per capita (current US$)	566.4	865.6	1 437.3
GNI: Gross national income per capita (current US$)	526.5	790.8	1 375.3
Gross fixed capital formation (% of GDP)	16.7	19.1	17.9
Exchange rates (national currency per US$)[a]	165.59	195.08	213.80
Balance of payments, current account (million US$)	1 337	624	−1 467
CPI: Consumer price index (2000=100)	100	174	292[b]
Agricultural production index (2004-2006=100)	83	98	138
Food production index (2004-2006=100)	83	98	138
Labour force participation, adult female pop. (%)	22.1	23.5	24.8
Labour force participation, adult male pop. (%)	71.1	71.1	71.7
Tourist arrivals at national borders (000)	73	336	536
Energy production, primary (000 mt oil equivalent)	21 639	20 080	14 988[c]
Telephone subscribers, total (per 100 inhabitants)	2.1	15.4	50.4
Internet users (per 100 inhabitants)	0.1	1.1	12.4

Total trade		Major trading partners			2010
	(million US$)[c]		(% of exports)[c]		(% of imports)[c]
Exports	6 259.0	China	25.2	United Arab Emirates	9.9
Imports	9 184.8	India	20.1	China	9.3
Balance	−2 925.8	Thailand	18.4	United States	6.4

Social indicators

Population growth rate (average annual %)	2010-2015	3.0
Urban population growth rate (average annual %)	2010-2015	4.8
Rural population growth rate (average annual %)	2010-2015	2.2
Urban population (%)	2011	32.3
Population aged 0-14 years (%)	2011	44.0
Population aged 60+ years (females and males, % of total)	2011	4.5/3.7
Sex ratio (males per 100 females)	2011	101.3
Life expectancy at birth (females and males, years)	2010-2015	67.7/64.5
Infant mortality rate (per 1 000 live births)	2010-2015	44.4
Fertility rate, total (live births per woman)	2010-2015	4.9
Contraceptive prevalence (ages 15-49, %)	2006-2010	27.7
International migrant stock (000 and % of total population)[d]	mid-2010	517.9/2.1
Refugees and others of concern to UNHCR	end-2010	508 355
Education: Government expenditure (% of GDP)	2005-2011	5.2
Education: Primary-secondary gross enrolment ratio (f/m per 100)[e]	2005-2011	57.1/76.1
Education: Female third-level students (% of total)	2005-2011	28.7
Seats held by women in national parliaments (%)	2011	0.3

Environmental indicators

Threatened species	2011	274
Forested area (% of land area)	2009	1.0
CO_2 emission estimates (000 metric tons and metric tons per capita)	2008	23 365/1.0
Energy consumption per capita (kilograms oil equivalent)	2009	282.0

a Official rate. b Series linked to former series. c 2009. d Includes refugees. e UNESCO estimate.

Zambia

Region	Eastern Africa
Currency	Kwacha (ZMK)
Surface area (square kilometres)	752 612
Population in 2010 (estimated, 000)	13 089
Population density in 2010 (per square kilometre)	17.4
Capital city and population in 2011 (000)	Lusaka (1 802)
United Nations membership date	1 December 1964

Economic indicators	2000	2005	2010
GDP: Gross domestic product (million current US$)	3 239	7 271	16 201
GDP: Growth rate at constant 2005 prices (annual %)	3.6	5.2	7.1
GDP per capita (current US$)	317.5	634.4	1 237.8
GNI: Gross national income per capita (current US$)	302.1	589.8	1 102.2
Gross fixed capital formation (% of GDP)	17.2	27.2	22.5
Exchange rates (national currency per US$) [a]	4 157.83	3 508.98	4 796.11
Balance of payments, current account (million US$)	−623	−731	386
CPI: Consumer price index (2000=100)	100	251	420
Industrial production index (2005=100) [b]	85 [c]	100	128 [d]
Agricultural production index (2004-2006=100)	79	100	143
Food production index (2004-2006=100)	86	98	144
Employment in industrial sector (% of employed)	5.8 [efg]	7.1 [h]	...
Employment in agricultural sector (% of employed)	71.6 [efg]	72.2 [h]	...
Labour force participation, adult female pop. (%)	75.1	73.8	73.3
Labour force participation, adult male pop. (%)	85.4	86.0	85.7
Tourist arrivals at national borders (000)	457	669	815
Energy production, primary (000 mt oil equivalent)	781	852	884 [d]
Telephone subscribers, total (per 100 inhabitants)	1.8	9.1	42.3
Internet users (per 100 inhabitants)	0.2	2.9	10.0

Total trade		Major trading partners			2010
	(million US$)	(% of exports)		(% of imports)	
Exports	7 200.3	Switzerland	51.0	South Africa	34.4
Imports	5 320.8	China	20.2	Dem. Rep. of Congo	23.8
Balance	1 879.5	South Africa	9.1	Kuwait	9.6

Social indicators		
Population growth rate (average annual %)	2010-2015	3.1
Urban population growth rate (average annual %)	2010-2015	4.2
Rural population growth rate (average annual %)	2010-2015	2.3
Urban population (%)	2011	39.2
Population aged 0-14 years (%)	2011	46.5
Population aged 60+ years (females and males, % of total)	2011	5.2/4.2
Sex ratio (males per 100 females)	2011	100.5
Life expectancy at birth (females and males, years)	2010-2015	50.0/49.2
Infant mortality rate (per 1 000 live births)	2010-2015	81.0
Fertility rate, total (live births per woman)	2010-2015	6.3
Contraceptive prevalence (ages 15-49, %)	2006-2010	40.8
International migrant stock (000 and % of total population) [i]	mid-2010	233.1/1.8
Refugees and others of concern to UNHCR	end-2010	48 182
Education: Government expenditure (% of GDP)	2005-2011	1.4
Education: Female third-level students (% of total) [j]	2005-2011	31.6 [k]
Seats held by women in national parliaments (%)	2011	11.0

Environmental indicators		
Threatened species	2011	68
Forested area (% of land area)	2009	66.8
CO$_2$ emission estimates (000 metric tons and metric tons per capita)	2008	1 887/0.2
Energy consumption per capita (kilograms oil equivalent)	2009	112.0
Rainfall in the capital city, total mean (millimetres)		843
Temperature in the capital city, mean °C (minimum and maximum)		14.9/26.4

a Official rate. b The indices are shown in terms of ISIC Rev. 3. c 2003. d 2009. e October. f Population census. g Age group 12 years and over. h November to December. i Includes refugees. j UNESCO estimate. k 2000.

Zimbabwe

Region	Eastern Africa
Currency	Zimbabwe Dollar (ZWR) [a]
Surface area (square kilometres)	390 757
Population in 2010 (estimated, 000)	12 571
Population density in 2010 (per square kilometre)	32.2
Capital city and population in 2011 (000)	Harare (1 542)
United Nations membership date	25 August 1980

Economic indicators	2000	2005	2010
GDP: Gross domestic product (million current US$)	7 549	6 223	7 204
GDP: Growth rate at constant 2005 prices (annual %)	−8.2	−4.1	9.0
GDP per capita (current US$)	603.4	495.0	573.1
GNI: Gross national income per capita (current US$)	581.8	487.1	531.1
Gross fixed capital formation (% of GDP)	11.8	2.1	7.0
Exchange rates (national currency per US$) [b]	0.06	80.77	...
CPI: Consumer price index (2000=100) [c]	...	28	103
Agricultural production index (2004-2006=100)	132	93	97
Food production index (2004-2006=100)	114	91	96
Employment in industrial sector (% of employed)	...	9.3[def]	...
Employment in agricultural sector (% of employed)	...	64.8[de]	...
Labour force participation, adult female pop. (%)	68.7	83.1	82.9
Labour force participation, adult male pop. (%)	81.5	90.1	89.5
Tourist arrivals at national borders (000) [g]	1 967	1 559	2 239
Energy production, primary (000 mt oil equivalent)	3 117	2 836	2 294[h]
Telephone subscribers, total (per 100 inhabitants)	4.1	7.8	64.3
Internet users (per 100 inhabitants)	0.4	8.0	11.5

Total trade		Major trading partners			2010
	(million US$)	(% of exports)		(% of imports)	
Exports	3 199.2	South Africa	54.2	South Africa	50.2
Imports	9 051.5	United Arab Emirates	10.3	United States	8.5
Balance	−5 852.3	China	7.4	China	6.2

Social indicators		
Population growth rate (average annual %)	2010-2015	2.2
Urban population growth rate (average annual %)	2010-2015	3.4
Rural population growth rate (average annual %)	2010-2015	1.3
Urban population (%)	2011	38.6
Population aged 0-14 years (%)	2011	38.2
Population aged 60+ years (females and males, % of total)	2011	6.7/5.2
Sex ratio (males per 100 females)	2011	97.3
Life expectancy at birth (females and males, years)	2010-2015	52.7/54.0
Infant mortality rate (per 1 000 live births)	2010-2015	47.3
Fertility rate, total (live births per woman)	2010-2015	3.1
Contraceptive prevalence (ages 15-49, %)	2006-2010	60.2[i]
International migrant stock (000 and % of total population) [i]	mid-2010	372.3/2.9
Refugees and others of concern to UNHCR	end-2010	5 031
Education: Government expenditure (% of GDP)	2005-2011	2.5
Education: Female third-level students (% of total)	2005-2011	45.0
Seats held by women in national parliaments (%)	2011	15.0

Environmental indicators		
Threatened species	2011	56
Forested area (% of land area)	2009	41.2
CO_2 emission estimates (000 metric tons and metric tons per capita)	2008	9 068/0.7
Energy consumption per capita (kilograms oil equivalent)	2009	261.0
Rainfall in the capital city, total mean (millimetres)		841
Temperature in the capital city, mean °C (minimum and maximum)		12.3/25.5

a Beginning 1 August 2008, 1 new Zimbabwe dollar = 1 billion old Zimbabwe dollars. **b** Official rate. **c** Index base 2009=100. **d** 2004. **e** June. **f** Excludes electricity, gas and water. **g** Arrivals of non-resident visitors at national borders. **h** 2009. **i** 2005-2006. **j** Includes refugees.

Technical notes

Below are brief descriptions of the indicators presented in the country profiles. The terms are arranged in alphabetical order. Numbers in square brackets refer to the primary sources of the data which are listed in the Statistical sources and references section.

Agricultural production index: The indices are calculated by the Laspeyres formula based on the sum of price-weighted quantities of different agricultural commodities produced. The commodities covered in the computation of indices of agricultural production are all crops and livestock products originating in each country. Practically all products are covered, with the main exception of fodder crops. Production quantities of each commodity are weighted by the average international commodity prices in the base period and summed for each year. To obtain the index, the aggregate for a given year is divided by the average aggregate for the base period 2004-2006. Indices are calculated without any deductions for feed and seed and are referred to as "gross" by the Food and Agriculture Organization of the United Nations (FAO).
Source of the data: FAOSTAT database [2] of the Food and Agriculture Organization of the United Nations, available at http://faostat.fao.org/site/612/default.aspx#ancor (23 February 2012 update).

Balance of payments is a statement summarizing the economic transactions between the residents of a country and non-residents during a specific period, usually a year. It includes transactions in goods, services, income, transfers and financial assets and liabilities. Generally, the balance of payments is divided into two major components: the current account and the capital and financial account. The data on balance of payments presented in the *World Statistics Pocketbook* correspond to the current account category. The current account is a record of all transactions in the balance of payments covering the exports and imports of goods and services, payments of income, and current transfers between residents of a country and non-residents.
Source of the data: International Monetary Fund, *International Financial Statistics (IFS)* database [5], (last accessed 1 December 2011).

Capital city: The designation of any specific city as a capital city is done solely on the basis of the designation as reported by the country or area. The city can be the seat of the government as determined by the country. Some countries designate more than one city to be a capital city with a specific title function (e.g., administrative and/or legislative capital). The data refer to the year 2011.
Source of the data: The United Nations Population Division, *World Urbanization Prospects: The 2011 Revision* [12], available at http://esa.un.org/unpd/wup/CD-ROM/WUP2011-F13-Capital_Cities.xls (last accessed 24 April 2012).

CO_2 **emission estimates** represent the volume of CO_2 (carbon dioxide) produced during the combustion of solid, liquid, and gaseous fuels, and from gas flaring and the manufacture of cement. Original data were converted to CO_2 emissions by using the conversion formula: 1 gram Carbon = 3.664 grams CO_2, as per http://cdiac.ornl. gov/pns/convert.html#3.

Source of the data: Global, Regional, and National Fossil-Fuel CO_2 Emissions, Carbon Dioxide Information Analysis Center [1], available at http://cdiac.ornl.gov/ ftp/ndp030/CSV-FILES/nation.1751_2008.csv (last accessed 18 October 2011).

Contraceptive prevalence refers to the percentage of women married or in-union aged 15 to 49 who are currently using, or whose sexual partner is using at least one method of contraception, regardless of the method used. Contraceptive methods include modern methods such as sterilization, oral hormonal pills, intra-uterine devices, condoms, injectables, implants, vaginal barrier methods and emergency contraception and traditional methods such as the rhythm, withdrawal, lactational amenorrhea method and folk methods. The data contain the most recent estimates of contraceptive prevalence between the years 2006 and 2010.

Source of the data: The Social Indicators website of the Demographic and Social Statistics Branch of the United Nations Statistics Division at http://unstats.un.org/ unsd/demographic/products/socind/Tables_Excel/table2d_Dec%202011.xls   [14] (December 2011 update).

CPI: Consumer price index measures changes over time in the general level of prices of goods and services that a reference population acquires, uses or pays for consumption. A consumer price index is estimated as a series of summary measures of the period-to-period proportional change in the prices of a fixed set of consumer goods and services of constant quantity and characteristics, acquired, used or paid for by the reference population. Each summary measure is constructed as a weighted average of a large number of elementary aggregate indices. Each of the elementary aggregate indices is estimated using a sample of prices for a defined set of goods and services obtained in, or by residents of, a specific region from a given set of outlets or other sources of consumption goods and services. Unless otherwise noted, the indices here generally refer to "all items" and to the country as a whole.

Source of the data: LABORSTA Internet [4], an International Labour Organization database, Table 7A: Consumer prices, general indices, at http://laborsta.ilo.org (last accessed 18 October 2011).

Currency refers to those notes and coins in circulation that are commonly used to make payments. The official currency names and the ISO currency codes are those officially in use, and may be subject to change.

Source of the information: United Nations Treasury's [21] website at http://www. un.org/Depts/treasury/as of 1 November 2011.

Technical notes (*continued*)

Deaths by assault: The rates are the annual number of deaths purposely inflicted by other persons, reported by sex for the year per 100 000 corresponding mid-year population. The data refer to the latest available year between 2005 and 2008.
Source of the data: United Nations Statistics Division's *Demographic Yearbook 2008* [15], Table 20: Death and death rates by cause and sex, classified under External causes, assaults. See also http:// unstats.un.org/unsd/demographic/products/dyb/dyb2008.htm.

Education: Female third-level students: The number of female students at the third-level of education is expressed as a percentage of the total number of students (males and females) at the same level in a given school year. Third-level education is that which is provided at university, teachers' college, higher professional school, and which requires, as a minimum condition of admission, the successful completion of education at the second level, or evidence of the attainment of an equivalent level of knowledge. Unless otherwise indicated, the data refer to the latest available year between 2005 and 2011.
Source of the data: the website of the UNESCO Institute of Statistics [8], Table 14: Tertiary indicators, available at http://stats.uis.unesco.org/unesco/TableViewer/tableView.aspx?ReportId=167 (January 2012 release).

Education: Government expenditure (% of GDP): Unless otherwise indicated, the data refer to the latest available year between 2005 and 2011. They show the trends in general government expenditures for educational affairs and services at pre-primary, primary, secondary and tertiary levels and subsidiary services to education, expressed as a percentage of the gross domestic product.
Source of the data: the website of UNESCO Institute for Statistics [8], Table 19: Finance indicators by ISCED level, available at http://stats.uis.unesco.org/unesco/TableViewer/tableView.aspx?ReportId=172 (January 2012 release).

Education: Primary and secondary gross enrolment ratio is the total enrolment in first and second levels of education, regardless of age, expressed as a percentage of the eligible official school-age population corresponding to the same level of education in a given school year. Education at the first level provides the basic elements of education (e.g. at elementary school or primary school). Education at the second level is provided at middle school, secondary school, high school, teacher-training school at this level and schools of a vocational or technical nature. Enrolment is at the beginning of the school or academic year. The gross enrolment ratio at the first and second level should include all pupils whatever their ages, whereas the population is limited to the range of official school ages. Therefore, for countries with almost universal education among the school-age population, the gross enrolment ratio will exceed 100 if the actual age distribution of pupils extends beyond the official school ages. Unless otherwise indicated, the data refer to the latest available year between 2005 and 2011.

Technical notes (*continued*)

Source of the data: The website of the UNESCO Institute of Statistics [8], Table 5: Enrolment ratios by ISCED level, available at http://stats.uis.unesco.org/unesco/TableViewer/tableView.aspx?ReportId=182 (January 2012 release).

Employment in agricultural and in industrial sectors: The "employed" comprise all persons above a specified age who, during a specified brief period, either one week or one day, were in "paid employment" or in "self-employment" as defined below. "Persons in paid employment" comprise all persons in the following categories: (a) "at work": persons who during the reference period performed some work for wages, salary or related payments, in cash or in kind; or (b) "with a job but not at work": persons who, having already worked in their present job, were absent during the reference period and continued to have a strong attachment to their job. "Persons in self-employment" comprise all persons (a) "at work": persons who during the reference period performed some work for profit or family gain, in cash or in kind; or (b) "with an enterprise but not at work": persons with an enterprise, which may be a business enterprise, a farm or a service undertaking, who were temporarily not at work during the reference period for any specific reason. Employers, own-account workers and members of producers' co-operatives should be considered as in self-employment and should be classified as "at work" or "not at work", as the case may be. (See ILO's *Current International Recommendations on Labour Statistics*). Unless otherwise indicated, the data refer to the 15 years and over age group who perform any work at all in the reference period, for pay or profit in industry (mining, manufacturing, electricity, gas and water and construction) and in agriculture. Agriculture comprises the following divisions of the International Standard Industrial Classification of All Economic Activities (ISIC), Rev. 4: crop and animal production, hunting and related service activities, forestry and lodging, and fishing and aquaculture. Data sources include the World Bank's Core Welfare Indicators Questionnaire, Eurostat's European Labour Force Survey, household income and expenditure surveys, household or labour force surveys, living standards surveys, official estimates and population censuses. The most common source of the data shown is the household or labour force survey; if other sources have been used they are indicated with a footnote.

Source of the data: The Key Indicators of the Labour Market database [3], prepared by the International Labour Organization (ILO), available at http://kilm.ilo.org/kilmnet/ (last accessed 10 November 2011).

Energy consumption per capita: Data on consumption refers to "apparent consumption", which is derived from the formula "production + imports - exports - bunkers +/- stock changes".

Source of the data: The Energy Statistics database of the United Nations Statistics Division (last accessed 24 April 2012) and the *Energy Statistics Yearbook* [16].

Technical notes (*continued*)

Energy production, primary, refers to the first stage of production of various forms of energy (from sources that involve only extraction or capture, with or without separation from contiguous material, cleaning or grading, before the energy embodied in that source can be converted into heat or mechanical work, converted into a common unit (metric ton of oil equivalent) (see United Nations publication *Concepts and Methods in Energy Statistics, with Special Reference to Energy Accounts and Balances*, 1982). The data refer to the following commercial primary energy sources: hard coal, lignite, peat, oil shale, crude petroleum, natural gas liquids, biodiesel, alcohol, natural gas, primary steam/heat, and electricity generated from hydro, nuclear, geothermal, wind, tide, wave and solar sources.
Source of the data: The Energy Statistics database of the United Nations Statistics Division (last accessed 24 April 2012) and the *Energy Statistics Yearbook* [16].

Exchange rates are shown in units of national currency per US dollar and refer to end-of-period quotations. The exchange rates are classified into broad categories, reflecting both the role of the authorities in the determination of the exchange and/or the multiplicity of exchange rates in a country. The market rate is used to describe exchange rates determined largely by market forces; the official rate is an exchange rate determined by the authorities, sometimes in a flexible manner. For countries maintaining multiple exchange arrangements, the rates are labelled principal rate, secondary rate, and tertiary rate.
Source of the data: The International Monetary Fund, *International Financial Statistics* [5] database (last accessed 1 December 2011). For those currencies for which the IMF does not publish exchange rates, non-commercial rates derived from the operational rates of exchange for United Nations programmes are shown, as published by the United Nations Treasury [21] at http://www.un.org/Depts/treasury/.

Fertility rate: The total fertility rate is a widely used summary indicator of fertility. It refers to the number of children that would be born per woman, assuming no female mortality at child bearing ages and the age-specific fertility rates of a specified country and reference period. Unless otherwise indicated, the data are the five-year average for the reference period 2010-2015.
Source of the data: The Social Indicators website of the Demographic and Social Statistics Branch of the United Nations Statistics Division at http://unstats.un.org/unsd/demographic/products/socind/Tables_Excel/table2c_Dec%202011.xls [14] (December 2011 update).

Food production index covers commodities that are considered edible and contain nutrients. Accordingly, coffee and tea are excluded because they have practically no nutritive value. The index numbers shown may differ from those produced by countries themselves because of differences in concepts of production, coverage, weights, time reference of data, and methods of evaluation. The data include estimates made by FAO in cases where no official or semi-official figures are available from the countries.

Source of the data: FAOSTAT database [2] of the Food and Agriculture Organization of the United Nations, available at http://faostat.fao.org/site/612/default.aspx#ancor (23 February 2012 update).

Forested area refers to the percentage of land area occupied by forest. Forest is defined in the Food and Agriculture Organization's *Global Forest Resources Assessment* as land spanning more than 0.5 hectares with trees higher than 5 metres and a canopy cover of more than 10 percent, or trees able to reach these thresholds in situ. It does not include land that is predominantly under agricultural or urban land use.

Source of the data: The FAOSTAT database [2] of the Food and Agriculture. Organization of the United Nations, available at http://faostat.fao.org/ (last updated 21 July 2011).

GDP: Gross domestic product is an aggregate measure of production equal to the sum of gross value added of all resident producer units plus that part (possibly the total) of taxes on products, less subsidies on products, that is not included in the valuation of output. It is also equal to the sum of the final uses of goods and services (all uses except intermediate consumption) measured at purchasers' prices, less the value of imports of goods and services, and equal to the sum of primary incomes distributed by resident producer units (see *System of National Accounts 2008*). The data in the *World Statistics Pocketbook* are in current United States (US) dollars and are estimates of the total production of goods and services of the countries represented in economic terms, not as a measure of the standard of living of their inhabitants. In order to have comparable coverage for as many countries as possible, these US dollar estimates are based on official GDP data in national currency, supplemented by national currency estimates prepared by the Statistics Division using additional data from national and international sources. The estimates given here are in most cases those accepted by the United Nations General Assembly's Committee on Contributions for determining United Nations members' contributions to the United Nations regular budget. The exchange rates for the conversion of GDP national currency data into US dollars are the average market rates published by the International Monetary Fund, in *International Financial Statistics* [5]. Official exchange rates are used only when free market rates are not available. For non-members of the Fund, the conversion rates used are the average of United Nations operational rates of exchange. It should be noted that the conversion from local currency into US dollars introduces deficiencies in comparability over time and among countries which should be considered when using the data. For example, comparability over time is distorted when exchange rate fluctuations differ substantially from domestic inflation rates.

Technical notes (*continued*)

Source of the data: The *National Accounts Main Aggregates Database* available at http://unstats.un.org/unsd/snaama/dnllist.asp (December 2011 update) and the *National Accounts Statistics: Analysis of Main Aggregates* [19], compiled from national data provided to the United Nations Statistics Division.

GDP: Growth rate at constant 2005 prices is derived on the basis of constant price series in national currency. The figures are computed as the geometric mean of annual rates of growth expressed in percentages for the years indicated.
Source of the data: The *National Accounts Main Aggregates Database* available at http://unstats.un.org/unsd/snaama/dnllist.asp (December 2011 update) and the *National Accounts Statistics: Analysis of Main Aggregates* [19], compiled from national data provided to the United Nations Statistics Division.

GDP per capita estimates are the value of all goods and services produced in the economy divided by the population.
Source of the data: The *National Accounts Main Aggregates Database* available at http://unstats.un.org/unsd/snaama/dnllist.asp (December 2011 update) and the *National Accounts Statistics: Analysis of Main Aggregates* [19], compiled from national data provided to the United Nations Statistics Division.

GNI: Gross national income per capita estimates are the aggregate value of the balances of gross primary incomes for all sectors in the economy divided by the population. GNI is equal to GDP less primary incomes payable to non-resident units plus primary incomes receivable from non-resident units. In other words, GNI is equal to GDP less taxes (less subsidies) on production and imports, compensation of employees and property income payable to the rest of the world plus the corresponding items receivable from the rest of the world. Thus GNI at market prices is the sum of gross primary incomes receivable by resident institutional units/sectors. It is worth noting that GNI at market prices was called gross national product in the 1953 SNA, and it was commonly denominated GNP. In contrast to GDP, GNI is not a concept of value added, but a concept of income (see *System of National Accounts 2008*).
Source of the data: The *National Accounts Main Aggregates Database* available at http://unstats.un.org/unsd/snaama/dnllist.asp (December 2011 update) and the *National Accounts Statistics: Analysis of Main Aggregates* [19], compiled from national data provided to the United Nations Statistics Division.

Gross fixed capital formation is measured by the total value of a producer's acquisitions, less disposals, of fixed assets during the accounting period plus certain specified expenditure on services that adds to the value of non-produced assets (see *System of National Accounts 2008*). The data are based on the percentage distribution of GDP in current prices.

Technical notes (*continued*)

Source of the data: The *National Accounts Main Aggregates Database* available at http://unstats.un.org/unsd/snaama/dnllist.asp (December 2011 update) and the *National Accounts Statistics: Analysis of Main Aggregates* [19], compiled from national data provided to the United Nations Statistics Division.

Industrial production index: The data shown here generally cover, unless otherwise noted, the International Standard Industrial Classification of All Economic Activities, Revision 4 (ISIC Rev. 4) sections B, C, D and E (i.e., mining and quarrying; manufacturing; electricity, gas, steam and air conditioning supply; and water supply, sewerage, waste management and remediation activities). The data that are footnoted as referring to ISIC Rev. 3 cover Tabulation Categories C, D and E (mining and quarrying; manufacturing; and electricity, gas and water supply).
Source of the data: Table 5 of the United Nations *Monthly Bulletin of Statistics* [18], available at http://unstats.un.org/unsd/mbs/ (last accessed 10 November 2011).

Infant mortality rate (per 1 000 live births) is the ratio of infant deaths (the deaths of children under one year of age) in a given year to the total number of live births in the same year. Unless otherwise noted, the rates are the five-year projected averages for the reference period 2010-2015.
Source of the data: The Social Indicators website of the Demographic and Social Statistics Branch of the United Nations Statistics Division at http://unstats.un.org/unsd/demographic/products/socind/Tables_Excel/table2b_Dec 2011.xls [14] (December 2011 update).

International migrant stock generally represents the number of persons born in a country other than that in which they live. When information on country of birth was not recorded, data on the number of persons having foreign citizenship was used instead. In the absence of any empirical data, estimates were imputed. Data refer to mid-2010. Figures for international migrant stock as a percentage of the population are the outcome of dividing the estimated international migrant stock by the estimated total population and multiplying the result by 100.
Source of the data: The United Nations Population Division, *Trends in International Migrant Stock: The 2008 Revision* [10] available at http://esa.un.org/migration/. Estimates of total population are obtained from the United Nations Population Division, *World Population Prospects: The 2008 Revision* available at http://www.unpopulation.org and include information received by UNSD as of 16 October 2009.

Internet users per 100 inhabitants are based on nationally reported data for users divided by the total population and then multiplied by 100. There are variations in data collection among countries: some use surveys that give a more precise figure for the number of Internet users, while others base their estimates on derivations from reported Internet Service Provider subscriber counts, calculated by multiplying the number of subscribers by a multiplier. Surveys may differ across countries in the user age and frequency of use they cover. Some figures may refer to only users above a certain age.

Source of the data: The World Telecommunication/ICT Indicators Database 2011 (15th Edition) of the International Telecommunication Union [7], available at http://www.itu.int/ITU-D/ict/ publications/world/world.html (last accessed 15 December 2011).

Labour force participation rate is calculated by expressing the number of persons in the labour force as a percentage of the working-age population. The labour force is the sum of the number of persons employed and the number of unemployed (see ILO's *Current International Recommendations on Labour Statistics*). The working-age population is the population above a certain age, prescribed for the measurement of economic characteristics. Unless otherwise noted, the data refer to the age group of 15 years and over.

Source of the data: The Key Indicators of the Labour Market database [3], produced by the International Labour Organization, available at http://kilm.ilo.org/kilmnet/ (last accessed 18 October 2011).

Life expectancy at birth is the average number of years of life at birth (age 0) according to the expected mortality rates by age estimated for the reference year and population. Unless otherwise indicated, the data are the five-year projected averages for the reference period 2010-2015.

Source of the data: The Social Indicators website of the Demographic and Social Statistics Branch of the United Nations Statistics Division at http://unstats.un.org/ unsd/demographic/products/socind/Tables_Excel/table2a_Dec%202011.xls [14] (December 2011 update).

Major trading partners shows the three largest trade partners (countries of destination and origin) in international merchandise trade transactions. In some cases, less than three countries may be shown, for example when one or more of the largest shares of exports and/or imports refer to regions or unspecified areas rather than to individual countries. Data are expressed as percentages of total exports and of total imports of the country or area.

Source of the data: The United Nations Statistics Division's Commodity Trade Statistics Database [13] (COMTRADE, see http://comtrade.un.org) and the United Nations *International Trade Statistics Yearbook* [17].

Population aged 0-14 years refers to the population aged 0-14 years of both sexes as a percentage of total population. Unless otherwise indicated, the data refer to the year 2011.

Source of the data: The Social Indicators website of the Demographic and Social Statistics Branch of the United Nations Statistics Division at http://unstats.un.org/

unsd/demographic/products/socind/Tables_Excel/table1b_Dec%202011.xls   [14] (December 2011 update).

Population aged 60 years and over refers to elderly men as a percentage of all males and elderly women as a percentage of all females. Unless otherwise indicated, the data refer to the year 2011.
Source of the data: The Social Indicators website of the Demographic and Social Statistics Branch of the United Nations Statistics Division at http://unstats.un.org/unsd/demographic/products/socind/Tables_Excel/table1b_Dec%202011.xls [14] (December 2011 update).

Population density refers to population per square kilometre of surface area. Data are derived from the population estimates for 2010 divided by the surface area. See also *population estimates* and *surface area*.

Population estimates: Data for "Population in 2010" refer to de facto population as of 1 July 2010. The total population of a country may comprise either all usual residents of the country (de jure population) or all persons present in the country (de facto population) at the time of the census; for purposes of international comparisons, the de facto definition is recommended.
Source of the data: Estimates for 2010 were prepared by the United Nations Population Division and published in the *World Population Prospects: The 2010 Revision* [11], available at http://esa.un.org/unpd/wpp/index.htm.

Population growth rate is the average annual percentage change in total population size. Unless otherwise indicated, the data refer to the period 2010-2015.
Source of the data: The Social Indicators website of the Demographic and Social Statistics Branch of the United Nations Statistics Division at http://unstats.un.org/unsd/demographic/products/socind/Tables_Excel/table1c_Dec%202011.xls   [14] (December 2011 update).

Rainfall in the capital city, total mean data are computed by adding average monthly measurements from the weather stations in the capital city, unless otherwise noted. The data are official climatological information supplied by national meteorological and hydrological services. Since the definition of mean rainfall and averaging periods may be different for different countries, care should be taken when comparing city climatologies.
Source of the data: The World Meteorological Organization website [25], available at http://www.worldweather.org/ (last accessed 13 January 2011).

Refugees and others of concern to the Office of the United Nations High Commissioner for Refugees (UNHCR): The 1951 United Nations Convention relating to the Status of Refugees spells out that a refugee is someone who, owing to a well-founded fear of being persecuted for reasons of race, religion, nationality, political opinion or membership in a particular social group, is outside the country of his or her nationality and is unable to, or owing to such fear, is unwilling to avail himself or herself of the protection of that country; or who, not having a nationality and being outside the country of his or her former habitual residence, is unable or, owing to such fear, unwilling to return to it. In this series, refugees refer to persons granted a humanitarian status and/or those granted temporary protection. Included are persons who have been granted temporary protection on a group basis. The series also includes returned refugees, asylum-seekers and persons displaced internally within their own country for reasons that would make them of concern to the UNHCR if they were outside their country of origin.

Source of the data: The *UNHCR Global Trends 2010*, Table 1: Refugees, asylum-seekers, internally displaced persons (IDPs), returnees (refugees and IDPs), stateless persons, and others of concern to UNHCR by country/territory of asylum, end-2010 [9], available at http://www.unhcr.org/statistics.html (Annexes, last accessed 7 July 2011).

Region: Macro geographical regions arranged according to continents and component geographical regions used for statistical purposes.

Source of the data: The *Standard Country or Area Codes and Geographical Regions for Statistical Use, Revision 4* (United Nations publication) [20], available at http://unstats.un.org/unsd/methods/m49/m49.htm.

Rural population growth rate data are based on the number of persons defined as rural according to national definitions of this concept. In most cases these definitions are those used in the most recent population census.

Source of the data: The United Nations Population Division, *World Urbanization Prospects: The 2011 Revision* [12] available at http://esa.un.org/unpd/wup/CD-ROM/Urban-Rural-Population.htm (last accessed 24 April 2012).

Seats held by women in national parliaments refer to the number of women in the lower chamber of national parliaments expressed as a percentage of total occupied seats in the lower or single House.

Source of the data: The Inter-Parliamentary Union [6], Women in National Parliaments, Situation as of 30 November 2011, available at http://www.ipu.org/wmn-e/classif.htm.

Sex ratio is calculated as the ratio of the number of men to that of 100 women. Unless otherwise indicated, the data refer to the year 2011.

Source of the data: The Social Indicators website of the Demographic and Social Statistics Branch of the United Nations Statistics Division at http://unstats.un.org/unsd/demographic/products/socind/Tables_Excel/table1a_Dec%202011.xls [14] (December 2011 update).

Technical notes (*continued*)

Surface area, unless otherwise noted, refers to land area plus inland water.
Source of the data: The United Nations *Demographic Yearbook 2009-2010* [15], Table 3, available at http://unstats.un.org/unsd/demographic/products/dyb/dyb2009-2010/Table03.xls (last accessed 22 November 2011).

Telephone subscribers, total per 100 inhabitants refer to the sum of main telephone lines and cellular mobile subscribers divided by the population and multiplied by 100.
Source of the data: The World Telecommunication/ICT Indicators Database 2011 (15th Edition) of the International Telecommunication Union [7], available at http://www.itu.int/ITU-D/ict/publications/world/world.html (last accessed 15 December 2011).

Temperature in the capital city, mean °C (minimum and maximum): Data were computed from average monthly measurements from the weather stations in the capital city, unless otherwise noted. The data are official climatological information supplied by national meteorological and hydrological services worldwide. Since the definition of mean temperature and averaging periods may be different for different countries, care should be taken when comparing city climatologies.
Source of the data: The World Meteorological Organization website [25], available at http://www.worldweather.org/ (last accessed 13 January 2011).

Threatened species represents the number of plants and animals that are most in need of conservation attention and are compiled by the World Conservation Union IUCN/ Species Survival Commission (SSC).
Source of the data: The IUCN *Red List of Threatened Species* [24] version 2011.2: Table 5, available at www.iucnredlist.org (last accessed 11 November 2011).

Total trade: exports and imports show the movement of goods out of and into a country. Goods simply being transported through a country (goods in transit) or temporarily admitted (except for goods for inward processing) do not add to the stock of material resources of a country and are not included in the international merchandise trade statistics. In the "general trade system", the definition of the statistical territory of a country coincides with its economic territory. In the "special trade system", the definition of the statistical territory comprises only a particular part of the economic territory, mainly that part which coincides with the free circulation area for goods. "The free circulation area" is a part of the economic territory of a country within which goods "may be disposed of without Customs restrictions". In the case of exports, the transaction value is the value at which the goods were sold by the exporter, including the cost of transportation and insurance, to bring the goods onto the transporting vehicle at the frontier of the exporting country (an FOB-type valuation). In the case of imports, the transaction value is the value at which the goods were purchased by the importer plus the cost of transportation and insurance to the frontier of the importing country (a CIF-

Technical notes (*continued*)

type valuation). Both imports and exports are shown in United States dollars. Conversion from national currencies is made by means of currency conversion factors based on official exchange rates (par values or weighted averages).

Source of the data: The United Nations Statistics Division's Commodity Trade Statistics Database [13] (Comtrade, see http://comtrade.un.org) and the United Nations *International Trade Statistics Yearbook* [17].

Tourist arrivals at national borders: An international tourist is any person who travels to a country other than that in which he or she has his or her usual residence but outside his/her usual environment for a period not exceeding 12 months and whose main purpose of visit is other than the exercise of an activity remunerated from with the country visited, and who stays at least one night in a collective or private accommodation in the country visited (see *Recommendations on Tourism Statistics* of the United Nations and the World Tourism Organization). Unless otherwise indicated, the data refer to arrivals of non-resident tourists at national borders.

Source of the data: The United Nations World Tourism Organization *Yearbook of Tourism Statistics* [23] (information received by UNSD as of 12 January 2012).

Unemployment refers to persons above a specified age who during a specified reference period were: "without work", i.e. were not in paid employment or self-employment as defined under employment; "currently available for work", i.e. were available for paid employment or self-employment during the reference period; and "seeking work", i.e. had taken specific steps in a specified recent period to seek paid employment or self-employment. In circumstances where employment opportunities are particularly limited and where persons not working do not have easy access to formal channels for seeking employment or face social and cultural barriers when looking for a job, the "seeking work" criterion should be relaxed. National definitions of unemployment often differ from the recommended international standard definitions and thereby limit international comparability. Inter-country comparisons are also complicated by the different types of data collection systems used to obtain information on unemployed persons. Unless otherwise indicated, the data refer to the 15 years and over age group and are national employment office statistics, usually labour force surveys, compiled by the ILO. (See ILO's *Current International Recommendations on Labour Statistics*, 2000 Edition).

Source of the data: The LABORSTA Internet [4] an ILO database, Short term indicators of the labour market, Main dataset, available at http://laborsta.ilo.org/sti/sti_E.html (last updated 29 February 2012).

United Nations membership dates: The United Nations is an intergovernmental organization whose members are the countries of the world. Currently there are 192 Member States of the United Nations, some of which joined the UN by signing and ratifying the Charter of the United Nations in 1945; the other countries joined the UN later, through the adoption of a resolution admitting them to membership. The process usually follows these steps: first, the country applies for membership and makes a declaration accepting the obligations of the Charter; second, the Security Council adopts a resolution recommending that the General Assembly admit the country to membership and finally the General Assembly adopts a resolution admitting the country.

Source of the data: The List of Member States, available at http://www.un.org/en/members/ [22].

Urban population and **urban population growth rate** series are based on the number of persons defined as urban according to national definitions of this concept. In most cases these definitions are those used in the most recent population census.

Source of the data: The United Nations Population Division, *World Urbanization Prospects: The 2011 Revision* [12] available at http://esa.un.org/unpd/wup/index.htm (last accessed 24 April 2012).

Statistical sources and references

Statistical sources

[1] Carbon Dioxide Information Analysis Center (Oak Ridge, Tennessee, USA), *Global, Regional, and National Fossil-Fuel CO_2 Emissions*, available at http://cdiac.ornl.gov/trends/emis/overview_2008.html.

[2] Food and Agriculture Organization of the United Nations, FAOSTAT database, available at http://faostat.fao.org/.

[3] International Labour Organization, *Key Indicators of the Labour Market, 7th edition* software, available at http://kilm.ilo.org/kilmnet/.

[4] _____, LABORSTA Internet database, available at http://laborsta.ilo.org/.

[5] International Monetary Fund (IMF), Washington, *International Financial Statistics (IFS)* database.

[6] Inter-Parliamentary Union, Women in National Parliaments, available at http://www.ipu.org/wmn-e/classif.htm.

[7] International Telecommunication Union (ITU), Geneva, the World Telecommunication/ICT Indicators Database 2011 (15th Edition) database, available at http://www.itu.int/ITU-D/ict/publications/world/world.html.

[8] United Nations Educational, Scientific and Cultural Organization (UNESCO) Institute for Statistics, Montreal, UNESCO statistics database, available at http://stats.uis.unesco.org.

[9] United Nations High Commissioner for Refugees, Global Trends 2010, available at http://www.unhcr.org/statistics.html.

[10] United Nations, Department of Economic and Social Affairs, Population Division, *Trends in International Migrant Stock: The 2008 Revision* (United Nations database, POP/DB/MIG/Stock/Rev.2008), available at http://esa.un.org/migration/.

[11] _____, *World Population Prospects. The 2010 Revision*, New York, 2010, available at http://esa.un.org/unpd/wpp/index.htm.

[12] _____, *World Urbanization Prospects: The 2011 Revision* available at http://esa.un.org/unpd/wup/index.htm.

[13] United Nations, Department of Economic and Social Affairs, Statistics Division, Commodity Trade Statistics Database (COMTRADE), available at http://comtrade.un.org/db/default.aspx.

[14] _____, Demographic and Social Statistics, Social Indicators website: http://unstats.un.org/unsd/demographic/products/socind/default.htm

Statistical sources and references (continued)

[15] _____, *Demographic Yearbook* (Series R, United Nations publication). See also http://unstats.un.org/unsd/demographic/products/dyb/dyb2.htm.

[16] _____, *Energy Statistics Yearbook* (Series J, United Nations publication).

[17] _____, *International Trade Statistics Yearbook* (Series G, United Nations publication).

[18] _____, *Monthly Bulletin of Statistics* (Series Q, United Nations publication). See also http://unstats.un.org/unsd/mbs/.

[19] _____, *National Accounts Statistics: Analysis of Main Aggregates* (Series X, United Nations publication). See also http://unstats.un.org/unsd/snaama/introduction.asp.

[20] _____, *Standard Country or Area Codes for Statistical Use* (ST/ESA/STAT/SER.M/49/Rev.4), New York, 1999 and http://unstats.un.org/unsd/methods/m49/m49.htm.

[21] United Nations, Department of Management, Office of Programme Planning, Budget and Accounts, Treasury website: http://www.un.org/Depts/treasury.

[22] United Nations Member States website: http://www.un.org/en/members/.

[23] United Nations World Tourism Organization (UNWTO), Madrid, UNWTO statistics database, *Compendium of Tourism Statistics* and *Yearbook of Tourism Statistics*. See also http://www.unwto.org.

[24] World Conservation Union, *The 2011 IUCN Red List of Threatened Species*, available at http://www.iucnredlist.org/.

[25] World Meteorological Organization, at http://www.worldweather.org/.

References

Food and Agriculture Organization of the United Nations (2010), *Global Forest Resources Assessment 2010* (Rome), available at http://www.fao.org/forestry/fra/fra2010/en/.

International Labour Organization (2000). *Current International Recommendations on Labour Statistics*, 2000 Edition (Geneva), available at http://www.ilo.org/public/english/bureau/stat/publ/currrec.htm.

United Nations (1951 and 1967). Convention relating to the Status of Refugees of 1951 (United Nations, Treaty Series, vol. 189 (1954), No. 2545, p. 137), art. 1) and Protocol relating to the Status of Refugees of 1967 (United Nations, Treaty Series, vol. 606 (1967), No. 8791, p. 267).

United Nations (1982). *Concepts and Methods in Energy Statistics, with Special Reference to Energy Accounts and Balances: A Technical Report. Statistical Office*, Series F, No. 29 and Corr. 1 (United Nations publication, Sales No. E.82.XVII.13 and corrigendum), available at http://unstats.un.org/unsd/publication/SeriesF/SeriesF_29E.pdf.

United Nations (2008). *Principles and Recommendations for Population and Housing Censuses Rev. 2.* Statistics Division, Series M, No. 67, Rev. 2 (United Nations publication, Sales No. E.07.XVII.8), available at http://unstats.un.org/unsd/publication/SeriesM/Seriesm_67rev2e.pdf.

United Nations (2008). *International Standard Industrial Classification of All Economic Activities (ISIC), Rev. 4.* Statistics Division, Series M, No. 4, Rev.4 (United Nations publication, Sales No. E.08.XVII.25), available at http://unstats.un.org/unsd/publication/SeriesM/seriesm_4rev4e.pdf.

United Nations (2004). *International Merchandise Trade Statistics: Compilers Manual,* Statistics Division, Series F, No. 87 (United Nations publication, Sales No. E.02.XVII.17), available at http://unstats.un.org/unsd/publication/SeriesF/seriesf_87e.pdf.

United Nations (2010).*International Merchandise Trade Statistics: Concepts and Definitions*, Statistics Division, Series M, No.52, Rev.3, (United Nations publication, Sales No. E.10.XVII.13), available at http://unstats.un.org/unsd/trade/EG-IMTS/IMTS%202010%20(English).pdf.

United Nations, European Commission, International Monetary Fund, Organisation for Economic Cooperation and Development and World Bank (2009). *System of National Accounts 2008 (SNA 2008), available at http://unstats.un.org/unsd/nationalaccount/sna2008.asp.*

Statistical sources and references (continued)

United Nations and World Tourism Organization (2008). *International Recommendations for Tourism Statistics 2008,* Series M, No. 83/Rev.1 (United Nations publication, Sales No. E.08.XVII.28).

World Health Organization (WHO, 2007*). International Statistical Classification of Diseases and Related Health Problems, Tenth Revision (ICD-10),* (Geneva), available at http://www.who.int/classifications/icd/en/.

Index of indicator notes and definitions

Index of indicator notes and definitions (*continued*)

Also of interest

See UN CountryStats – an app for iPhones and iPads - which has been adapted from the print version of the *Pocketbook* and can be downloaded free of charge from the Apple store.

The *World Statistics Pocketbook* can also be viewed online in PDF format at http://unstats.un.org/unsd/pocketbook/ and in UNdata at http://data.un.org/CountryProfile.aspx.

Other statistical publications offering a broad cross-section of information which may be of interest to users of the *World Statistics Pocketbook* include:

- the *Monthly Bulletin of Statistics* (MBS) in print and the Monthly *Bulletin* of Statistics Online (at http://unstats.un.org/unsd/mbs/app/DataSearchTable.aspx

- the *Statistical Yearbook* (SYB) in print and online in PDF format at http://unstats.un.org/unsd/syb/

Both publications are available for sale in print format (see below for instructions on how to order them).

For more information about other publications and online databases prepared by the UN Statistics Division, visit: http://unstats.un.org/unsd/pubs/ and http://unstats.un.org/unsd/databases.htm

For additional information about the work of the United Nations Statistics Division, visit http://unstats.un.org/unsd.

To order United Nations publications, please visit www.un.org/publications or contact:

United Nations Publications
300 East 42nd Street
New York, NY 10017
Tel: 1-888-254-4286
Fax: 1-800-338-4550
E-mail: publications@un.org

Please let the Statistical Dissemination Section team, which is responsible for producing the *World Statistics Pocketbook,* the *Monthly Bulletin of Statistics* and the *Statistical Yearbook,* know how you like these statistical products and how you made use of the data, by sending your feedback and suggestions to statistics@un.org.